Investment Strategies of Hedge Funds

For other titles in the Wiley Finance series
please see www.wiley.com/finance

Investment Strategies of Hedge Funds

Filippo Stefanini

John Wiley & Sons, Ltd

Adapted and updated from the original Italian, first published in 2005 by Il Sole 24 Ore.
Translation by Laura Simontacchi.

Other Wiley Editorial Offices

John Wiley & Sons Inc., 111 River Street, Hoboken, NJ 07030, USA

Jossey-Bass, 989 Market Street, San Francisco, CA 94103-1741, USA

Wiley-VCH Verlag GmbH, Boschstr. 12, D-69469 Weinheim, Germany

John Wiley & Sons Australia Ltd, 42 McDougall Street, Milton, Queensland 4064, Australia

John Wiley & Sons (Asia) Pte Ltd, 2 Clementi Loop #02-01, Jin Xing Distripark, Singapore 129809

John Wiley & Sons Canada Ltd, 22 Worcester Road, Etobicoke, Ontario, Canada M9W 1L1

Wiley also publishes its books in a variety of electronic formats. Some content that appears in print may not be available in electronic books.

Library of Congress Cataloging-in-Publication Data

Stefanini, Filippo.
 [Hedge funds. English]
 Investment strategies of hedge funds / Filippo Stefanini.
   p.   cm. — (Wiley finance series)
 "Adapted and updated from the original Italian, first published in 2005 by Il Sore 24 Ore"—
 Includes bibliographical references and index.
 ISBN-13: 978-0-470-02627-4 (cloth : alk. paper)
 ISBN-10: 0-470-02627-8 (cloth : alk. paper)
 1. Hedge funds. I. Title. II. Series.
 HG4530.S795 2006
 332.67′253—dc22   2006016527

British Library Cataloguing in Publication Data

A catalogue record for this book is available from the British Library

ISBN 978-0-470-02627-4 (H/B)

Typeset in 10/12pt Times by Integra Software Services Pvt. Ltd, Pondicherry, India
Printed and bound in Great Britain by CPI Antony Rowe, Chippenham, Wiltshire

Contents

Foreword

Hedge Funds. Rarely has a financial term stimulated such a broad spectrum of conflicting views. Hedge funds have been vilified by some people, and blamed for almost every negative occurrence in financial markets. This accusation is predominantly based on one famous hedge fund meltdown in 1998 which, some say, came close to toppling the global banking system. Hedge funds are often perceived to be the riskiest and most volatile of investments, buccaneers operating in an unregulated environment, using irresponsible and unwarranted leverage to deliver their returns. Hardly a week goes by without an article in the international press casting a shadow over the industry.

Other people have a diametrically opposed view. They exalt hedge funds as the best performing investments around and laud their managers as financial geniuses, turning some into superstars of the financial industry. This view maintains that hedge funds are able to protect investors' capital efficiently in times of financial market strife.

The truth, as is almost always the case, lies somewhere in between. Some hedge funds are populated by some of the best brains in the financial industry using sophisticated and very efficient investment strategies to deliver outstanding returns. Others are populated by mediocre talent and are run in a risky manner. The hedge fund industry is nothing more than a sophisticated part of the general investment industry as a whole, with money managers investing in an extremely diversified and extensive range of strategies.

Where does that leave most investors who want to evaluate and understand the hedge fund universe and take advantage of the talent that exists therein? In the vortex of opinion, counter-opinion and argument, investors need a guiding hand. Hedge fund investing requires a level of sophistication to understand both the risks involved and also the suitability of any investment relative to the objectives of the investor. Although such an assessment continues to be the role of an investment professional, publications such as this book are contributing to a much greater understanding of hedge fund investing among the wider investor audience.

In his book Filippo Stefanini has striven to demystify the hedge fund industry, shedding light on various strategies used to deliver returns. Filippo has reaffirmed the attributes I have come to know over the course of our professional collaboration these last four years – diligence, precision and attention to detail – and combined these with the ability to present complex financial strategies and their background, clearly and succinctly.

This publication is a great educational tool for existing and potential investors in hedge funds.

Michael Perotti
Alternative Asset Management Group
Union Bancaire Privée

Preface

The growth of the asset management industry was also fostered by the expansion of the range of products, honed to best satisfy the specific and diversified needs of investors.

In addition to traditional asset management products, such as mutual funds, so called alternative investments gradually grew in prominence. The main alternative investment products are hedge funds and funds of hedge funds, but they also include private equity and venture capital funds (Figure 0.1).

Alternative investments are characterized by a low correlation with traditional investments.

Since the first hedge fund was launched in 1949 by Alfred Winslow Jones, the hedge fund industry has grown impressively reaching the size of $1.3 trillion and 8000 hedge funds. Often hedge funds are responsible for a big slice of the daily trading volumes of financial markets and they are counted among the best clients for brokers, given the level of trading fees they generate.

This exponential growth has led regulators to take a closer look at this phenomenon. The US Securities and Exchange Commission (SEC) has recently decided to increase the regulation requiring the registration of the investment advisors of the US hedge funds and the Financial Services Authority (FSA) already requires the investment advisors to be registered in the UK.

Nevertheless, this remarkable phenomenon is still surrounded by an aura of mystery. So, the goal of this book is to help readers to understand in detail the investment behavior of hedge funds.

Each chapter of this book is structured to cover the following subjects:

- strategy history;
- strategy's theoretical description;
- description of securities involved and size of the securities market;
- hedging techniques and possible use of derivatives;
- some trading examples;
- liquidity;
- leverage;
- risks and risk management.

We shall not get into the performances generated by single hedge funds, both to avoid investment solicitation and because past performances are not indicative of future returns.

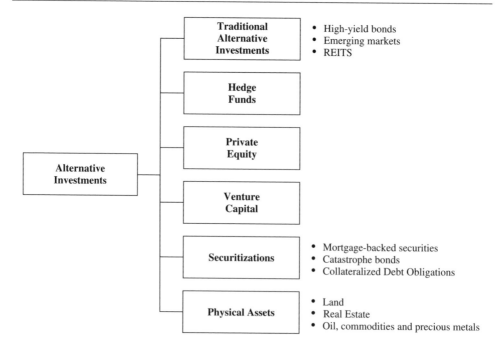

Figure 0.1 Alternative investments

This approach is consistent with the book's aim, which is not intended to offer financial products, but rather to describe how hedge fund managers make a profit, and sometimes suffer a loss, following a market-uncorrelated approach.

At times we shall make use of investment examples to better clarify investment modalities, but these examples are in no way meant to form a judgment on the shares of listed companies. In most cases, they are examples of past deals that are closed, and therefore the conclusions reached by way of said examples may not be current anymore, and even more importantly may not be shared by the companies concerned. It should never be forgotten that past performances are not indicative of future performances.

Any performance entails the need to take a risk, so with this in mind we tried to carry out a critical analysis of the opportunities and risks of the many investment strategies adopted by hedge funds.

Just as during the Italian Renaissance apprentices would learn their crafts and art from great artists, today generations of young money managers are forming around great managers, so that one day they will leave the "shop" to launch their own hedge fund. Only a few exceptionally talented managers can manage successful hedge funds. There are things that can be taught and things that can be learnt only through practice. Investing is a discipline lying halfway between art and exact science. Maybe the only way to get hold of the secrets of this industry is to work in a privileged observatory, as fund of hedge fund managers do, meeting or talking daily with hedge fund managers.

There is no school where investment strategies can be taught, because each strategy is unique and original, and can be learnt only through hands-on experience.

Finally, we discourage new managers from trying to implement these very same investment strategies: this is no manual, and it is not intended to explain how to implement an investment strategy. The theoretical aspect is but the first step. However, should any of our readers feel tempted to implement these strategies, just bear in mind that practice can widely differ from theory.

Strategy is easy, execution is hard!

Filippo Stefanini
Milan, April 2006

Acknowledgments

My special thanks go to my wife Silvia for her patience, insight and encouragement, and to my parents Carlo and Laura and my grandmother Dina, without whose help this book would never have been written.

I would like to thank Giovanni Maggi, Stefano Ticozzi and Davide Elli, my colleagues in Aletti Gestielle Alternative SGR, for reviewing the drafts of my book. In particular, I thank Davide Elli for helping me with the description of trading examples and with volatility trading, and Stefano Ticozzi for having helped me find all the Bloomberg pictures for this book.

I am grateful to Bruno Redini, consultant with Aletti Gestielle Alternative SGR, for helping me correct the book's drafts and for his invaluable comments.

I would like to thank François-Serge Lhabitant, Professor of Finance at Edhec in Paris and at the Ecole des Hautes Etudes Commerciales of the Lausanne University, for his advice on the work's structure; Alessandro Fassò, Professor of Statistics at the Faculty of Engineering with the University of Bergamo, for helping me with the statistical analysis of hedge fund index performances; and many hedge fund managers for helping me assemble trading examples.

Over the years, I have had the privilege of meeting a group of exceptional hedge fund managers: I would like to thank each of them for helping me understand their working approach.

It is evident that any mistakes in the book are the author's sole responsibility.

About the Author

Filippo Stefanini is deputy Chief Investment Officer in Aletti Gestielle Alternative SGR, an Italian alternative investment company that specializes in managing funds of hedge funds. This company is part of the banking group Banco Popolare di Verona e Novara and at December 31st 2005 has assets under management of €1.5 billion.

In 1998 he graduated with first-class honors in Industrial Engineering from Bergamo University, and began working as a consultant for Accenture in the Asset Management and Investment Banking areas in 1999. Since 2001 he has worked for Aletti Gestielle Alternative SGR, having participated in the start-up project. He was co-author of the 2002 book *Hedge Funds: to invest for generating absolute returns*. In 2005, he authored the book *Hedge Funds: the investment strategies*. Both books were published in Italy by Il Sole 24 Ore.

He is fluent in English and French and is married to Silvia Locatelli.

1
A Few Initial Remarks

1.1 WHAT IS A HEDGE FUND?

In the United States, the country where they first appeared and enjoyed the greatest development, there is no exact legal definition of the term "hedge fund" that outlines its operational footprint and gives a direct understanding of its meaning.

Yet, to rely on the literal meaning of hedge fund, i.e. "investment funds that employ hedging techniques", could be misleading, because it relates merely to just one of the many traits of hedge funds and makes reference to only one of the many investment techniques they deploy.

A more fitting definition in our opinion is the following: "A hedge fund is an investment instrument that provides different risk/return profiles compared to traditional stock and bond investments".

To appreciate the meaning fully, however, it is necessary to remark that hedge funds make use of investment strategies, or management styles, that are by definition alternative, and that they do not have to fulfill special regulatory limitations to pursue their mission: capital protection and generation of a positive return with low volatility and low market correlation.

Hedge funds are set up by managers who have decided to take the plunge into self-employment, and whose backgrounds can be traced to the world of mutual funds or proprietary trading for investment banks.

The differences between hedge funds and mutual funds are manifold.

The performance of mutual funds is measured against a benchmark, and as such it is a relative performance. A mutual fund manager considers any tracking error, i.e. any deviation from the benchmark, as a risk, and therefore risk is measured in correlation with the benchmark and not in absolute terms. In contrast, hedge funds seek to guarantee an absolute return under any circumstance, even when market indices are plummeting. This means that hedge funds have no benchmark, but rather different investment strategies.

Mutual funds cannot protect portfolios from descending markets, unless they sell or remain liquid. Hedge funds, however, in the case of declining markets, can find protection by implementing different hedging strategies and can generate positive returns. Short selling gives hedge fund managers a whole new universe of investment opportunities. It is not the general market performance that counts, but rather the relative performance of stocks.

The future return of mutual funds depends upon the direction of the markets in which they are invested, whereas the future return of hedge funds tends to have a very low correlation with the direction of financial markets.

Another major difference between hedge funds and mutual funds is that the latter are regulated and supervised by Regulatory Authorities, and are bound by limitations restricting their portfolio makeup and permitted instruments. Moreover, investors are further protected by obligations burdening the management company in terms of capital adequacy, proven robust organization and business processes. On the contrary, the absence of a stringent regulatory framework for hedge funds leaves the manager with greater latitude to set up a fund characterized by unique traits in terms of the financial instruments to be employed, the management style, the organizational structure and the legal form.

Therefore, the hedge fund industry is marked by a great heterogeneity, in that it is characterized by different investment strategies and by funds of a wide variety of sizes.

Although hedge funds immediately bring to mind the image of innovative investment strategies within the financial landscape, the first hedge fund came into existence more than half a century ago.

1.2   HISTORY OF HEDGE FUNDS

This section details some of the important events in the history of hedge funds.

Back in 1949, Alfred Winslow Jones, a former reporter for *Fortune*, started the first hedge fund with an initial capital of only US$100 000. Jones' core intuition was that by correctly combining two speculative techniques, i.e. using both short sales and leverage, it would be possible to reduce total portfolio risk and construct a conservative portfolio, featuring a low exposure to the general market performance. Jones also had two other major ideas: to cater to investors, he had invested all his savings in the fund he managed, and his profit came from a 20 % stake in the generated performance rather than from the payment of a fixed percentage of assets under management. This approach made it possible to bring the interests of manager and investor together.

Today, the archetype described above characterizes only a small number of hedge funds: the term is now used to refer to a vast realm of different management models.

At present, a hedge fund has five main characteristics:

- The manager is free to use a wide range of financial instruments.
- The manager can short sell.
- The manager can use leverage.
- The manager's profit comes from a management fee, which is fixed and accounts for 1.5–2.5 %, and from a 20–25 % fee on profits. Generally, the performance or incentive fee is applied only if the value of the hedge fund unit grows above the historical peak in absolute terms or over a one-year period.
- The manager invests a sizable part of his personal assets in the fund he manages, so as to bring his own interests in line with those of his clients.

In 1952, Jones opened up his partnership to other managers and started to hand over to them the management of portions of the portfolio, and within a short period of time he assigned them the task of picking stocks. Jones would allocate the capital among his managers, monitor and supervise all investment activities and manage the company's operations. The first hedge fund in history turned into the first multi-manager fund in history.

In 1967, Michael Steinhardt started Steinhardt, Fine, Berkowitz & Company with eight employees and an initial capitalization of $7.7 million. Steinhardt began his career as a stock picker and then, as his hedge fund grew, shifted to a multi-strategy fund. In the 1980s Steinhardt became head of a hedge fund group with roughly US$5 billion of assets under management and with over 100 employees. Steinhardt ended his hedge fund career in 1995 after suffering big losses in 1994.

By 1969, the US Securities and Exchange Commission (SEC) had started to keep a watchful eye over the blossoming industry of hedge funds as a result of the rapid growth in the number of new hedge funds and of assets under management. At that time, the commission estimated that approximately 200 hedge funds were in existence, with $1.5 billion of assets under management. 1969 was also the year that George Soros created the "Double Eagle" hedge fund, the predecessor of the more renowned Quantum Fund.

The first fund of hedge funds[1] was Leveraged Capital Holdings, created in Geneva in 1969 by Georges Karlweis of Banque Privée Edmond de Rothschild, which had the purpose of investing in the best single-managers of the time. Leveraged Capital Holdings also represents the first European hedge product.

In 1971, the first US fund of funds was started by Grosvenor Partners, and in 1973, the Permal Group launched the European multi-manager and multi-strategy fund of funds, called Haussmann Holdings N.V. The people who were given the task of creating the investment team for Permal were Jean Perret and Steve Mallory (hence the name Permal).

Then, in 1980, Julian Robertson and Thorpe McKenzie created Tiger Management Corporation and launched the hedge fund Tiger with an initial capital of $8.8 million. In 1983, Gilbert de Botton started Global Asset Management (GAM), a company specializing in the management of funds of hedge funds, which in 1999 was acquired by UBS AG and by the end of 2004 had some €38 billion of Assets under Management (AuM).

At the beginning of the 1990s, Soros, Robertson and Steinhardt managed macro funds worth several billion dollars and invested in stocks, bonds, currencies and commodities all over the world, trying to anticipate macro-economic trends.

In 1992, alternative investment instruments started to draw the attention of the press and of the financial community, when George Soros's Quantum Fund made huge profits anticipating the depreciation of the British pound and of the Italian lira.

The early 1990s were the heyday of macro funds. The exit of the British pound and the Italian lira from the European Monetary System in September 1992 allowed Soros to cash in an incredible profit of $2 billion.

On 4th February 1994, the Fed unexpectedly introduced the first rate hike of one quarter of a percentage point, which caused US treasuries to topple and led to a temporary drain of liquidity on the markets. The twin effect of panic on the markets and leverage proved disastrous for Steinhardt Partners, which in 1994 suffered a loss of 31 %. Steinhardt decided to retire at the end of 1995, despite the fact that during that year he had been able partly to recover the 1994 losses, ending 1995 up 26 %.

Later on, hedge funds bounced back into the headlines when in the first nine months of 1998 Long Term Capital Management, managed by John Meriwether and a think tank including two Nobel laureates in Economics (Myron Scholes and Robert Merton), generated a staggering $4 billion loss, starting a domino effect that left many banks, financial institutions and big brokers in many countries teetering on the brink of default. Only the prompt intervention of a bail-out team led by the Federal Reserve of Alan Greenspan avoided the onset of a systemic crisis.

In October 1998, when the Japanese yen appreciated against the dollar, Robertson suffered a loss of about $2 billion. In 1999, his long/short equity strategy, based on the analysis of fundamentals of listed companies, did not work at all in the market driven by the tail wind of the New Economy. After withdrawals from investors, assets under management had plunged from $25 billion in August 1998 to less than $8 billion at the end of March 2000.

---

[1] Ineichen, A.M. (2003) *Absolute Returns: The Risk and Opportunities of Hedge Fund Investing*, John Wiley & Sons, Inc.

At the end of March 2000, when the "dot-com" speculative bubble was at its peak, Robertson announced the liquidation of the Tiger Fund.

In April 2000, George Soros changed his chief investment strategist and soon after the CEO of Soros Fund Management LLC as well. Soros announced to his investors that he would stop making large leveraged macro investments. To reduce the risk he would downsize his return objectives.

1.3 PROPRIETARY TRADING

The world of hedge funds borders with that of proprietary trading in investment banks.

Proprietary trading desks are made up of groups of managers, who manage the proprietary book of banks following the same techniques and financial instruments employed by hedge funds. This affinity is further evidenced by the fact that many hedge fund managers have a past experience in proprietary trading desks for the most prestigious investment banks. The main difference lies in the fact that in a hedge fund the manager is also the owner, whereas proprietary trading managers are employees of the banks and only part of their variable wage is linked to the performance of the portfolio they manage.

Another difference is that the hedge fund industry puts an emphasis on monthly results, whereas the time horizon on which the performance of proprietary trading desks is measured is tied to the bank's quarterly reports.

Before the crisis in August 1998, proprietary trading played quite a role in the income statement of financial institutions. Immediately after the financial crisis of August 1998, which led to sharp losses, many proprietary trading desks were closed or segregated off the balance sheet by creating hedge funds. At present, proprietary trading is making a comeback, even though there is no one single model.

1.4 THE GROWTH OF THE HEDGE FUND INDUSTRY

Hedge Fund Research estimates that the number of hedge funds has gone from 610 in 1990 up to 7436 in 2004 (not including funds of hedge funds). Assets managed by hedge funds went from an estimated $38.9 billion in 1990 to approximately $973 billion in 2004.

According to Tremont Capital Management Inc., at the end of 2004 the hedge fund industry reached $975 billion of assets, in addition to another $300 billion held in managed accounts, totaling $1275 billion of AuM. Various sources agree in estimating that the number of active hedge funds is running at about 9000, with approximately 3500 managers.

In the period between 1990 and 2003, as shown in Figure 1.1, assets under management grew at a compound annual growth rate of 26 %, while the number of funds grew at a rate of 20 %.

A trillion dollars accounts for about 1.3 % of the total capitalization of financial markets, excluding the leverage, or 3.5 % including the leverage. Therefore the hedge fund industry can be considered a niche sector.

Why then bother with an industry that accounts for only 3–4 % of the assets of global financial markets? First, because it is estimated that hedge funds make up 10 % of market trade volumes, and second because this is the industry where some participants seem to be able to generate a market-uncorrelated performance.

Figure 1.2 compares the cumulative returns of the hedge fund industry with the cumulative returns of stock and bond markets in the period between 1994 and 2004. Note that as of March 2000, while global stock markets started to slip, hedge funds on average were able to protect their capital and to generate positive returns with a low volatility.

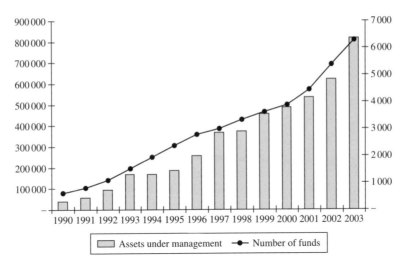

Figure 1.1 The growth of the hedge fund industry. The left scale represents the assets under management in billion US dollars and the right scale is the number of hedge funds from 1990 to 2003. Source: Hedge Fund Research, Inc. © HFR, Inc.2004, www.hedgefundresearch.com. Reproduced by permission of Hedge Fund Research, Inc.

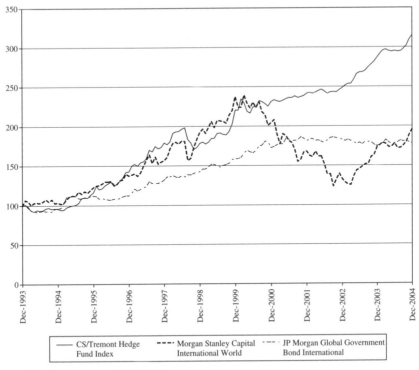

All indices are expressed in US dollars.

Figure 1.2 Cumulative returns of the hedge fund industry compared with cumulative returns of stock and bond markets from 1994 to 2004. Source: Bloomberg L.P.

1.5 MAIN CHARACTERISTICS OF THE CURRENT INDUSTRY

Hedge funds are characterized by the use of alternative management styles or investment strategies, which is in fact what this book intends to analyze.

Figure 1.3 shows the makeup of the hedge fund industry by investment strategy at the end of 2004, measured as a percentage of assets under management. It is clear that the two main investment strategies are long/short equity, with 33%, and the event driven style, which accounts for 19% of the market share.

It is also worth examining the hedge fund industry distribution by size. For this type of analysis, we took into consideration only hedge funds that had been operating for at least five years, and we examined asset data as of 31st December 2004 supplied by the LIPPER TASS database. Since the hedge fund assets supplied by this database are denominated in various currencies, we translated all of them into dollars at the exchange rate in force on 31st December 2004.

The resulting industry's actual profile is illustrated in Figure 1.4: each bar of the chart represents the sum of the assets of all hedge funds that belong to that size bracket. Size brackets have been arbitrarily chosen to be seven.

Clearly, the hedge fund industry proves to be heterogeneous in terms of fund size.

In reality, the industry's actual profile should also include the myriads of hedge funds that have little assets under management, that were launched a short time ago, and that are not releasing their performance data to any database yet.

The low barriers to entry characterizing the hedge fund universe lead us to assume a size distribution with a completely different shape: see the curve in Figure 1.4. Let us rotate the bar chart 360° around the dotted axis shown in the chart. Figure 1.5 shows the industry shape subdivided by homogeneous size brackets: we obtain a "vase" shape. According to some journalists we have opened up Pandora's box! Successful hedge funds are those that have reached a bigger size and over time have achieved a consistent performance. The base of

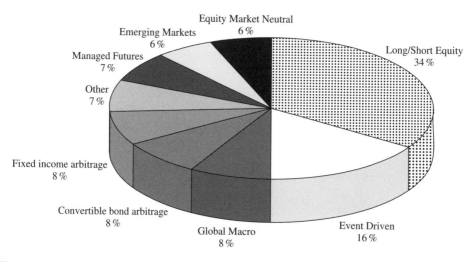

Figure 1.3 Makeup of the hedge fund industry by investment strategy at the end of 2004 (percentages of assets under management). Source: LIPPER TASS, Tremont Capital Management, Inc.

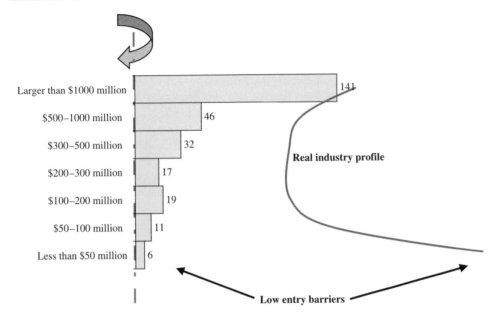

Figure 1.4 Profile of the hedge funds industry for dimensional classes at the end of 2004. Source: calculation on LIPPER TASS data

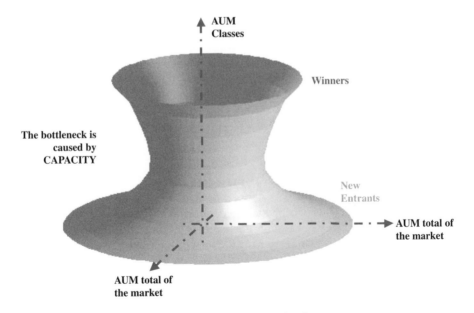

Figure 1.5 Pandora's box?

the "vase" is represented by new entrants, as well as by hedge funds that are having trouble generating returns.

The hedge fund industry is characterized by low barriers to entry for new managers: investment banks roll out the red carpet for managers who wish to launch a new hedge fund. The reason is that hedge funds are great clients for investment banks, as a result of the substantial brokerage fees they pay on the purchase and sale of financial instruments. In addition to brokerage services, investment banks even provide them with office space, technological infrastructures, risk management systems, and through their *capital introduction* systems, they also take care of the fund's marketing among final investors.

Low barriers to entry and the appealing fee structure brew an explosive mixture fostering the proliferation of new hedge funds. This phenomenon is heightened further by the strong demand for quality hedge funds on the part of investors. For a successful manager it is very easy to raise money to invest. As we will see in some numerical examples later on, every hedge fund manager knows all too well that the greater the amount of money he manages, the higher the fees he is going to earn. Why then do the assets managed by hedge funds not grow exponentially? The reason lies in the so-called capacity issue, which is what determines the bottleneck in the "vase" depicted in Figure 1.5.

1.6   CAPACITY

The largest equity mutual fund is Vanguard's index fund S&P 500, with more than $94 billion of assets under management, while the biggest fixed income fund is Pacific Investment Management Company's Total Return Fund, with a capital of €73 billion at the end of 2003. Vanguard and Fidelity manage $675 and $955 billion, respectively.

Often, hedge funds that are closed to new capital do not disclose their performance to databases and therefore elude the classifications of journalists who have but a hazy knowledge of the hedge industry. In recent years, no two similar classifications have been published with regard to major hedge funds when weighted by assets under management.

The hedge fund business is no scalable business, due to the inherent diseconomies of scale. Assets managed by a hedge fund cannot exceed a certain limit, called capacity, without negatively affecting its performance. Beyond given limits, additional capital prevents the replication of relative value strategies and dilutes returns, obliging hedge funds to take on a greater directional risk in the attempt to keep up their performance.

Because capacity limits the size of hedge funds, the assets managed by the largest hedge funds are definitely less than those managed by the largest mutual funds.

1.7   COMMISSIONS

Some funds have become famous for their performance, their size, the aura of mystery surrounding them – since they release information only to their investors and are closed to new investors – and for their commissions, which have been said by some investors to be "outrageous". If we analyze the most extreme cases, we find a group with annual management fees of 6–7% and performance fees of 20%; another group charges no management fees but its performance fees are 50% of profits; other groups charge a 3% annual management fee and performance fees account for 30% of profits.

Most hedge funds charge their clients with performance fees accounting for about one fifth of profits, but you can get as high as one fourth, one third or even half the gains generated by the hedge fund.

A hedge fund's rewarding system is asymmetric. Fund managers receive a portion of the profits but do not share in the losses. If a manager suffers a loss, he tends to take on greater risks to start showing a profit again.

The best way to solve this asymmetry is when managers also own fund units, i.e., when they share a personal interest in the fund management: managers invest their own savings in the same place where hedge fund customers put their money. Ownership is a direct and powerful incentive that can guarantee a careful asset management.

According to Van Hedge Fund Advisors International LLC, on 31st December 2003, 78 % of hedge fund managers had invested at least $500 000 of their own savings in their hedge funds.

1.8   INDUSTRY PERFORMANCE OVERVIEW

Let us take a look at the hedge fund index data, whose structure will be analyzed in each chapter of the book.

The percentage of positive months is good (71 %), with an average performance in positive months of +1.9 %. The annualized performance is greater than the selected equity index and bond index, while volatility lies halfway between that of the equity index and the bond index.

Figure 1.6 shows the monthly returns of the CS/Tremont Hedge Fund Index from 1994 to 2004.

Figure 1.7 depicts the historical performance trend as a function of risk for the CS/Tremont Hedge Fund Index between 1994 and 2004. The chart is a squiggle showing the 12-month moving average of the average annual return as a function of the 12-month moving average of the annualized mean standard deviation. Each dot represents the average risk/return in the previous 12 months and the squiggle joining the various dots shows the historical track of the index on a risk-return plane. The moving average is used to reduce data noise. The concentration ellipsoid shows that in the last three years the hedge fund industry in general shifted towards a low volatility. The cluster represents the normality, while the "wriggles" lying outside the cluster represent deviations from normality.

Figure 1.8 becomes particularly interesting in the light of the so-called high water mark. According to Van Hedge Fund Advisors International LLC, on 31st December 2003, 93 % of hedge funds had high water marks. As the term implies, technically speaking a high water mark defines the value the fund must reach to take performance fees. The performance fee is not applied if the value of the fund unit, although higher than the previous month, does not grow above the initial value of the unit calculated in any previous month.

The chart in Figure 1.8 highlights the sharp and sudden drawdown that took place in August 1998. In that month there was a strong *flight-to-quality* caused by the default of Russia's domestic currency debt. The drawdown lasted three months, and it took 13 months to recover the losses.

Figure 1.8 was obtained by ignoring positive performances generated in a period of no drawdown, while in the other cases we considered only the negative performances of the hedge fund industry and the time it took to recover from the negative performance and emerge from the drawdown. We observe that from 1994 to 2004 hedge funds often went "underwater". In those below-the-watermark periods, on average hedge funds did not collect performance fees, because they had to work to return to their pre-loss levels. The periods in which hedge funds do not earn performance fees are quite tense for the management company organization. Losses could turn out to be excessive, so that some employees,

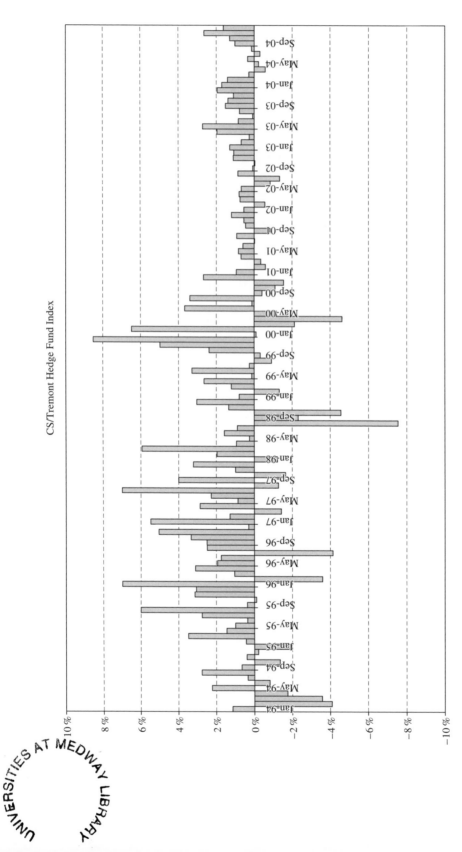

CS/Tremont Hedge Fund Index

Figure 1.6 Monthly returns of CS/Tremont Hedge Fund Index from 1994 to 2004. Source: CS/Tremont Index LLC, www.hedgeindex.com. Copyright © 2006, Credit Suisse/Tremont Index LLC. All rights reserved*

* See page 298 for full copyright notice.

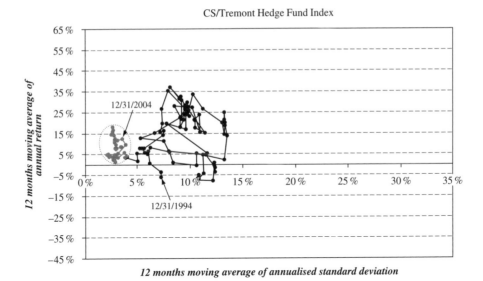

Figure 1.7 Historical performance trend of return as a function of risk for CS/Tremont Hedge Fund Index from 1994 to 2004. Source: CS/Tremont Index LLC, www.hedgeindex.com. Copyright © 2006, Credit Suisse/Tremont Index LLC. All rights reserved*

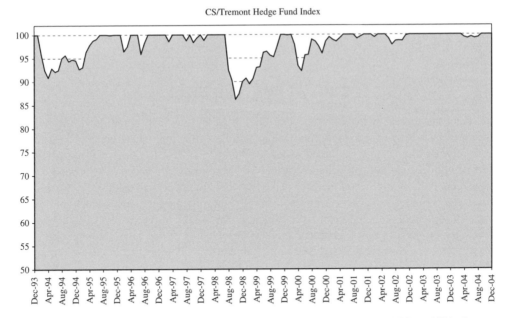

Figure 1.8 Underwater periods for CS/Tremont Hedge Fund Index from 1994 to 2004. Source: CS/Tremont Index LLC, www.hedgeindex.com. Copyright © 2006, Credit Suisse/Tremont Index LLC. All rights reserved*

---

instead of working to recover the losses, may decide to resign and go to work for hedge funds that are performing well. The management company may also decide to liquidate the hedge fund that has incurred substantial losses, or even worse, the manager might take too many risks to recover the losses. Hennessee Group calculated the *attrition rate* of hedge funds (i.e., the rate of liquidated funds) based on its proprietary database. In 2004, the attrition rate was 5.3 %, while the annualized attrition rate over a six-year period was about 5 %. The rate of attrition also includes funds that shut down for reasons other than the fund's performance.

It is clear that hedge fund investors need to be aware and carefully monitor this issue.

1.9   THE HEDGE FUND MANAGER

As has already been remarked, each hedge fund tends to be unique. Hedge funds are characterized by a strong entrepreneurship and the absence of a stringent regulatory framework. Every hedge fund has its unique organizational and legal structure, particular business culture, management style, and manager's professional experience, age and education. In every hedge fund it is the manager who sets the rules of the game in full latitude: management style, investment time horizon, return and volatility objectives, target market and the fund's optimal capacity.

Perhaps the most singular aspect is the manager's experience, with quite a motley collection of backgrounds: there are sculptors, journalists, Noble laureates, nuclear engineers, physicists, mathematicians, chess champions, IT engineers, geologists, biologists, physicians, strategic consultants, lawyers, investment bankers, brokers, etc. Often the greatest innovations come from people who draw from a very different experience than most of the other players, because they can look at problems from a fresh slant.

1.10   ALPHA AND BETA

Based on the theory of the Capital Asset Pricing Model, we can break down the returns generated by a hedge fund into a linear alpha and beta function, where alpha measures the extra-return which cannot be linked to market trends and beta measures the sensitivity of rates of return to market performance variations. The returns of a hedge fund depend on the manager's skill, as well as on market conditions, that are not related to the single talents of managers. However, when analyzing single investment strategies, we shall see that this model does not fit in well with hedge fund performance. The source of returns varies significantly, depending on the different investment strategies adopted by hedge funds, among individual hedge funds, and over time. Hence, we would rather use a theoretical model that allows for a more efficient explanation of the performance of hedge funds, and to this end we distinguish between traditional beta and alternative beta, and between structural alpha and "skill" alpha (Figure 1.9).

Traditional sources of beta are the stock market, bond duration and credit spreads. Even though these factors are not normally distributed and, as such, their risk is not well measured by beta, we find it valuable to identify the sources of beta.

Alternative sources of beta are liquidity, volatility, correlations, the risk inherent in corporate events, beta of commodity markets and the complexity inherent in the modeling of corporate events or structured products.

Figure 1.9   Break up of the hedge fund return. Source: Copyright Harcourt

Structural alpha is linked to the structural advantages enjoyed by hedge funds, for example the greater regulatory freedom, the latitude offered by having no benchmark, flexibility and nimbleness, and limited size.

Alpha linked to the manager's talent is represented by his analytical skills, the ability to produce fresh investment ideas, and his portfolio management and risk management skills. Alpha appears in the presence of a highly talented manager who enjoys an information advantage. Real time information today is a commodity, because of the Internet. An excellent manager is a person, who with special insight digests a huge amount of information and is able to attach a meaning to it. Consider for example a manager who has been working for 15 years in a strategic consulting company, dealing only with the car industry. His knowledge of the car industry has been acquired in the field through the delivery of strategic plans of many car companies. This person could thus build an in-depth knowledge of the industry's dynamics, together with a network of liaisons with managing directors of the major companies of this sector, and knowledge about the suppliers of car manufacturers, customers and internal competition. This example clearly illustrates the existence of the hedge fund manager's alpha. A piece of news covering a specific car manufacturer or the price trends of raw materials will not just click on a light in the manager's head, but rather an entire Christmas tree flooding with lights. A given piece of news takes on quite a different meaning for him than for most other investors, and this gives him an information advantage, i.e. a unique competitive edge.

Throughout this book, for each hedge fund investment strategy, we shall refer to Figure 1.9 to identify the market factors that affect hedge fund performance.

1.11   INVESTMENT STRATEGIES

Mutual funds are classified by breaking them down into the markets and sectors in which they invest, whereas hedge funds are classified first by the investment style followed by the manager and second in terms of market or sector. However, often hedge funds are managed along multiple styles and therefore they may straddle various categories. Within a given investment strategy, there are managers who have such a peculiar style as to be unique. This book is not intended to solicit investments or express judgments on the validity of one strategy over another. Its aim is to describe the "state-of-the-art" of hedge fund investment strategies and give an overview of the heterogeneous hedge fund industry. Investment strategies are so vast and complex that a whole book could be written for each of them.

An investment strategy stems from the manager's experience and creativity, endowing it with nuances that make it almost unique. There is no single classification of hedge fund strategies, and what is more, hedge fund strategies are no static universe, rather they are subject to constant change and expansion.

In 1735, the Swedish botanist Carl von Linné, best known under the Latinized name of Carolus Linnaeus, published the book *Systema Naturae*, where he designed a classification system for plants and animals, from which the current system takes origin. Linnaeus assigned a binomial Latin name to each species: first the genus of belonging, then the specific "shorthand" name.

Confronted with a huge variety of investment strategies adopted by hedge funds, we may well apply Linnaeus's classification system to hedge funds, and thus identify five similar "genera":

1. Relative value
2. Event driven
3. Directional/Trading
4. Long/short equity
5. Other strategies

Each genus is then subdivided into different identified species, as in Figure 1.10.

Classifications are by themselves limited, but they do help us gain a better understanding of the vast and heterogeneous world of hedge funds.

Relative value strategies are arbitrage transactions that seek to profit from the spread between two securities rather than from the general market direction. Relative value strategies include merger arbitrage, convertible bond arbitrage, fixed income arbitrage, mortgage-backed arbitrage and capital structure arbitrage.

Event driven strategies seek to capitalize on opportunities arising during a company's life cycle, triggered by extraordinary corporate events, such as spin-offs, mergers, acquisition, business combinations, liquidations and restructuring.

Directional/Trading strategies seek to take advantage of major market trends rather than focusing their analysis on single stocks. Directional/Trading strategies include the managed futures and macro strategies.

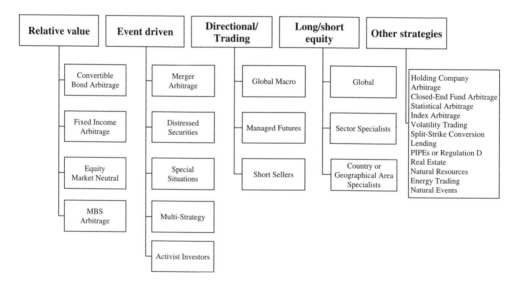

Figure 1.10   The investment strategies

Long/short equity strategies is where the manager takes a long position on stock he feels the market is underpricing and short sells stock he perceives is being overpriced. This is by far the largest discipline among hedge funds, maybe the easiest to understand but at the same time one of the most difficult to implement.

Other strategies is a residual category where we included all the most recent and innovative strategies.

The hedge fund industry is always on the shift, and since the early 1990s it has completely reshaped, as shown in Figure 1.11: according to Hedge Fund Research, in 1990, 71 % of the industry was made up of hedge funds managed along the macro strategy. The losses incurred by this strategy in 1994 and 1998 brought about a deep change throughout the whole hedge fund business.

To date, approximately 50 % of the hedge fund industry is comprised of relative-value based funds, while in the last decade the weight of the long/short equity strategy remained practically unchanged, starting at about one third, inching up to 50 % in 1999 and 2000, and then slipping down again to 36 %.

The change in the weight of the various strategies over time reflects the ups and downs of their returns. In the twilight of macro funds, the hedge fund industry shifted towards arbitrage strategies and the long/short equity strategy.

The analysis of hedge fund investment strategies helps understand that they should not to be made to bear the blame if some listed stocks go down the drain. Sweeping generalizations are never correct: from a philosophical point of view it is like deriving a general principle from a particular instance, making it clear that the logical process of induction is not applicable.

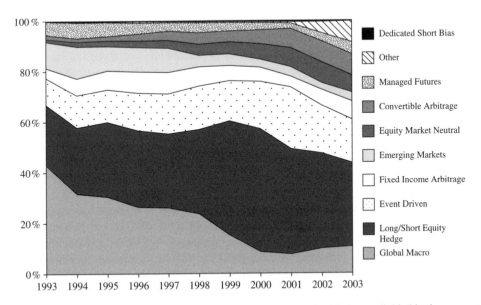

Figure 1.11 Shift of the assets under management of the hedge fund industry divided by investment strategy from 1993 to 2003. Source: calculation on TASS Research, Tremont Capital Management, Inc. data

1.12   EXPLORERS AND FRONTIERS

According to a metaphor introduced by Professor Goetzmann of Yale University, hedge funds are explorers that operate on the frontiers of markets. Once discovered, analyzed and "cleared", the frontier recedes and explorers must constantly re-adapt to new frontiers.

Today, it is the emerging markets such as Russia, China, India and Korea that represent geographical frontiers.

New frontiers are also new types of assets, as options were at the end of the 1970s, securitizations in the 1980s, index derivatives in the 1980s and 1990s, credit derivatives at the end of the 1990s, and as energy trading and structured finance are today. Hedge fund managers are market makers for these new assets. When a new financial market is created for a new asset, it is affected by the problem of low liquidity, as investors are not familiar with the new financial instruments.

Hedge fund managers spend time analyzing the information structure and digesting information so as to be always surfing out in the front of the information flow. Transparency removes the motivation to explore and develop new frontiers, but new investment styles shall emerge and disappear as the financial market frontier shifts.

The macro-frontier is represented by the development of models for making links across the different economies. The new research micro-frontier is represented by models to track market trends.

1.13   SEC'S VIGILANCE

The exponential growth enjoyed by the hedge fund industry led the US Securities and Exchange Commission (SEC) to take a closer look at this phenomenon. In September 2003, the SEC conducted a comprehensive study (*Implications of the growth of hedge funds*, a 113 page report) on US hedge funds, based on which, on 26th October 2004, it introduced the requirement for hedge fund management companies with at least 15 clients and $30 million of assets under management to register with the Commission starting from 1st February 2006. Only the hedge funds with at least two years lock-up are exempted from registering.

The registration means that management companies will be required to make periodical disclosures regarding their organizational structure, and they will be subject to periodical compliance examinations by the Commission staff.

1.14   CONSIDERATIONS ON PERFORMANCE
SUSTAINABILITY

To examine and reflect on the hedge fund business, we have identified a number of short *business cases* that allow us to draw some useful considerations. Let us start with a very simple example, and take an individual willing to invest an initial capital of €100 000 on financial markets. If the investment generates a 20 % net profit yearly for ten years running, and if profits are reinvested, at the end our investor will own a capital of €619 174, with a six-fold increase over the initial capital. However, although on year one he should earn €20 000, on year ten he should earn €103 196, that is, five times the profit realized on year one. As Table 1.1 shows, with each passing year it gets more and more difficult for our investor to meet the objective of a net 20 % annual performance, because each year he has to gain more and more money.

Table 1.1

Year	Capital at year-end	Gain during the year
0	€ 100 000	
1	€ 120 000	€ 20 000
2	€ 144 000	€ 24 000
3	€ 172 800	€ 28 800
4	€ 207 360	€ 34 560
5	€ 248 832	€ 41 472
6	€ 298 598	€ 49 766
7	€ 358 318	€ 59 720
8	€ 429 982	€ 71 664
9	€ 515 978	€ 85 996
10	€ 619 174	€ 103 196

A hedge fund manager needs to find new opportunities quickly enough to keep up with the growth in assets under management. This explains why a very successful hedge fund at some point or another has to redeem to its investors part of their investments due to capacity saturation.

It also explains why, once they reach a given size, successful hedge funds must necessarily turn into macro or multi-strategy funds to generate satisfactory returns.

1.15 CAPACITY AND PERFORMANCE SUSTAINABILITY

Let us take into consideration a macro hedge fund that starts managing $5 billion and generates a 30 % performance per year for 32 years in a row.

The fund's capitalization at the end of year 32 would amount to approximately $22 000 billion, namely equal to the current capitalization of US equity markets: this means that this hypothetical fund would own all the stocks traded on US markets. Clearly a paradox. It is now quite intuitive that high performances can be sustained only on relatively small AuM.

1.16 ABILITY OR CHANCE?

Another very simple example allows us to understand how every year there are some investors who can boast exceptional performances. Let's assume that every year there are n investors who, lacking any managing skill, invest at random, and let's assume that the probability they will achieve a positive return is 1 out of 2, and the probability they get a negative result is once again 1 out of 2. Let's assume that k is the number of investment years. The probability that among n managers there are a few who obtain k consecutive positive returns is measured by the following formula:

$$\binom{n}{k} \cdot \left(\frac{1}{2}\right)^k \cdot \left(\frac{1}{2}\right)^{n-k}$$

where

$$\binom{n}{k} = \frac{n!}{k! \cdot (n-k)!} \quad \text{and where } n! = 1 \cdot 2 \cdot \ldots \cdot n$$

The probability of having 10 positive results in a row is 0.10 %, namely 1 out of every 1000 investors.

The probability of having 9 or 10 positive results over a 10-year period is 1.07 %, or 10 out of 1000 investors.

The probability of having 8 or more positive results over a 10-year period is 5.47 %, or 50 out of 1000 investors.

The hedge fund picker will always bump into a fund that started to short the NIKKEI in 1990 or the NASDAQ on March 2000, but it is difficult to determine if it was by pure chance or due to the manager's skills. True enough, past performance is not indicative of future returns, but no doubt it provides us with precious information on the manager's behavior when confronted with successes or failures along his managing business.

1.17   THE IMPORTANCE OF AVOIDING LOSSES

This last example tells us how important the first investment rule is: never lose. According to Warren Buffett, this rule should be etched into the mind of investors.

Let us assume that an investor wants to get a net annual 20 % profit and instead suffers a 20 % loss in year five. On year six, to recover the loss and to meet his return objective of 20 % per year, the investor cannot just generate a 20 % or even 40 % performance, but rather has to get up to +80 %. This clearly shows that it is extremely difficult to recover a loss (Table 1.2).

In the book, *Creative Destruction*,[2] it is suggested that long-term studies on the creation, survival and disappearance of US companies clearly show that the corporate equivalent of El Dorado, i.e. a golden firm that is constantly over-performing, has never existed: it is a myth. Consider, for example, that in 1917 the US monthly magazine *Forbes* published the list of the top 100 US companies. Seventy years later, in 1987, *Forbes* published once again the original list and showed that 61 companies of the original top 100 had gone out of business. More than that: the surviving 39 companies had down-performed the market by 20 %.

Table 1.2

Year	Capital at year-end	Gain during the year	Performance (%)
0	€100 000		
1	€120 000	€20 000	+20 %
2	€144 000	€24 000	+20 %
3	€172 800	€28 800	+20 %
4	€207 360	€34 560	+20 %
5	€165 888	€− 41 472	−20 %
6	€298 598	€+ 132 710	+80 %
7	€358 318	€59 720	+20 %
8	€429 982	€71 664	+20 %
9	€515 978	€85 996	+20 %
10	€619 174	€103 196	+20 %

[2] Foster, R. and Kaplan, S. (2001) *Creative Destruction: Why Companies That Are Built to Last Underperform the Market – And How to Successfully Transform Them*, New York: Doubleday.

We may well draw an analogy with the hard sustainability of hedge fund performance. It is evident that those who wish to invest in this asset class would be better off relying on fund of hedge fund managers, who are in a position to manage a periodical portfolio turnover, while conducting a due diligence on hedge funds included in the portfolios.

1.18 DECREASING RETURNS WITH LONGER INVESTMENT HORIZONS

Let us assume we invest €100 000 in a stock that turns out to be a great investment. Let's say that we sell the same stock for €150 000. It is self-evident that the longer the time necessary to close our investment, the greater the return decrease. However, it might be surprising to visualize how rapidly our return actually deteriorates. Let's see what happens to our return if, instead of one year, we have to wait longer to sell (Table 1.3).

The annual return declines rapidly from +50 % to +8.4 % after five years. How important the time necessary to close an investment turns out to be!

Table 1.3

Years	Annual return (%)
1	+50.0 %
2	+22.5 %
3	+14.5 %
4	+10.7 %
5	+8.4 %

1.19 BUSINESS CASE: A HEDGE FUND START-UP

Let us consider as an exemplification the start-up of a hedge fund. Let's try and estimate the profit of a fund management company, whose fee structure is 1.5 % management fee and 20 % performance fee. To make things simple, let's say that fees are collected at year-end, capital follows a linear growth, management fees are collected first, followed by performance fees, and that management fees are calculated based on the average asset value. We won't consider income taxes. Let's assume also that overhead costs, namely personnel costs, office rents and the depreciation of IT equipment, like servers and PCs, amount to $1.5 million per year (Table 1.4).

Table 1.4

Case number	Gross performance generated by the manager (%)	Initial capital of the hedge fund in million dollars	Profits generated by the management company in million dollars
1	10 %	$ 100	$ 1.76
2	20 %	$ 100	$ 3.82
3	10 %	$ 200	$ 5.02
4	20 %	$ 200	$ 9.14

It is clear that the manager would make a much greater profit than the wage he would get as an employee in charge of a proprietary trading desk for an investment bank.

But the other side of the coin is what happens if during the year the manager starting a hedge fund with an initial capital of $100 million delivers a gross performance of -10%? In this case, the management company would suffer a $75 000 loss. With such a poor performance, however, few investors would keep their money invested in the fund, and therefore the fund could be hit by a wave of redemptions that might cause its liquidation.

This example shows clearly how appealing the idea of opening a new hedge fund may be for a talented manager.

The next chapter describes the meaning of arbitrage in the hedge fund world in order to be able to later understand the arbitrage strategies. It is one of the most important chapters of the book, because arbitrage plays such an important role in much of the hedge funds thinking.

2
Arbitrage

There is no free lunch.
Old Stock Exchange adage

Arbitrage strategies are very popular in the hedge fund world, but before turning to their description, it is necessary to clarify the specific meaning of the term "arbitrage" in this context.

From an academic point of view, an arbitrage stands for a risk-free transaction that generates an instant profit: a theoretical example of arbitrage is the concurrent purchase and sale of the same security on different markets at different prices. By buying the same security at a lower price and selling it right away at a higher price, an arbitrageur earns an immediate profit at no risk, saving the settlement and delivery risks.

But in the hedge fund business the term arbitrage has developed a different sense, in that it does not refer to risk-free positions, but rather to positions involving risks other than the market risk. Hedge fund arbitrages in practice are directional positions on spreads: if the spread widens or narrows as anticipated, the manager makes a profit; otherwise he suffers a loss. Therefore we must not be misled by the word arbitrage: a hedge fund may·well suffer a loss even when it has constructed an arbitrage position – what it takes, is for the spread to widen or narrow contrary to predictions.

An arbitrage opportunity may appear when given technical, geographical, legal or administrative barriers interfere with the correct interaction between two markets trading the same security, thus preventing the security from having the same price on both markets.

In a perfect world, there would be no arbitrage opportunities, and in the real world most arbitrage opportunities tend to disappear quickly, unless there are high transaction costs that hamper frequent arbitrages. Over time, inevitably, other arbitrageurs will get organized to take advantage of arbitrage opportunities, narrowing down the price difference until it disappears. Arbitrage opportunities draw various arbitrageurs to the market, and they will erode each other's profits by competing against one another. Once again, to make a return it is necessary to take on risks!

It is important to note that arbitrageurs are not asked to forecast the absolute movement of two securities, but rather the relative movement of one over the other, irrespective of market direction.

Any arbitrage opportunity faces so-called *steamroller risks*. Through a colorful analogy, an arbitrageur is seen as somebody who picks up a few coins from the ground in front of a moving steamroller: the man runs no risk provided he never forgets that the steamroller is forging ahead towards him. In order to earn a few coins the man runs the risk of being steamrolled.

Risks can also come from regulatory or tax changes, which may force the arbitrageur to close a position while losing money. Or, as illustrated below in the ADR arbitrage example, sometimes conditions regulating the short sale of a security may change suddenly, and the security may be called in by the owner; or sometimes the borrowed security may pay out a dividend, which is going to represent an unexpected cost for the arbitrageur.

The greater the number of arbitrageurs operating on a given market, the higher the competition, which means that the returns realized by the arbitrageurs will be lower. The current trend in the hedge fund business is that the massive money flow towards arbitrage strategies makes it more and more difficult for managers to generate interesting returns.

Most of the low-hanging fruits have already been picked!

2.1   THE TRANSACTION COSTS BARRIER

Transaction costs are made up of the brokerage fees that the hedge fund pays to brokers to buy and sell securities. Arbitrage opportunities will generate profits only if they are large enough to exceed transaction costs.

In Figure 2.1 we depict the barrier represented by transaction costs. In the chart we have plotted the difference between the actual price and the theoretical price for a financial instrument selected by a hedge fund manager. As evidenced by the chart, the trading opportunities offered to the manager taper off as time passes, due to the growing competition of other arbitrageurs. In black, we show the profit opportunities for most arbitrageurs: it is clear that these opportunities peter out and disappear over time. In gray, we show the additional profits that can be cashed in by those hedge funds that are able to negotiate lower brokerage fees with their brokers.

All managers attach great importance to reducing transaction costs, so as to expand the opportunity universe of profitable trades. To do so, they need to examine the market microstructure and the impact of transaction costs on viable trading opportunities. The Monte Carlo simulation method is often used to this end.

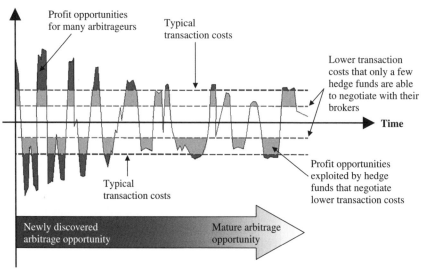

Figure 2.1   The transaction costs barrier

Typically, transaction costs present economies of scale: the greater the size of the fund, the greater the trading frequency, and the lower the transaction costs that the manager is able to negotiate with his counterparties. As a result, the largest funds with the highest trading frequency will enjoy a broader universe of arbitrage opportunities.

2.2   ADR ARBITRAGE

ADR (*American Depositary Receipt*) is a certificate issued by a US bank, traded in the United States as domestic shares, with settlement in the United States. It is a receipt certifying the number of shares of a foreign-based corporation held by the US bank in the country of origin. The receipt can also represent multiples of the foreign shares.

GDR (*Global Depositary Receipt*) is a certificate issued by a bank and traded in the same country as the bank of issue as domestic shares. The receipt certifies the number of shares of a foreign-based corporation held by the bank in the country of origin.

In India, Korea, Taiwan, Thailand, Hong Kong and Australia, ADR and GDR may trade at a premium or at a discount against the local share prices. This opens up arbitrage opportunities between ADR (or GDR) and local shares: it is an arbitrage between similar shares, traded simultaneously on two different markets. The impact of different buy or sale flows on different markets and exchange rate changes causes the prices of the ADR or of the underlying share to fluctuate. The barriers to entry for this arbitrage strategy are transaction costs and the speed of transaction execution both on the ADR and on the underlying share.

Figure 2.2 shows an example of ADR arbitrage using the company Infosys. The figure plots the premium at which the ADR is traded over the local share. The ADR trades at a

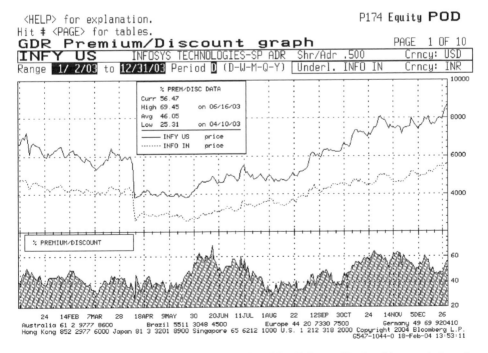

Figure 2.2 Arbitrage between local share and ADR: Infosys. Used with permission from Bloomberg L.P.

premium of 57 % against the local share, so the hedge fund manager takes the following position: long on the local share and short ADR. (Infosys Technologies Ltd is a multinational based in Bangalore, India, with more than 21 000 employees worldwide. It provides Information Technology advisory services and software services, including e-business, program management and supply chain solutions. The services include application development, product co-design, system implementation and engineering in sectors such as the insurance, banking, telecommunications and manufacturing industries. The share is traded on the NASDAQ (INFY) and in India on the National Stock Exchange (INFY NS), Bombay Stock Exchange (INFY BO) and Bangalore Stock Exchange.)

2.3 ARBITRAGE BETWEEN OFF-THE-RUN AND ON-THE-RUN THIRTY-YEAR TREASURY BONDS

The arbitrage between off-the-run and on-the-run thirty-year Treasury Bonds was devised in the 1970s by a group of arbitrageurs, the Bond Arbitrage Group of Salomon Brothers, headed by John Meriwether. Let's see how it is constructed.

A few months after the issue of a thirty-year Treasury Bond, the presence of many long-term investors leaves very few notes outstanding, thus reducing their liquidity. However, the US Treasury is still issuing new thirty-year Treasury Bonds. The Treasury notes issued a few months earlier are said to be *off-the-run*, whereas the newly issued ones are called *on-the-run*. Since the off-the-run notes are less liquid, they are traded at a slight discount over on-the-run notes.

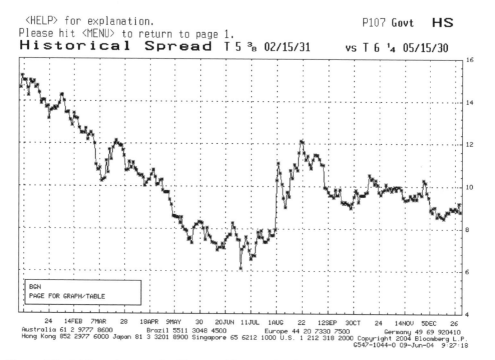

Figure 2.3 Arbitrage between the thirty-year Treasury Bond on-the-run and the thirty-year Treasury Bond off-the-run. Used with permission from Bloomberg L.P.

Arbitrageurs open a convergence position on the spread between the two Treasury notes and make a profit if the spread narrows. Since the spread is very small, to make an interesting return it is necessary to resort to leverage.

Figure 2.3 shows the spread between the thirty-year Treasury Bond issued on 15th February 2001 (on-the-run) and the thirty-year Treasury Bond issued on 15th February 2000 (off-the-run). As evidenced by the figure, the spread narrows down throughout 2003, from about 15 bps to approximately 9 bps. By buying thirty-year Treasury Bonds due on 15th February 2031 and selling short the same amount of thirty-year Treasury Bonds due on 15th February 2030, a hedge fund manager could have made a profit out of the spread convergence.

The next chapter will describe short selling, the enabler of all the hedge fund strategies. The structure of the following chapters comes from a classification of the arbitrage opportunities sought in equities, mergers and acquisitions, convertible bonds, fixed income securities and in special situations.

3
Short Selling

You'll never be the most popular guy at the party
if you say the emperor has no clothes.
A hedge fund manager

Remember Hans Christian Andersen's tale *The Emperor's New Suit*, in which all the courtiers strive to please their Emperor, and all are afraid to speak their minds? Can we see this applying to today's emperors, namely the managing directors of large corporations listed on financial markets?

The hedge fund manager may use this tale to say that people who have a mind of their own and do not go with the crowd may prove rather annoying. In the tale, no courtier has the courage to tell the emperor that he is actually naked, because they all fear they will be considered unfit for their jobs. Today, financial markets are all biased towards good news: if somebody says a company should be sold because it is destroying value, he is not going to be very popular! Short sellers who pin down poorly managed companies are not widely appreciated, but they can be considered the market's independent voice, and are therefore very important for markets as a warning signal against excesses.

3.1 A BRIEF HISTORY OF SHORT SELLING

This section details some of the important events in the history of short selling, and shows the repeated – failed – attempts to outlaw it.

In his book *Devil Take the Hindmost: A History of Financial Speculation*, Edward Chancellor suggests that the first case of short selling took place in 1609, when the Dutch merchant, Isaac Le Maire, organized short sales on stocks of the Dutch East Indies Company VOC listed on the Amsterdam Stock Exchange. In 1610, the VOC directors convinced the Dutch States-General to declare short selling illegal because bearish speculators were "incommensurably damaging innocent shareholders, among which are widows and orphans". Since the illegal activities continued anyway, instead of forbidding them, in 1689 the Dutch government decided to levy a tax on profits from short sales.

In the 18th and 19th centuries, short sales were banned time and again in Great Britain, France and Germany. Only rarely however were these bans actively enforced, and operators found it easy to circumvent them.

In 1720, the South-Sea speculative bubble burst in Great Britain: in a frantic rush to acquire rights to trade with Latin American countries, the shares of the South Seas Company shot up from £325 to £1200. Later on, the shares of the company tumbled to £86 and short sellers were blamed. In 1734, short sales were banned: however, the law remained unapplied and was abrogated in 1860. In 1866 a new wave of panic swept the financial markets, causing many banks to go bust. The blame for this crash was put on short selling, and in

1867 the Parliament passed another law forbidding short sales on banking shares, but once again the law went unapplied. In 1868, a testimony at the Royal Commission demonstrated that the stock market crash had not been caused by short sales, but rather by insane banking practices and by a poor asset quality.

In France in 1724 a royal decree prohibited short selling. Even Napoleon declared this practice illegal, because he believed that short sales drove treasury prices down, interfering with the financing of his expansionary plans. Together with his Finance Minister Mollien, he maintained that short sellers were traitors because they wished treasuries to collapse.

In 1812, the New York state issued a ban on short sales in the wake of the speculation spate at the outbreak of war against England. The ban proved to be unsuccessful and was lifted during the depression between 1857 and 1859. In 1864, the US government tried to put a bridle on short selling through the Gold Speculation Act, but in just two weeks the price of gold rose from $200 up to almost $300 and the ban was revoked.

Before 1900, stock manipulation and cornering[1] were widespread in particular on railway company stocks.

In Germany, in 1897, the Reichstag issued a law prohibiting future trades on corn and flour, and forward trades on shares of mining and manufacturing companies. So traders physically left the stock exchange to continue to trade futures, and trades were redirected onto the London and Amsterdam stock exchanges. The law was abolished in 1909 with regard to the chapters referring to shares and in 1911 for commodities.

During World War I, the warring nations banned short selling on their stock markets, to prevent enemy agents from playing havoc with their markets, and to avoid speculative excesses.

The strength of feeling against short selling is shown by the fact that in the Wall Street crash of 1929, Ben Smith, a short seller, had to hire bodyguards after being threatened by ruined shareholders.

In September 1931, the turmoil provoked by the British decision to pull out of the "gold standard" led the NYSE to ban short sales, but two days later they reconsidered and backed off.

A wide debate was started on short selling during the 1930s, and in 1938 this led the SEC to pass Rules 10a-1 and 10a-2. Under the up-tick rule, exchange-listed securities on US markets may not be sold short unless the last trade prior to the short sale at a different price was not lower than the price at which the short sale is executed. This rule can be easily circumvented, however, by resorting to cross-border trades or with options. The original up-tick rule does not apply to over-the-counter market or to shares listed on the NASDAQ.

In 1949, Alfred Winslow Jones, a former reporter for *Fortune*, created the first hedge fund. He raised $100 000 and started managing an equity fund. The fund was structured as a partnership to avoid SEC controls and to retain maximum flexibility when setting up the portfolio. His strategy was to combine long positions on undervalued shares with short positions on overvalued shares. Thus, short selling became the keystone of the first hedge fund and of all the ones to follow.

In 1982, the first group destined to focus on short selling was created: the Feshbach Brothers were three Californian brothers who specialized in spotting terminal shorts; that is, companies afflicted by frauds, accounting anomalies, or on the brink of bankruptcy. McBear was another manager who specialized in short selling in 1983.

---

[1] Share buy-up to force investors who sold short to repurchase the securities to cover the shares called in by brokers.

In 1985, James Chanos founded Kynikos Associates in New York, an independent investment company specializing in short selling. At present, Kynikos Associates has more than $1 billion of assets under management and is considered the world's largest company specialized in short selling.

It is worth noting how hedge funds specializing in short selling became popular after the stock market crashes in 1987 and 2000.

A quick survey of how short selling has developed on the Japanese markets may prove instructive. The Japanese market of securities lending started towards the end of the 1980s. According to one hedge fund manager, the first institutional investor to lend its Japanese equity portfolio to the investment bank Morgan Stanley was the College Retirement Equities Fund, one of the largest pension systems worldwide. The same source reveals that Salomon's proprietary desk in Tokyo was the first to borrow Japanese shares from foreign institutional investors in order to carry out arbitrages on Japanese convertible bonds.

Back then, this hedge fund manager worked for the Japanese bank Sumitomo Trust NYC, and he recollects that the lent shares were called in by the end of March every year, because the bank wanted to exercise its voting rights during GAMs. Later on, at the beginning of the 1990s, institutional investors who did not wish to exercise their voting rights in general meetings started to lend their Japanese equity portfolio, thus providing a greater liquidity to the securities lending market.

At present, the Japanese securities lending market is liquid, and brokerage companies compete against one another to borrow the portfolios of institutional investors. At the start, institutional investors were skittish and some were not willing to lend out their Japanese equity portfolios for short selling, but today their attitude has changed, and they show a much greater predisposition, lured by the profits coming from the commissions they get for lending the securities.

Today, it is not difficult to find borrowable shares for most stocks listed in Japan enjoying a good trade volume, but it is still mostly foreign investors who lend their Japanese equity portfolios.

The Japanese market adopted the up-tick rule in April 2002.

In Hong Kong, restrictions on short selling have been eased up, but they are still in force in many Asian countries. Nevertheless, as far as we know, bans on short selling can be sidestepped by using derivatives or swaps.

This brief historical overview clearly indicates that short selling has long been a controversial practice on capital markets. The dislike for short sales is recurrent and gets worse every time markets are hit by panic or by falling prices. The moral diffidence against this practice and the fear it might engender a market disturbance has prompted numerous attempts to prohibit or limit short selling.

Despite this dislike and diffidence against short sales, many studies show that short sellers actually favor the stabilization of falling markets, because you need to buy in the borrowed shares to close out short positions, while short sales provide liquidity to the market when there is a dearth of buyers.

Today, pure short selling is a niche strategy: there are altogether some 10–15 managers exclusively dedicated to this type of management due to the prolonged bull market period in the 1990s. This is also a consequence of the fact that the galaxy of securities with a tumbling profitability is much more limited than the universe of healthy companies.

According to the LIPPER TASS database, as of 31st December 2004, out of a total of 2361 hedge funds there were 18 hedge funds, both on-shore and off-shore, following a "dedicated short bias" strategy. To date, hedge funds specializing exclusively in short selling are rather rare and many of them switched to a long short equity strategy with a net short position, or short bias.

A myth that should be exploded is that these funds are the cause of market crashes: as of 31st December 2004 these funds accounted for about 0.24 % of total hedge funds. At the end of 2004 the hedge fund industry had estimated assets under management of about $1275 billion. The estimated capitalization of US equity markets is approximately $20 000 billion: this means that the weight of these funds on world equity markets is 0.015 %. These figures by themselves are evidence that short-only hedge funds cannot possibly be the cause of crashing equity markets.

3.2 WHAT IS SHORT SELLING?

Short sellers follow the conventional wisdom, according to which you should buy low and sell high. Here, however, the stock is sold first and bought later! Figure 3.1 illustrates the flows in the process of short selling.

Short sellers borrow shares and sell them on the market with the idea of buying them back later at a lower price. To short sell a stock, it is necessary to borrow it from a broker and immediately sell it on the market; then you have to deliver the stock back to the counterparty

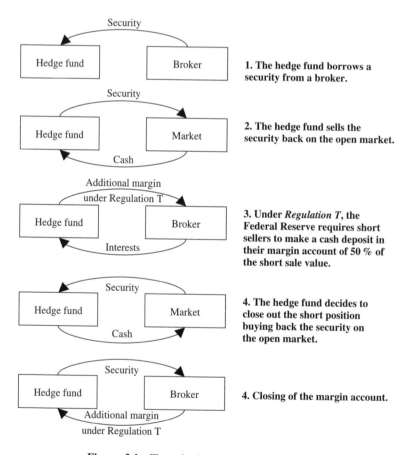

Figure 3.1 Flows in the process of short selling

by buying the same amount of shares later on the open market. If the repurchasing price is lower than the initial selling price there is a profit, otherwise the manager will suffer a loss. Short sellers also make money from the liquidity interest originating from selling the stock short, a liquidity which is held as *restricted credit* by the brokerage company lending the shares: the short seller will earn interest on these cash proceeds, called *short interest rebate*.

The outcome of the transaction depends on the manager's stock picking ability and market timing. Profits from short sales are taxed at the short-term capital gain rate, irrespective of how long the position remained open.

Unlike traditional investors, who look for undervalued companies, short selling managers look for overvalued ones.

Short selling hedge funds do not disclose the names of the companies they are selling short to their investors, for fear that the market might stand in the way and try to cause a squeeze. It is common practice among hedge fund managers to comment on short sales only after they have been closed out.

If a manager believes a stock is overvalued, he will ask his broker to sell the stock short: the broker will then lend the desired number of shares to the manager, requiring the manager to return them within a given period of time, defined in advance. As soon as the manager receives the shares, he sells them on the open market and receives liquidity that generates an interest income. The broker is compensated based on the loan value, and in any case will require the manager to set up a margin account as a loan collateral.

If the share price goes down, the manager can purchase the stock back at a lower price than he originally sold it for, and can therefore return the shares to the broker, profiting from the difference between the sale price and the following repurchase price, in addition to the interest income he got from the cash proceeds from the short sale of stock. Short selling exposes the short seller to a potential unlimited downside risk: if the share price goes up, he will have to repurchase the stock whatever its price at contract maturity.

Some readers may wonder how is it possible to make money on stock you do not own. Even after this explanation on how short selling works, it may still appear confusing, especially if one tries to compare this mechanism with everyday life. It is actually rather difficult to imagine going to the market to short sell cherries that a grocer is selling at a high price, hoping to buy them later at a lower price!

3.3 A SIMPLIFIED EXAMPLE OF SHORT SELLING ON US MARKETS

Short selling is a marginable transaction, i.e., it is necessary to set up a margin account with a broker by signing an agreement, which says the customer will pledge his stocks as margin. Short sellers borrow stock from a broker and sell it back on the open market. Under *Regulation T*, the Federal Reserve requires short sellers to make a cash deposit in their margin account of 50% of the short sale value, or 100% in fully paid securities. Once the short sale has been carried out, the broker measures the position's profit or loss on a daily basis: if the share price has gone down, the short seller has more money available to use as he wishes, while if the share price has gone up, the short seller must deposit an additional margin. Below is an example of a short sale[2]: to make it simpler, this example does not

---

[2] Staley, K.F. (1997) *The Art of Short Selling*, New York: John Wiley & Sons, Inc.

consider any fees due to the broker or any interest income generated by the liquidity coming from the short sale.

A customer sells 100 shares short at a unit price of $100. As a result he has to set up a margin account as follows:

$10 000	Liquidity generated by the short sale
$5000	Additional margin under Regulation T
$15 000	Margin account balance at short sale inception

If the share price goes down to $80, the customer makes a $2000 profit:

$15 000	Margin account balance at short sale inception
$-8000	Necessary outlay to repurchase shorted shares
$7000	Margin account balance after closing out the short sale

$7000	Margin account balance after closing out the short sale
$-5000	Additional margin under Regulation T
$2000	Profit

Whereas, if the share price goes up to $120, the customer suffers a $2000 loss:

$15 000	Margin account balance at short sale inception
$-12 000	Necessary outlay to repurchase shorted shares
$3000	Margin account balance after closing out the short sale

$3000	Margin account balance after closing out the short sale
$-5000	Additional margin under Regulation T
$-2.000	Loss

In this case, however, the margin account stands for 25 % of the share repurchasing price: the New York Stock Exchange (NYSE) requires a minimum 30 % margin and most brokers require at least 35 %. To comply with the rules imposed by NYSE, the short seller must deposit an additional $600 (30 % of $12 000 is $3600).

Most hedge funds make a profit from the cash proceeds from short sales (*short rebate*) ranging between 60 % and 90 % of the interest income applied by the broker on the cash deposit. The difference between the interest income and the *short rebate* is the broker's compensation for lending the stock.

3.4   WHO LENDS SECURITIES FOR SHORT SELLING?

The availability of borrowable securities depends on their owners and not on the hedge fund community. The incentive to lend is given by the fact that the shareholder gets a compensation, which for shares is typically equal to an annual rate ranging between 1 % and 5 %. Share borrowers also agree to refund any dividends paid out by the stock during the lending period to the original owner. So the shareholder enhances the return on his shares, because in addition to the dividend yield, he gets also a lending fee, that is, a compensation for lending the shares. This is an attractive incentive for institutional investors, who have large equity portfolios. In addition, share lenders have the right to call in the shares at any time, for example when general shareholders' meetings are due that the shareholder wishes to attend.

For example, according to an article issued by Reuters on 10th March 2004, the investment bank Credit Suisse First Boston was given the mandate to borrow $50 billion shares from the California Public Employees' Retirement System, CalPERS, to better serve its hedge fund customers.

In the United States, stock lending is a widespread practice, while in Europe it mainly involves large cap securities. In Japan, the availability to lend a stock is closely correlated to its presence in the portfolios of foreign institutional investors. On some emerging markets, securities lending is illegal. Still, emerging market shares that have a corresponding ADR or GDR are generally available for lending.

3.5   REGULATIONS GOVERNING SHORT SELLING

Short selling on US markets is subject to many rules:

- the open short interest, which we will define later, is published every month by the NYSE and the NASDAQ for each listed company;
- short sales are subject to the up-tick rule;
- Regulation T requires the deposit of a 50 % margin of the value of the shorted shares;
- the liquidity generated by short sales represents a collateral and is not available for other short sales;
- many institutional investors, such as mutual funds and pension funds, cannot short sell.

At present, in the United States investors must file the 13D report with the Securities and Exchange Commission (SEC) when their position exceeds 5 % of the equity of a company. With short selling, there is no similar obligation to report one's position should a given threshold be exceeded.

The Full Disclosure Coalition association is requiring that short sellers be obliged to report their short positions with the SEC, so as to pin down possible manipulation attempts by short sellers.

On 10th April 2003, William Donaldson, Chairman of the SEC, declared to the US Senate Banking Committee that as part of a study on the opportunity to regulate the hedge fund business, the SEC was addressing the issue of short selling.

The SEC recently issued Regulation SHO, which replaces Regulations 3b-3, 10a-1 and 10a-2 and changes the up-tick rule. The new regulation allows short sales only when the price is $0.01 higher than the best bid quote. The new regulation will be applied to all markets, including the NASDAQ, which until now had been exempted.

The SEC also launched a one-year pilot program involving about one third of the more liquid shares included in the Russell 3000 index, during which the rules forbidding short selling when the share price is falling are temporarily suspended, so as to evaluate the impact on volatility, liquidity and share price stability.

Finally, the SEC introduced harsher rules against the so-called *naked short selling*[3], under which brokers will be required to check in advance and inform the short seller whether the shares are available or can be borrowed for short selling.

---

[3] Selling short without having borrowed the securities beforehand to make delivery.

3.6 THE RISKS OF SHORT SELLING

Short-only hedge funds are funds that adopt an investment strategy which is the exact contrary of the one followed by traditional mutual funds, that go for a long-only strategy. Although short selling may theoretically be considered symmetrical to the purchase of a security, in reality short selling entails very specific risks:

- The downside of a short sale position is potentially unlimited. When all goes wrong, the worst that happens to a share is that it drops to zero, whereas on the upside it can rise forever. Faced by this statement, short sellers argue that according to their experience there are many more shares tumbling to zero than skyrocketing to heaven! In any case, a risk asymmetry exists between a long and a short position.
- The risk of a *short squeeze*, when a broker demands the immediate delivery of lent securities. The short sale agreement gives the broker the right to call in lent securities at any time. Lent securities can be called in for various reasons: to take part in the company shareholders' meeting or for extraordinary equity events, such as mergers.
- The risk of a *dividend payout*. If the share pays out a dividend, the dividend amount is charged to the short seller and is paid out to the broker who lent the securities. Changes to existing tax laws can be dangerous for short sellers. For example, in the United States on 28th May 2003, President George W. Bush passed the "Job and Growth Tax Relief Reconciliation Act", introducing a change in share dividend taxation: whereas before dividends earned by single individuals were taxed at a maximum marginal rate of 38.6 %, once the Act was passed the maximum rate was brought down to 15 %, like long-term capital gains, thus acting as an incentive for companies to increase the distribution of dividends to shareholders.
- The impossibility of setting up a short sale as a result of the *up-tick rule*. Hedge funds, just as any other market participant, must comply with the regulations enacted in 1938 by regulatory authorities (in this case the SEC, but SEC's regulations apply only to stock listed on NYSE or NASDAQ), allowing short sales only if the latest price change of the security being shorted was an upward movement (SEC rule 3b-3). In practice, short sales are authorized only if there was an "up-tick" (an upward movement between two immediately following prices) in the share price. As a result, it is forbidden to short a stock while its price is falling. In 1994, the SEC approved an experimental regulation, called "bid-test", to stop short sales on stock listed on the NASDAQ at prices equal to or lower than the bid quote when the price is lower than the previous bid quote.
- The *liquidity shortage risk*. Generally, managers set up short sales only on large cap companies, which have a greater liquidity and therefore their shares are more available to be borrowed from a broker, and where the short squeeze risk is smaller. Often it is not possible to short sell small and medium cap stock, because the market for borrowing the securities has become tight. Short selling should be allowed only on financial instruments that are considered liquid enough to close out the short position by repurchasing the financial instrument. In the case of very severe crises, the financial instruments concerned are generally suspended, which puts the parties involved in a short selling contract under a liquidity risk.

Short selling is more complicated than long-only. Borrowing a stock may be difficult, expensive, and the share can be called in at any time. A successful short position narrows more and more as the share price declines, while an unsuccessful position grows in size.

The emergence of large private equity funds is the most recent risk for the short selling activity. Private equity firms in 2004 raised $85 billion, a huge amount of money if we consider that they can use leverage in addition. Private equity funds can target underperforming small and mid cap companies and can offer a premium on the current market prices for the control of some companies. The activity of private equity funds can be an obstacle to short selling, making it trickier to short companies.

3.7   SHORT INTEREST AND SHORT INTEREST RATIO

Short interest is defined as the number of shorted shares that have not been delivered yet. High short interest levels say that many sellers have sold short in anticipation of a bearish trend. Many traders however believe that a high short interest level is an important indicator of an impending rise in the share price, because the future stock demand from short sellers who have to close out their position will push the share price up. Data covering the short interest of individual stock are of public domain and are published for shares listed on the following markets: American Stock Exchange (AMEX), NASDAQ, New York Stock Exchange (NYSE) and Toronto Stock Exchange.

On a monthly basis, NYSE and NASDAQ calculate the number of short positions settled on the 15th of every month, or if the 15th is a holiday, on the next working day to come. NYSE (see Figure 3.2) and AMEX publish these data four working days after the transaction settlement date. NASDAQ publishes these data at the end of the month. So for stocks listed on US markets, short interest data are not available daily, but only on a monthly basis with a few days delay. As for shares listed on European markets, to the author's knowledge there are no short interest data available. At present, the US securities lending market is larger and more active than the European one.

Short interest ratio is defined as the ratio between short interest and the average daily volume over a given period (generally 30 days): it represents the number of days it would take for short sellers on average to repurchase all the borrowed shares, assuming that all daily transactions are used to close out short sales. A high short interest ratio may indicate

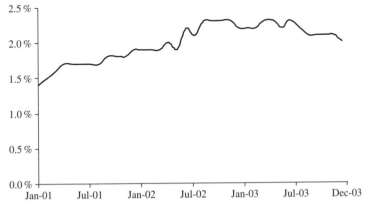

Short interest is calculated as the number of shares sold short and not yet closed out, divided by the number of the outstanding shares traded at NYSE

Figure 3.2   Short interest at NYSE (from January 2000 to December 2003). Source: www.nyse.com

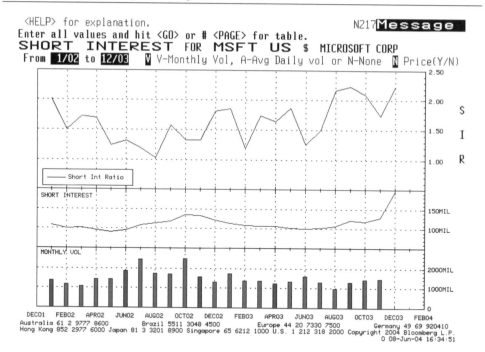

Figure 3.3 Short interest ratio on Microsoft stock in 2002 and 2003. Used with permission from Bloomberg L.P.

that it will be difficult for short sellers to cover their positions. If unexpected good news were announced on a share with a high short interest ratio, the share prices could rise and force short sellers to buy the shares before their price rises even further.

Data covering the short interest and short interest ratio of an individual share are available on Bloomberg machines upon entering the following command: *ticker <Equity> SI*.

Figure 3.3 shows the short interest on Microsoft stock in 2002 and 2003. The chart is subdivided into three sections: the upper part shows the short interest ratio, the short interest is in the middle, and the bottom section gives the share monthly volume.

3.8   WALL STREET'S ALTER EGO

Short sellers are accused of being cynics. According to some observers, just like the followers of the Greek philosopher Diogenes, they are characterized by sheer indifference to ideals and feelings, and contempt for any social tradition and custom.

Financial markets are a meeting point of traders who agree on the price of a transaction but disagree on its value: the buyer believes that the price is lower than the value, while the seller believes the price is higher than the value. Hence, financial markets thrive on price consensus and value disagreement. Short sellers are the disagreeing voice against the false optimism of market players towards listed companies, against an irrational ebullience, against corporate frauds, against market hypes.

One thing that short sellers do is provide the market with corporate information. In a research study conducted in 1996 by the Harvard Business School, Paul Asquith and Lisa Meulbroek identified a strong correlation between short interest and negative corporate results. The study was based on monthly short interest data covering all companies listed on the NYSE and the NASDAQ between 1976 and 1993.

Similarly, Professor Owen A. Lamont of the University of Chicago, in a study spanning 1977–2002, found empirical evidence that the shares of companies that try to oppose short sellers are generally overvalued.

3.9 STOCK PICKING IN SHORT SELLING

The fact that a stock is overvalued is not enough on its own to trigger short selling: for example, the market might be rewarding a business reorganization. The company must be going through a down-performing period.

Let's examine the necessary characteristics for a company to be an ideal short sale target:

- Deteriorating fundamentals and onset of a *catalytic event*, namely, an event that may have a negative impact on the company in the short term (for example, announcing lower profits than expected by analysts, accounting problems, adverse regulatory changes, funding problems). In particular, before setting up a short position on a stock, it is necessary to identify a catalytic event, because a stock can go on being overvalued for years. This brings to mind a maxim attributed to John Maynard Keynes, who, speaking about market irrationality, said: "Markets can remain irrational longer than you can remain solvent".
- Companies belonging to distressed industries negatively affected by external changes.
- Changes in the equity structure.
- Companies with inflated share prices characterized by:

  – low cash flow
  – high price earning
  – strong leverage.

- Companies whose management lies to its investors, for example by adopting aggressive accounting practices, through "accounting tricks" with stock options, "accounting tricks" with pension funds, one-off depreciations, reports with pro-forma data instead of actual data. Warren Buffett maintains that EBITDA (*Earnings Before Interest, Taxes, Depreciation and Amortization*) is profit net of bad news, something you would want to take with great caution.
- Companies who are destroying value: i.e., companies with a low return on equity and a high price/earning ratio, who are putting their liquidity in investments whose return is lower than their return on equity, and are therefore bound to erode their profit structure.
- Companies with a high *insider selling*, i.e., with lots of shares being sold by the company's managers. (Do not confuse insider selling, which is legal, with insider trading, which is illegal.) Insider selling data are published periodically by the SEC.

A useful exercise to spot short sale target companies is to read public documents, such as the *Company Annual Report* (10K filing), the *Company Quarterly Report* (10Q filing) and other reports published by the SEC (SEC filing). Another document is Form 144, which has to be filled out by company executives whenever they place a personal order to sell their company's shares. Top managers must also fill in Form 4 within ten days of the month end to report on the purchases and sales of their company's shares. When an investor owns a stake of 5 % or more, he must file Form 13-D with the SEC. Every year, during their general annual meeting, companies must file a proxy statement with the SEC aimed at informing the shareholders on which items they can vote. This document also reports how many shares are held by management, executive remuneration, shareholders with a greater than 5 % stake in the company's equity, pending legal disputes and a lot of other useful information.

It is useful to analyze the executive compensation packages, in particular incentives (stock options, loans extended by the company to top managers, fringe benefits, golden handshakes, insurance policies, private airplanes, apartments), to understand whether the company is managed for the benefit of shareholders or of top managers.

Additional information on a short sale target company can be obtained by interviewing the company management, competitors, suppliers, customers, trade associations, advisors, journalists, independent analysts, etc. This information can then be used to form a personal idea as to the assumptions made in the company's business plan.

Before getting into a short sale, it is necessary to gain a macro-view: you must identify sector dynamics and deteriorating industries, economic cycles, the state of public finance, capital flows and emerging trends.

Many traders feel it is also necessary to read technical analysis indicators, such as trend indicators, oversold/overbought trends, momentum indicators, Fibonacci's indicator, money flow indicators. And it is important to monitor the volume of options traded on the company.

A further step is the collection of reports issued by brokers to measure analyst consensus of the company and the expectations of the financial community.

Hedge fund managers follow a strict discipline for short selling, fixing target prices that represent a threshold that, once reached, leads to the sale or closing out of the position.

Generally, short selling managers do not resort to leverage, in that short selling is an inherently leveraged strategy. One of the greatest risks short selling managers run is that once they have spotted an overvalued company and they have sold it short, a buyer steps in, offering to take the company over and paying a premium to shareholders.

Shorting a company with good fundamentals because it is experiencing temporary problems or based on an excessive valuation is risky, because a good management team can rapidly fix problems.

Short sellers try not to be deceived by the apparent story represented by financial statements; they try to scratch the surface and see what lies behind the numbers. To evaluate the health of a company, analysts study the financial reports of the last two years (10Q, 10K and possibly 8K). Great attention must be devoted to footnotes, and in particular it is important to figure out what has not been written in reports that should have been. Analysts look for accounting items whose actual value is lower than their balance-sheet value: securities that have not been marked to the market, real estate with inflated prices, inventory made up of obsolete products, receivables unlikely to be collected, etc.

Most of the recommendations expressed by brokers on shares go from buy to add to hold, and only a few analysts are willing to express a sell, reduce or underperform guidance on a stock. Analysts are constrained by corporate finance relationships or by the need to protect their business relationships with corporate management. This is why brokerage firms tend to be rather biased towards optimism.

This is the hard kernel of conflicts of interest between the investment banking industry and its customers. And this is why hedge fund managers who go for a short selling strategy use their own internal research to spot short selling targets.

But things are not as easy as they may seem. In his book *The Alchemy of Finance*, George Soros, one of the most famous macro managers, admits he lost money by starting to short

Internet securities too soon during the new economy equity boom, indicative of the fact that managers cannot neglect to take money flow into consideration.

In a bull market, even a perfect short selling candidate may cause a short seller substantial losses. During market rallies, even the stock of a company that shows no profits and assets on its bottom line can raise in expectation of future gains. Many of these companies belong to the technological or bio-technological industry and have new products in their pipeline. It is extremely difficult to figure out when the market is going to appreciate the fact that the expectations attached to these new fabled products are in fact an illusion. Only by throwing a cynical look at business plans can investors try to understand which innovating companies will make it, and which will fail. Being right in anticipating the demise of a business is one thing, deciding when it is actually going to go belly up and timing one's short selling accordingly is a whole different story. There could be people willing to extend loans that would keep struggling companies, whose financial conditions are worse than those of a terminal patient, alive: these operations are appropriately called *rescue financing*.

A distressed company can drive the price of its shares up outright by announcing that it intends selling part of its assets, for example through a real estate securitization.

A golden rule for short sellers is: *If you can't read it, short it.* Some companies write reports that are totally unintelligible to people with a good accounting background, others make it impossible even to experts to understand their reports. According to Kathryn Staley, experience teaches that when a report (for example the *Company Annual Report* or *Company Quarterly Report*) is incomprehensible, corporate managers are hiding something, and often the hidden problem is the tip of the iceberg: we are talking about *creative accounting*.

A contribution to the good returns obtained in 1999 by this strategy was actually made by aggressive accounting procedures adopted by many companies. Expense deferrals, goodwill, intangible costs, cost capitalizations, off-balance-sheet debts and non-recurring revenues should be analyzed with great care.

With regard to creative accounting Warren Buffett said: "Managers thinking about accounting issues should never forget one of Abraham Lincoln's favorite riddles: How many legs does a dog have if you call his tail a leg? Answer: Four, because calling a tail a leg does not make it a leg".

Below is an example that will shed some light on the above points.

A hedge fund manager started to follow Enron in October 2000, after reading an article published in *The Texas Wall Street Journal* covering accounting practices in large energy trading companies (see Figure 3.4). Many of these companies adopted the *gain-on-sale* accounting procedure to account for their long-term energy trades. Under this accounting method, a company can estimate the future profitability of a trade executed today and recognize a profit today based on the present value of future estimated profits. Based on his experience, the fund manager knew that the temptation for the management of companies adopting this accounting method to be excessively aggressive in their future assumptions is too large to be ignored. Indeed, if the management's optimistic assumptions do not materialize, the profits recognized under the *gain-on-sale* method must be written down: however, in this case there is the temptation to carry out new and larger trades that generate profits, which are immediately accounted for again under the *gain-on-sale* method, and cover up the write-downs. According to the manager, once a company enters this spiral, it is very difficult to get away from it.

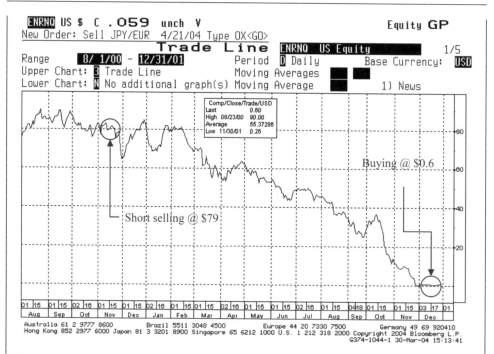

Figure 3.4   Enron share price from 1st August 2000 to 31st December 2001. Used with permission from Bloomberg L.P.

The first document the fund manager examined was the 1999 Form 10K filing, and he was immediately struck by Enron's low profitability, considering its accounting methods and the dominant position it enjoyed on the market: ROE was about 7%, while the cost of capital was probably brushing 9%, which meant that Enron was destroying value, in spite of the fact that it was showing "profits" for its shareholders.

The fund manager started selling Enron shares short on November 2000, when the share was at $79.

One thing the manager could not sort out was *related party transactions*. He was made suspicious by the high amount of Enron shares sold by Enron's top management.

At the end of 2000, Enron announced that its bandwidth capacity trading initiatives in the telecommunications field could be worth $20–30 per share. According to the fund manager, who right then was short selling companies belonging to the telecom and bandwidth industry, the assumptions were highly unlikely, especially considering the excess output capacity in the telecommunication industry.

In Spring 2001, some top managers left Enron and in August 2001 the CEO, Jeff Skilling, suddenly resigned for "personal reasons". As a result of this, the hedge fund manager increased his short selling position on Enron.

In December 2001, Enron filed for bankruptcy. The hedge fund manager closed out his position in December 2001, when Enron's share price was at $0.6.

3.10   THE ART OF CONTRARY THINKING

Often the best bargains are reached by buying when everybody else wants to sell or selling when everybody else wants to buy. For example, buying skis and a windbreaker in summer or a fan in December. It might seem trivial to say this, but most of us, in our daily life, do exactly the reverse: we buy skis in December and fans in summer. These are amusing examples, but such things make a much more serious impact in the stock market. Humans, by their very nature, tend to feel a greater level of fear following a dreadful event, and a greater sense of optimism after a pleasant event. As a result, the average investor believes he can make out the market trend, but what happens more often is that he buys at highs and sells at lows, losing money. 2003 exemplifies this statement: after almost three years of losses, small investors quit the market, but in 2003 the stock markets actually attained the best performance of the last five years.

In his book *The Art of Contrary Thinking*, written in 1954, Humphrey Neill handed down an epigram that summarizes his thought: "When everyone thinks alike, everyone is likely to be wrong".

Market sentiment indicators try to assess the prevailing psychological trends on the market. If these indicators form a trend and remain on historically moderate levels, they tend to confirm the market's general trend, but when they reach extreme values they become *contrarian indicators*. At the top of optimism (think of the "irrational exuberance" mentioned by Alan Greenspan when referring to the new economy) or at the bottom of pessimism, the sentiment is most likely going to vaporize and the trend will reverse. The rule-of-thumb of the art of contrary thinking is that in times of market turning points most investors take the wrong move.

Experience suggests that at the peak of optimism, it is better to be more prudent, while at the bottom of pessimism it is good to start overcoming one's fears. Let's look at some examples of how contrarian indicators can help us understand whether we are in a phase of excessive pessimism or optimism:

- percentage of shares in balanced mutual funds: when the percentage hits the ceiling, optimism on the market is also flying high;
- percentage of capital allocated on equity funds compared to fixed income funds on the global mutual fund market: when this percentage is at the top, optimism on the market is also at its peak;
- oversold and overbought indicators that can point to trend reversals;
- market consensus surveys: when optimism is at the top, it may signify that a trend reversal is about to occur;
- *short interest*: when this indicator shows high levels it points at a deeply negative market sentiment, yet also at a future demand for stock to close out short sales;
- *put/call ratio*: this indicator is the ratio of trading volume in index and equity put options to the trading volume in index and equity call options. A high ratio (put/call ratio >1.0) points at a very negative market sentiment whereas a low ratio (put/call ratio <0.4) points to an excessive optimism. When investors nurture positive expectations, they buy more call options than put options. Beware however: this indicator is built on disagreement, as for each trader who bought an option, there is another one willing to sell it, and both believe they have made a bargain!

Contrarian indicators are most useful when they hit extreme values, in that they signal market hypes and therefore a possible trend reversal: but they say nothing of the trend reversal timing. This is why people talk of the art of contrary thinking: it is not a scientific theory in the Popperian sense, in that it cannot be falsified. However, it can turn people's attention to market hypes and to the importance for market operators to be disciplined and to keep in close touch with their emotions. In other words, rather than forming a prediction system, contrary indicators are an antidote to the general forecasting system.

Being a contrarian on the market is inevitably going to be extremely uncomfortable: it takes courage and a high stress tolerance.

According to James Chanos, Chairman of Kynikos Associates Ltd, short selling is very difficult because every day CEOs and investor relators repeat that short sellers were wrong. The barrage directed at short sellers by all those who have a vested interest in shorted companies is an obstacle to their work.

To be a contrarian, you also need to have a clear understanding of the market expectations.

3.11   MEASURING THE STRATEGY'S HISTORICAL PERFORMANCE

Let's start analyzing the historical behavior of this strategy by examining the monthly returns of the CS/Tremont Hedge Fund Index Dedicated Short Bias. Again, how an investment performed in the past is not necessarily an indicator or a guidance as to its future return. However, we still believe that the examination of historical data is a useful exercise to reason on which scenarios are favorable to this strategy, and which are not.

The statistical analysis of the CS/Tremont Hedge Fund Index Dedicated Short Bias data between 1994 and 2004 gives the outcome shown in Table 3.1.

Table 3.1

	CS/Tremont Dedicated Short	Morgan Stanley Capital International World in USD	JP Morgan Global Govt Bond Global International
Value at Risk (1 month, 95%)	−7.10%	−6.40%	−1.90%
Value at Risk (1 month, 99%)	−8.40%	−10.40%	−3.60%
Best month Performance	22.70%	8.90%	7.00%
Average Performance in positive months	4.20%	3.20%	1.60%
Worst month Performance	−8.70%	−13.50%	−5.10%
Average Performance in negative months	−3.70%	−3.50%	−1.00%
% Positive months	45%	61%	57%
Compound Annual Growth Rate (CAGR)	−3.60%	6.30%	5.40%
Annualized monthly volatility	17.70%	14.20%	6.20%
Skewness	0.91	−0.6	0.65
Kurtosis	2.18	0.59	2.21
Largest drawdown*	−46.50%	−48.40%	−8.60%
Duration of the largest drawdown in months	76	30	4
Time to recovery** in months	n.d.	n.d.	9
Drawdown start	30th Sep. 1998	30th Apr. 2000	28th Feb. 1994
Drawdown end	31st Dec. 2004	30th Sep. 2002	31st May 1994

* The largest drawdown is defined as the maximum value of any "peak to trough decline" over the specified period. The subsequent minimum is not determined until it has reached a new high.
** Time to recovery is the time necessary to recover from the largest drawdown.

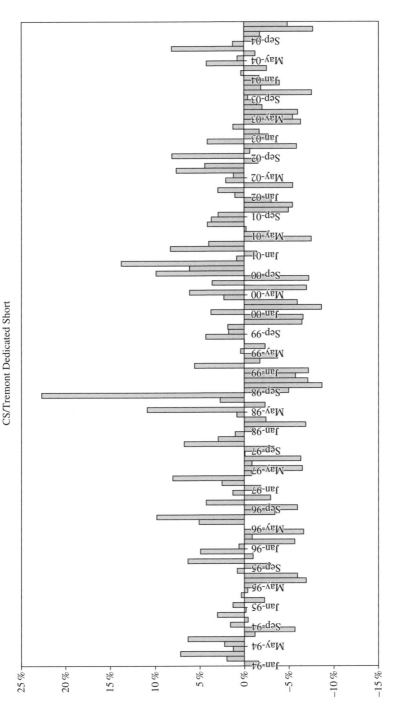

CS/Tremont Dedicated Short

Figure 3.5 Monthly returns of CS/Tremont Dedicated Short from 1994 to 2004. Source: CS/Tremont Index LLC, www.hedgeindex.com. Copyright © 2006, Credit Suisse/Tremont Index LLC. All rights reserved*

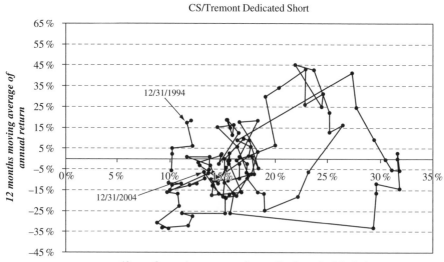

Figure 3.6 Historical performance trend of return as a function of risk for CS/Tremont Dedicated Short from 1994 to 2004. Source: CS/Tremont Index LLC, www.hedgeindex.com. Copyright © 2006, Credit Suisse/Tremont Index LLC. All rights reserved*

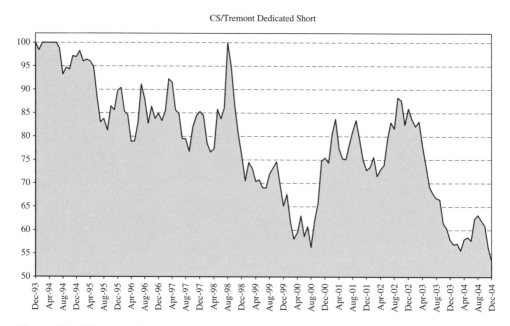

Figure 3.7 "Underwater" periods for CS/Tremont Dedicated Short from 1994 to 2004. Source: CS/Tremont Index LLC, www.hedgeindex.com. Copyright © 2006, Credit Suisse/Tremont Index LLC. All rights reserved*

The performance of the hedge funds specialized in short selling is historically the worst among all the other hedge fund strategies, with an annualized return of -3.6% between 1994 and 2004. In addition, monthly returns have been very volatile (17.7%). The percentage of positive months is very low (45%) even when compared to the selected equity and fixed income indices. The largest drawdown has been huge (-46.5%) and very long (not yet recovered). The historical distribution of monthly returns is pretty symmetric (skewness close to zero) with tails shorter than those of the Gaussian distribution (kurtosis less than 3).

Figure 3.5 shows the monthly returns of the CS/Tremont Hedge Fund Index Dedicated Short Bias from 1994 to 2004.

Figure 3.6 illustrates the historical return performance as a function of risk for the CS/Tremont Hedge Fund Index Dedicated Short Bias between 1994 and 2004. (Figure 3.6 does not include the concentration ellipsoid, due to the erratic nature shown by the risk/return structure of these hedge funds over time.)

Figure 3.7 shows that between 1994 and 2004 hedge funds were often "below-highwatermark". The chart must be analyzed taking drawdown data into consideration: throughout the drawdown and during the time to recovery periods, the hedge funds adopting this strategy were under the high water mark. See Chapter 1, Section 1.8, for more details on the setup and meaning of Figures 3.6 and 3.7.

As we can see from the "underwater" chart, between 1994 and 2004 there were many dips and the largest drawdown was a staggering -46.5%, which has not been recovered yet.

Between 1994 and 2004, numerous events took place that were highly consequential for markets, like the unexpected interest rate rise started in February 1994 by the Fed.

Notice, how the CS/Tremont Hedge Fund Index Dedicated Short Bias hit its highest monthly performance ($+22.7\%$) in August 1998, right in the middle of a strong *flight-to-quality* movement triggered by Russia's default.

3.12 CONCLUSIONS

To conclude this chapter, we quote the final part of the Enron speech given by the hedge fund manager James Chanos on 6th February 2002 in front of the Committee on Energy and Commerce of the United States House of Representatives. James Chanos proudly vindicates the role of short sellers on modern capital markets:

Finally, I want to remind you that, despite two hundred years of "bad press" on Wall Street, it was those "unAmerican, unpatriotic" short sellers that did so much to uncover the disaster at Enron and at other infamous financial disasters during the past decade (. . .) While short sellers probably will never be popular on Wall Street, they often are the ones wearing the white hats when it comes to looking for and identifying the bad guys!

4

Long/Short Equity

Buy cheap and sell expensive
Old Stock Exchange adage

The long/short equity strategy is the portfolio management approach that most resembles the one originally followed by the first hedge fund. Like A.W. Jones, the father of hedge funds, long/short equity managers aim at setting up an equity portfolio whose returns are not correlated to market performance, but rather to their stock selection skills. They look for shares that they believe the market is undervaluing, as well as shares they perceive are being overvalued, then they buy the first (long position) and short sell the second ones (short position). The portfolio can also be hedged without resorting to short selling, namely by using equity index derivatives: often managers sell equity index futures so as to be able to change the portfolio's exposure rapidly in response to market changes.

Long/short equity managers make money when long positions go up and short positions go down; if the reverse occurs, they suffer losses.

Managers who adopt this strategy make use of the same fundamental, technical and statistical analyses employed by traditional equity managers and trade on the same reference market. A hedge fund, however, is structurally distinguished from a traditional mutual fund by short selling, leverage and the manager's incentive system.

The concept in itself is easy to understand and fairly easy to implement: however, money management lies halfway between being art and science, and so the challenge is to implement the concept with success.

The long/short equity strategy is by far the largest investment strategy among hedge funds: according to the LIPPER TASS database, on 31st December 2004, long/short equity funds represented 33 % of the whole sector.

This is the hedge fund strategy that from a conceptual point of view compares the most to the traditional benchmark-related strategy. Equity weights that are greater or smaller than the weight implied in the benchmark are replaced respectively by long and short positions in absolute terms. The portfolio of any fund linked to a reference benchmark can ideally be broken down into the sum of a set of long and short active positions (a long/short portfolio) with a portfolio that passively replicates the benchmark. Implicitly, in any portfolio that has a benchmark and is actively managed, short positions can be visualized as underweights relative to the benchmark. The advantage for the long/short manager is that by having no reference benchmark, he does not come up against the weights of the securities in the benchmark to decide the overweights or underweights: in fact, a long/short equity hedge fund manager does not manage his portfolio relative to a benchmark, but rather in absolute terms. Hence, for many traditional managers, the long/short equity strategy is the door to the hedge fund world.

In a long/short portfolio, short positions have a double advantage: they provide a negative exposure to securities which are believed to be overvalued and reduce the portfolio's market exposure by hedging the systematic risk.

All short positions must stand on their own two feet. Short positions must be constructed to generate a profit, rather than to hedge long positions. The adoption of a strategy with both long and short position widens the gamut of possible alternatives available to the investor, in that it makes it possible to make a profit from the relative performance of two stocks.

A portfolio managed along the long/short equity style can take four main positions:

- *straight long*, namely, long positions on the stock of a corporation the manager likes (for example a long position on General Electric);
- *straight short*, namely, short positions on the stock of a corporation the manager dislikes (for example, a short position on Intel);
- *relative value*, which is going to be described later in this chapter under the name *share class arbitrage*;
- *pair trades*, namely, a position on the relative value of two securities (for example long Deutsche Telekom versus short Vodafone).

4.1 HISTORY OF THE FIRST HEDGE FUND

As already said in Chapter 1, Alfred Winslow Jones (1923–1989) is considered the father of the first hedge fund. During World War II he was a writer and editorfor *Fortune* magazine covering a variety of topics from finance, to politics, to the war effort. By 1948 he had left *Fortune* but was working on a freelance article for the magazine entitled "Fashions in Forecasting". It was while researching this piece that he interviewed the most successful money managers of the time and began to formulate ideas for a new type of fund. Jones was not convinced of his ability to predict the direction of the market consistently. He thought he had good stock picking skills but admitted that he was not able to predict the direction of market trends.

His fundamental insight was that a fund manager could use two techniques: buying stocks with leverage, and selling short other stocks. Each technique was already well known by the market and was considered highly speculative, but when properly combined together could reduce the overall portfolio risk and result in a conservative portfolio, with a low market exposure.

The realization that one could use speculative techniques to conservative ends was the most important step in forming the hedge fund.

In 1949, Jones formed a general partnership with four friends, became the Managing Partner, and started a long/short equity fund. To attract investors, Jones invested his own savings in the hedge fund and chose to be paid with 20 % of the fund performances, instead of fixed fees. The first hedge fund was born.

4.2 MARKET EXPOSURE

The manager can decide to hold a deliberate positive market exposure (*net long bias*), to take advantage of a generalized bullish period, or he may hold a net negative market exposure (*net short bias*). For this reason, the long/short equity strategy can be classified among directional strategies.

Generally, the net market exposure is positive (*long bias*), even though occasionally some funds, driven by the manager's strong macro-economic view, may have a net short exposure. As a result, the performance of long/short equity hedge funds tends to show a positive correlation to the performance of the reference equity markets. When markets are bearish, these types of funds generally tend to be negatively correlated, and yet outperform the market.

In order to understand why the net market exposure is positive, it is instructive to think of what would happen to a long/short equity hedge fund with a focus on the US market and a short bias. If in one year the S&P 500 index should score +10 % and the hedge fund should lose 5 % due to its short bias, investors would probably not forgive the manager and would ask for redemption. The fund would be obliged to close down and liquidate its portfolio.

It is much easier for a manager to follow a traditional investment strategy due to the potential shortage of securities available for short selling and to the psychological barriers that have to be overcome to sell short.

People say that an ideal hedge fund should be able to earn two thirds of the market return when the latter is performing well and lose only one third of the market loss when the market is underperforming. What may seem a rather dull objective turns out to be quite the opposite: if we carry out a short historical simulation and apply this golden rule, we can see that the ideal hedge fund performs much better than any index with a lower volatility. Figure 4.1 illustrates an example of an ideal hedge fund earning two thirds of the monthly return of the Morgan Stanley Capital International World index, when the latter is making a profit, and shedding only one third of monthly losses, when the index is suffering a loss. The figure shows the cumulative performance of such an ideal hedge fund from 1994 to 2004: in the bull market lasting until March 2000, this hedge fund has a cumulative return aligned with that of Morgan Stanley Capital International World in US dollars. Then, during the bear market lasting until mid-2002, this hedge fund achieves the goal of capital protection and clearly overperforms the index. Finally, during the bull market from mid-2002 to the end of 2004, the hedge fund participates again to the index rise. So, clearly, the ideal hedge fund overperforms the Morgan Stanley Capital International World index. This example shows the power of the logic of capital protection and that in the long term it is more important to preserve the capital during bear markets than to participate completely in bull markets.

Let's now define two fundamental indicators used to characterize a long/short equity hedge fund: net exposure and gross exposure. Remember, in the case of a stock, beta measures the stock's performance against market performance, i.e., it measures the sensitivity of the stock to market movements.

w_i is the stock's weight in the portfolio (as a percentage of the fund's net asset value) and β_i is the stock's beta relative to the market. If the stock is sold short, w_i will be negative. L stands for the number of long positions and S for the number of short positions in the portfolio. The net market exposure (*net exposure*) equals the sum of the weights of the long positions less the absolute value of the sum of the weights of short positions:

$$\text{net exposure} = \sum_{i=1}^{L} w_i - \left| \sum_{i=1}^{S} w_i \right|$$

However, we must not be deceived by the concept of net market exposure. We might be led to think that a hedge fund with a net market exposure equal to zero is hedged: on the contrary, this manager might lose money on both the long and the short positions, and so

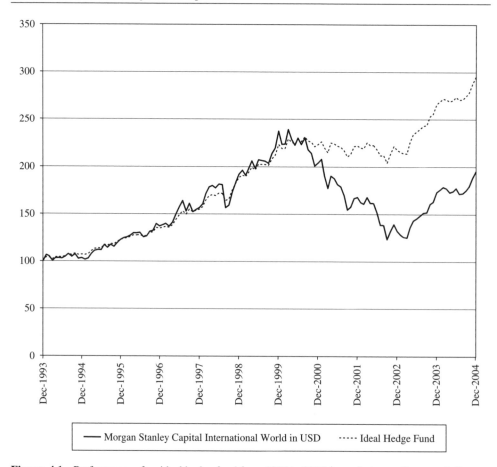

Figure 4.1 Performance of an ideal hedge fund from 1994 to 2004 (cumulative performance). Source: Bloomberg L.P.

actually lose much more rapidly than a traditional fund. To analyze the behavior of a hedge fund performance, it is therefore necessary to add another unit of measure in addition to the net market exposure.

The gross market exposure (*gross exposure*) equals the sum of the weights of long positions plus the absolute value of the sum of the weights of short positions:

$$\text{gross exposure} = \sum_{i=1}^{L} w_i + \left| \sum_{i=1}^{S} w_i \right|$$

The gross market exposure tells us how much money the manager has actually put to risk.

Let's now consider a long/short equity hedge fund with only two stocks in portfolio: a long position of 80 % of the fund's net assets and a short position of 40 % of net assets. The net exposure is +40 %, while the gross exposure is +120 %. This means that the hedge fund has opened positions accounting for 120 % of its net asset value, so the hedge fund used leverage.

Typically, the maximum leverage used by long/short equity hedge funds is twice their capital (100 % long position and 100 % short position).

Net exposure by itself is not enough to analyze a portfolio's exposure to systematic risk, since it gives equal weight to all positions, neglecting their sensitivity to market changes. Actually, a portfolio may be made up of positions with a strong sensitivity to market changes (high beta securities), whose weight in the portfolio is not comparable to the weight of more defensive securities (low beta securities).

Hence, it is necessary to introduce the concept of beta adjusted net market exposure (*beta adjusted exposure*):

$$\text{beta adjusted exposure} = \sum_{i=1}^{L+S} w_i \cdot \beta_i$$

Net exposure may be equal to zero, but the beta adjusted exposure might not. Net exposure is a static measure, whereas the beta adjusted exposure tells us the net market exposure considering the different sensitivities to market movements.

In the example in Figure 4.2, assuming that the beta of the long position is 0.5 and the beta of the short position is 1.5, we get a beta adjusted net exposure equal to:

$$80\% \cdot 0.5 - 40\% \cdot 1.5 = -20\%$$

This is surprising: the net exposure is equal to $+40\%$, but the beta adjusted exposure is -20%. So, although at first glance the portfolio seemed to have a long net market position, on deeper examination we find out that, when considering the securities' different sensitivities to market changes, net exposure turns out to be negative.

Moreover, a net portfolio according to the beta adjusted exposure may not be neutral with regard to sectors, and if it is made up of many small cap securities, it may have little liquidity. Hence, the need to monitor two important indicators:

* the beta adjusted exposure of each single sector comprising the portfolio;
* the portfolio's liquidity, measured for example as the average number of days necessary to liquidate a portfolio without affecting the stock price. Based on a stock's daily average trading volume, it is possible to calculate the mean time necessary to close a position without negatively affecting a stock price.

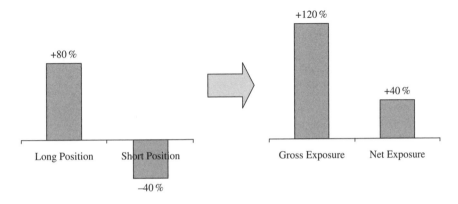

Figure 4.2 Meaning of gross exposure and short exposure: an example

It is interesting to examine what happens to the long and short positions in a long/short equity hedge fund portfolio as a function of stock performance. If the performance goes in the manager's favor:

- long positions increase their value;
- short positions decrease their value.

As a direct consequence of this movement, the long portion of the portfolio grows bigger, while the short portion narrows down; this means that the hedge fund's net exposure has decreased. This might be an undesired effect, and the manager may have to take action to stop losses and rebalance the positions.

If instead performance goes against the manager:

- long positions decrease their value;
- short positions increase their value.

As a direct consequence of this movement, the long portion of the portfolio gets smaller, while the short portion grows bigger; this means that the hedge fund's net exposure has increased. Here again the manager may have to take action to rebalance the portfolio positions.

This trivial consideration on performance tells us that managing a long/short equity hedge fund is more difficult than might be expected at first glance.

4.3   MANAGEMENT STYLES

Long/short equity hedge funds may be better characterized using the following elements, which we will examine in turn in this section:

- net long or net short;
- bottom-up, top down or stereoscopic;
- value or growth;
- large cap or small cap stocks;
- short-term oriented, or more on a longer-term investment horizon;
- diversified or concentrated;
- followers of the reference market's prevailing trend (momentum) or forerunners of trend reversals (counter trend or contrarian);
- global[1] or specializing on a domestic market or a geographical area;
- market generalists or industry specialists.

As already mentioned, long/short equity hedge funds may have a long net exposure, and only rarely a short net exposure. The hedge fund manager may display one the following approaches:

- *bottom-up*, when the manager closely examines the fundamentals of single companies and selects the ones he wishes to buy or sell sort. Typically, these managers are stock pickers;
- *top down*, when the manager constructs his positions based on a macro-economic view, deciding the geographical and sector allocation first, and only then selecting stocks.

---

[1] In practice, these funds have a positive US equity market bias as a result of sheer size.

Typically, these managers follow a sector rotation, trying to anticipate the market's sector preference depending on the economic cycle;

- *stereoscopic*, when the manager combines these two approaches.

The *value* style is based on the analysis of the fundamentals of listed companies. Often, the manager and his analysts meet with the management of the listed company, and talk to their suppliers, customers and competitors. However, considering the importance of timing an investment, when dealing with a volatile stock, managers often use technical analysis.

As to the frequency of trades, a portfolio can be adjusted with trades within the same day, or on a medium to long term.

Value managers seek to identify companies whose intrinsic value has not yet been appreciated by the market: companies whose potential has not been uncovered by the market; companies that trade under the sum-of-the-parts evaluation; or companies that trade at discounted market multiples compared to peer companies, for example P/E, EV/EBITDA, etc.

Many managers prefer using liquidity measures rather than accounting measures. As an adage goes: "Cash does not lie", whereas other balance-sheet indicators could be manipulated by creative accounting.

A company's cash flow can be:

- distributed to shareholders with dividends or invested through a share buyback plan;
- retained in the company and invested in new projects.

Generally, the market attaches a more generous valuation to earnings distributed as dividends or used for a share buyback plan, rather than when they are reinvested in the company.

However, a company's growth relies on the sustainability of its current Return On Equity (ROE), which in turn depends on the profitability generated by reinvested liquidity. If the cash flow reinvested in the company has a return on investment (ROI) greater than its ROE, the company's profitability appears sustainable and growing; otherwise it means that a worsening of the company's profit structure is looming ahead.

A widely used indicator by managers is the so-called *director dealing*, i.e. deals in their company's shares by top management. Although it is true that top managers can sell their company's shares for many reasons, there is only one reason why they buy: when they believe that their company's shares are undervalued. Director dealing data are reported to market regulatory authorities for disclosure.

Even if a stock is strongly undervalued, it may remain so for a long time unless a catalytic event takes place, clearly revealing to the market the downward bias: if a manager invests in a similar stock, he gets caught in the so-called *value trap*. A manager may run the risk of falling in love with the investment stories surrounding the positions he has constructed, and may thus make major valuation mistakes. A manager's talent also rests in his humbleness and ability to recognize mistakes promptly. A manager need not be infallible: to attain a good performance it is sufficient to maintain a good balance between winning and losing ideas; that is, on average you need to be right more than you are wrong.

By analyzing the past behavior of equity markets, one realizes that sometimes growth stocks are favorite and other times it is value stocks. Figure 4.3 illustrates the relative valuation of shares with a low Price/Book ratio compared to shares with a high Price/Book ratio. The figure shows that at the beginning of the 1990s, the market rewarded "value" shares, whereas at the beginning of 2000, with the new economy bubble, "growth" shares overperformed value shares.

Price/Book Ratio

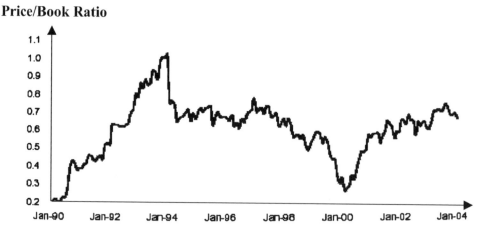

The chart shows the relative median valuation between stocks of the lowest quartile respect to stocks of the highest quartile. Portfolios have been rebalanced quarterly. The investment universe used is formed by 500 biggest companies of the FTSE World Index.

Figure 4.3   The relative valuation of shares with a low Price/Book ratio compared to shares with a high Price/Book ratio. Source: Lehman Brothers, WorldScope, FTSE, Exshare

Also, we should not take for granted that small cap securities will show a better relative performance over large cap securities, or for that matter high beta shares over low beta shares. Historical charts show fluctuations in market preferences.

The Standard & Poor's Smallcap 600 is a capitalization-weighted index measuring the performance of US small cap securities. Figure 4.4 compares the Price/Earning ratio of small cap and large cap securities.

As you can see in Figures 4.3 and 4.4, no management style is always winning; it is up to the manager to understand where he stands along the economic cycle and what management style is to be favored.

Talking with many managers specializing in the long/short equity strategy, we noticed that each manager created his own "indicator dashboard" to examine market characteristics. The dashboard can comprise indicators ranging from the Treasury note interest rate curve, the ratio between company upgrades and downgrades, company default rates, estimate revisions by analysts, the Price/Earnings (P/E) ratio, etc., up to original indicators such as the ratio between traded call and put options, the analysis of the performance of stocks considered to be forerunners of the economic cycle, etc. The ability to generate returns stems also from the independent research of hedge funds. Performance can be repeated only when it is based on a structured investment process, capable of constantly producing trading ideas.

The concept of a "margin of safety" introduced by Graham[2] is basic for investors, ensuring they are hedged if something wrong suddenly occurs.

Small caps, for example, are defined on the US market as shares with a market capitalization below $1 billion (there are about 5000 in the USA). The low liquidity of small caps prevents many investors from taking advantage of market opportunities. The coverage of small caps by analysts of brokerage companies is scarce: consider that, if on average an S&P

[2] Graham, B. (1973) *The Intelligent Investor*, New York: HarperBusiness.

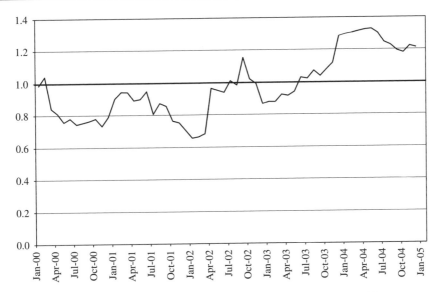

Figure 4.4 Price/Earning ratio of small cap securities from S&P 600 index and large cap securities from S&P 500 index from 1999 to 2004. Source: Bloomberg L.P.

500 company is covered by the research studies of 14 analysts, Russell 2000 companies, with a market cap below $500 million, are covered on average by only three analysts. Typically, larger long/short equity hedge funds have a pro-larger cap companies bias.

Managers may follow a management style with an intense short-term oriented trading, or a low portfolio turnover with a more long-term oriented investment horizon.

Portfolio *diversification* in long/short equity hedge funds is widely heterogeneous. Should we try to classify them by size, we could go from highly concentrated portfolios with about 30–40 securities to much more diversified portfolios comprising 200–300 securities. It is extremely important to understand the weight of the most important stock in the portfolio, and the weight of the first five securities in order of importance. Here, the approach of managers differs widely.

Momentum managers seek to make a profit from a so-called performance persistence effect, according to which, securities, industries and markets that have overperformed will go on doing so. It's like saying that they set up a position to leverage the persistence of trends. Since trends do not go on forever, sooner or later a reversal occurs, and market excesses are wiped out. This is the so-called mean reversion effect, which leads some managers to behave differently from their colleagues above, and to try to anticipate trend reversals (*counter trend* or *contrarian*).

Finally, long/short equity managers can specialize in a reference market, or in a reference economic sector, depending on the manager's field of expertise that in his opinion provides him with a competitive edge over the other traders.

4.4 SPECIALIZED LONG/SHORT EQUITY FUNDS

Unlike global and generalist managers, many managers have decided to reduce their investment universe and specialize by geographical areas or economic sectors.

We can find hedge funds with geographical focus by country (United States, United Kingdom, Japan, etc.), as well as by geographical region (Europe, Asia, etc.). Among the geographical specializations, emerging markets are particularly important, such as Brazil, Russia, India, China, Korea, etc.

In the 1990s, there was a mushrooming of hedge funds specialized in high-growth sectors, like technology, telecommunications, biotechnologies, financial services, natural resources, etc. Based on this specialization, the manager offers a focused sector exposure, trying to put his past working experience in a given field to work. Typically, these managers set up the hedge fund portfolio along a bottom-up approach, and compared to generalist hedge funds, they often have a greater concentration in single positions, are more aggressive and have a long bias on a single industry or a single geographical area.

4.4.1   Long/short Equity Technology-Media-Telecommunication (TMT)

The technology sector has three main characteristics:

1. there are few winners and many losers;
2. product cycles are more important than economic cycles, because product cycles in technology are short (from six months to three years);
3. technology stocks are generally very volatile.

It is surprising to note that the weight of technology stocks in the NASDAQ Composite Index is only 55 % and this should be borne in mind when using this index.

Technology gives access to a series of new applications that open up new investment opportunities. Hedge fund managers specializing in the TMT sector seek to spot the winners and losers when new applications are launched.

For example, in the near future the mobile communication revolution will make it possible to consolidate voice, video and data and this will have an important impact on some neighboring sectors. Mobile communication systems – UMTS (*Universal Mobile Telecommunications Systems*), also called 3G (3rd generation technology) – are expected to enjoy a strong growth, along with Bluetooth technology, videoconferences, liquid crystal displays (LCDs) and GPS systems for satellite navigation. Also, Internet voice communication providers enable free and high quality voice communications between users connected to the Internet anywhere in the world and low cost connectivity to traditional fixed and mobile telephones. This is going to revolutionize the way in which people communicate through the Internet, and it is going to erode market share of traditional telecom companies in the high margin segment of international phone calls.

Another promising sector is nanotechnologies applied to the production of new materials featuring completely different physical and chemical properties from the ones known up to now.

Other technology industries, however, are burdened by high pressure on prices, growing competition and waning demand. Products that once represented the state of the art in technological innovation are now being dismissed as low technological innovation products. Indicative of this is the fact that at the beginning of December 2004, IBM announced the disposal of its PC division to Lenovo Group Limited, a Chinese company that is a leader in the manufacturing and sale of personal computers in China and Asia.

4.4.2 Long/short Equity Biotech

The most interesting and rapidly growing areas for biotechnologies are oncology, stem cells, cardiovascular diseases, inflammatory diseases, infectious diseases and biomedical equipment. Now that the human genome has been fully mapped, new incredible fields of research have cracked open for the treatment of diseases through gene therapy.

In the United States, the Food and Drug Administration (www.fda.gov) must approve drugs before they can be launched on the market. The approval or rejection of a drug causes sharp movements in the price of manufacturing companies. The largest biotechnology communities are based in San Francisco and Boston in the US and Munich in Germany.

These hedge funds seek an information advantage and try to assess the potentials of the new drugs and treatments so as to correctly predict the changes in the manufacturing companies' value. These hedge funds hire scientific advisors, and at times even have Nobel Laureates in their ranks.

Biotech funds invest prevailingly on biotech companies listed on the NASDAQ (Figure 4.5). The biotech industry is characterized by a lively M&A activity, because many traditional pharmaceutical companies are cash rich and sometimes find it more interesting to buy small and successful biotech companies that are going to develop interesting new drugs, than to invest internally in research projects whose outcome is uncertain.

The sales of some smaller biotech companies are highly concentrated on a few drugs, hence valuating a company of this kind practically means assessing the options on the treatment efficacy of their drugs. Population aging in Western countries and in Japan will increase drug demand.

The biotechnology industry is a high growth sector when compared to the traditional pharmaceutical industry. Recently, the pharmaceutical industry has been downgraded from growth to value. The healthcare sector has been hit hard by events – such as the rejection of the flu vaccine by Chiron and the withdrawal from the market of Vioxx manufactured by

Top 6 companies	Market capitalization in billion USD
Amgen	71.7
Genentech	51.6
Biogen Idec	19.6
Gilead	16.5
Genzyme	12.1
MedImmune	7.0
Chiron	6.1
Total	**184.6**

Following top 10 companies	Market capitalization in billion USD
Celgene	5.1
ImClone	4.3
Millennium	3.7
OSI Pharm.	2.6
Amylin	1.9
PDLI	1.8
Eyetech	1.8
Neurocrine	1.7
Onyx	1.5
Icos	1.4
Total	**25.8**

Figure 4.5 Main biotech companies listed on the NASDAQ (data as of 19th October 2004). Source: Bloomberg L.P.

Merck – that raised many worries as to the vulnerability to lawsuits and prompted regulatory authorities to clamp down their controls on drug safety.

4.4.3 Long/short Equity Gold

Hedge funds that follow this strategy open long and short positions on investments related to gold and precious metals. Historically, gold was used as a protection against inflation, although more recently it has started to be employed as a hedge against currencies.

The manager takes long or short positions when gold or precious metals exceed the threshold beyond which they are not supported by fundamentals. These managers can also invest in commodities.

4.4.4 Long/short Equity on Emerging Markets

Signori imperadori, re e duci e tutte altre genti che volete sapere le diverse generazioni delle genti e le diversità delle regioni del mondo, leggete questo libro dove le troverrete tutte le grandissime maraviglie e gran diversitadi delle genti d'Erminia, di Persia e di Tarteria, d'India e di molte altre province (Marco Polo, Il Milione).

Emperors, kings and dukes and ye other people who wish to learn about different populations and different regions of the world, read this book, that will guide you along the great wonders and diversities of the people from Armenia, Persia and the land of Tartars, India and many other provinces (Marco Polo, *The Travels of Marco Polo*, Chapter 1)

The wonder we feel today when we try to follow the development of emerging countries does not lie too far from the one the merchant of Venice, Marco Polo, experienced in the 13th century in his journey in the Far East. By emerging countries we mean Brazil, Russia, India, China, Korea, etc. Emerging markets are a heterogeneous set from a geographical, economic and political point of view (Figure 4.6).

Hedge fund managers are attracted to emerging markets by their growth potential and the diversification they offer in comparison to more developed countries, and for the opportunities that may come from young markets that have not reached maturity yet. However, emerging markets are characterized by a strong volatility. On some of these markets selling short is still very difficult: see Chapter 3 for a more extensive coverage of short selling.

India and China are two huge countries in demographic terms: in 2003 China had 1.3 billion inhabitants, and India had 1 billion. In 2003, direct foreign investments amounted to $53.5 billion in China and $3.6 billion in India.

The strong investments carried out by Western companies to delocalize their manufacturing plants, especially for labor-intensive products, caused lasting changes in the consumption of oil, natural gas and coal, because the production of electric power in China could not keep up with the power requirements of manufacturing companies. This led to the so-called Chinese paradox, with China exercising both an inflationary and deflationary pressure on the West: China exports deflation with its low cost products, but at the same time exports inflation due to the strong demand for raw materials.

India, on the other hand, has become the center of software and IT service outsourcing, mainly as a result of the availability of workers who speak English and have a university education.

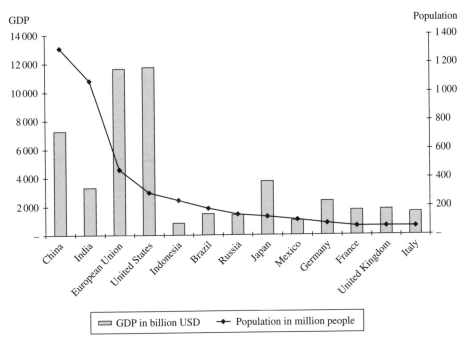

Figure 4.6 GDP and population for the biggest countries in the world (estimates as of July 2005).
Source: www.cia.gov, The World Factbook

Growth in these countries will depend on numerous factors: political stability, political reforms, the construction of infrastructures, the opening up to foreign trade and investments, education levels, public debt, exchange rates, taxes and interest rates, etc.

One of the favored themes followed by long/short equity managers on emerging markets is trying to use trading ideas to take advantage of the lasting changes brought about by a growing middle class, especially in China and India, which is starting to show consumption habits similar to the West and is responsible for a high growth in retail consumption.

We will not analyze the CS/Tremont Emerging Markets Index in this context because it comprises funds that we would classify as long/short equity on emerging markets, as well as hedge funds that we consider to be Debt Emerging Markets, which will be dealt with in Chapter 14 on global macro.

Straight long

British Land Company plc is a real estate company specializing in commercial property in the United Kingdom. British Land Company plc invests in rental property and real estate, trying to maximize growth and potentials. The company trades, funds and develops real estate property. Its real estate portfolio is mainly made up of offices, supermarkets, shopping centers and industrial areas.

A hedge fund manager bought the British Land Company plc share for 550p, after meeting with the company's managing director. The reasons underlying the investment in British Land Company plc shares are illustrated below:

- the commercial real estate industry in the United Kingdom was outperforming the bond market;
- the property portfolio is of top quality (high quality tenants);
- the share price was at a discount of about 30 % over shareholders' equity.

Due to the sharp rise in the price of the British Land Company plc share during 2004, the share's discount on shareholders' equity went down to 10 % and the manager decided to pocket part of the profits, reducing his position at the beginning of December 2004. Figure 4.7 depicts the hedge fund manager's trading activity: it was a very profitable investment idea for the hedge fund.

Straight short

A hedge fund manager learnt that interesting short selling ideas could be found in companies that carry out large acquisitions relative to their market capitalization, in particular companies that make acquisitions outside of their domestic market. According to the manager, there is strong empirical evidence suggesting that this type of acquisition hardly live up to the profit targets set by the management, and can destroy shareholder value in the medium term.

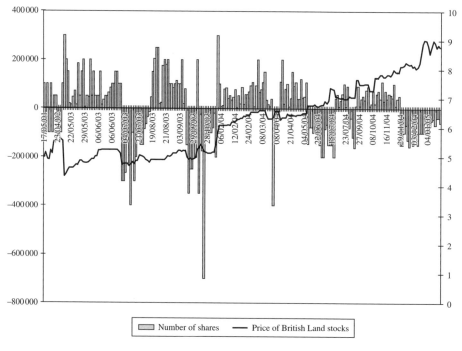

Figure 4.7   British Land

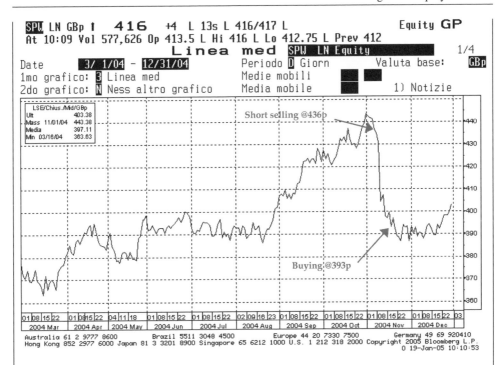

Figure 4.8 Scottish Power share price (Italian labels). Used with permission from Bloomberg L.P.

Scottish Power (Figure 4.8) is a company that produces and sells electric power in the United Kingdom; it has been diversifying its production more and more outside the United Kingdom, and in 1999 it acquired the company PacifiCorp in the USA.

The manager closely monitored its development, and talks with energy producers in the United States underlined a growing pressure on returns while the capital expenditure plan had to be accelerated due to customer demand. This led the manager to believe that Scottish Power might be forced to announce to its investors that the returns from PacifiCorp would be lower than expected and that the current capex plan would not generate the predicted profits.

The manager confirmed his investment decisions during meetings with the management throughout 2004 and in his latest meeting with Scottish Power he grew convinced that the regulatory pressure was mounting up.

The fundamental analysis of the company's sum of the parts, mainly based on adjusted cash flows to account for lower returns from the US, gave a target price of 390p per share. Since the shares were being traded at 430p, the manager identified a potential to open a short selling position. The short sale was executed at a price of 436p.

To monitor these positions, among others, the manager checks the price performance relevant to the target price indicated by the fundamental analysis model, and if a position reaches the target price, the manager adjusts the trade either to set a new target price or to close out the position.

> The share price of Scottish Power slipped rapidly towards the target price set by the manager. The manager's analysis process concluded that some analysts had started to downgrade Scottish Power and as a result the market was pricing in news of lower returns.
>
> While utility stocks were hiking abruptly, Scottish Power did not partake, which caused its valuation to be cheaper compared to the other companies belonging to the same industry.
>
> The manager thought it unlikely that the share price of Scottish Power would get lower, but rather believed it might start rising, so he decided to close out his short position at 393p, very close to the target price.

4.5   SHARE CLASS ARBITRAGE

Share class arbitrage is a special kind of arbitrage on a company's capital structure, for example, the arbitrage between saving shares, preferred stock and common stock. Let's take a closer look at the differences between the various classes of stock.

Common stock does not provide shareholders with any privilege with regard to dividend distribution or asset allocation in case of business liquidation.

Preferred stock provides shareholders with a prior claim on dividends and capital refund in case the company is closed down; however, it limits voting rights.

Saving stock does not confer any voting rights or the right to participate in general or special shareholder meetings; however, it enjoys capital privileges over common shock, under the articles of association of the issuer. In general, in the case of dividend payout, saving shares are assigned a minimum annual dividend and a minimum difference on the dividend of common shares in the case of liquidation.

As a result of market forces and in particular following corporate events, these three share classes may be traded at prices that are not congruent with one another, thus giving rise to an arbitrage opportunity.

4.6   PAIRS TRADING

Pairs trading is a *relative value* position created by matching a long position on a stock with a short position on another stock belonging to the same industry. If the two investments have the same size, the position will have a zero net exposure. Otherwise, it will be a long or short net exposure, reflecting the manager's bias towards the market.

In order to understand how interesting a pairs trading strategy may be, we describe how it works by way of a practical example featuring Wal-Mart and Albertson's supermarkets.

> Wal-Mart Stores, Inc. is a retailing business with supermarkets and hypermarkets selling a variety of goods from clothes to household articles and appliances, electronics and hardware. Wal-Mart is present in the United States, Canada, Argentina, Brazil, Germany, Mexico, Korea, United Kingdom and Puerto Rico.
>
> Albertson's, Inc. is a store chain selling food and drugs in various states of the US. The company's stores are a combination of food–drug stores, traditional supermarkets and warehouses. Retailing is supported by distribution centers owned by Albertson's.

The investment assumption followed by the hedge fund manager is that Wal-Mart Stores has reached a big enough size to create economies of scale for group purchasing, which allow the company to snatch market shares away from the other supermarket chains, for example Albertson's. The competitive pressure on prices exerted by Wal-Mart Stores narrowed Albertson's margins.

Investment example:

- purchase of $1200 worth of Wal-Mart Stores shares;
- concurrent short sale of $1000 worth of Albertson's shares.

Let's say that the interest rate at which Albertson's shares are lent is 0.5 % per year and that the manager can invest his cash proceeds at a 2 % rate per year.

In the time span between 1st January 2003 and 31st July 2003, the manager's performance can be broken down as follows:

- the long position went up by +8.4 %, generating a $100 profit;
- the short position went down by −19.9 %, generating a $199 profit;
- investing for seven months, the cash proceeds from the short sale generated a $20 profit;
- borrowing Albertson's shares for seven months generated a $5 loss.

If we assume a 50 % margin for the short sale and set brokerage fees aside, the long/short position generated a total profit of $314 on an initial invested capital of $700, i.e., a total return of about +45 %.

Note that the position is also profitable when both stocks go down, as shown in Figure 4.9. The money lost on the long position on Wal-Mart is recovered by the short position on Albertson's. This is the hedge fund's recipe to generate profits in downturning markets as well.

If both stocks had gone up, the manager would have profited from the long position on Wal-Mart and would have suffered a loss on the short position on Albertson's. This position generates a profit or a loss depending on whether the profit made on Wal-Mart is greater than the loss suffered on Albertson's.

As a result, the profit or loss of a *pairs trading* position depends on the relative strengths of the two securities and not on their absolute performance. The gray area is the spread between the two stocks in favor of the hedge fund manager. The return source is not correlated to a market risk, but instead to the manager's skills.

Ex-post, the strategy to purchase Wal-Mart Stores stock and simultaneously short sell Albertson's stock proved successful. What would have happened if the manager had got his analysis wrong and had short sold Wal-Mart Stores stocks and purchased Albertson's stock instead? The manager would have suffered a loss, which shows that the long/short equity strategy is not risk free. Its success depends on the manager's ability to construct a portfolio with numerous positions, each with uncorrelated investment ideas to one another.

With regard to risk, the long/short equity strategy brings with it an important advantage over traditional strategies. In pairs trading, short selling turns a highly correlated stock into a negatively correlated stock, hence the performance of the pairs trading position depends on the overperformance of one stock over the other.

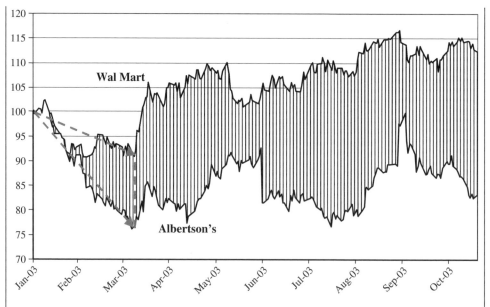

Figure 4.9 Spread between Wal-Mart and Albertson's (common base 100 as of 1st January 2003). Source: Bloomberg L.P.

4.7   COVERED CALL AND COVERED PUT OPTIONS SALE

If no catalytic events are looming ahead, the price of the shares selected by the manager may stay undervalued for a long time and the manager can fall into the "value trap", i.e., he bought a highly undervalued stock, but this remains undervalued for a long time.

To increase his portfolio performance, the hedge fund manager can decide to sell *out-of-the-money* put options to buy the shares at the target price, or sell *out-of-the-money* call options to sell the owned shares at the target price. In this case, the catalytic event is the option maturity, and the manager is "synthetically" producing a catalytic event to push its position towards a more rapid outcome.

Sale of "out-of-the-money" call options[3]

The manager buys Microsoft shares at $25 because based on his valuations the target price is $30. To improve the fund performance, the manager sells European *out-of-the-money* calls[4] whose exercise price is equal to the target price of $30 and he receives the option premium. At maturity, the manager will find himself in one of the following three situations, depending on the price of the Microsoft shares:

---

[3] The figures in this example are purely illustrative.
[4] Options that can be exercised only upon maturity.

- > $30: the buyer of the calls will exercise his right to buy at $30 and the manager will be obliged to deliver the Microsoft shares he holds in his portfolio. The manager is obliged to deliver the Microsoft shares at $30 when maybe the market price for Microsoft is $35. So the manager is losing out on any gain above the $30, but he still achieves his goal of selling the shares at the target price of $30.
- = $30: calls are exercised at $30 and the manager will be obliged to deliver the Microsoft shares he holds in his portfolio. However, since Microsoft has reached the target price set by the manager, Microsoft shares are sold at a profit.
- < $30: calls will not be exercised. The manager has earned the premium, and has thus improved the hedge fund performance.

Sale of "out-of-the-money" put options[5]

The manager short sells Intel stock at $24 because based on his valuations the target price is $20. To improve the fund performance, the manager sells European *out-of-the-money* put options whose exercise price is equal to the target price of $20 and he receives the option premium. At maturity, the manager will find himself in one of the following three situations, depending on the price of the Intel shares:

- < $20: the buyer of the puts will exercise his right to sell Intel shares at $20 and the manager will be obliged to buy back the Intel shares from the put holder to turn them in to the original lender of the Intel shares. The manager does not participate anymore in the further decline of the Intel shares under $20, in that he has to cover his short position at $20. The manager still achieves his goal of buying back the shares he had sold short at a target price of $20.
- = $20: put options will be exercised at $20 and the manager is obliged to buy Intel shares from the put holder to close out his short sale, delivering the shares to the original lender. However, since Intel has reached the target price set by the manager, the Intel shares are bought back at a profit.
- > $20: puts will not be exercised. The manager has earned the premium, and thus he has improved the hedge fund performance.

4.8   STRATEGY'S HISTORICAL PERFORMANCE ANALYSIS

Let us analyze the historical behavior of the long/short equity strategy based on the monthly returns of the CS/Tremont Long/Short Equity Index. Again, the past performance of a given investment is not necessarily indicative of a future return for the same investment. Still, we believe it is useful to examine historical data to understand which scenarios are favorable to this strategy and which are not.

The statistical analysis of the CS/Tremont Long/Short Equity Index data between 1994 and 2004 produces the results shown in Table 4.1.

---

[5] The figures in this example are purely illustrative.

Table 4.1

	CS/Tremont Long/Short Equity	Morgan Stanley Capital International World in US$	JP Morgan Global Govt Bond Global International
Value at Risk (1 month, 95 %)	−3.30 %	−6.40 %	−1.90 %
Value at Risk (1 month, 99 %)	−6.40 %	−10.40 %	−3.60 %
Best month Performance	13.00 %	8.90 %	7.00 %
Average Performance in positive months	2.50 %	3.20 %	1.60 %
Worst month Performance	−11.40 %	−13.50 %	−5.10 %
Average Performance in negative months	−2.00 %	−3.50 %	−1.00 %
% Positive months	67 %	61 %	57 %
Compound Annual Growth Rate (CAGR)	12.20 %	6.30 %	5.40 %
Annualized monthly volatility	10.60 %	14.20 %	6.20 %
Skewness	0.23	−0.6	0.65
Kurtosis	3.69	0.59	2.21
Largest drawdown*	−15.00 %	−48.40 %	−8.60 %
Duration of the largest drawdown in months	29	30	4
Time to recovery** in months	17	n.a.	9
Drawdown start	31st Mar. 2000	30th Apr. 2000	28th Feb. 1994
Drawdown end	31st Jul. 2002	30th Sep. 2002	31st May 1994

* The largest drawdown is defined as the maximum value of any "peak to trough decline" over the specified period. The subsequent minimum is not determined until it has reached a new high.
** Time to recovery is the time necessary to recover from the largest drawdown.

Historically, the CS/Tremont Long/Short Equity index had an annualized average performance of +12.2 % with a monthly annualized volatility of 10.6 % against a performance of world equity markets of +6.3 % with a volatility of 14.2 %. The correlation between CS/Tremont Long/Short Equity and the MSCI World Index is +0.61, a positive and significant correlation.

The percentage of positive months is pretty high (67 %).

The Value at Risk (one month, 99 %) means that "We have a 99 % probability of not losing more than −6.4 % of the investment in the next month". Instead we have observed a monthly performance of −11.4 %. There is nothing wrong because, as usual, we must read statistics very carefully. The distribution of monthly returns is pretty symmetric (Skewness equal to 0.23) and with fat tails (Kurtosis greater than 3) and this implies that we cannot use the VaR to estimate an extreme value of the distribution, because we need many more observations.

The largest drawdown has been significant (−15 %) and lasted for more than two years (29 months). Then the index needed 17 months to recover the largest drawdown.

Figure 4.10 shows the monthly returns of the CS/Tremont Long/Short Equity index between 1994 and 2004.

Figure 4.11 illustrates the historical performance as a function of risk of the CS/Tremont Long/Short Equity index between 1994 and 2004. (The figure does not include the concentration ellipsoid, due to the erratic nature shown by the risk/return structure of these hedge funds over time.)

Figure 4.12 shows that between 1994 and 2004 hedge funds were often "underwater". The figure must be analyzed taking drawdown data into consideration: throughout the drawdown and the time to recovery period, the hedge funds adopting this strategy were under the

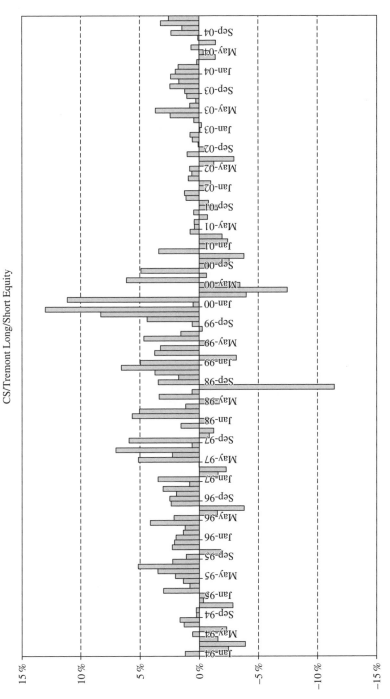

CS/Tremont Long/Short Equity

Figure 4.10 Monthly returns of CS/Tremont Long/Short Equity from 1994 to 2004. Source: CS/Tremont Index LLC, www.hedgeindex.com. Copyright © 2006, Credit Suisse/Tremont Index LLC. All rights reserved*

---

* See page 298 for full copyright notice.

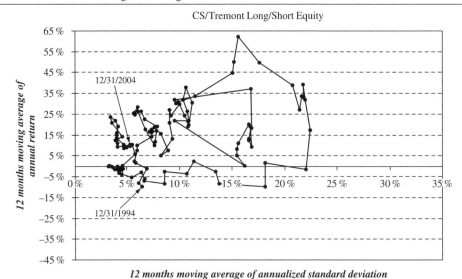

Figure 4.11 Historical performance trend of return as a function of risk for CS/Tremont Long/Short Equity from 1994 to 2004. Source: CS/Tremont Index LLC, www.hedgeindex.com. Copyright © 2006, Credit Suisse/Tremont Index LLC. All rights reserved*

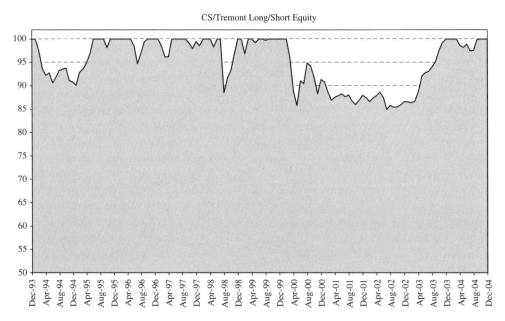

Figure 4.12 Underwater periods for CS/Tremont Long/Short Equity from 1994 to 2004. Source: CS/Tremont Index LLC, www.hedgeindex.com. Copyright © 2006, Credit Suisse/Tremont Index LLC. All rights reserved*

---

high water mark. See Chapter 1, Section 1.8, for more details on the setup and meaning of Figures 4.11 and 4.12.

The unexpected interest rate rise started in February 1994 by the Fed triggered the first drawdown. In August 1998 there was a strong *flight-to-quality* movement caused by Russia's default, which brought about the second drawdown. In March 2000 the new economy bubble burst, leading to the worst drawdown for long/short equity funds. Finally, there was the gruesome Twin Towers attack in New York on 11th September 2001. The March 2000 drawdown was very long and lasted 29 months. It took 17 months to recover the losses.

Finally, note that a sine-qua-non condition for the performance of a long/short equity hedge fund to be repeatable over time, although not sufficient by itself, is that the manager's decisions must be based on a structured investment process, capable of generating new trading ideas nonstop. Only larger management companies seem to be in a position to pursue this objective.

4.9   EQUITY MARKET NEUTRAL

A long/short equity strategy variation is the one used by equity market neutral funds characterized by holding a market neutral portfolio, i.e., its performance is not correlated to market movements. Even though they are close relatives, equity market neutral funds differ from long/short equity funds for their systematic risk level.

According to the LIPPER TASS database, on 31st December 2004, equity market neutral funds accounted for only 6 % of the hedge fund industry.

During market uptrends, equity market neutral funds make a profit if long positions go up more rapidly than the drop in value incurred by the short positions in portfolio. Vice versa, in market downtrends, they make a profit if short positions go up at a faster rate than the rate at which long positions are going down.

A beta adjusted net exposure close to zero is a target for every truly equity market neutral portfolio. Notwithstanding, an equity market neutral portfolio may have a beta adjusted net exposure that is very close to zero, but its beta adjusted net exposure with regard to sectors or geographical areas will not be zero, and therefore it may be subject to specific risks, like for example sector risks or country risks. This should not come as a surprise, because our common sense tells us that if we eliminate all systemic risks, we are also giving up performance. A truly equity market neutral portfolio must be very diversified (i.e. more than 100 equities) in order to be able to minimize the sector exposures and the country exposures. Furthermore, every equity position should be hedged with another equity or a basket of equities of the same sector.

At this point, it is time to talk about the Capital Asset Pricing Model (CAPM), a statistical mathematical model of the securities market, which represents a hypothetical state of equilibrium and simplifies reality. According to this model, the expected return of a specific investment depends on two parameters: the expected return on risk-free assets, and the average risk premium (which is the difference between the returns on a risky investment and a risk-free one).

α (alpha) and β (beta) are the coefficients of the linear regression line obtained by plotting the portfolio's historical performance (R_p) compared to the reference market performance (R_m),

$$R_p = \alpha + \beta \cdot R_m$$

Alpha measures the expected excess return on each undervalued stock, and it is the difference between the average expected return and the predicted return based on the market risk premium and the stock's beta. Thus, alpha represents the manager's stock picking skills when constructing a portfolio.

The manager's aim when following a market neutral strategy is to maximize both the long and the short alphas, by managing them in an integrated and not separate way, as a global portfolio.

It is often maintained that the aim of an equity market neutral strategy is to seek a positive α (alpha) and set up a portfolio with β (beta) close to zero, so that the generated returns are not correlated to the market. However, this is not correct, because a beta close to zero is not a guarantee for no market correlation. To better appreciate this, we have to resort to some mathematical analysis.

The correlation between stock returns and market returns can be formalized as follows:

$$\beta = \frac{cov\,(R_i, R_m)}{var\,(R_m)} = \rho_{i,m} \cdot \frac{\sigma_{R_i}}{\sigma_{R_m}}$$

where $\dfrac{\sigma_{R_i}}{\sigma_{R_m}}$ is the scale factor

So beta is equal to the portfolio's market correlation times a scale factor that magnifies or reduces the correlation by a factor equal to the ratio between portfolio risk and market risk.

This mathematical formula allows us to better understand that if the portfolio's beta is close to zero, it is too early to draw the conclusion that the portfolio is market neutral. The scale factor explains how a low beta may well go hand in hand with a high market correlation.

Thus, beta is not an adequate measure of market risk for financial assets whose risk is low relevant to market risks.[6]

It should also be noted that in practice a manager cannot keep the portfolio's beta always down to zero, because any change in the prices of the stocks in the portfolio is going to change the weights. To be beta neutral, it would be necessary to carry out immediate portfolio adjustments.

Finally, we should point out that these measures of risk are by themselves not truly valid, because the underlying distributions are clearly not Gaussians, as shown below by performance statistics.

4.9.1   Equity Market Neutral Strategy's Historical Performance Analysis

Let us analyze the historical behavior of the market neutral strategy based on the monthly returns of the CS/Tremont Equity Market Neutral Index. Again, the past performance of a given investment is not necessarily indicative of a future return for the same investment. Still, we believe it is useful to examine historical data to understand which scenarios are favorable to this strategy and which are not.

---

[6] Giovanni Beliossi, *Prendere la via lunga e quella corta*, Risk Italia, December 2001.

Table 4.2

	CS/Tremont Equity Market Neutral	Morgan Stanley Capital International World in US$	JP Morgan Global Government Bond Global International
Value at Risk (1 month, 95%)	−0.5%	−6.4%	−1.9%
Value at Risk (1 month, 99%)	−1.0%	−10.4%	−3.6%
Best month Performance	+3.3%	+8.9%	+7.0%
Average Performance in positive months	+1.1%	+3.2%	+1.6%
Worst month Performance	−1.2%	−13.5%	−5.1%
Average Performance in negative months	−0.4%	−3.5%	−1.0%
% Positive months	84%	61%	57%
Compound Annual Growth Rate (CAGR)	+10.3%	+6.3%	+5.4%
Annualized monthly volatility	3.0%	14.2%	6.2%
Skewness	0.29	−0.60	−0.65
Kurtosis	0.28	0.59	2.21
Largest drawdown*	−3.6%	−48.4%	−8.6%
Duration of the largest drawdown in months	5	30	4
Time to recovery** in months	4	n.a.	9
Drawdown start	31st Jul. 1994	30th Apr. 2000	28th Feb. 1994
Drawdown end	30th Nov. 1994	30th Sep. 2002	31st May 1994

* The largest drawdown is defined as the maximum value of any "peak to trough decline" over the specified period. The subsequent minimum is not determined until it has reached a new high.
** Time to recovery is the time necessary to recover from the largest drawdown.

The statistical analysis of the CS/Tremont Equity Market Neutral Index between 1994 and 2004 produces the results shown in Table 4.2.

The percentage of positive months is very high (84%) and the average performance of positive months is +1.1%.

The performance has been very strong, with an annualized return of 10.3% between 1994 and 2004, with a surprisingly low volatility (3%).

The distribution of monthly return is symmetrical (Skewness close to zero) and the tails are shorter than those of the Gaussian distribution (Kurtosis less than 3).

The largest drawdown has been small (−3.6%), lasted for five months and was recovered in a short time (four months).

Figure 4.13 shows the monthly returns of the CS/Tremont Equity Market Neutral Index from 1994 to 2004.

Figure 4.14 illustrates the historical performance as a function of risk for the CS/Tremont Equity Market Neutral Index between 1994 and 2004. The concentration ellipsoid shows that historically the risk/return profile of the Equity Market Neutral strategy remained confined to a well-defined area within the risk/return space, and in particular it had a very low volatility.

Figure 4.15 shows that from 1994 to 2004 there have been no relevant "underwater" episodes for Equity Market Neutral hedge funds. The figure must be analyzed taking

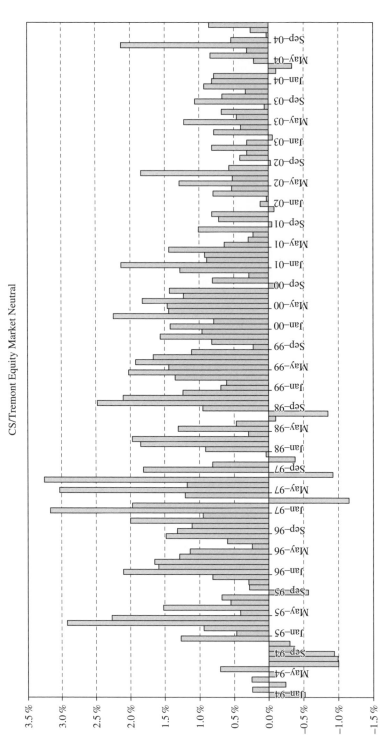

Figure 4.13 Monthly returns of CS/Tremont Equity Market Neutral from 1994 to 2004. Source: CS/Tremont Index LLC, www.hedgeindex.com. Copyright © 2006, Credit Suisse/Tremont Index LLC. All rights reserved*

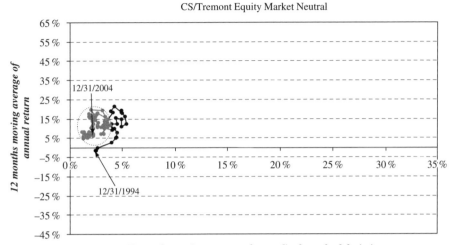

Figure 4.14 Historical performance trend of return as a function of risk for CS/Tremont Equity Market Neutral from 1994 to 2004. Source: CS/Tremont Index LLC, www.hedgeindex.com. Copyright © 2006, Credit Suisse/Tremont Index LLC. All rights reserved*

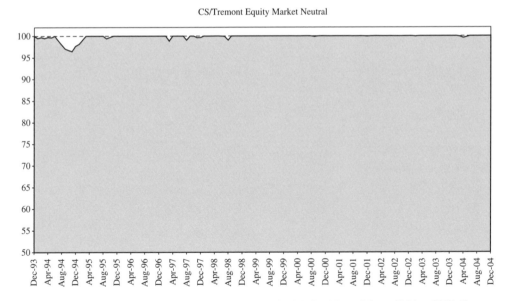

Figure 4.15 Underwater periods for CS/Tremont Equity Market Neutral from 1994 to 2004. Source: CS/Tremont Index LLC, www.hedgeindex.com. Copyright © 2006, Credit Suisse/Tremont Index LLC. All rights reserved*

---

drawdown data into consideration: throughout the drawdown and the time to recovery period, the hedge funds adopting this strategy were under the high water mark. See Chapter 1, Section 1.8, for more details on the setup and meaning of Figures 4.14 and 4.15.

The equity market neutral strategy withstood many events that strongly affected the market between 1994 and 2004.

5
Merger Arbitrage

The merger arbitrage strategy seeks to seize the opportunities arising from extraordinary corporate events, such as mergers and acquisitions (M&A) or leveraged buy-outs, by trading the stocks of the companies involved in the deal. In general, in these transactions common stock is exchanged for cash, other common stock, or a combination of cash and stocks. The merger arbitrage strategy is more properly called *risk arbitrage*, because it is an arbitrage strategy whose outcome purely depends on the risk associated with the deal outcome. Its success totally depends on the finalization of the mergers and acquisitions.

The hedge fund manager takes a directional position on the spread:

- in the case of acquisition, between the value offered for the acquisition and the current market value of the company to be acquired;
- in the case of merger, between the theoretical exchange ratio of the stock of the two merging entities and the exchange ratio currently expressed by the market.

The greater the risk of a deal failure, the greater is the spread. All mergers/acquisitions are exposed to the risk that the deal is not closed as announced initially. If the deal fails, generally the value of the target company shares drops sharply.

The hedge fund manager opens arbitrage positions on mergers and acquisitions where he expects the current market spread to converge towards the offered one. The manager will make a profit if the spread narrows, and will lose money if the spread widens.

In the case of an acquisition, the acquiring company generally has to pay a premium to take over the target company, therefore the bid is at a premium on the market value of the company being acquired before the acquisition is announced. Still, it would be an oversimplification to think that the acquisition arbitrage strategy consists in just going long on the stock of the target company and selling short the stock of the acquiring company. This is what generally happens, but there can be circumstances under which taking a convergence position means doing the exact opposite: namely, going long on the acquiring company and short on the company being acquired, as shown in Figure 5.7 as part of an example later in the chapter.

The existence of managers performing merger and acquisition arbitrages explains why, when an extraordinary corporate transaction is announced, trading volumes swell.

The manager performing merger and acquisition arbitrages may choose between two approaches:

- take a position after the transaction has been announced;
- try to anticipate the merger or acquisition event, taking a position before the announcement.

Generally, hedge fund managers trade after the deal has been announced. To invest seeking to anticipate an event means to invest on rumors or, which is even worse, on confidential information, which translates into the illegal practice of *insider trading*.

A merger or an acquisition is not a binary event: it is not as simple as the transaction either being completed or not. These deals are often very complicated and profiting from them requires skills, expertise and abilities in the fields of financial engineering and risk management.

The key questions a manager tries to answer are:

- Does the deal make sense both in strategic and financial terms?
- Are there other potential purchasers that may make a higher bid for the target company?
- If the deal fails, what is the possible loss?
- What is the probability of the deal being completed and what is its expected time-to-completion?

A hedge fund manager specializing in this strategy tries to understand the economic rationale underlying the merger or acquisition: value creation; cost cutting; synergies; economies of scale; possible staff redundancies; fiscal implications; the costs, time and difficulties entailed by the integration process; possible opposition by the acquired company management.

Then the manager will build a position – the size of which depends on the risk associated with the highest loss and the expected time to completion – and try to trade on the volatility spread.

5.1   A BRIEF HISTORY OF M&A

The arbitrage on mergers and acquisitions is a classic arbitrage strategy, which has been performed for more than half a century. The invention of this strategy dates back to the mid-1940s and it is attributed to Gustave Levy, partner of the investment bank Goldman Sachs. His successor was Robert Rubin, partner of Goldman Sachs and subsequently Secretary of the US Treasury. Throughout the 1980s, Goldman Sachs's Risk Arbitrage department was the most profitable after that of M&A.

Brealey and Myers[1] observed that in the history of the United States mergers have come in waves, and they have considered the determinants of these waves as one of the open issues of finance. Brealey and Myers identified five major merger waves, each characterized by the fact that it started during a changeover to new business structures and it ended during a recession period[2]:

- the "trustification" of industrial America between 1898 and 1903;
- the introduction of the assembly line between 1923 and 1929;
- conglomerates in the 1960s;
- the second major restructuring in the 1980s;
- the consolidation caused by deregulation in the 1990s.

A significant number of mergers and acquisitions are caused by industrial shocks, like technological changes, deregulation, changes in raw material prices and globalization.

The first wave of mergers dates back to the period between 1898 and 1903, when many small and medium enterprises consolidated to set up monopolies in the oil, steel and manufacturing industries. It was a reaction to the deflation that took place at the end of the

[1] Brealey, R. and Myers, S. (2000) *Principles of Corporate Finance*, 6th edition, New York: McGraw Hill.
[2] Kerschner, E. and Geraghty, M. (2004) *Riding the Wave: An Elongated M&A cycle*, Citigroup, 30th July 2004.

19th century. The first wave ended as a result of President Roosevelt's intervention aimed at limiting "trustification", and of the economic recession that had started in 1902.

In 1904, the Supreme Court supported the government by enforcing the antitrust laws against Northern Securities Company. The antitrust laws were applied once more by President Taft in 1911 against Standard Oil and the American Tobacco Company. In 1914, the Clayton Act prohibited anti-competitive share acquisitions, but not asset acquisitions.

The second wave took place between 1923 and 1929, and was characterized by the consolidation of many sectors through the creation of oligopolies in the power and gas industries, as well as in the manufacturing industry. At the time, the high technology and high growth manufacturing industries were the auto and airplane industries, the radio and television sector, and the power industry. The second wave ended with the crash of the stock market in 1929 and the onset of the Great Depression.

In 1950, worried about the growing consolidations, the Congress passed an amendment aiming at strengthening antitrust laws. It was still allowed, however, to merge into conglomerates.

The third wave of mergers took place in the 1960s, when big economic conglomerates were formed through the merger of companies belonging to different industries. In those years, many investment banks started to create their own merger and acquisition arbitrage groups, making substantial profits. The third wave ended at the beginning of the recession of the 1970s, which caused conglomerate profits to sink, followed by their shares.

The fourth wave took place during the 1980s, as a result of disinflation and foreign competition. In those years, the number of hostile bids exploded, favored by low interest rates and by a favorable regulatory framework. The oil, natural gas, financial services, regional banks and food industries were swept up in a consolidation process.

Following the financial scandals involving some of the prominent figures of the merger arbitrage community, the golden age of mergers and acquisitions ended abruptly in October 1989, when the leveraged buy-out[3] of American Airlines failed, because its managers and employees could not obtain the necessary financing. Many leveraged companies filed for bankruptcy, including the investment bank Drexel Burnham Lambert, leader on the junk bond market. In the mid-1990s, the economy was engulfed in a new recession. Among the negative historical figures of merger and acquisition arbitrage we may cite Michael Milken and Ivan Boesky. Michael Milken was the founder and head of the high yield bond department in Drexel Burnham Lambert and during the 1980s he became famous for financing corporate raids with the issuance of junk bonds. In 1989, the government charged him with securities/reporting violations. He pleaded guilty for some securities and tax law violations. He paid a $200 million fine and served a 22 month sentence in prison. Ivan Boesky, manager of the Hudson Fund, a hedge fund specialising in merger arbitrage, in 1986 was arrested and settled insider trading charges with the SEC for sanctions that included a $100 million payment.

The fifth wave of mergers took place in the second half of the 1990s. As illustrated in Figure 5.1, it is the most relevant in terms of numbers and size of M&A deals. The left axis shows the value of the M&A transactions in billion dollars, while the right axis shows the number of M&A deals.

Figure 5.2 measures the number of announced merger and acquisition deals as a percentage of gross domestic product between 1991 and 2004. The figure shows that in the United States the M&A activity was livelier than in Europe.

---

[3] Takeover of a company using borrowed funds.

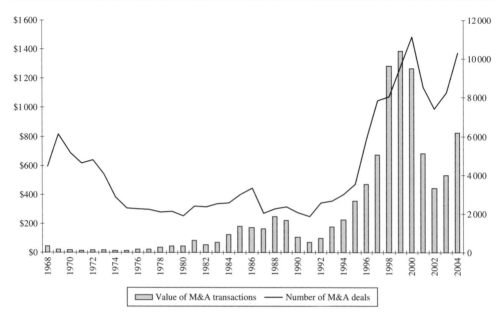

Figure 5.1 M&A activity in United States and cross border. The left axis shows the value of the M&A transactions in billion dollars, while the right axis shows the number of M&A deals. Source: www.mergerstat.com

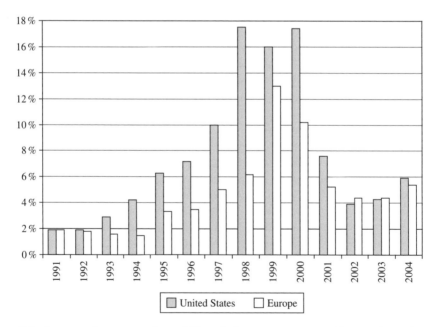

Figure 5.2 Announced merger and acquisition deals as a percentage of gross domestic product between 1991 and 2004. Source: Morgan Stanley

The reasons of this fifth wave can be traced back to technological changes, globalization and market liberalization. In particular, deregulation swept across the financial, telecommunication and utilities industries, which turned into dynamic businesses, focused on innovation, on mergers and on cost-cutting. This wave of mergers and acquisitions ended with the burst of the new economy bubble and the onset of recession in 2001.

In parallel, the European market of mergers and acquisitions also started to pick up. It is a very interesting area for hedge fund managers, as until now it has proved to offer more attractive spreads than in the United States.

Some academic studies demonstrated that merger waves differ from one another because they tend to involve a limited number of different industries between one wave and the other.[4] This confirms the observation that a great proportion of mergers are caused by an industry-wide shock.

Nowadays, major investment banks that act as corporate advisors dominate the merger and acquisition market.

Let us now focus our attention on what has happened in recent years.

As shown in Figure 5.3, after a peak in 1999 the M&A market reached its lowest point in 2002 and then began to grow, sustained by the high level of cash in corporate balance sheets and by the pressure for consolidation in many sectors.

Figure 5.4 shows the breakdown by sector of M&A activity, globally and from 1997 to 2005: telecom and banks have been the most active sectors in the period. As a matter of fact, the search for a critical size is a success factor to survive the high level of competition in the telecom and banking sectors.

Although between 1998 and 2000 all share exchange deals accounted for about 30 % of transactions worth more than one billion dollars, only 15 % of the greatest deals in 2003 was on a share exchange basis, mainly as a direct effect of the low interest rates throughout 2003: 61 % of deals over one billion dollars in 2003 was on a purely cash exchange basis.

Many of the larger acquisitions carried out by European companies in recent years targeted non-European companies. Despite the strong Euro, in 2003 European companies spent

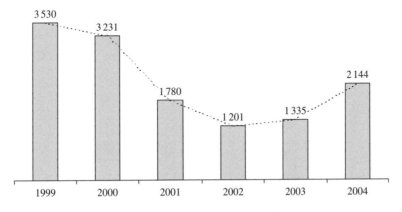

Figure 5.3 M&A global activity from 1999 to 2004 (data in billion USD). Source: Bloomberg L.P.

[4] Andrade, G., Mitchell, M. and Stafford, E. (2001) "New evidence and perspectives on mergers," *Journal of Economic Perspectives*, **15**(2), 103–120.

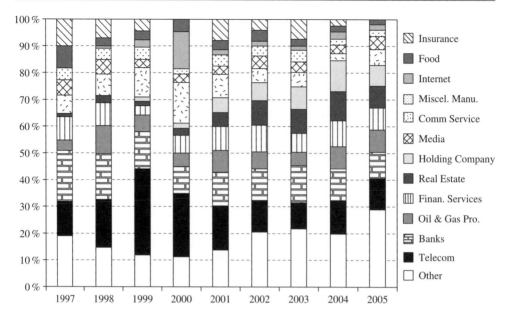

Figure 5.4 Most active sectors in M&A globally from 1997 to 2005 (% of volume in USD). Source: Bloomberg L.P.

50 % less on acquiring non-European companies compared to 2001: as a whole, European companies spent $158 billion on acquiring non-European companies.

A climate of confidence has a strong impact on the merger and acquisition sector. Large M&A deals are announced when the managing directors trust both the price of their stock, and the political and macro-economic backdrop. Even though deal volumes grew in 2003, arbitrageurs did not benefit from it, and obtained only mediocre results. As a matter of fact trading volumes increased, yet spreads were not very attractive, reaching on average about 5 % (Figure 5.5).

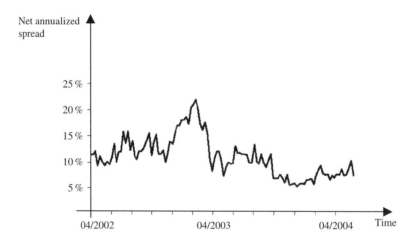

Figure 5.5 Historical trend of the net annualized spread in M&A deals. Source: Lehman Brothers

Table 5.1 The main M&A deals in history from 1996 to 31st January 2005 (only deals with an announced value exceeding $50 billion). Source: Bloomberg L.P.

Announce date	Target Company	Acquirer	Seller	Total amount announced in million US$	Type of payment	Status of the deal as of 31st January 2005
10-Jan-2000	Historic Tw Inc	Time Warner Inc		186 236	Stock	Complete
14-Nov-1999	Vodafone Ag	Vodafone Group Plc		185 066	Stock & Debt	Complete
05-Oct-1999	Sprint Corp	Worldcom Inc-Worldcom Group		110 065	Stock & Debt	Terminated
04-Nov-1999	Warner-Lambert Co	Pfizer Inc		87 319	Stock	Complete
20-Apr-1999	Telecom Italia SpA/Old	Deutsche Telekom Ag-Reg		80 402	Stock & Debt	Terminated
01-Dec-1998	Mobil Corp	Exxon Mobil Corp		80 338	Stock	Complete
28-Oct-2004	Shell Transprt&Tradng Co Plc	Royal Dutch Shell Plc		80 138	Stock	Pending
09-Jul-2001	Comcast Cable Comm Holdings	Comcast Corp-Cl A	AT&T Corp	76 057	Stock	Complete
26-Jan-2004	Aventis SA	Sanofi-Aventis		72 704	Cash and Stock	Complete
17-Jan-2000	SmithKline Beecham Plc	GlaxoSmithKline Plc		72 445	Stock	Complete
28-Jul-1998	GTE Corp	Verizon Communications Inc		71 127	Stock	Complete
06-Apr-1998	Citicorp	Citigroup Inc		69 892	Stock	Complete
11-May-1998	Ameritech Corporation/Del	SBC Communications Inc		68 219	Stock	Complete
11-Feb-2004	The Walt Disney Co.	Comcast Corp-Cl A		67 309	Stock	Terminated
04-Nov-1999	Warner-Lambert Co	Wyeth		65 488	Stock	Terminated
15-Jul-2002	Pharmacia Corp	Pfizer Inc		64 264	Stock	Complete
13-Apr-1998	Bankamerica Corp (Old)	Bank Of America Corp		57 466	Stock	Complete
05-Jan-1999	Vodafone Americas Asia Inc	Vodafone Group Plc		57 355	Cash and Stock	Complete
28-Jan-2005	Gillette Company	Procter & Gamble Co		52 279	Stock	Pending
11-Apr-2000	Nortel Networks Corp	Shareholders	BCE Inc	56 029	Stock	Complete
11-Aug-1998	Amoco Corp	BP Plc		55 947	Stock	Complete
22-Mar-1999	Mediaone Group Inc	Comcast Corp-Cl A		55 890	Stock & Debt	Terminated
22-Apr-1999	Mediaone Group Inc	AT&T Corp		55 422	Cash, Stock & Debt	Complete
14-Jan-2004	Bank One Corp	JPMorgan Chase & Co		55 066	Stock	Complete
11-Mar-1999	Tim SpA	Telecom Italia SpA/Old		54 514	Stock	Terminated
23-Oct-2000	Honeywell International Inc	General Electric Co		52 668	Stock	Terminated
05-Jul-1999	Elf Aquitaine	Total SA		52 297	Stock	Complete

The two main reasons why spreads remained so narrow are the high number of arbitrageurs trading on the same transactions, and the low interest rates. At present, managers are facing the challenge of developing a more flexible and creative approach, allowing them to take advantage of corporate events other than mergers and acquisitions. Citigroup[5] maintains that most probably M&A activity is on the verge of a new significant wave, taking into account the historical perspective. In this sixth wave, the shock is represented by the integration of the Internet and of the new information technologies in corporate key areas, causing corporate processes to be reconfigured. Since historically merger and acquisition activities were focused only on a small number of industries, according to Citigroup the sectors that will most probably consolidate are finance, media and healthcare. The need to merge may also stem from the urge to consolidate in response to global competition.

In 2004, M&As were favored by a sustained economic growth, low interest rates and high corporate cash flows. Spreads are not very attractive and are closely correlated to interest rates. In the United States, the internal rate of return for a deal is on average 5 %, which is 3–4 times lower compared to 1999 and 2000. Spreads are so narrow that sometimes the risk a deal will fail is not sufficiently remunerated.

In Europe, spreads are slightly higher, since less capital is being allocated to this strategy and its entry barriers are higher, due to the complexity of deals and the regulatory peculiarities of EU countries.

Table 5.1 shows the main M&A deals in history: it covers the period from 1996 to 31st January 2005 and we selected only deals with an announced value exceeding $50 billion.

5.2   STRATEGY DESCRIPTION

Hedge fund managers carry out a case study on the announced merger or acquisition deal so as to assign a given probability to each possible outcome. Their information sources are the companies' public documents, company reports, Internet websites, analyst reports and SEC filings (10K[6], 10Q[7], proxy, tender document, merger agreement, etc.). Another precious source of information is the network of contacts the hedge fund manager has built within the sector with investment bank analysts, the management of the companies concerned, advisors specialized in the sector, the management of companies belonging to the same sector, and legal offices.

Also, a large part of the manager's work consists in analyzing the worst case scenario, i.e. the deal failure, and the resulting potential loss suffered by the hedge fund.

Managers calculate the value of the shares of the companies involved in the extraordinary event and verify whether the exchange ratio between the two companies' stock is fair. If not, managers can challenge the acquisition and require that the buyer raise his offer. Hedge funds can therefore play a very important role in the renegotiation of the terms and conditions of an acquisition.

The merger or acquisition process is made up of the following steps:

1. preliminary agreement;
2. final agreement specifying the terms and conditions along which the transaction is performed and the withdrawal terms for each party;

---

[5] Kerschner, E. and Geraghty, M. (2004) *Riding the Wave: An Elongated M&A cycle*, Citigroup, 30th July 2004.
[6] *Company Annual Report*
[7] *Company Quarterly Report*

3. audit of the financial reports of the company being acquired, or in the case of merger, of both companies by an auditing company expressly hired;
4. shareholders' approval for both companies in the case of merger or for the company being acquired in the case of acquisition;
5. approval by market regulatory authorities and anti-trust authorities;
6. legal outcome of the deal.

A further source of risk is a delay in the completion of the deal, in that stretching out the investment period inevitably squeezes the return.

In addition to checking that the exchange ratio is fair, it is also important for the hedge fund manager to determine how long the invested capital will remain locked up before the deal is over. It is a very complicated evaluation, in that it requires for example assessment on possible delays due to legal issues, and there is the risk of extraordinary events that may slow down the deal finalization.

In the case of hostile takeover, a new buyer can materialize, called the *white knight*, who intervenes by making a higher bid. The company will still be acquired, but at least it may have a more friendly buyer as the following example shows.

On 12th December 2004, according to the online issue of *The Wall Street Journal*, Honeywell decided to acquire Novar Plc, an industrial holding in the United Kingdom, for $1.52 billion.

Honeywell offered 185 pence per Novar Plc share, about 28 % more than the competitor Melrose Plc had offered the month before during a hostile bid. Novar had rejected the $1.2 billion Melrose bid, and was looking for a new buyer. Novar's board of directors accepted Honeywell's offer, and Honeywell also took over £300 million worth of Novar's debts.

In this example, Honeywell was Novar Plc's *white knight*.

5.3   RISK ASSOCIATED WITH THE OUTCOME OF AN EXTRAORDINARY CORPORATE EVENT

Until the deal is completed, the share prices of the two companies factor in the market's uncertainty as to the outcome of the deal. Said uncertainty may be triggered by various factors, such as financial difficulties, regulatory hurdles, disagreement between the two management teams or the disclosure of negative information on one of the two companies concerned. Often, as a result of this uncertainty, the target company's stock is traded at a discount until the deal is over.

Merger arbitrage managers are highly skilled in the analysis of the risks associated with deal failure. A deal may fail for many reasons:

- shareholders do not approve the deal: this may happen when shareholders are not satisfied with the exchange ratio offered in the case of merger or with the bid in the case of acquisition;
- deal terms may be renegotiated due to pressures by the shareholders or the target company management;
- the anti-trust authorities and the market regulatory authorities do not give the green light;
- fiscal or regulatory issues;

- a new buyer steps in, who is on more friendly terms with the current management of the target company;
- defensive actions by the management of the target company, for fear of layoffs or deep changes in the management structure;
- other unforeseen factors.

When a hostile takeover is attempted, the top management of the target company falls under the regulations governing takeover bids in the country where the company has its legal domicile. Depending on these regulations, the top management of the target company may be obliged to limit its activities to the ordinary business, and thus is prevented from taking defensive actions against the hostile takeover.

When possible, a company may challenge a hostile takeover through the following actions: poison pill, staggered board and special share classes.

The so-called *poison pill* is the free of charge distribution by the takeover-target company to its current shareholders of preferred stock convertible to dividends, in such a number as to at least match the number of outstanding shares. Shareholders will not want to exercise their right to convert to gain access to the dividend distribution, except in the case of takeover. A takeover attempt will raise the target company's share price, thus making it more expensive to take it over.

A *staggered board* is a board of directors in which only a portion of the directors are elected each year, to thwart unfriendly takeover attempts, since potential acquirers would have to wait at least one year to take full control of the company's board. The purchasing company will thus have to win two ballots in two different shareholders' meetings, instead of winning a single ballot in the meeting at the time of the offer.

There are companies that issue *special share classes*, for example class A and class B, with different voting rights. This method is used when a majority shareholder wishes to retain control over a company, by holding the shares with more favorable voting rights and floating the other class of shares.

The spread between the announced exchange ratio and the market exchange ratio is greater in the case of hostile bids, in that there is a higher risk that the deal will fail. Wider spreads are also justified by the greater legal implications and complexities brought forth by conflicting situations.

When merger arbitrage managers enter a deal, there is no certainty as to the timing of the events.

The greater the uncertainty as to the deal outcome, the larger the merger arbitrage spread becomes. This widening causes a loss to the manager who has already carried out the arbitrage transaction, and if the deal is not completed, the manager will be obliged to cover his short sales, and the situation may get even worse if the market is tight.

Generally, managers tend to increase their position in a single deal little by little as it approaches a positive ending. For a hedge fund manager, the greatest loss comes when a deal fails close to the date of completion. Clearly, the probability of the success of a deal changes over time, increasing along the way until the deal smoothly reaches its positive conclusion.

The risk/return profile of a merger or acquisition arbitrage is highly asymmetrical: there is a high probability of gaining a narrow spread and a very little probability of losing a lot of money.

Let's see an example of deal failure.

On 22nd October 2000, General Electric announced that it intended acquiring Honeywell International with an offer of 1.055 General Electric shares for each Honeywell International share. Most analysts gave a positive opinion to this merger, and it was estimated that it would produce a cost saving of $1.5 billion per year. On 30th September 2000, General Electric's market capitalization was about $573 billion, while Honeywell International's was $28 billion. In view of the size of the two companies, many hedge fund managers went headlong into merger arbitrage.

On 2nd May 2001, at the end of a study on the effects of competition on the manufacturing of airplane engines, automation controls and industrial sensors, the US Department of Justice approved the merger. This strengthened the merger's probability of success. However, on 14th June 2001, after a number of negotiations, Mario Monti – EU competition commissioner – announced the commission's intention to reject the merger, despite the fact that General Electric had expressed its willingness to liquidate assets for $2.2 billion. The decision was based on the fact that the European Union was worried that the resulting company would have a dominant position in the market of airplane engines and electronics. This was the first time the European Union reached a different conclusion from the US antitrust authorities.

This decision caught the entire financial community unawares, and the merger failed, inflicting a hard blow on arbitrageurs.

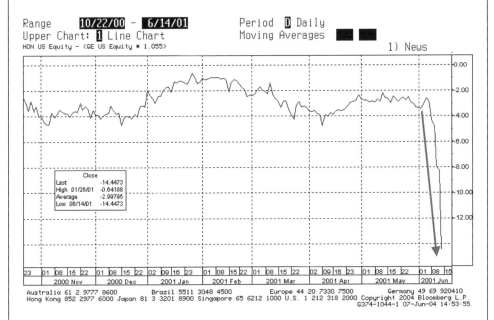

Figure 5.6 Example of deal failure. The spread in basis points between the actual Honeywell share and the Honeywell share theoretically measured as being 1.055* General Electric. Used with permission from Bloomberg L.P.

5.4   TYPES OF MERGERS AND ACQUISITIONS

There are several different types of mergers and acquisitions:

- Cash mergers or tender offers
- Stock swap mergers or stock-for-stock mergers
- Stock swap mergers with a collar
- Multiple bidder situations
- Leveraged buyouts and hostile takeovers
- Spin-offs

5.4.1   Cash Mergers or Tender Offers

In the case of cash mergers, the purchasing company offers a fixed cash amount for each share of the target company. Generally, the price offered for the shares includes a premium on the market price of the shares before the offer. Following the announcement, the price of the shares of the target company should rise naturally, but it does not immediately reach the price offered by the acquiring company. The percentage difference between the initial price of the offer and the closing share price of the target company the day after the announcement of the acquisition is called *merger arbitrage spread*. This spread varies as a function of the risk the deal may fail. In the case of cash merger, the hedge fund manager purchases the shares of the target company without short selling the shares of the purchasing company.

Gucci, the Italian fashion house listed on the New York Stock Exchange (NYSE) and on the Euronext Amsterdam N.V., was caught in the middle of a battle for its control between Moët Hennessy–Louis Vuitton (LVMH) and Pinault Printemps Redoute (PPR, which started in 1999.

The battle ended on 10th September 2001 with an agreement between LVMH, PPR and Gucci, envisaging:

1. the purchase in October 2001 by PPR of a package of Gucci shares held by LVMH at a price of \$94 for a total amount of \$806 million;
2. the payment by Gucci of a \$7 dividend per share in December 2001;
3. the obligation for PPR to launch a takeover bid for all Gucci shares it did not hold yet in March 2004 at a unit price of \$101.50.

The September 11 terrorist attack caused the prices of luxury stocks to drop considerably. Even though the agreement did not contain any provision governing withdrawal in the case of adverse conditions, the Dutch securities commission (Securities Board of the Netherlands, STE; today called Netherlands Authority for the Financial Markets) had to give its unconditional approval by 24th September 2001. STE approved the agreement without introducing additional terms.

A hedge fund manager realized that the agreement caused the Gucci share to turn into a kind of convertible bond, that is, a bond issued by PPR and convertible into Gucci shares: the bond would then pay out a special coupon equal to the dividend distributed by Gucci in December 2001.

This hedge fund manager modeled the convertible bond. PPR was an *investment grade* issuer and it was therefore easy to hedge against the issuer's credit risk. When comparing

Gucci with a basket of luxury shares, the hedge fund manager also grew convinced that the more conservative estimates indicated that the convertible bond was underpriced.

The hedge fund bought the Gucci shares. To hedge against PPR's credit risk, the manager bought *credit default swaps* on PPR with a notional value of 1.7 times the Gucci share price. The interest rate risk was hedged by purchasing *Eurodollar futures*. To be delta neutral with respect to the convertible bond, the hedge fund manager sold short a basket of luxury shares.

In June–July 2002, corporate bonds started to widen their credit spread with respect to Treasuries with a similar maturity, due to the worrisome corporate accounting scandals and the bankruptcy of issuers that used to have an *investment grade* creditworthiness.

PPR shares tumbled from €125 to €80, but also the luxury share basket that the manager had sold short dropped sharply, generating a profit of 10 % of the market value of Gucci shares for the manager.

5.4.2   Stock Swap Mergers or Stock-for-Stock Mergers

In this case, the acquiring company offers its shares in exchange for the shares of the target company, based on the relation indicated by the *exchange ratio*. Unlike the cash merger, the price offered for the target company is not fixed, but it depends on the price ratio between the two companies. To make a profit it is not sufficient to buy the shares of the target company and convert them into shares of the acquiring company, because as a result of the offer, the price of the shares of the purchasing company may decrease substantially and the converted shares may end up costing less than the initial purchasing price.

The manager constructs a position that brings the real exchange ratio as expressed by market values towards the theoretical exchange ratio. He is not concerned with the absolute changes in the share prices, but instead he is only interested in relative price changes.

Hence, the manager takes a directional position on the spread between the theoretical exchange ratio and the actual exchange ratio: said position does not depend upon the global market performance, so it is market neutral. However, bullish stock markets may jeopardize the outcome of many transactions based on the value of the shares of the purchasing company.

Recently, merger spreads have narrowed down, but merger arbitrages are typically short-term investments: by using leverage, modest short-term returns can be translated into interesting annualized returns.

On 1st September 2003, France Telecom announced the acquisition of Orange, providing investors with the following event schedule:

- 1st September 2003: announcement of the bid on not yet held Orange shares with 11 France Telecom shares in exchange for 25 Orange shares;
- 9th September 2003: approval by the regulatory authorities;
- 12th September 2003: opening of the booking period;
- 6th October 2003: France Telecom shareholders vote on the Orange buyout;
- 6th October 2003: closing of booking;
- 20th October 2003: bid results;
- 24th October 2003: settlement.

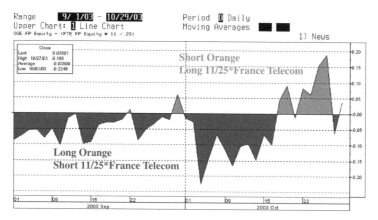

Figure 5.7 The spread in basis points between the actual Orange share and the Orange share theoretically measured as being 11/25*France Telecom. Used with permission from Bloomberg L.P.

The hedge fund manager takes action immediately after the announcement of the deal. He believes that the actual exchange ratio converges with the announced one, thus he carries out a dynamic hedging as a function of the mismatches between the shares and the theoretical exchange ratio.

Figure 5.7 shows the spread in basis points between the actual Orange share and the Orange share theoretically measured as being 11/25*France Telecom. Note that the spread is variable, in that it reflects mainly the probability that the deal shall be completed. The manager trades so as to have no spread between Orange and "theoretical Orange", that is, to lead the spread between the two stocks towards zero until it disappears upon the deal completion. As a result, when the spread is negative, the hedge fund manager has the following open position:

- Long 25 Orange shares; and
- Short 11 France Telecom shares.

When the spread is positive, the manager has the following open position:

- Short 25 Orange shares; and
- Long 11 France Telecom shares.

Note from Figure 5.7 that since the spread between Orange and "theoretical Orange" ranges between −20 bps and +20 bps, the hedge fund manager will probably resort to leverage and will increase his leverage as the deal drives closer to completion. In the dark gray areas, the manager has a long position on the shares of the acquired company (Orange) and a matching short position on the shares of the purchasing company (France Telecom). On the contrary, in the light gray areas, the manager went long on the shares of the acquiring company (France Telecom) and short on the shares of the acquired company (Orange).

As anticipated, this example confirms the fact that it would be an oversimplification to believe that merger arbitrage is nothing more than going long on the shares of the target company and selling short the shares of the purchasing company.

5.4.3   Stock Swap Mergers with a Collar

A stock swap merger with a collar, or fixed rate stock swap merger, is a complex merger situation where the exchange ratio is based on the price of the acquiring company at the date of completion, or, in extreme cases, when the target company has the right to cancel the merger if the value of the share of the bidding company goes below a given value, called the *collar*.

The outcome of the merger depends on the price of the shares of the purchasing company, therefore this type of deal is highly sensitive to the volatility of the underlying stock.

A hedge fund manager analyzes the collar as if it were an option. The outcome of more complicated mergers is marked by a greater uncertainty and generally spreads are wider.

Company A offers to buy company B as follows (see Figure 5.8):

- if share A is traded under $46, company A offers 0.478 shares in exchange for 1 share B;
- if share A is traded between $46 and $58, B shall receive $22 in share value;
- if share A is traded above $58, company A offers 0.379 shares in exchange for 1 share B.

Company A is making a collar bid, to set the minimum and maximum number of own shares to be issued. The collar is defined based on the share price of the bidding company at the date of completion of the bid.

Before the bid price is determined, the hedge fund manager has the opportunity to delta hedge by trading the option value.

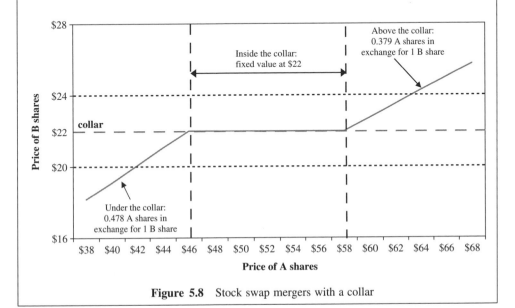

Figure 5.8   Stock swap mergers with a collar

5.4.4   Multiple Bidder Situations

The multiple bidder situation is also a complex scenario involving many companies in a web of mergers and acquisitions.

For example, on 17th March 1999, Global Crossing announced the acquisition of Frontier Corporation. On 17th May 1999, US WEST Inc. announced the merger with Global Crossing. To make things even more complicated, on 14th June 1999, Qwest, a competitor of Global Crossing, announced a hostile takeover bid for Frontier Corporation and US WEST. We shall not dwell on the intricacies of this example, in that it is well beyond the scope of this book, but will just emphasize that at times mergers and acquisitions can be highly complex, and at times may call for uncommon analytical skills.

In the case of multiple bidder situations, spreads are wider compared to less complex situations.

5.4.5   Leveraged Buyouts and Hostile Takeovers

A leveraged buyout (LBO) is an extraordinary corporate event entailing the acquisition of a controlling interest in the stock of a company using borrowed funds. A leveraged buyout is a financial engineering transaction, through which a company is acquired by making a wide use of leverage to minimize the outlay of capital. Funds are raised by giving the target company's assets as collateral, and the loan is paid out of the cash flows of the acquired company. The loan will be paid back using the cash flows or selling part of the assets of the acquired company.

In the so-called *cash merger* technique, an ad hoc company is formed, which becomes the special purpose vehicle (SPV) for the acquisition. The company is capitalized by the raiders and borrows money to acquire the target company with a cash offer. Banking institutions that take part in this transaction can grant bridge loans or underwrite part of the junk bonds that may be issued by the SPV. Once the acquisition is over, the two companies merge so that the acquiring company's initial debt is passed on to the acquired company. Therefore, LBOs are targeted at companies that have a sound financial position; the acquiring company gives the target company's shares as security against the loans it has received. Considering the characteristics of this deal, the target company must meet special requirements:

- low indebtedness;
- stable and abundant cash flows;
- no need for short and medium term investments.

The end result of this transaction is the change in ownership of the target company and the debt transfer from the acquirer to the acquired company.

In contrast, a management buyout (MBO) is an LBO carried out by the company management. The management acquires a controlling interest in the stock of their company by borrowing money and offering the acquired company's stock as collateral.

In 2004 and 2005, private equity activity is sustaining the M&A deal flow, especially in Europe. Private equity firms in 2004 raised $85 billion, a huge amount of money. As a consequence, the LBO market is booming and the boundaries of the private equity business are being redefined in a number of ways:

- primarily in terms of size, because private equity companies are going after far larger businesses than they have done in the past;
- the multiples EV/EBITDA are often far more aggressive than the multiples currently priced by the equity market.

Autostrade constructs, maintains, and operates toll highways in Italy, the United Kingdom, and the United States. Autostrade also consults on highway projects in Europe, Asia, Latin America, and the Middle East. It manages gas stations along its Italian freeways.

On 1st November 2002, Schemaventotto, Autostrade's major shareholder with a 30 % stake, announced a takeover bid on the company's residual equity, offering €9.5 per share for a total of €7.98 billion. Schemaventotto shareholders were Edizione Holding (60 %), the holding company of the Benetton family, Fondazione Cassa di Risparmio di Torino (13.33 %), Acesa (12.83 %), Generali (6.67 %), UniCredito (6.67 %) and Brisa (0.5 %).

The bid was launched by a special purpose vehicle called NewCo28, fully controlled by Schemaventotto, and financed by a banking syndicate led by UniCredito and Mediobanca. Conditional to the bid was meeting the threshold of 66.7 % of the equity stake controlled by Schemaventotto. This threshold would allow NewCo28 to gain a qualified majority, based on which, during the special shareholder meeting, the merger with Autostrade after the takeover could be approved: the aim was to transfer the debt over to the operating company Autostrade and pay the acquisition out of the high cash flows generated by Autostrade.

However, after two days of suspended trading for the Autostrade stock, when trading was resumed on 4th November 2002, the Autostrade stock quotation had already exceeded the bid price of €9.5.

The price offered by Schemaventotto for the full control of Autostrade had been considered inadequate by a major investment bank, since it entailed a premium of just 13 % on the average price of the Autostrade share in the previous six months. The market expected Schemaventotto to make a higher bid, and there were rumors that a third party may step in with a hostile counter bid on Autostrade.

On 11th February 2003, NewCo28 decided to increase its bid, offering €10 per share. On 21st February 2003, the takeover was completed successfully and Schemaventotto was in control of 83.8 % of Autostrade's equity.

On 28th March 2003, the Board of Directors of Autostrade SpA. and the sole administrator of NewCo28 SpA. approved the plan to merge Autostrade into NewCo28. On 21st May 2003, the merger was approved by the shareholders of Autostrade and NewCo28 convened in a special meeting. At the end of the deal, Schemaventotto gained full control of the entity resulting from the merger, with a stake of about 62.7 %, based on the results at the end of the takeover. The immediate effect of the merger was the increase of the net consolidated financial debt of Gruppo Autostrade by the exact amount of NewCo28's net financial debt.

Some hedge funds entered the deal, which was rather big in size: about €8 billion cash. In this case, we cannot talk about an arbitrage because Schemaventotto's stock was not listed. These hedge funds went long on Autostrade, in that they considered the premium to be paid to take control over Autostrade to be higher than the one offered in the first bid. Anyway, we can still talk about a hedging position, since the cash offer represented a downside protection.

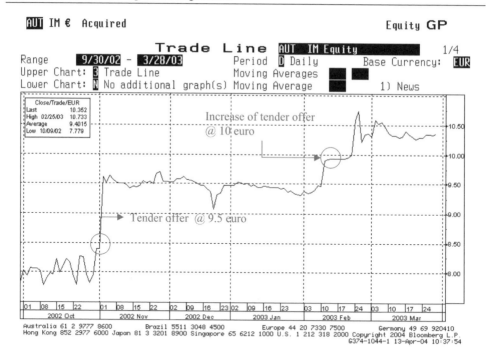

Figure 5.9   Takeover bid of NewCo28 on Autostrade. Used with permission from Bloomberg L.P.

5.4.6   Spin-offs

A spin-off is a form of corporate divestiture resulting in a new independent company. A spin-off gives rise to a new entity, which is typically the divestiture of a subsidiary or a division by the parent company. The shares of the new company are distributed on a pro rata basis to the parent company's shareholders or sold to new shareholders through an initial public offering.

In general, spin-off shares tend to decline immediately after the spin-off: first, because the distribution ratio may be for instance 1 new share for every 20, so many institutions will tend to liquidate them because the size of the stake would not be considered worth the monitoring effort; and second, because often the market is not in a position to measure the profitability of spin-offs correctly, as very little is known with regard to the allocation of overhead expenses and administrative costs between the new and the original entity.

5.5   RISK MANAGEMENT

We saw that the major risk inherent in merger or acquisition arbitrages is that the deal may fail or be postponed.

The most effective way for hedge fund managers to control risk is through diversification. A portfolio spreading across many mergers and acquisitions diversifies the risk associated with the single deals.

Many managers use leverage because often the spreads between the securities involved in the deal are small and would generate limited returns. Clearly, the use of leverage increases the risk that the manager might be obliged to divest his positions along a timing that is far from optimal.

Managers tend to trade on mergers between large cap companies, so as to be sure they have a sufficient liquid market for the short sale.

5.6   STRATEGY'S HISTORICAL PERFORMANCE ANALYSIS

Let's now analyze the historical behavior of this strategy based on the monthly returns of the CS/Tremont Risk Arbitrage index. Again, the past performance of a given investment is not necessarily indicative of a future return for the same investment. Still, we believe it is useful to examine historical data to understand which scenarios are favorable to this strategy and which are not.

The statistical analysis of the CS/Tremont Risk Arbitrage Index between 1994 and 2004 produces the results shown in Table 5.2.

The Value at Risk (1 month, 99 %) means that "We have a 99 % probability of not losing more than -2.7% of the investment in the next month". Instead we have observed a monthly performance of -6.2%. There is nothing wrong because, as usual, we must read statistics very carefully. The distribution of monthly returns is asymmetric (Skewness equal to -1.31) and with fat tails (Kurtosis greater than 3) and this implies that we cannot use the VaR to estimate an extreme value of the distribution, because we need many more observations.

The percentage of positive months is very high (80 %) and the average performance in positive months is $+1.1\%$. Hedge fund managers take a directional position on a spread, but not with respect to capital markets: actually the merger arbitrage strategy has a very low correlation to the performance of financial markets.

Table 5.2

	CS/Tremont Risk Arbitrage	Morgan Stanley Capital International World in USD	JP Morgan Global Government Bond Global International
Value at Risk (1 month, 95 %)	−1.30 %	−6.40 %	−1.90 %
Value at Risk (1 month, 99 %)	−2.70 %	−10.40 %	−3.60 %
Best month Performance	3.80 %	8.90 %	7.00 %
Average Performance in positive months	1.10 %	3.20 %	1.60 %
Worst month Performance	−6.20 %	−13.50 %	−5.10 %
Average Performance in negative months	−1.10 %	−3.50 %	−1.00 %
% Positive months	80 %	61 %	57 %
Compound Annual Growth Rate (CAGR)	8.20 %	6.30 %	5.40 %
Annualized monthly volatility	4.30 %	14.20 %	6.20 %
Skewness	−1.31	−0.6	0.65
Kurtosis	6.34	0.59	2.21
Largest Drawdown*	−7.60 %	−48.40 %	−8.60 %
Duration of the largest drawdown in months	4	30	4
Time to recovery** in months	7	n.a.	9
Drawdown start	30th Jun. 1998	30th Apr. 2000	28th Feb. 1994
Drawdown end	30th Sep. 1998	30th Sep. 2002	31st May 1994

* The largest drawdown is defined as the maximum value of any "peak to trough decline" over the specified period. The subsequent minimum is not determined until it has reached a new high.
** Time to recovery is the time necessary to recover from the largest drawdown.

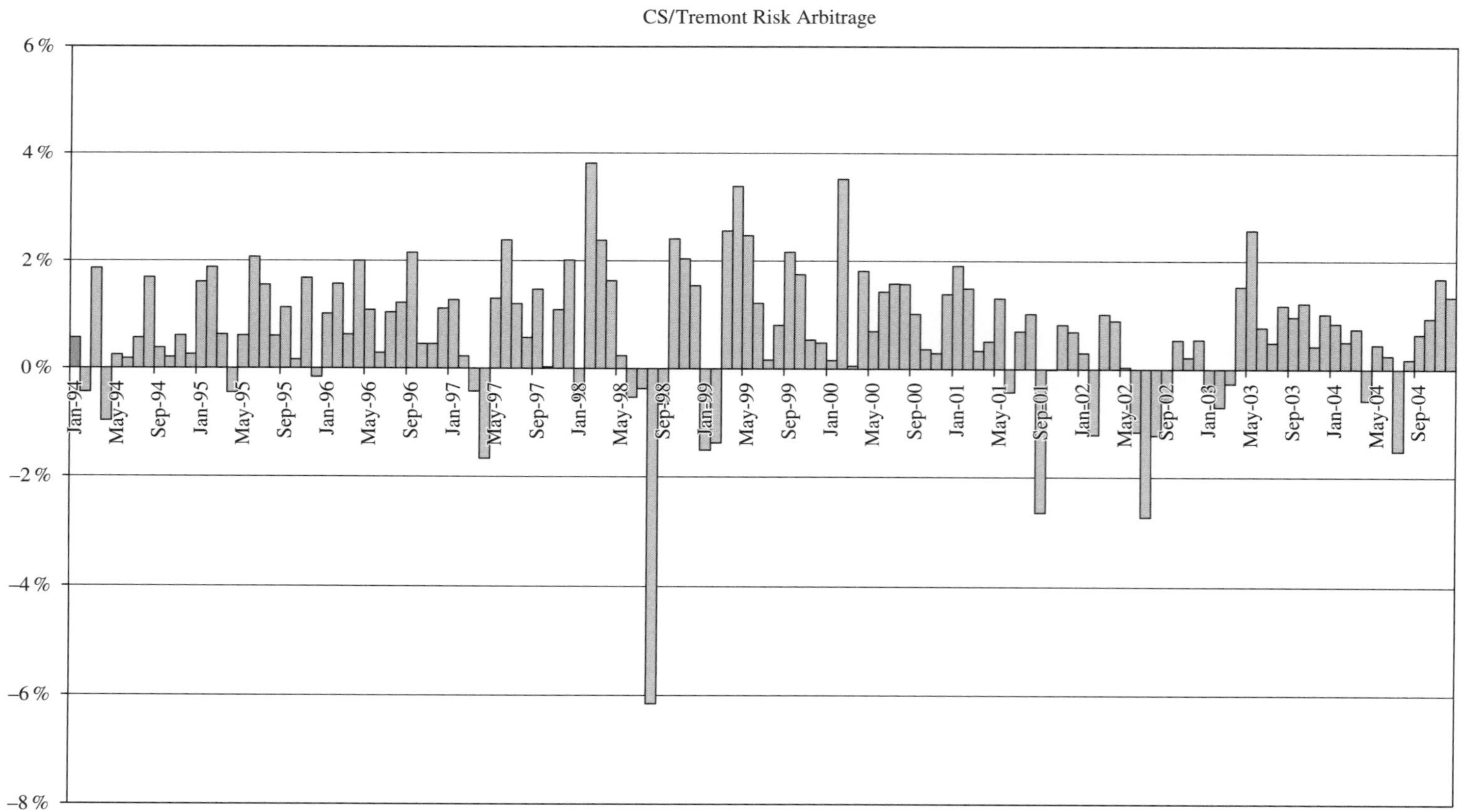

CS/Tremont Risk Arbitrage

Figure 5.10 Monthly returns of CS/Tremont Event Driven – Risk Arbitrage from 1994 to 2004. Source: CS/Tremont Index LLC, www.hedgeindex.com. Copyright © 2006, Credit Suisse/Tremont Index LLC. All rights reserved*

The largest drawdown has been significant (−7.6%) and lasted for only four months. Then the Index needed seven months to recover.

Figure 5.10 shows the monthly returns of the CS/Tremont Risk Arbitrage Index from 1994 to 2004.

Figure 5.11 illustrates the historical performance as a function of risk of the CS/Tremont Risk Arbitrage Index between 1994 and 2004. The concentration ellipsoid shows that historically this strategy stayed within a well-defined area of the risk/return range. (See Chapter 1, Section 1.8, for more details on the setup and meaning of Figures 5.10 and 5.11.)

As shown on Figure 5.12, between 1994 and 2004 there were two important "underwater" dips. The chart must be analyzed taking drawdown data into consideration: throughout the drawdown and the time to recovery period, the hedge funds adopting this strategy were under the high water mark. August 1998 was the worst month for the merger and acquisition arbitrage strategy.

The first drawdown concerned Long Term Capital Management. This company had invested in Ciena Corporation, a telecommunications company that was merging with Tellabs Inc. On 21st August 1998, the merger was postponed and the Ciena stock plummeted to $25.5 down from $31.25. In one single trade, Long Term Capital Management lost $150 million due to the longer time needed to complete the merger.

Merger and acquisition arbitrage positions are not correlated to the direction of financial markets. The risk that the deal fails is not a systematic risk, except for extreme events, like the spread widening during the August 1998 market crisis.

The second drawdown, in the Summer of 2002, came together with a very weak stock market, which acted as a brake on mergers and acquisitions.

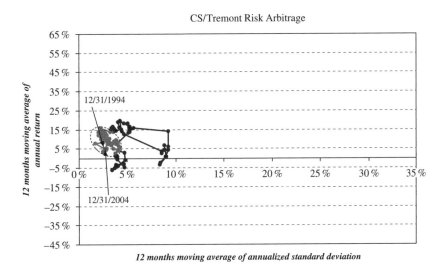

Figure 5.11 Historical performance trend of return as a function of risk for CS/Tremont Event Driven – Risk Arbitrage from 1994 to 2004. Source: CS/Tremont Index LLC, www.hedgeindex.com. Copyright © 2006, Credit Suisse/Tremont Index LLC. All rights reserved*

---

* See page 298 for full copyright notice.

CS/Tremont Risk Arbitrage

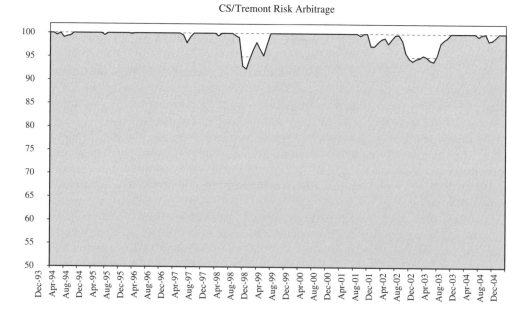

Figure 5.12 Underwater periods for CS/Tremont Event Driven – Risk Arbitrage from 1994 to 2004.
Source: CS/Tremont Index LLC, www.hedgeindex.com. Copyright © 2006, Credit Suisse/Tremont
Index LLC. All rights reserved*

The performance of a merger arbitrage strategy is mainly dependent upon two factors: the
number of mergers or acquisitions and the premium offered for the deal's success (merger
spread).

The number of announced deals is cyclical and is affected by the economic cycle. The
money of exchange for many of these deals is the share value, therefore prolonged periods
of bearish stock markets slow down mergers and acquisitions, since they can increase their
costs. Bullish stock market periods favor stock-swap mergers. One example of how high
share prices have driven the number of acquisitions up is represented by Internet shares. In
contrast, low interest rates favor leveraged buyouts.

The success of this strategy depends upon a sufficient number of mergers and acquisitions
such as to allow the manager to construct a diversified portfolio, and on the width of the
spreads on successful deals, offsetting failing ones. Clearly the spread width is proportional
to the risk that the deal may fail.

5.7 CONCLUSIONS

Merger and acquisition arbitrages were once considered the hunting preserve of a few Wall
Street talented traders, who well understood their dynamics. Retail and institutional investors
gave up the opportunity to make a profit out of announced deals because they lacked the
expertise in extraordinary corporate events. However, a big supply associated with a low
demand led to good returns, and since the 1980s opportunities have flourished, more and

---

more people have gained the insight and expertise necessary to deal with mergers and acquisitions and the art of arbitrage has become less obscure for a wider circle of investors. The perceived risk decreased and spreads started inexorably to shrink. Today, buyers and sellers are drawn from a similar background and experience and the merger arbitrage market has become fairly crowded. The progressive ripening of the merger arbitrage strategy led to a prolonged but constant decrease in returns from the merger and acquisition arbitrage strategy.

Classical plain vanilla arbitrages on announced deals are too crowded with arbitrageurs, so they are not very interesting in terms of correct risk/return profile. Hedge fund managers are therefore asking their investors to trust them with wider investment powers so as to invest along an event driven, special situation strategy, or to act before a transaction is announced.

However, acting before a transaction is announced means possessing an in-depth knowledge of the industry and the company valuations, identifying the acquirers and the potential targets, while always keeping in mind the regulatory hurdles. In practice, this is the profile of an analyst of the M&A department of an investment bank. Once again, we see a close correlation between hedge funds and some investment bank departments.

Looking back to Figure 1.9 in Chapter 1, let's identify the key factors we can use to break down the performance of merger arbitrage managers:

- traditional beta: stock market beta (when the stock market is underperforming, the number of transactions decreases and the time to completion gets longer);
- alternative beta: risk that the announced deal fails and legal risks;
- structural alpha: none;
- skill alpha: skillful deal analysis and selection, risk management.

6
Convertible Bond Arbitrage

Convertible bond arbitrage should be seen as a real business. In its simplest form,
it's a business of lending money to corporations in the
form of convertible debt and collateralizing that loan with common stock.
A hedge fund manager

Convertible bonds are bonds that give their holders the right to periodic coupon payments and, as of a fixed date, the right to convert the bonds into a fixed number of shares. If the bond-holder decides to exercise his conversion right, instead of being paid back the par value of the bonds, he will receive a fixed number of shares in exchange. For example, in 2003 Siemens Finance BV issued €2.5 billion of bonds convertible into Siemens AG shares paying a fixed annual coupon of 1.375 %, due on 6th April 2010.

In most cases these shares are common stock of the issuer, yet sometimes it can be shares from another company, should the issuer decide to sell an equity investment it holds in another company by issuing a convertible. For example, in 2003 Unicredito Italiano Bank (Ireland) PLC issued €1.148 billion of bonds convertible into Generali shares paying a fixed annual coupon of 2.5 %, due on 19th December 2008 with an exercise date for the conversion right as of 19th December 2005.

Convertibles are ideal securities for arbitrage because the convertible itself, namely the underlying stock and the associated derivatives, are traded along predictable ratios and any discrepancy or misprice would give rise to arbitrage opportunities for hedge fund managers.

A convertible bond is called *plain vanilla* if it simply comprises of a bond and a call option on the underlying stock (the right to convert the bonds into a fixed number of shares). A "plain vanilla" convertible bond can also be viewed as a stock plus a put option whose exercise price is equal to the conversion price.

If we figure the convertible as comprised of a bond from the same issuer plus a call option giving the right to buy the underlying stock on expiration, it is easier for us to understand that to have the call option, the convertible must have a lower coupon compared to the common bond. We also realize that a call option gives the holder the possibility of an unlimited upside. The bond side of the convertible offers capital protection, except of course for the issuer credit risk.

If we figure the convertible as comprised of a stock plus a put option with exercise price equal to the conversion price, it is easier for us to understand that it gives the holder of a convertible the guarantee that the conversion value be paid (except for the issuer credit risk). It also gives exposure to a rise of the underlying stock, but the buyer must pay a premium on the stock's current price.

Convertible bonds are hybrid securities, which can be rearranged into many different financial instruments:

- long position in a pure bond that pays out to its holder a periodic coupon and upon maturity pays back its par value;
- long position in an American call option to convert the bond into the underlying stock. The option is of the American type, i.e., it gives the holder the right to exercise at any time prior to expiration;
- short position in an American call option expiring after the bond. The option can be exercised by the issuer only under certain circumstances, which are often linked to the share price. It is as if the convertible bond holder had sold to the issuer the right to call in the convertible bond loan at a fixed value, giving rise to a compulsory conversion;
- short position in an American option to issuer's default. It could be seen also as the sale of a put option on the deep-out-of-the-money stock;
- long position in an out-of-the-money American put option, because in case of bankruptcy, the downside risk is limited by the bond recovery value, which shall be defined at the end of the bankruptcy procedure.

In this list we should include the exposure to exogenous risks that are not associated with the issuer, for example the issuing company being acquired by another company. When companies with in-the-money or at-the-money convertible bond issues are acquired, bonds shed their premium and converge onto the value offered by the acquirer for the target company shares. The onset of other corporate events may play a substantial role in the evaluation of convertible bonds.

The prospectus backing convertible bond issues (not issued along the procedure envisaged for *private placements*) is very complicated and includes many clauses and provisions that a hedge fund manager must analyze thoroughly before investing:

- screw clause;
- special dividend;
- takeover protection;
- non-dividend ranking stock;
- non-conversion period;
- call election pitfall.

The standard terms for a plain vanilla convertible bond are:

- 5 year maturity;
- coupon of 2–3 %;
- premium of 25–30 %;
- option for the issuer to require conversion after 3 years.

A convertible bond is an interesting financial instrument for buyers because it gives them the opportunity to participate in the growth of the underlying stock, if the share price goes up, or to limit losses, if the share price goes down.

If you take the opposite perspective, a convertible bond is also a very interesting financial instrument for companies who wish to raise capital.

6.1 WHY ISSUE A CONVERTIBLE BOND?

A company may decide to raise capital:

- by borrowing from banks, generally for short-term loans;
- by issuing new shares, if shareholders are willing to underwrite the capital increase or if the majority shareholders do not lose their control over the company;
- by issuing bonds, if the company's rating does not make the use of this form of funding too expensive.

But there are several reasons why a company may decide to raise capital by issuing convertible bonds:

- the issuer believes that at present its stock is undervalued by the market and therefore wants to sell it forward at a premium. If, when the loan expires, the shares have actually gone up, reaching or exceeding the price the issuer believes to be fair, the holders of the convertibles will exercise their conversion right and buy the shares at the price that had originally been considered adequate by the issuer;
- the issuer resorts to convertibles to enjoy a lower cost of funding compared to what it would be forced to pay with the issue of non-convertible bonds;
- the issuer wants to raise capital on the market, but the controlling group does not want to surrender its majority or wants to delay capital dilution at least until maturity of the convertible bond;
- the issuer wants to sell an equity investment in another company at a premium.

Hence, the issuer of convertible bonds can sell its stock at a premium, or the stock of another company it holds in its equity portfolio, in exchange for the payment of a lower interest rate compared to the issue of non-convertible bonds.

6.2 A BRIEF HISTORY OF CONVERTIBLE BONDS

The first convertible bonds were issued in the 19th century as a sweetener to arouse the interest of investors in railway construction in the United States. For example, the railway company Chicago, Milwaukee & St. Paul Railway resorted to many convertible bond issues between 1860 and 1880. After some twenty years of absence, at the beginning of the 20th century other convertible bonds started to be issued again by other railway companies, for example in 1901 a $15 million issue by Baltimore & Ohio Railroad and a $100 million issue by Union Pacific Railroad. Many more issues followed, and not only by railway companies, as shown in 1906 by the $150 million issue by American Telephone & Telegraph Co.

In his book *Arbitrage in Securities* published in 1931, Meyer H. Weinstein observes that the advent of convertibles, beginning with the consolidation of railroads around 1860, ushered in the first arbitrage trades and techniques. Since no option pricing theories and no computers were yet available, most of the arbitrage transactions described in Meyer's book were based on selling short just one fourth, half, three quarters of the share against a long position on the convertible.

The modern convertible bond market came into existence in the 1950s, again in the United States. At that time, airlines used these notes to strengthen their capital structure, paying lower interest rates than with traditional funding forms, while avoiding a dilution of their shareholding structure.

In 1967, Edward O. Thorp and Sheen T. Kassouf wrote the book *Beat the Market,* which for the first time tackled the topic of convertible bond arbitrage from a mathematical standpoint. These authors were the first to bring up the concept of breaking down a convertible into a bond and a warrant, and of valuing each component separately to identify arbitrage opportunities. This marked the beginning of the application of mathematics to convertibles, laying the foundation for the complex quantitative models used today by traders who perform convertible bond arbitrages.

Many convertibles were issued during the bear market of the 1960s: International Telephone & Telegraph acquired many companies by issuing preferred convertible bonds. Also many small to medium sized companies turned to convertible bonds to gain access to capital to finance their growth. This contributed to creating the myth that convertibles were issued by companies with a poor creditworthiness. In 1984 IBM carried out a convertible issue with an AAA rating that changed the perception investors had of the convertible market.

Between the end of the 1980s and the beginning of the 1990s, the banking industry started to issue convertibles to meet the capital requirements set by regulatory authorities. Also during the 1980s, the convertible private placement market grew, propelled by its characteristic of offering a fast track to the market, skipping the many regulatory constraints of a public offering.

On 30th April 1990, in the United States the Securities and Exchange Commission (SEC) introduced rule 144A, exempting from registration requirements under the Securities Act of 1933 resales of certain restricted securities to given qualified investors. This rule allowed issuers to gain an easier access to the market and improved the liquidity of private placements on the secondary market.

In the 1990s, high-tech companies often resorted to convertibles.

6.3   THE CONVERTIBLE BOND MARKET

Figure 6.1 clearly shows the growth of the convertible market, giving evidence of the increasing popularity of this financial instrument. The pace of new issues shows a booming

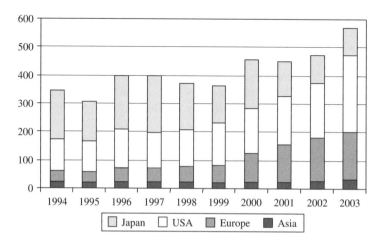

Figure 6.1   Convertible bonds market from 1994 to 2003 in billion of USD. Source: Deutsche Bank Securities, www.dbconvertibles.com

growth in the last decade. In 2001, it was mainly US high-tech companies propelling the peak in new issues. In 2003, the peak in new convertible issues was mainly driven by a strong refinancing activity: many convertible bonds had expired, which caused many issuers to resort once again to the issue of convertible bonds for refinancing purposes. In contrast, in 2004 the convertible bond market shrank.

Figure 6.2 details the relative weight of the different geographical regions in the world convertible market in 2003. The United States and Europe accounted for 75 % of the whole convertible market pie.

Convertible bonds, as with all other bond notes, differ in terms of issuer credit rating assigned by international rating agencies such as Standard & Poor's, Moody's Investors Service or Fitch Ratings (Figure 6.3). Issuers that have been directly downgraded from investment grade to below investment grade (BB or lower) are called *fallen angels*, while *rising stars* are issuers that initially were below investment grade and have been upgraded to investment grade.

Domestic convertible markets, namely United States, Europe, Japan and Asia-Pacific, have different characteristics.

As shown in Figure 6.2, the US has the largest market share, accounting for about 45 % of the world market. The US convertible bond market is organized as an *over-the-counter* market, because most issues are performed along the *private placement* procedure (SEC Rule 144A). These issues are not backed by a prospectus, are reserved to qualified investors and cannot be offered to the public at large.

The European convertible bond market accounts for about 30 % of the world market and is rapidly growing. The European market can be roughly broken down as follows: 33 % French issues, 17 % German issues, 15 % UK issues, and 10 % Italian issues. Worldwide, issues from the telephone, insurance, technology and media industries dominate the convertible market.

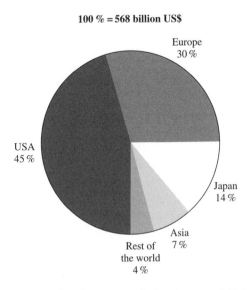

Figure 6.2 Convertible bonds markets by geographical regions as of 31st December 2003. Source: Deutsche Bank Securities, www.dbconvertibles.com

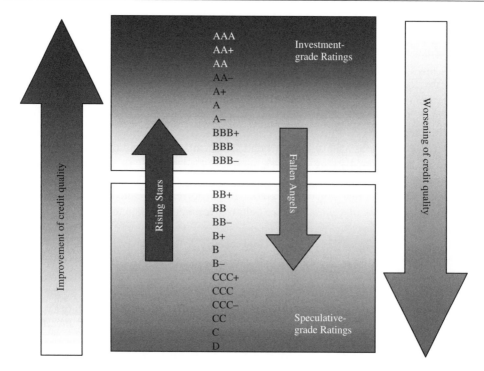

Figure 6.3   Bond ratings. Source: Standard & Poor's Global Fixed Income Research

It is interesting to see how the European and the US markets bear different characteristics with regard to the size of the issuers and the credit rating of convertible bond issues. Most European issues come from large companies, with a market cap above $10 billion, compared to only 25 % of the US market.

The issuers' creditworthiness is higher in Europe: 65 % of the market in Europe is comprised of *investment grade* convertible bonds (BBB or higher), against only 40 % in the United States. In Europe, however, there is a higher percentage of convertibles that have no rating: 24 % of the European market against only 18 % in the United States (Figure 6.4).

The Japanese convertible bond market is made up of a large number of very small domestic issues, listed and traded on the Tokyo stock exchange.

In addition, the Asia-Pacific area is turning into a significant source of convertible issues: with the exception of the Hong Kong stock exchange, there are more frequent mispricings between actual and theoretical prices due to the difficulties of selling short and the great complexity of conversion procedures. In 2003, 22 % of new issues took place in Europe (Figure 6.5).

The delta of the bonds is getting greater, and there is a growing number of "balanced" convertible bonds: this is causing arbitrageurs to shift to credit trading and gamma trading.

Implied volatility, which we will explain later in this chapter, is at historical low levels. There is an ongoing debate on why volatility is so low now. A possible explanation lies in the fact that many highly leveraged traders used the VXO index as a generic global hedge against the world systemic crisis, and sold the VXO when they reduced their leverage.

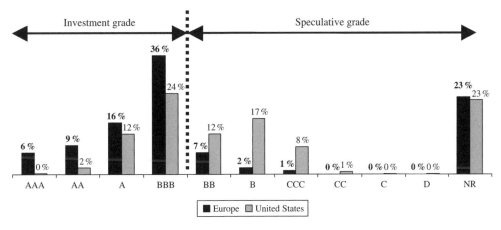

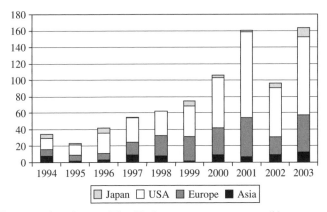

Figure 6.4 The issuers' creditworthiness in convertible bonds market as of 31st December 2004. Source: Goldman Sachs Convertible Strategy estimates, MACE

We count all company issued convertibles. We do not count reverse convertibles.

Figure 6.5 New issues of convertible bonds market in billion USD. Source: Deutsche Bank Securities, www.dbconvertibles.com

Another concomitant cause may be the significant number of CDO issues (which will be described in Chapter 8), leading to a volatility sale on the market.

The implied volatility of convertible bonds in 2004 remained at historically very low levels.

Credit spreads are stable and there is a low carry. According to some hedge fund managers interviewed by the author, in 2005 the European and Asian markets offer more profitable convertible bond arbitrage opportunities.

Based on estimates, a large part of convertible bonds are held by hedge funds. Assuming that the convertible bond market is worth $568 billion (source: Deutsche Bank on 31st December 2003), that funds performing convertible bond arbitrages account for 8.31% (source: LIPPER TASS on the same date) of total assets under management by hedge funds (about $750 billion in single manager hedge funds plus some estimated $250 billion in private managed accounts), and that the average leverage is 2 times,[1] hedge funds could be holding convertibles for a total estimated value of $166 billion, which accounts for an estimated market share of about 30 % of convertible bonds outstanding. According to UBS estimates, trades generated by the arbitrage of convertible bonds (carried out by hedge funds and proprietary trading desks) account for 65 % of the convertible bond market. Again UBS estimated a strong presence of hedge funds in new convertible issues.

As of 31st December 2004, hedge funds pursuing a *convertible bond arbitrage* strategy accounted for 8 % of the hedge fund industry, according to the LIPPER TASS database.

6.4 DEFINITIONS

The issuance of a convertible bond, not issued along the private placement procedure, is backed by a prospectus, describing all its characteristics and provisions for the exercise of the existing rights, which can be very complex.

The *maturity* is the date on which the issuer must offer to redeem for cash the par value of the convertible bond.

The *coupon* is the payment of the bond interest, usually in constant installments paid at fixed intervals throughout the life of the bond.

The *conversion ratio* is the fixed number of shares of common stock into which a bond is exchangeable.

The *conversion value* or *parity* is the market value of the shares into which the bond can be converted at a given time. The conversion value represents the lower limit of the convertible bond value: if this were not so, it would be possible to make an arbitrage profit by purchasing the convertible bond and immediately exercising the conversion right, then selling the stock on the market. Still, there are convertibles that are under parity, due to transaction costs, as well as to the risk of receiving the converted stock late. A delay in the delivery of the converted stock pins the arbitrageur into a highly risky position, in that, when applying for conversion, he waives his privileges of creditor, but is not yet a shareholder, since he has not received the converted shares yet. To offset this risk, arbitrageurs enter the trade only if the convertible's discount to parity allows for an acceptable safety margin. The convertible's discount to parity depends on the expected delay in the delivery of the converted stock, on volatility and on the liquidity of the underlying stock. If the underlying stock can be borrowed, it can be sold before the converted shares are delivered, thus the arbitrage can take place and a convertible will not trade at a discount to parity. However, if the share is not borrowable, a delay of a few weeks in the delivery of converted shares on some emerging markets triggers discounts of about 10–30 %.

The *premium* of a convertible bond is the difference between the convertible's market value and its conversion value, and it is expressed as a percentage of the conversion value. Usually, investors are willing to pay a premium on the conversion value of the convertible bond because the bond characteristics of a convertible offer a downside protection and, generally, higher returns compared to share dividends. A low premium means that the convertible will be highly sensitive to changes in the underlying stock price, whereas in the case of high premium, the convertible will be more sensitive to changes in factors affecting

---

[1] Goldman Sachs Convertible Strategy.

the bond price, for example interest rate changes. The conversion premium is the value attached to the option of converting the bond into a share: it is the premium investors are willing to pay on top of the conversion value of the convertible bond to obtain a downside protection and generally higher returns.

Bond floor or *straight bond value* is the present value of future cash flows of the convertible as a straight corporate bond, i.e. non-convertible (coupons plus final redemption) discounted at the LIBOR rate plus a spread that depends on the issuer's credit rating. The value of the non-convertible bond component alone represents the lower limit to the value of the convertible, in that it measures only the bond component without all the other characteristics. To measure the bond floor of a convertible bond, it is necessary to know the interest rate and assess the credit risk of the issuer.

The *credit spread* is the interest rate difference paid by the convertible bond compared to the risk-free interest rate. The higher the credit spread, the greater the probability of default by the issuer.

$$(\text{Credit Spread}) = (\text{Bond Yield}) - (\text{Government Bond with the same maturity})$$

6.5   QUANTITATIVE MODELS TO VALUE CONVERTIBLE BONDS

At maturity, a convertible bond may either be worth its par value or the market value of the shares for which it is exchangeable, depending on which is higher. Before maturity, the valuation is much more complex. The value of a convertible bond is a function of the price of the underlying stock and can be represented as shown in Figure 6.6.

Throughout its life a convertible bond can go through four potential stages as shown in Figure 6.7:

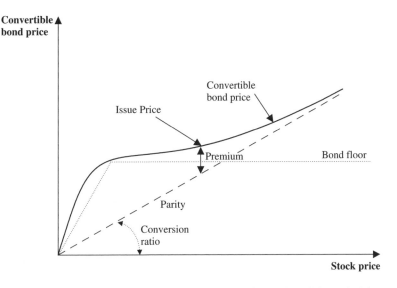

Figure 6.6   The price of a convertible bond in function of the price of the underlying stock

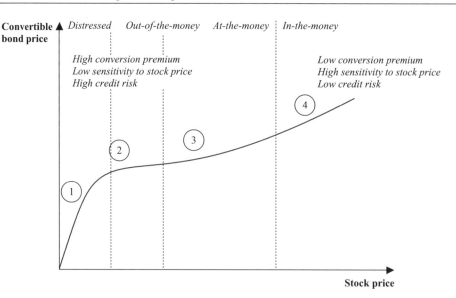

Figure 6.7 The four stages in a convertible bond

1. *Distressed*: when the share price is very low and the issuer's ability to pay the bonds is questionable.
2. *Bond proxy*: when the share price is low, the conversion right is unlikely to be exercised, and the conversion option is out-of-the-money.
3. *True convertible*: when the share price is close to the conversion price, and the option is at-the-money.
4. *Equity proxy*: when the share price is very high, conversion is very probable and the conversion option is in-the-money.

If a convertible bond is trading close to its bond floor, the value of the convertible's bond component will be more sensitive to interest rate changes compared to a convertible that is trading at a premium, which in turn, will be more sensitive to changes in the underlying share price.

Quantitative models for the valuation of convertibles can be subdivided into:

- analytical models;
- numerical models.

Traders use quantitative models to identify convertible bonds whose market value differs from the theoretical price.

6.5.1 Analytical Models

In 1976, Ingersoll[2] proposed a valuation model for convertible bonds based on the option theory and on the Black–Scholes option pricing model.

---

[2] Ingersoll, J. (1977) "A Contingent-Claims Valuation of Convertible Securities", *Journal of Financial Economics*, May, **4**, 289–321. The document can be downloaded from the website www.yale.edu.

The main assumptions of the Ingersoll model are: markets operate continuously; no transaction costs; share prices follow an Ito diffusion process; securities prices have a log normal distribution; and the underlying stock volatility is constant.

Ingersoll's model assumes that prices vary continuously, i.e., there is always liquidity on the market and there are no limits to securities lending and short selling. It also assumes that the company's market value follows an Ito diffusion process, i.e. a continuous Brownian motion. Under this assumption, it is possible to set up a closed analytical formula to calculate the value of a convertible bond.

Ingersoll's model can be applied only to European convertibles, namely, convertibles that can be exercised only upon expiration. This model shows the complexity of the valuation of convertible bonds, and it provides a highly interesting theoretical reference in that it can reach an analytical solution to the valuation of convertibles.

Yet, we know all too well that interest rates, credit spreads, currencies and dividends are not constant, and the clauses and provisions written in the prospectus of a convertible are often highly varied and complicated, making it fairly difficult to apply analytical valuation models. This is why it is necessary to turn to numerical approximation models.

6.5.2 Numerical Models

The most widely used mathematical models among hedge fund managers for the valuation of convertible bonds are numerical methods, among which we may include binomial and trinomial trees, the 3-dimensional binomial model and the Monte Carlo simulation model.

The binomial tree model was published in 1979 by Cox, Ross and Rubinstein.[3] This model allows the building of a tree of possible share prices between now and the convertible's maturity. This tree is then used to find the convertible's current value, by calculating its value along all the tree nodes. In the binomial tree model, the tree has two branches that develop from every node, while in the trinomial tree model there are three branches diverging from each node. The higher the number of nodes, the more accurate is the model. The binomial model makes it possible also to value an American option, which would otherwise find no solution in a closed form.[4] If the number of time steps grow bigger, the binomial tree tends towards Black and Scholes' continuous formula for European options.

The trinomial tree model was introduced by Boyle in 1986. The share price can move in three directions from every single node and therefore the number of time steps can be reduced to reach the same precision obtained with the binomial tree.

The Monte Carlo method, named after the casino of the Principality of Monaco, is a statistical simulation method, according to which data obtained through the generation of random numbers coming from a given statistical distribution is considered empirical and is used to estimate the parameters under consideration. Thousands of random samples are generated, derived from the assumed statistical distribution which takes as parameters the maximum likelihood estimators using real data, and then these data are used to estimate the parameters under examination.

---

[3] Cox, J.C., Ross, S.A. and Rubinstein M. (1979) "Option Pricing: A Simplified Approach," *Journal of Financial Economics*, October, 229–263.
[4] For readers who wish to learn more about the model, see Hull, J.C. (2000) *Futures, Options and Other Derivatives*, 4th edition, New Jersey: Prentice Hall.

All these models are helpful when making a decision, but many of the options embedded in a convertible do not fit the models and therefore the fund manager's skill and a rigorous risk management discipline become all the more valuable. The manager's art lies in finding innovative ways to evaluate convertible bonds without being swamped with too many details.

6.6 IMPLIED VOLATILITY AND HISTORICAL VOLATILITY

Implied volatility is the volatility the marketplace is implying through the price of the convertible bond.

Implied volatility is the value of σ that, when included in the convertible valuation formula chosen by the hedge fund manager (where all the other variables have been fixed or estimated), makes it possible to obtain a theoretical value of the convertible bond identical to the market price.

Implied volatility can be used to verify the market opinion on the expected volatility of a given security.

Historical volatility, in contrast, refers to the price fluctuations of a stock over a specific period of time in the past (typically 100 days, 180 days or 250 days). To calculate historical volatility, we must calculate the standard deviation of the stock's historical series of rates of return at fixed intervals (generally 1 day).

Generally, the option embedded in the convertible bond is traded at a lower implied volatility than the historical volatility of the underlying stock.

6.6.1 Credit Spreads, Implied Volatility and Risk Appetite

Both credit spreads and implied volatility are a measure of the potential return premium expected by investors, given the perceived risks. The greater implied volatility and credit spreads are, the greater the risk level perceived by investors. Both indicators have decreased significantly in 2003 and 2004. This means that either investors believe there is a much lower risk than in the past, or that compared to the past they are willing to receive a lower return for the same risk, or both.

6.7 CONVERTIBLE BOND ARBITRAGE

Most convertible bond arbitrage deals are constructed with a long position on the convertible bond, hedged with a concurrent short sale of the underlying common stock.

Convertible bonds are hybrid securities that, as we have already seen, can be rearranged into many other financial instruments, which, as a result of market forces, can display valuation discrepancies. The goal of the hedge fund manager is thus to identify convertible bonds that have a substantial market price difference compared to the theoretical value and to carry out trades that allow him to extract that value, while being protected against market risks. Generally, the risk of interest rate fluctuations is hedged on the convertible long position by using interest rate swaps, and sometimes the convertible issuer's credit risk is also hedged against (risk that the spread widens and issuer default risk) by resorting to credit default swaps.

Hedge fund managers seek convertible bonds that bear the following characteristics:

- high volatility of the underlying stock, to profit from delta trading and gamma trading;
- good liquidity of the convertible issue and easily borrowable underlying stock;
- low conversion premium, because the convertible is less sensitive to interest rate risk and credit risk;
- stock paying no dividends or with a low dividend, to avoid having to pay out a dividend to the shareholder from whom the shorted shares were borrowed;
- high convexity of convertibles, to profit from gamma trading;
- issues with a low implied volatility.

The complexity of valuation models and the variety of deals clearly indicate that to carry out an arbitrage strategy on convertible bonds it is necessary to rely on a complex and expensive technological infrastructure, which represents a significant barrier to entry.

Said technological infrastructure must be able to monitor the convertible bond markets constantly through the application of valuation models, looking for opportunities that the fund manager may take advantage of by using a specific arbitrage strategy.

Fund managers must assess the risk/return profile of each position individually and of the entire portfolio as a whole. The portfolio must be analyzed in terms of issuer creditworthiness, and risks must be diversified by sector, as well as by issuer market capitalization, so as to make sure the portfolio can rely on an adequate liquidity; the portfolio Greeks must be monitored, together with the portfolio sensitivity to interest rate changes and its behavior in case of share price fluctuations. The fund manager must diversify the portfolio and use leverage, and must also rely on strict selling rules for each position making up the portfolio.

A hedge fund manager can establish various type of arbitrages:

1. cash-flow arbitrage;
2. volatility trading;
3. gamma trading;
4. credit arbitrage;
5. skewed arbitrage;
6. carry trade;
7. refinancing play;
8. late stage restructuring play;
9. multi-strategy.

6.7.1 Cash-flow Arbitrage

A hedge fund manager buying a convertible bond and selling the underlying stock short is constructing a position that generates a high cash flow. The proceeds from the stock short sale are used to finance the purchase of the convertible bond.

Let's assume for example that a convertible bond has been purchased at a 10 % premium at $110 and the underlying stock is sold short for $100. To make it simpler, we won't consider the margin account for the short sale and will say that the arbitrageur must finance the transaction only with the difference, equal to $10. This is indicative of the fact that convertible bonds with a borrowable underlying stock never trade at a discount.

Let's assume that our convertible generates an annual 5 % yield (once again, to make it simple we will say the issuer credit risk remains unchanged throughout the arbitrage), i.e.,

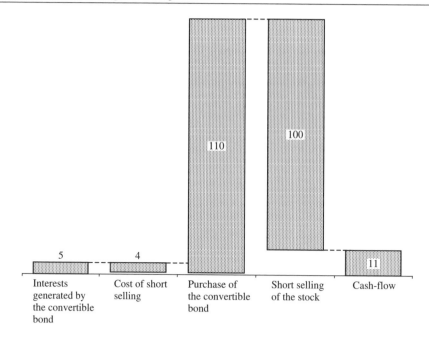

Figure 6.8 Cash flow generated by a convertible bond arbitrage position

$5 during the year, and let's say that the short sale cost is 2% per year ($2) and that the dividend paid by the underlying stock during the year is 2% ($2). The position is giving the arbitrageur a $1 return on an invested capital of $10, namely 10% (Figure 6.8).

In reality, with such an interesting return, other arbitrageurs are bound to spot the opportunity and will drive the convertible price up, raising the premium. So, for example, a 15% premium drives the return down to 6.7%, while a 20% premium pushes the return down to 5%. Without considering the actual numbers, which are purely indicative, this clearly shows how convertible bonds, with a borrowable underlying stock, trade at a substantial premium over par.

Cash-flow arbitrage is actively used in situations where there is no bond floor, for example in mandatory convertibles, because they have a higher coupon compared to a convertible bond and generally have a similar risk to that of stock.

The static return is represented by the payment of the fixed coupon, the return from the cash proceeds generated by the short sale, and it may be decreased by the payment of dividends and by the cost of leverage. Convertible bonds are generally undervalued with respect to their theoretical value for at least three reasons:

- most issuers have a speculative rating and only few investors are interested in these notes, which leads to a thin liquidity on the market;
- many convertible issues come in small sizes and are neglected by analysts;
- investors tend to prefer plain vanilla securities, which are clearly identifiable.

If one happens to identify an undervalued convertible, it is possible to take advantage of the premium expansion.

Transaction costs, that is, the fees collected by brokers for the trades and the interest rate on the loans necessary for the leverage, narrow down arbitrage possibilities.

6.7.2 Volatility Trading

For traders, volatility is the most important variable in the option pricing models (Black–Scholes). Traders can visualize volatility as a "synthetic" security, which can be negotiated as any other security.

When a convertible is traded close to its bond floor, it still generates a cash flow, but the real gain for hedge fund managers comes from volatility.

The *delta* of a convertible bond is the convertible price sensitivity to the underlying share price changes. Analytically, delta is the first order derivative of the convertible price compared to the underlying stock price. Graphically, delta is represented by the slope of the tangent to the curvature of the convertible price as a function of the underlying share price, at a fixed share price (Figure 6.9).

Most convertible bond arbitrages are constructed with a long position on the convertible and a concurrent short position on the underlying share for a fixed number of shares defined by the delta of the convertible. The long position on the convertible captures the convertible discount to the theoretical value and the short position on the underlying stock reduces the stock exposure.

The *hedge ratio* is the number of shares that must be sold short to get a delta-neutral portfolio of convertibles and shares.

Let's assume that the convertible price is $1000 and that the current market price of the underlying stock is $50 with a conversion premium of 50 % so that the value of the conversion premium is $75.

The delta of the convertible represents the rate of change in the price of the convertible with respect to a 1 % change in the stock price. Let's assume that the bond has a delta of 0.65. The hedge ratio is equal to ($1000/$75)*0.65 = 8.6667.

As illustrated in Figure 6.9, the tangent approaches the convertible curvature only for small changes in the price of the underlying share. The change in the delta of the convertible with respect to the change in the underlying stock price implies that the size of the short position must be dynamically adjusted to remain delta neutral.

A delta neutral position yields positive returns irrespective of whether the stock goes up or down: this is determined by the fact that the delta rises when the stock goes up and declines when the stock goes down. Graphically, we can see that the slope of the curvature of the convertible price as a function of the underlying share grows when the share price grows, until it approaches a maximum of 100 %.

The different variables affecting the price of the convertible start changing once the initial position has been constructed, therefore the fund manager must constantly adjust the hedge so as to remain delta neutral. This constant adjusting of the hedge to keep the portfolio delta neutral is called *delta hedging*.

To keep a position delta neutral, when the stock price goes up, also driving up the delta, the fund manager must sell short more shares, whereas when the share price goes down, also pulling down the delta, the fund manager must partly cover his short sales.

This means that to keep a position delta neutral, the fund manager must buy shares when they are going down and sell shares when they are going up. Surprisingly enough, and contrary to the suggestions of a certain type of press coverage, in the case of delta hedging, fund managers are actually carrying out a share price stabilizing action!

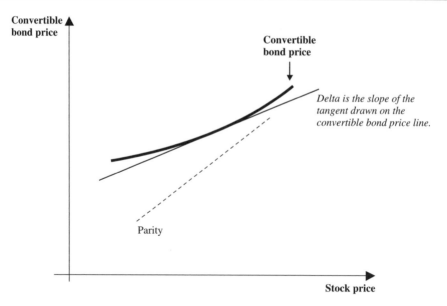

Figure 6.9 Graphical meaning of the convertible bond delta

The convexity of the curvature of the convertible price favors the arbitrageur: if the share price rises sharply, the convertible price should increase more rapidly than the losses on the short position, and if the share price drops significantly, the convertible price should fall less rapidly than the gains that can be obtained on the short position.

Delta hedging can also be interpreted from the point of view of the value of the option embedded in the convertible: if the share price goes up, the embedded option approaches the exercise price, the convertible becomes more sensitive to stock fluctuations and the fund manager must sell short more shares; however, if the share price goes down, the embedded option sheds value and the fund manager must buy back shares.

A delta neutral position is long on volatility: *it's as if you bought the volatility of the underlying stock*. This is what we refer to when we talk about *volatility trading*. With delta hedging, it is possible to make a profit if the volatility of the underlying share grows, which means that it is possible to make a profit when markets become edgy or are going through a crisis. Being long on volatility is like buying a protection against capital market crises. If the volatility of the underlying share in a given period is higher than the volatility implied in the convertible price at the time of purchase, the trade will yield a positive return.

The *vega* of a convertible bond is the sensitivity of the bond price to the changes in volatility of the underlying stock. Analytically, the vega is the first order derivative of the convertible price with respect to the volatility of the underlying stock.

Volatility is a complex concept and can be measured in different ways depending on the time horizon (10 days, 30 days, 90 days, etc.) and on which volatility is being considered: realized, implied, historical, future, etc. The volatility implied in the option price also depends on whether the option is at-the-money, in-the-money or out-of-the-money. Volatility can be regarded as a financial security that can be bought or sold. It is interesting to note how volatility can never go to zero, unless markets are closed.

In order to understand the opportunities available to hedge fund managers with volatility trading, it is worth following the performance of the VXO index. The VXO index (Chicago Board Options Exchange OEX Volatility Index) is an estimate of the short-term future volatility on the stock market, calculated as the weighted average of the implied volatility of 8 OEX S&P 500 calls and puts. VXO is a useful gage of volatility both in absolute terms and as a trend: however, VXO captures the volatility of the US large cap equity market, whereas the issuers of convertible bonds come from all over the world and generally have a lower market cap and lower credit ratings, with the result that their stock tends to be potentially more volatile (Figure 6.10).

Let's consider for example a hedge fund manager who is long a convertible bond for a given amount and short the underlying stock for an amount equal to the delta. The fund manager waits for something to happen to the price of the underlying share: either for the stock price to go up or down.

If the share price goes up, the fund manager converts the bond and returns the borrowed shares. He will lose the conversion premium he paid when he bought the convertible, but if the position is generating a positive cash flow, the longer the position can be kept outstanding, the sooner the premium is paid back. If the fund manager can count on a minimum period to keep the arbitrage position open, for example the time to the first available date for the conversion, then the fund manager can easily compute the maximum conversion premium he might lose to close the arbitrage position at breakeven. If the breakeven point is easily reached, the position can be kept open for a long time.

However, if the share price goes down, the convertible starts building a premium and the hedge fund manager can "break down" his position by buying back the shorted shares

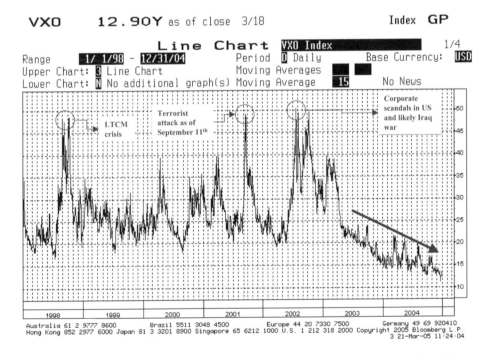

Figure 6.10 VXO index from 1998 to 2004. Used with permission from Bloomberg L.P.

and selling the convertible at a higher premium than at the time of purchase. When the convertible reaches its bond floor, profit grows at the same rate at which the share price decreases. The profit generated by the premium increase is much higher than the positive cash flow generated by the arbitrage position.

In this example, if the stock price goes down, the fund manager makes a much higher profit compared to the profit that could be made out of a share price increase.

Figure 6.11 depicts the return profile of a long position on a convertible bond for a given amount and a short position on the underlying stock for the same amount. The chart shows the risk/return profile as a function of the price of the underlying stock.

Arbitrageurs do not like the asymmetry of the returns generated by volatility trading in this example, because they want to be *market neutral*, namely, they want their return profile to be symmetrical so as to be able to make the same profit irrespective of whether the share goes up or down.

Figure 6.11 also depicts the return profile of a long position on a convertible bond. The chart shows the risk/return profile as a function of the price of the underlying stock. When the share price goes up, profit rises slowly while the convertible premium is eroded, then the slope of the profit curvature rises until it asymptotically reaches that of an equity investment. Whereas when the share price goes down, the convertible price approaches the bond floor and the convertible premium rises until the convertible is so close to the bond floor that it is not sensitive anymore to stock fluctuations.

It is interesting to note that the return profile of an investor who is long a convertible is specular to that of an investor who is at the same time long a convertible and fully covered with the underlying share. It is therefore easy to understand that by holding both positions simultaneously, the return profile is symmetrical. Again, Figure 6.11 also depicts the return

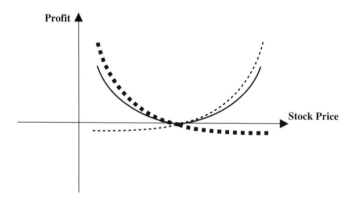

Figure 6.11 Return profiles

profile of an investor who holds two convertible bonds and has shorted only one underlying share: delta is equal to 50 %. Delta hedging creates profit symmetry.

This theoretical example shows a profit symmetry with a delta of 50 %, however reality is more complicated than that. Convertibles with a delta close to 50 % are called *balanced convertibles*. Often, new convertible issues tend to have a delta close to 50 %, which explains why hedge funds are often willing to pay a high price for newly issued convertibles.

Measuring the delta is crucial in an arbitrage strategy, and valuation models call for some experience. Moreover, transaction costs and the liquidity of securities are some of the major constraints in establishing convertible bond arbitrages.

As shown in Figure 6.11, the greater the share price change, the higher the potential profit for the arbitrageur: in this case we talk of volatility trading. Hence, arbitrageurs tend to be more interested in buying convertibles with highly volatile underlying stock.

A low liquidity or high trading units, called round lots, may be an obstacle to arbitrage.

Finally, it is important to consider the *time decay* of a convertible, i.e., the premium deterioration as the convertible comes closer to expiration.

The *theta* of a convertible is the convertible price change over time. Analytically, theta is the first order derivative of the convertible price with respect to time.

The *time decay* of a convertible can be interpreted as the time decay of the call option embedded in the convertible.

At the beginning of 1999, some Internet companies issued convertible bonds on the US market. The convertibles appeared very expensive to *long-only* investors, but since the underlying stock was so volatile that it would display movements of 20 % within the same trading day, the same convertibles highly appealed to hedge fund managers because volatility arbitrages were extremely profitable.

For example, in 1999, Amazon.com issued a convertible bond by way of $1.25 billion private placement, paying a coupon of 4.75 % and due on 1st February 2009. In this case, volatility arbitrage was highly profitable.

For small share price changes, the short position on the stock acts as a protection against the decrease of the bond price, since part of the valuation of a convertible comes from the conversion value. This helps create a market-neutral position, whereby the return depends only on the coupon paid by the bond.

During volatile market periods, this protection busts and a sharp fall in the underlying share price generates a profit that stems from the fact that the gain on the short position on the stock is greater than the loss suffered on the long position on the bond.

Indeed, a sharp rise in the share price also yields a profit, because the profit generated by being long the bond is greater than the loss suffered being short the underlying stock.

Moreover, we should also add to the profit generated in both situations the income from the convertible bond coupon, plus interest income on the cash proceeds from the short sale of the underlying stock.

6.7.3 Gamma Trading

In addition to delta trading, hedge fund managers can capture an additional profit by trading the underlying stock in response to delta changes.

The *gamma* of a convertible bond is the convertible's delta sensitivity to changes in the underlying stock price. Analytically, gamma is the first order derivative of the delta of the convertible price with respect to the share price or, in consideration of the delta definition, the second order derivative of the convertible price with respect to the share price. Graphically, the gamma is represented by the convexity of the curvature of the convertible price as a function of the underlying stock price, at a fixed price of the underlying share.

Gamma hedging or gamma trading is the delta hedge adjustment process in response to market movements. Fund managers gamma hedge to capture the volatility/profit of the underlying stock. Every day the fund manager executes sell or buy orders for the underlying stock. In most cases the trading range is a multiple between 1 and 2 times the daily volatility of the share. There are various ways to calculate the optimal multiplier: the fund manager can back test the intraday prices of the last 50 days using different trading ranges and taking into account transaction costs. The order size depends upon the size of the bond issue, the gamma of the convertible and the round lot size. If gamma is small in absolute terms, the delta changes very slowly and it is not necessary to carry out frequent adjustments to keep the portfolio delta neutral. However, if gamma is big in absolute terms, the delta is highly sensitive to the changes in the underlying stock price and it is now necessary to carry out frequent adjustments to keep the portfolio delta neutral.

The greater the convexity, the greater the hedge ratio error following the share movements. The greater the gamma, the greater the potential profit for the hedge fund manager.

As long as markets are volatile, delta hedging and gamma trading can generate profits. A hedge fund manager adopting these two strategies will suffer losses when market volatility falls below a certain level.

It is interesting to note that for companies whose convertible bond issues are significant in size with respect to the total shares outstanding, the gamma trading activity reduces the volatility of the underlying share as it always acts against the direction of the share price movements.

Example 1

Typically, arbitrage starts out with a convertible having a delta of 50 %. If as a result of the market forces the share price goes up, the convertible turns away from the bond floor and becomes more sensitive to the share price. In gamma trading, unlike delta trading, instead of waiting for a further rise in the share price, the hedge fund manager short sells additional shares at a higher price to keep his return profile symmetrical. If after the sale the share price goes back down to the original value, the fund manager will buy back the same amount of shorted shares and make a profit.

Let's assume the fund manager has bought for $100 a bond convertible into 100 shares of stock. Assuming that the valuation model used by the fund manager establishes that the return profile is symmetrical for a delta of 50 %, the fund manager short sells 50 shares at a price of say $0.80. In so doing, the fund manager receives $40, and now his position costs $100 − $40 = $60.

If the share goes up 25 % to $1, let's assume that the valuation model used by the fund manager computes a delta of 70 %. The fund manager will short sell 20 more shares at a price of $1 each. If as a result of the sale the share price goes back down to $0.80, the fund manager buys back the 20 shares at $0.80. The fund manager is back to his original position now, but gamma trading generated a $0.20 profit times 20 shares, which is equal to $4. A $4 profit out of a position that costs the fund manager $60 means a 6.7 % profit in addition to the cash flow generated by the open position.

Example 2

Let's consider the bonds Kfw-Kredit Wiederaufbau convertible into Deutsche Telekom shares, due on 8th August 2008, fixed coupon of 0.75 % and a €50 000 round lot (see Figure 6.12). This is a €5 billion issue and offers a good liquidity. It is also backed by the guarantee of the German Government, therefore the credit risk is almost nonexistent, and Standard & Poors' rating is AAA.

The implied volatility level is appealing (25 % on 8th August 2003 against a historical 100 day volatility of Deutsche Telekom of 37 %) and the fund manager decides to open a convergence position between the convertible's implied volatility and the historical volatility of the Deutsche Telekom stock.

The fund manager performs a gamma trading on the Deutsche Telekom stock, while being protected against interest rate risks.

The position is opened on 8th July 2003 and is closed on 6th October 2003. In three months the fund manager generated a +2.33 % profit. Said profit stemmed from the position with +1.30 %, adjustments with +0.73 % and coupons with +0.30 %.

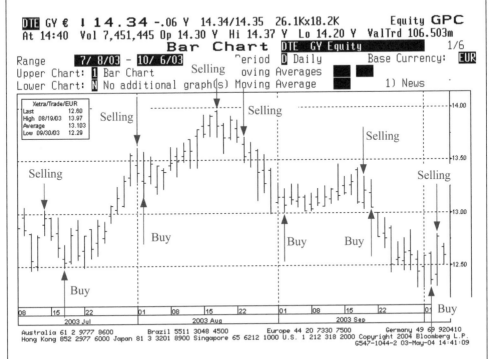

Figure 6.12 Deutsche Telekom stock and gamma trading from 8th July 2003 to 6th October 2003. Used with permission from Bloomberg L.P.

Table 6.1 shows in detail the various trades the fund manager executed in the first two days of gamma trading.

Table 6.1

Date and time	Security	Amount bought or sold
8th July 2003 06.12	Deutsche Telekom	−€14 494 346
8th July 2003 06.12	Deutsche Telekom	−€2 190 475
8th July 2003 06.12	Deutsche Telekom	−€23 023 973
8th July 2003 11.58	Kfw ex Deutsche Telekom 0.75 % 2008	€100 000 000
8th July 2003 18.59	Kfw ex Deutsche Telekom 0.75 % 2008	€40 000 000
9th July 2003 08.49	Kfw ex Deutsche Telekom 0.75 % 2008	−€7 755 188
9th July 2003 09.31	Deutsche Telekom	€1 559 564
9th July 2003 11.03	Kfw ex Deutsche Telekom 0.75 % 2008	−€5 087 500
9th July 2003 11.38	Kfw ex Deutsche Telekom 0.75 % 2008	−€763 500
9th July 2003 13.08	Kfw ex Deutsche Telekom 0.75 % 2008	−€10 748 400
9th July 2003 13.38	Deutsche Telekom	€3 924 279
9th July 2003 13.45	Deutsche Telekom	€1 846 000
9th July 2003 14.22	Deutsche Telekom	−€1 222 965
9th July 2003 14.26	Deutsche Telekom	€1 854 450
9th July 2003 14.26	Kfw ex Deutsche Telekom 0.75 % 2008	−€5 092 500
9th July 2003 14.57	Deutsche Telekom	−€6 329 218
9th July 2003 14.58	Deutsche Telekom	−€1 769 170
9th July 2003 16.59	Deutsche Telekom	−€2 797 050
9th July 2003 17.00	Deutsche Telekom	€286 000
9th July 2003 19.18	Kfw ex Deutsche Telekom 0.75 % 2008	€5 068 750

High convexity convertibles

Some convertible issues are characterized by the fact that they go up in value more rapidly than they go down in response to changes in the underlying share price. This characteristic is known as convexity, or gamma, and it is particularly important under an especially high market volatility.

Convertibles with a high convexity offer a value increase when the underlying share value rises (high level of sensitivity to changes in the underlying share price) and a limited downside risk because of the convertible's bond floor.

A big gamma implies that the slope of the tangent to the curvature of the convertible price changes rapidly as the underlying share price changes. The premium expands when the stock goes down, whereas it shrinks when the stock goes up.

Generally a convertible has a big gamma if its conversion premium is relatively low and has a low premium on the investment value.

6.7.4   Credit Arbitrage

The greatest and potentially most damaging risk for delta trading and gamma trading is the credit risk of the convertible issuer. When the share price falls so low as to push the convertible into the distressed area, what has been described for delta trading and gamma trading no longer applies. This may happen rarely, but the worst scenario for hedge funds following a convertible bond arbitrage strategy is for credit risk to grow systematically, affecting all the positions simultaneously. In recent times this happened in 1994 and in 1998, and it brought convertible bond arbitrage hedge funds to their knees: back then the credit spreads between corporate bonds and sovereign bonds widened.

Some fund managers prefer to focus on the convertible issuer's creditworthiness. The aim is to assess the issuer's fundamentals, that is, assess the likelihood that coupons are paid and on maturity the par value, to verify whether this probability is factored into the convertible's price. The closer a convertible bond trades to its bond floor, the more important this fundamental analysis becomes.

Busted convertibles are bonds whose issuer is in financial distress, with the share price tumbling rapidly and the credit quality of the bonds deteriorating. In this case, the price of the convertibles can go below the value of their bond component. Busted convertibles have a low stock sensitivity and trade like fixed-income investments.

If the price of the underlying stock drops sharply, the convertible bond will be valued like a simple bond and will generally reach its bond floor. Typically, this happens when the financial situation of the issuer has deteriorated, causing the credit spreads to widen and the discount rates to increase, while the bond sheds value.

To hedge against the credit risk of an issue, the hedge fund manager can buy a credit default swap. By paying a premium for the option, the fund manager is hedged against the issuer bankruptcy risk. The option writer on the other hand has received the premium, certain that the issuer credit quality is going to improve.

A *credit default swap* is a contract that offers a protection against a company's risk of default. The buyer of the protection receives the right to sell at par a given bond of the company when the latter defaults. The buyer makes periodic payments to the seller up to the expiration of the contract or until the company defaults. Generally, the event of default entails the payment of a final installment by the buyer. Usually, in case of default, the credit default swap is settled by cash delivery: the cash settlement is equal to the par value of the bond less the average market price of the bond on a specific date. Credit derivatives offer investors the chance to buy or sell protection against a borrower defaulting. It has also given investors a chance to express negative views on credits.

Credit derivatives have experienced an explosive growth and today the face value of outstanding credit default swaps is equal to $5000 billion.[5] The value of the stock underlying credit default swaps has exceeded the value of the entire high-yield fixed-income market (see Figure 7.7 in the next chapter).

According to a survey conducted by the International Swaps and Derivatives Association (www.isda.org) on a sample of 120 companies, to mid-2004 the notional amount for outstanding credit derivatives was $5440 billion, up 44 % compared to the beginning of 2004. In the first half of 2003, the growth rate had been 33 %. This market is becoming vast, deep, complex and more and more liquid.

An *interest rate swap* is an agreement whereby a company promises to pay the counterparty a predetermined fixed rate for a given number of years and based on a given principal, called notational principal amount. The counterparty in exchange will pay the other a floating interest rate on the same notional amount, for the same number of years.

---

[5] British Bankers Association.

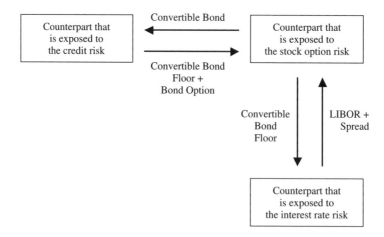

Figure 6.13   Credit default swap and interest rate swap

When interest rates rise, investors are attracted by the higher interest rates and the value of the debt issued at lower rates decreases. Hence, an interest rate increase causes a decrement of the value of the convertible's bond component.

A hedge fund manager can eliminate the interest rate risk by entering a swap agreement with a counterparty, whereby it pays a fixed rate equal to the coupon of the convertible bond, and receives a floating rate, typically the LIBOR rate plus a spread.

With a credit default swap and an interest rate swap, it is possible to break the convertible bond down into its components: call option on the stock, floating and fixed rate bond. Thus, each counterparty is exposed to the desired risk, while passing the undesired risks onto the other counterparties (Figure 6.13).

Volatility trading hedge funds transfer the credit risk and the interest rate risk to other counterparties by using swaps. According to a survey conducted by the International Swaps and Derivatives Association (www.isda.org) on a sample of 120 companies, to mid-2004 the notional principal outstanding volume of interest rate derivatives was about $164 500 billion.

Credit arbitrage hedge funds transfer the interest rate risk and eventually the stock option risk to other counterparties by using swaps. They will make a profit if the issuer's credit quality improves over time, or if it worsens over time as anticipated by the fund manager.

In the case of a swap between a credit investor and a volatility trading hedge fund, on expiration of the convertible bond there are two scenarios to be considered and several possible outcomes:

- If the issuer goes bankrupt, the hedge fund manager does not exercise the option and upon liquidation the credit investor will receive the recovery value of the convertible bond, if any.
- If the issuer does not go bankrupt, there are two possible outcomes:

    – if at expiration the option embedded in the convertible is out-of-the-money, the hedge fund manager does not exercise the option. The credit investor shall be paid back the par value of the convertible bond by the issuer;

- if at expiration the option embedded in the convertible is in-the-money, the hedge fund manager exercises the option and will pay the bond par value to the credit investor. The issuer in turn will deliver to the fund manager the amount of shares due based on the conversion ratio; in this case, the difference between the conversion value and the bond par value represents the fund manager's profit.

- If the issuer calls the convertible bonds, there are two possible outcomes:

  - if the option embedded in the convertible is out-of-the-money, the fund manager does not exercise the option. The issuer will pay the credit investor at *call price*;
  - if the option embedded in the convertible is in-the-money, the fund manager will call the bond from the credit investor and will pay him the *call value*. The hedge fund manager shall exercise the convertible bond and will receive the parity value, which is higher than the payment made to the credit investor.

Compared to a few years ago, today there are many more traders on the market who have gained substantial experience in assessing credit risk and who take on this risk with full knowledge.

Infineon Technologies AG designs, develops, manufactures and markets semi-conductors, for applications in the wireless and wireline communication, automotive, industrial computer security and chip card industries. Infineon Technologies AG has more than 35 000 employees worldwide, and in the financial year 2003–2004 generated sales for €7.19 billion.

Infineon Technologies AG issued convertible bonds for €1 billion, paying a 4.25 % coupon, due 6th February 2007, convertible into 1411.2334 Infineon Technologies AG shares for each €50 000 of nominal amount of the convertible bond. The convertible bond was not rated by rating agencies and has a provisional call clause in its prospectus.

A study conducted by the hedge fund's credit analysis department indicates that Infineon Technologies AG enjoys a good competitive position in a sector burdened by a recurring output overcapacity. In the case of recovery, the company has a good operating leverage. With its €1 billion size, the bond issue liquidity is good, and moreover there has been an additional issuance of convertible bonds for €800 million, due in 2010 and with a 5 % coupon.

The fund manager believes that good news from the semiconductor industry should drive the convertible's underlying share way up. He seeks to benefit from the narrowing of the convertible bond's credit spread. The share rise makes the conversion into stock of the new convertible bond more likely and it improves the debt ratio.

The position was opened on 30th April 2003 and closed on 6th October 2003.

The Infineon Technologies AG share rose from €7 to €12 and the implied credit spread narrowed from 700 bps down to 380 bps.

The trade closed with a positive return of +5.28 %. The performance came +3.40 % from the position and +1.88 % from the coupons (see Figure 6.14).

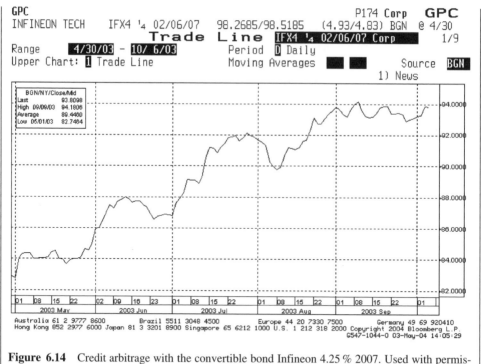

Figure 6.14 Credit arbitrage with the convertible bond Infineon 4.25 % 2007. Used with permission from Bloomberg L.P.

6.7.5 Skewed Arbitrage

This is an investment strategy available to macro hedge funds. In the above example, the fund manager sold the stock short and with the proceeds from this trade he financed the purchase of the corresponding convertible bond. By paying only the convertible premium, the fund manager constructed a high-leverage position. This position is different from the purchase of a put, because it generates a cash flow when held, and it has a longer life with respect to an option. In this way, the fund manager constructs a bearish position with a limited downside risk and with a long time horizon.

6.7.6 Carry Trade

A carry trade consists of buying bonds with a higher yield than the money you borrowed to buy them. Needless to say, the higher yield is associated with a higher risk. (For a more extensive discussion, not restricted to the convertible market alone, please refer to Section 7.8 in Chapter 7.)

For example, a carry trade is a strategy aimed at making a profit from a short-term convertible bond. This transaction rests on the assumption that the financial position of the issuer is sound enough to pay back the convertible bond. In carry trades, the primary source of return is accrued interests and not volatility.

Carlton Communications plc is a media company providing a variety of services, such as television program production and distribution, film production and Internet website management. Carlton is active in the United States and in the United Kingdom.

Carlton Communications plc issued convertible bonds for €638.7 million, paying a 2.25 % coupon, due on 4th January 2007, convertible into Thomson shares (24.2718 Thomson shares every €1000 of face value of the convertible bond). The convertible bond rating is BBB. The convertible bond has provisional call and clean up call clauses in its prospectus (see Figure 6.15).

The catalyst event triggering the deal closure is Carlton Communications' credit spread narrowing and/or a significant rise of the Thomson share. An additional profit may potentially come from the option on Thomson.

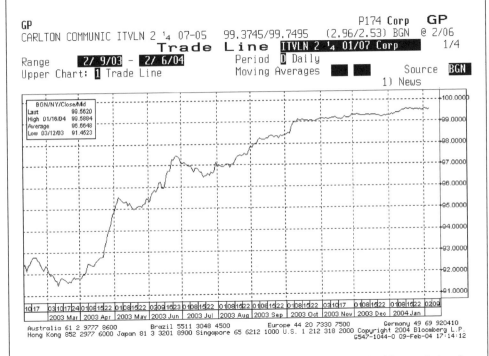

Figure 6.15 Carlton Communications ex Thomson 2.25 % 2007. Used with permission from Bloomberg L.P.

Table 6.2

	Date	Carlton convertible price	Credit spread	Thomson share price
Open	9th July 2003	0.97	132 bps	14.30
Close	30th October 2003	0.99	28 bps	17.72

The transaction closed with a positive return of +2.76 %. The performance came +2.06 % from the position (of which about 1 % was from the credit spread narrowing) and +0.70 % from the coupons.

6.7.7 Refinancing Plays

There are convertible bonds that are held for their high credit spread, whereby the expected catalyst event is the announcement of a new financing plan, which can dispel doubts on the issuer's ability to meet its redemption obligations at maturity of the convertible bond. The fundamental analysis of the issuer's credit position allows the hedge fund manager to form an opinion on the likelihood that the company is going to look for a new financing.

6.7.8 Late Stage Restructuring Plays

When the issuer of a convertible becomes part of the distressed world, its shareholders and management try to restructure the issuing company to set it back on its feet. For companies that underwent a restructuring, the survival odds have often improved, but the assessment of their creditworthiness remains severe.

In this phase, most convertible bond-holders are distressed investors, who bought at lower prices and are now seeking to make a profit and move somewhere else. As a general rule, buyers are very rare, because the picture of the issuer's recent distress is still vivid in the minds of investors. As a result, there are few buyers in a market where there are many sellers, which leaves hedge fund managers with the possibility of reaping market opportunities.

6.7.9 Multi-Strategy

This is an approach that includes all the arbitrage techniques analyzed up to now. It is a strategy followed by hedge funds that can count on a relatively large organization (even with hundreds of people), and have groups of specialized traders and analysts who follow a single investment strategy. The hedge fund's head of investments will then decide on the asset allocation to the various groups of traders, depending on existing market opportunities. This also permits a more rapid allocation of money in and out of a single strategy.

6.8 MANDATORY CONVERTIBLES

Mandatory convertibles are equity-linked hybrid securities that automatically convert to stock upon maturity, compared to bond convertibles where the exchange is optional. Mandatory convertibles pay a high coupon to investors, offering them significantly higher returns with respect to share dividends. Due to these benefits, upon issuance a mandatory convertible pays a premium on the share price and it provides investors with a limited participation in the underlying share rise.

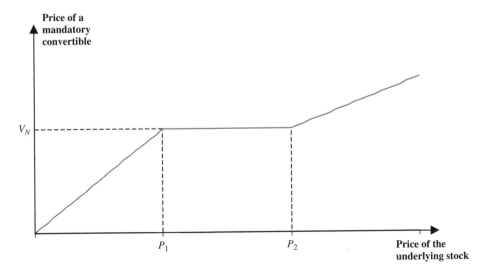

Figure 6.16   Mandatory convertibles

On expiration, mandatory convertibles are converted into a number of shares that depends on the price of the underlying share, as shown in Figure 6.16:

1. a fixed number of shares, if the share price is below a given price (lower exercise price P_1);
2. a variable number of shares if the share price lies between the two exercise prices, so that the value of the received shares remains constant (V_N) between the two exercise prices;
3. a fixed number of shares lower than that at point 1, if the share price is above a given price (upper exercise price P_2).

A mandatory convertible has no bond floor and therefore features no downside protection, because on expiration it automatically converts to stock. Mandatory convertibles are the bond issues that most resemble shares and include acronyms like DECS, PERCS, PRIDES, ELKS, etc.

Figure 6.17 shows the range of financial instruments, from those resembling shares to those resembling bonds.

Companies may decide to issue a mandatory convertible rather than a bond convertible for the following reasons:

- reduce the cost of capital with tax-deductible coupons;
- avoid cash redemptions on expiration;
- de-leverage the balance sheet, as generally mandatory convertibles are treated like shares;
- make a deferred sale of shares at a premium to the current price;
- raise capital at lower commission costs with respect to direct financing through shares;
- benefit from the way rating agencies treat mandatory convertibles as equity-like instruments.

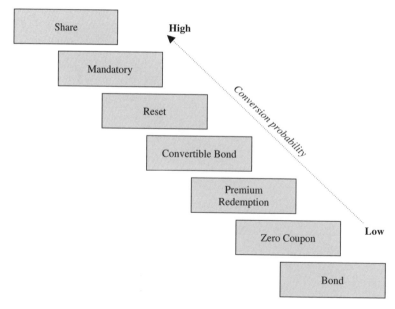

Figure 6.17 The range of financial instruments, from those resembling shares to those resembling bonds. Source: UBS

> On 24th February 2003, Deutsche Telekom AG issued a mandatory convertible through its Dutch financial company Deutsche Telekom International Finance B.V. The size of the issue was €2.2885 billion. The mandatory convertible paid a 6.5 % coupon once a year, expiration date 1st June 2006. The holders have the option to convert the mandatory convertible into Deutsche Telekom AG stock as of 1st July 2003 until 30th April 2006. To get an idea of the complexity of mandatory convertibles, the prospectus for this issuance is 296 pages long. The Deutsche Telekom AG share price on issue is €11.80 and the maximum conversion price is €14.632 (the conversion premium is 24 %). The mandatory convertible will be accounted for in Deutsche Telekom's balance sheet as a debt, until its maturity and its conversion into stock.

6.9 STRATEGY'S HISTORICAL PERFORMANCE ANALYSIS

Let's analyze the historical behavior of this strategy based on the monthly returns of the CS/Tremont Convertible Bond Arbitrage Index. Again, the past performance of a given investment is not necessarily indicative of a future return for the same investment. Still, we believe it is useful to examine historical data to understand which scenarios are favorable to this strategy and which are not.

The statistical analysis of the CS/Tremont Convertible Bond Arbitrage Index between 1994 and 2004 produces the results shown in Table 6.3.

Note that the percentage of positive months is very high (80 %) and the average performance in positive months is +1.3 %. The performance has been strong, with an annualized return of 9.8 % between 1994 and 2004, with a low volatility (4.7 %).

Table 6.3

	CS/Tremont Convertible bond arbitrage	Morgan Stanley Capital International World in US$	JP Morgan Global Government Bond Global International
Value at Risk (1 month, 95%)	−1.40%	−6.40%	−1.90%
Value at Risk (1 month, 99%)	−4.20%	−10.40%	−3.60%
Best month Performance	3.60%	8.90%	7.00%
Average Performance in positive months	1.30%	3.20%	1.60%
Worst month Performance	−4.70%	−13.50%	−5.10%
Average Performance in negative months	−1.20%	−3.50%	−1.00%
% Positive months	80%	61%	57%
Compound Annual Growth Rate (CAGR)	9.80%	6.30%	5.40%
Annualized monthly volatility	4.70%	14.20%	6.20%
Skewness	−1.45	−0.6	0.65
Kurtosis	3.81	0.59	2.21
Largest Drawdown*	−12.00%	−48.40%	−8.60%
Duration of the largest drawdown in months	2	30	4
Time to recovery** in months	10	n.a.	9
Drawdown start	31st Aug. 1998	30th Apr. 2000	28th Feb. 1994
Drawdown end	31st Oct. 1998	30th Sep. 2002	31st May 1994

* The largest drawdown is defined as the maximum value of any "peak to trough decline" over the specified period. The subsequent minimum is not determined until it has reached a new high.
** Time to recovery is the time necessary to recover from the largest drawdown.

The distribution of monthly return is asymmetrical (Skewness lesser than zero) and the tails are fatter than those of the Gaussian distribution (Kurtosis greater than 3).

The largest drawdown has been significant (−12%) and lasted for only two months. Then the index needed ten months to recover the losses.

Figure 6.18 shows the monthly returns of the CS/Tremont Convertible Bond Arbitrage Index from 1994 to 2004. Figure 6.19 illustrates the historical performance as a function of risk of the CS/Tremont Convertible Bond Arbitrage Index between 1994 and 2004.

In 2004, the risk/return profile of this strategy deviated from the concentration ellipsoid and landed on a low return and low volatility area.

Figure 6.20 shows that between 1994 and 2004 there were three important "underwater" dips for hedge funds following this strategy. The chart must be analyzed taking drawdown data into consideration: throughout the drawdown and the time to recovery period, the hedge funds adopting this strategy were under the high water mark. (See Chapter 1, Section 1.8, for more details on the setup and meaning of Figures 6.19 and 6.20.)

The three drawdowns were triggered by events that had relevant consequences on the markets: first, the unexpected interest rate rise started in February 1994 by the US Federal Reserve; second, in August 1998, there was a strong *flight-to-quality* movement caused by Russia's default; third, in summer 2002, following the disclosure of the accounting frauds in Adelphia and Worldcom, credit spreads on corporate bonds widened, causing big losses across all credit-oriented strategies.

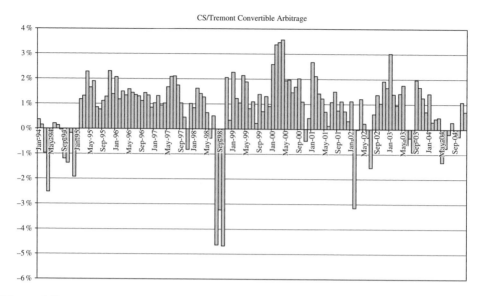

Figure 6.18 Monthly returns of CS/Tremont Convertible Arbitrage from 1994 to 2004. Source: CS/Tremont Index LLC, www.hedgeindex.com. Copyright © 2006, Credit Suisse/Tremont Index LLC. All rights reserved*

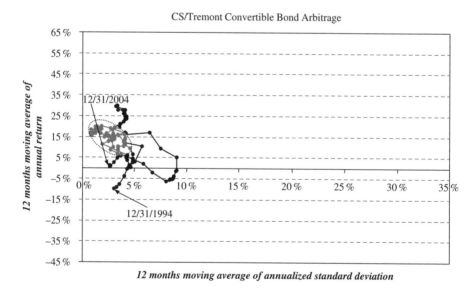

Figure 6.19 Historical performance trend of return as a function of risk for CS/Tremont Convertible Arbitrage from 1994 to 2004. Source: CS/Tremont Index LLC, www.hedgeindex.com. Copyright © 2006, Credit Suisse/Tremont Index LLC. All rights reserved*

CS/Tremont Convertible Arbitrage

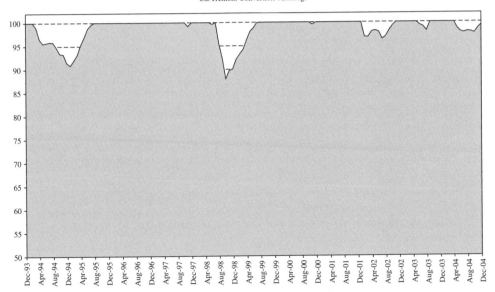

Figure 6.20 Underwater periods for CS/Tremont Convertible Arbitrage from 1994 to 2004. Source: CS/Tremont Index LLC, www.hedgeindex.com. Copyright © 2006, Credit Suisse/Tremont Index LLC. All rights reserved*

There are four main market conditions that are adverse to convertible bond arbitrageurs:

• The first scenario is when bond prices go down while share prices remain unchanged. This happened in 1994.
• The second scenario is when both shares and convertible bonds go down. This occurs when companies go bankrupt or do not pay back the bond upon expiration. This happened in 2002, when credit markets deteriorated and equity markets went down.
• The third scenario takes place during sudden market movements, like *flight-to-quality* and *flight-to-safety*, in which financial markets are unstable and share prices plummet. Credit spreads widen and share prices go down: on the market there is no liquidity. What happened in 1998, with a systemic liquidity crisis, is a good example of this.
• The fourth scenario is when there is a surprising capital structure movement, where the riskiest part of the capital, equities, jumps at a time when the less risky part of the capital, bonds, drops. This happened in May 2005 when the tender offer by Kirk Kerkorian on 4.95 % of General Motors shares drove the GM stock price higher, while Standard & Poor's downgraded the GM credit to sub-investment grade status.

Under extreme market conditions, leverage may force the fund manager to sell financial instruments with a wrong timing to pay in the required margins.

Goldman Sachs Convertible Strategy estimates that between 2000 and 2003 there was a slowdown in the use of leverage by a representative sample of convertible bond arbitrage hedge funds. Leverage went from about 10 times to about 3 times. Goldman Sachs Convertible Strategy also notes that neither the leverage nor the hedge fund size showed a statistically

---

significant correlation with the fund's performance. The hedge fund performance relies exclusively on the individual management approach that is unique to each hedge fund manager.

In 2004, credit-related sub-strategies performed better than volatility-related ones, mainly due to the credit spread squeeze and the low implied volatility levels. In 2004, the poor performance of the convertible bond arbitrage strategy triggered widespread redemptions that further increased the pressure on convertible valuations. 2004 was also characterized by low convertible issue levels with respect to investor demand.

As shown in Figure 6.10, realized volatility is at historical low levels, even lower than implied volatility, and this penalizes volatility trading.

Funds with a credit or special situation exposure had an above average performance in 2004. Some fund managers are shifting towards a multi-strategy investment approach, which also includes event-driven and capital structure arbitrage investments.

2004 was characterized by a low level of new issues and the overall size of the convertible market decreased from the previous year.

Volatility trading funds represent a low cost market hedge against equity market crisis risks, which typically coincide with a surging volatility.

6.10   RISK CONTROL

All the components of a convertible bond represent an investment opportunity but also a risk: credit, interest rates, the equity component and volatility.

Interest rates stand for the cost of capital: when interest rates go up, investors will be attracted by higher interest rates and the value of the debt issued at lower rates will go down. Hence, an increase in interest rates will cause a decrease in value of the bond component of a convertible bond.

Hedge fund managers can hedge against the risk of an interest rate rise by using interest rate futures, forwards and interest rate swaps. They can also hedge against the issuer default risk by buying credit default swaps.

Let's analyze the main risks to which convertible bond arbitrage is exposed:

1. Equity market risks. If the hedging is not equity market-neutral, the arbitrage is exposed to the risk of market fluctuations.
2. Interest rate risk. The convertible price moves in an inversely proportional manner with respect to the changes in interest rates, and the closer the convertible trades to its bond floor, the higher its interest rate sensitivity is. A rise in interest rates decreases the value of convertibles, but usually an interest rate hike is bad news for equity markets, therefore a short position on the underlying stock should act as a protection against interest rate rises. The value of the option embedded in the convertible grows as the interest rate grows, and therefore it provides a further hedge against interest rate rises, because when the value of the underlying stock decreases, the option to convert into a fixed number of shares becomes more valuable. Arbitrageurs can also hedge against interest rate risks by buying an interest rate swap.
3. Credit risk. Risk of widening credit spreads. The short position on the underlying stock partly reduces this risk because when credit spreads widen, share prices go down. Arbitrageurs can hedge against the risk of spread widening by buying a credit default swap.
4. Leverage is often used to amplify returns, but it can significantly increase risk.

5. The risk of special events, like a dividend payout. If the company pays a dividend, the fund manager who is short the company's stock must pay the amount of the dividend to the counterparty from whom he borrowed the stock. So the hedge fund manager who is delta hedging is exposed to the risk that the company pays a dividend. This risk may increase as a result of regulatory or fiscal changes: an example we mentioned when tackling short selling is the US "Jobs and Growth Tax Relief Reconciliation Act" in May 2003.

6. Liquidity risk. The risk that the bid/ask spread on the convertible bond and the share widens. This may be particularly true for securities of companies with a low credit-worthiness. The liquidity risk is higher for small convertible issues. Arbitrageurs cannot hedge against this risk.

7. Short selling exposes the risk of a *short squeeze*, namely a sudden call for the shares to be returned.

8. A shortage of borrowable shares may prevent the fund manager from establishing the hedge.

9. The prospectus of some issues may contain provisions that give the issuer the right to:

   – force the bond conversion in case the conversion of a given percentage of the total convertible bond issue is called (*clean-up call*);
   – force the bond conversion in case the stock dividend yield falls below the interest rate paid by the convertible (*provisional call*);
   – be exempt from paying accrued interest on bonds in case the bond holder exercises the conversion right (*screw clause*).

10. Currency risk. This happens when the portfolio is diversified across multiple currencies. The fund manager can hedge against these risks with a forward contract.

In order to reduce risk, hedge fund portfolios are typically diversified over a large number of different issues, with issuers featuring different credit ratings and belonging to different business sectors.

6.11   CONCLUSIONS

Convertible bond arbitrage is an example of a non-directional strategy whose return is not correlated to capital markets, but rather depends on the fund manager's ability to capture and take advantage of directional spreads.

It is a classical strategy in the hedge fund world, which has become too crowded due to the presence of too many traders and where there is a strong competition among hedge funds to carry out arbitrages. This erodes the profitability of arbitrages and tempts hedge fund managers into taking on directional risks based on their market expectations.

The current trend shows that hedge fund managers are shifting from a pure convertible bond arbitrage strategy to a multi-strategy approach, with a greater propensity to side a classical convertible bond arbitrage with strategies like PIPEs, statistical arbitrage, event-driven arbitrage, special situation arbitrage and even long/short equity.

There are convertible bond arbitrage fund managers who even resemble macro fund managers, because they take on directional risks on all components of the convertible bond: equity, credit, interest rate and volatility. This happens with larger hedge funds, with assets under management of €2–5 billion, or funds with a high leverage (over 5 times), which once again is associated with the need to manage a larger fund.

New financial instruments are emerging, like mandatory convertibles, which means that for a hedge fund manager the ability to analyze the characteristics of single issues and understand even the most complex structures may prove a competitive advantage, allowing him to explore the new frontiers of capital markets where rich investment opportunities may be at hand.

7
Fixed Income Arbitrage

Figure 7.1 will surprise people who think that the fixed income market consists mainly of treasuries. This figure shows that treasuries account for only 16.6 % of all bonds outstanding in the United States as of 30th September 2004. In fact, treasuries are surpassed by two other bond classes in terms of size: corporate bonds represent 20.1 %, but maybe more surprising is that 23.4 % is made up of mortgage bonds. Treasuries rank first in terms of daily average trading volumes. In the first nine months of 2003, the notes issued by the US Treasury were by far the most traded debt securities (Figure 7.2).

According to the LIPPER TASS database, on 31st December 2004, *fixed income arbitrage* funds accounted for 7 % of the hedge fund industry. Diverse trading strategies can be identified:

1. *Issuance driven arbitrage (snap trade)*: the arbitrageur anticipates that the prices of the latest treasuries issued (on-the-run) and the prices of the next to last treasuries having very similar maturity dates will converge when the demand for on-the-run treasuries slows down as a result of a new treasury issue.
2. *Yield curve arbitrage*: the fund manager expects changes in the slope of the various areas of a specific interest rate curve. A type of yield curve arbitrage is the so called butterfly trade, whereby you open a position having a relative value between a seven year treasury that is more expensive with respect to two treasuries at six and eight years.
3. *Intermarket spread trading*: the fund manager trades between two yield curves of different currencies.
4. *Futures basis trading (basis trading)*: strategy seeking to take advantage of mismatches between the price of a future contract and the price of the instruments to be delivered at contract expiration.
5. *Swap spread trading*: the fund manager seeks to take advantage of changes in a particular swap spread which is the difference between the fixed return a market participant is willing to pay to a counterparty in an interest rate swap and the yield of a treasury having a similar duration.
6. Other types of spread trade, like the spread between municipal bonds and treasury bonds, whereby the fund manager seeks to take advantage of temporary deviations of the relationship observed between the prices of related financial instruments and the theoretical relationship existing between them.
7. *Capital structure arbitrage.*
8. *Long/short credit or credit pair trading.*
9. *Carry trade.*
10. *Break-even inflation trade.*
11. *Emerging markets fixed income* (see the Debt Emerging Markets Strategy in Chapter 14 on Macro Funds).
12. *Cross-currency relative value trade.*

13. *Treasuries over eurodollars spread* (*international credit spread*).
14. *Leveraged loans.*
15. *Structured finance*: this will be discussed in Chapter 8.
16. *Mortgage trade*: the fund manager seeks to profit from an apparent mispricing between mortgage instruments, mortgage derivatives and related financial instruments. Mortgage-backed securities arbitrage will be covered more extensively in Chapter 9.

Fixed-income arbitrageurs take long and short positions ("offsetting"), seeking to take advantage of temporary mismatches between related securities. Generally, considering the exiguity of the mismatches, leverage is used. Portfolios are constructed in such a way as to have no correlation with interest rate changes, trying to nullify or at least minimize the portfolio's total duration.

Fixed income arbitrage seeks to seize the opportunities arising from minor misprices while being hedged against an interest rate change risk.

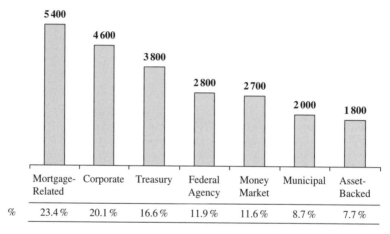

Figure 7.1 Outstanding bond market debt in the US as of 30th September 2004 (data in billion dollars). Source: Federal Reserve System, US Treasury, GNMA, FNMA, FHLM, Bloomberg; The Bond Market Association estimates

Figure 7.2 Average daily trading volume in the first three quarters of 2004 in the US (data in billion dollars). Source: Federal Reserve System, US Treasury, GNMA, FNMA, FHLM, Bloomberg; The Bond Market Association estimates

In most cases, fund managers open arbitrage positions on securities whose prices are mathematically or historically correlated, and that as a result of external events are being mispriced. The securities traded by fund managers could be treasuries, corporate bonds, agency securities, municipal bonds and treasury securities of emerging countries.

The fixed income market is segmented because large institutional investors, such as pension plans, insurance companies and central banks, generally have different investment objectives and constraints. Hedge fund managers try to exploit structural anomalies and segmentation effects in fixed-income markets around the world.

As the prices of fixed-income securities depend upon various factors, fund managers use sophisticated analytical models run by powerful computers to identify existing misprices on the market. We could say that fund managers profit from the complexity of the valuation of fixed-income securities and from their ability to analyze factors affecting the prices of these securities.

Since in general misprices are very small, fixed income arbitrage managers use leverage to maximize profit opportunities.

It is important to remember that the fund manager who is short selling a bond must pay all the detached coupons to the counterparty from whom he borrowed the bond throughout the length of the short sale. This means that a bond short sale has a negative carry, i.e., time tends to go against the position: the more the fund manager keeps the position open, the more he loses.

7.1   ISSUANCE DRIVEN ARBITRAGE OR SNAP TRADE

The performance of trades on securities with close maturity dates depends on factors associated with the issuance cycles. These arbitrages seek to profit from distortions in the yield curve rather than from the slope of the curve. A classical example of a trade whose performance depends on issuance is the arbitrage between 30-year off-the-run and on-the-run Treasury Bonds, which we described in Chapter 2.

At the other end of the spectrum of yield curve arbitrages there are trades involving securities with different maturity dates, whose relation depends on macroeconomic factors rather than on simple misprices, as is the case with the yield curve arbitrage.

7.2   YIELD CURVE ARBITRAGE

The *yield curve* is the curve traced by the yield of fixed income treasury securities issued by a given country at their different maturity dates. The shape and slope of the yield curve change as a function of the creditworthiness of the issuing government, the central bank policy, the issuance of new treasuries by the government, the meeting point between supply and demand, as well as the different economic cycle conditions the government is undergoing.

A yield curve arbitrage is an arbitrage whereby the trader takes long and short positions on different points of the yield curve of the treasuries of a given country so as to profit from treasuries misprices along those different points. These misprices lead to yield curve distortions that represent profit opportunities for arbitrageurs. However, there are treasuries whose yield lies outside the yield curve, which could be due to the fact that there might be no borrowable securities left or the lending cost makes the arbitrage unprofitable.

A yield curve arbitrage can be of two types:

- *intra-curve*: if the fund manager trades securities of the same country, i.e.. within one yield curve only;
- *inter-curve*: if the fund manager trades securities issued by different countries, i.e., between two yield curves of different currencies.

The different transactions can be classified in terms of the bond maturity of the long and short positions.

There are three intra-curve arbitrages:

- *yield curve flattener*: you go short the bonds that are closer to expiration and long the bonds with a longer expiration. It is an implicitly long position on volatility (Figure 7.3);
- *yield curve steepener*: you go long the bonds that are closer to expiration and short the bonds with a longer expiration. It is an implicitly short position on volatility (Figure 7.4);
- *yield curve butterfly*: the yield curve should have a smoothed shape. This type of arbitrage involves the yields corresponding to three maturity dates. When the yield curve displays a trough, the arbitrage will require to go long the bonds whose expirations lie on the butterfly's wings and short the bond in the butterfly's body. If, however, the yield curve displays a hump, the arbitrage will require to go short the bonds with maturity dates on the wings of the butterfly and long the bond on the body of the butterfly. The fund manager will make a profit if the current yield curve turns into the future yield curve traced in Figure 7.5 or runs parallel to it.

The flattening or steepening of the yield curve depends on macroeconomic factors, like inflation, GDP growth and the monetary policy pursued by central banks. These are directional positions that express the fund manager's macroeconomic view. Through these

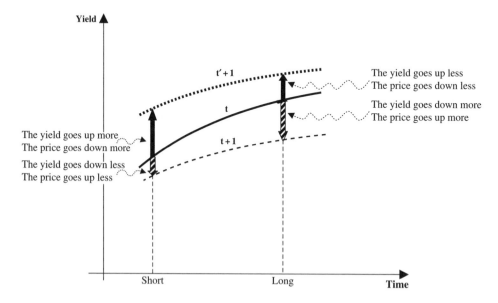

Figure 7.3   Yield curve flattening

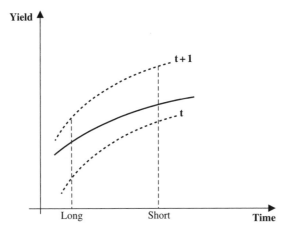

Figure 7.4   Yield curve steepening

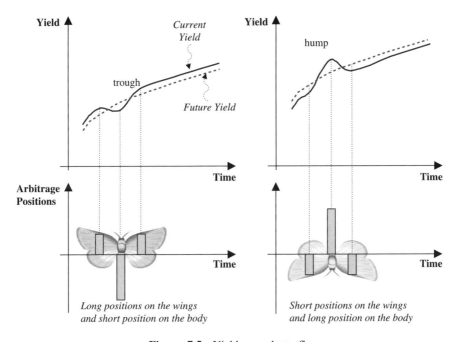

Figure 7.5   Yield curve butterfly

positions, the fund manager makes a forecast as to the shape of the yield curve and not a forecast on interest rate levels.

For example, the fund manager can execute:

* a steepener in the short-term tail of the British pound yield curve;
* a steepener in the short-term tail of the Japanese yen yield curve;
* a flattener in the US yield curve.

7.3   INTERMARKET SPREAD TRADING

The intermarket spread trading is an inter-curve yield curve arbitrage whereby the fund manager trades securities of different governments, i.e., between two yield curves of different currencies. Each currency has its own yield curve.

For example, the fund manager can go long on the 10-year Treasury Bond and short on the 10-year German Bund.

7.4   FUTURES BASIS TRADING OR BASIS TRADING

A futures contract on Treasury Bonds on expiration requires that the Treasury Bond indicated in the contract be delivered to the futures holder. Generally, in a Treasury Bond futures contract the counterparty who has to deliver the securities can choose the treasuries to be delivered from within a basket of predetermined debt securities, so as to avoid short squeezes and preserve market liquidity. On expiration of a Treasury Bond futures, the "cheapest to deliver" (defined below) securities will be delivered. So upon expiration of the futures contract, the price of the "cheapest to deliver" bond and the price of the futures contract will converge. Since it is uncertain which bond will be the "cheapest to deliver" on expiration, this can open up profit opportunities for arbitrageurs.

The basis of a futures contract on a single security is the difference between the securities spot price and its future price. The difference between the cash market price and the futures price give rise to profit opportunities for arbitrageurs.

When a given bond is delivered on expiration of the futures contract, the bond price results from the price of the futures contract for the bond conversion ratio plus the accrued interest. The *conversion ratio* for a bond to be delivered is approximately equal to the price at which the bond would generate a 6 % yield upon expiration of the first delivery day. The bond's *converted futures price* is defined as the bond's futures price subdivided by the bond's conversion ratio. The bond with the lower converted futures price is called the "*cheapest to deliver*", and will be the delivered bond under the contract.

When the yields of deliverable bonds change, it is most likely that the "cheapest to deliver" bond changes as well.

The delivery option embedded in the futures contract is represented by the probability stemming from the change in the "cheapest to deliver" bond and when within the delivery month to deliver the bond. Technically, the transaction portion holding the short position on the futures contract is at the same time long the delivery option. The most difficult aspect of the futures pricing exercise is measuring the value of the delivery option. Hedge fund managers create various, progressively sophisticated, mathematical models to price a futures contract.

Periodically, the futures market is misaligned with respect to its parallel bond and bond option markets, due to the different money flows reaching the different markets. These money flows by traditional investors generate interesting arbitrage opportunities for hedge fund managers.

7.5   SWAP SPREAD TRADING

A swap spread trade is the arbitrage on the spread between a swap and a Treasury Bond. The interest rate swap market has a notional outstanding volume of more than $140 billion.[1]

---

[1] ISDA Year-End 2003 Market Survey.

Borrowing at the short-term rate to buy a Treasury Bond generates the exit of a floating rate and the entry of a fixed rate. This position is equivalent to an interest rate swap paying a floating rate and receiving a fixed rate for exchange at a given nominal value and for a given period of time.

The swap curve is the curve formed by the interest rate swap fixed rates at the various maturity dates. The fixed rate of the swap generally does not coincide with the yield rate of Treasury Bonds. The widening or narrowing of the resulting spread can give rise to arbitrage opportunities for hedge fund managers.

Each currency has its own swap curve: the dollar, the euro, the yen, the pound sterling, the Norwegian crown, etc.

For example, the fund manager can execute:

- a steepener on the swap curve of the Australian dollar;
- a butterfly on the swap curve of the pound sterling;
- a steepener on the long tail of the swap curve of the US dollar;
- a flattener on the short tail of the swap curve of the Norwegian crown.

7.6 CAPITAL STRUCTURE ARBITRAGE

Investors segment financial instruments and specialize in single chunks of corporate capital structures, thus giving rise to inconsistencies in the relative valuations of the different parts making up the capital structure. This can turn into profit opportunities for traders who can move freely among the various constituents of the capital structure.

Merton's model[2] interprets equity and bonds as different types of options having the value of a company as underlying. Shareholders own the residual value of a company after debts have been paid down, therefore shares may be seen as an option on the value appreciation of that company. Bond-holders, however, are exposed to the risk that the assets of a company may fall below the amount of outstanding debt, when the company is insolvent, and therefore bonds may be seen as an option on the value depreciation of that company.

Merton's model interprets debt as being similar to a short position on a put option on corporate assets and interprets equity as a long position on a call option on corporate assets where the exercise price is equal to the book value of the company's debt. Based on the

---

[2] Merton's model assumes the value V of a company to satisfy the following differential equation, having a random walk:

$$dV = (\alpha V - C)dt + \sigma V dz$$

This equation implies that the company value (V) grows at a return rate α with a constant volatility equal to σ. There is the company's total pay-out by time unit. Let's assume that the company has issued a debt whose value at time T is equal to D_T and let's assume that at time T the company has to pay B to its bond-holders. If the value V of the company exceeds B at time T, the bond-holders will actually receive B, otherwise they will receive V_T. Hence, the debt value at time T is:

$$D_T = \min(V_T, B)$$

The share value S_T is simply equal to the value V of the company less the value of the debt. Therefore, at time T the share value is equal to:

$$S_T = \max(0, V_T - B)$$

Source: Merton, R.C. (1974) "On the Pricing of Corporate Debt: The Risk Structure of Interest Rates", *Journal of Finance*, **29**, 449–470.

In 1997 Robert C. Merton and Myron S. Scholes were awarded the Nobel Prize in Economic Sciences for their new derivative pricing model.

option pricing theory, the value of corporate assets can be derived from the equity price distribution.

Based on corporate financial statements, the asset value is equal to the market value of debt plus that of equity. If we deduct the equity market value to derive the debt market value, we obtain a spread implied in the shares for the company's credit. Hence, stock and bonds form a continuum represented by a company's capital structure (Figure 7.6).

In the case of the issuer going bankrupt, claims are liquidated starting from senior bank loans, then senior bonds, then subordinated bonds, and last, if there is still residual liquidity, shareholders. A simple arbitrage on a company's capital structure is established by buying senior bank loans and selling short subordinated bonds.

The capital structure arbitrage strategy seeks to capture price differentials between the various components of the capital structure of a single issuer. A hedge fund can invest simultaneously on all the securities of a company (corporate bonds, convertible bonds, common shares, preferred shares, secured senior debt and mezzanine or subordinated debt) to seize the arbitrage opportunities available within a company's capital structure. Capital structure arbitrage seeks to take advantage of price disparities or misalignments between two securities of the same issuer. The strategy is based on the relative value of the two securities, which allows the fund manager to hedge against the systematic market risk. If a capital structure arbitrage is well constructed, it can be isolated from the bond price plunge of a defaulting company.

The alpha generated by the fund manager depends on his ability to appreciate the more complex, less followed and less conspicuous relations between capital structure securities. For example, complexity can be increased by claim seniority, contract rights, legal issues for companies under bankruptcy, etc.

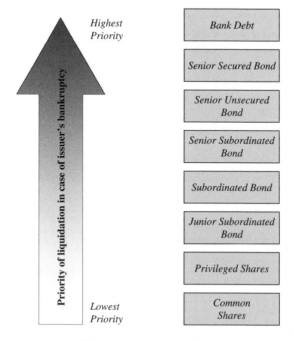

Figure 7.6 Capital structure of a company

There are different types of trade:

- *bonds versus equity*: temporary suspension of value perception between equity investors and fixed-income investors;
- *bonds versus bonds*: there are different levels of preferential claim or collateral guarantee among bonds, which are not priced in by current bond values on the market;
- *bonds versus credit default swap*: opportunities arising from temporary imbalances between supply and demand;
- *credit default swap versus stock options*: misalignments between the embedded volatility priced in by credit default swap and stock options;
- *bank debt versus credit default swap;*
- *Euro denominated versus USD denominated;*
- *secured debt versus unsecured debt.*

Credit Curve Arbitrage

In the second half of 2002, a company ABB was close to bankruptcy. By March 2003, after delivering on major asset sales, the short end of the credit curve had substantially recovered. A hedge fund manager concluded that the core business of ABB would return to positive cash flow and that the new management was very competent. The main uncertainty seemed to be asbestos, so the risk was much more front-ended and the credit curve would flatten. The hedge fund manager entered in the following trade: he went long the long-dated bond with the lowest price, which was the Sfr.$3\frac{3}{4}$% 2009 trading at 50 and he went short the €$5\frac{1}{4}$% 2004 at 93.

In a bankruptcy scenario, he would make 43 bond points, less negative carry of $1\frac{1}{2}$ points over six months. In the opposite scenario in which the credit recovered, as the manager expected, he would benefit from the tightening of spread between the two bonds. The main risk was that if the credit neither recovered nor fell into bankruptcy the trade would earn negative carry.

Date of Entry: March 2003
Entry price: Sfr50 and €93
Date of Exit: September 2003
Exit Price: Sfr88 and €98

Yield Curve Flattening

In April 2004, a hedge fund analyst visits Fiat's chief financial officer and a technical center in Italy. According to the analyst, Fiat has not really solved the business issues it faces, and he concludes that an investment upgrade is not close. The Fiat bond rating is Ba3 according to Moody's.

In July 2004, the analyst's concerns solidify as sales projections and profit targets for 2004 are likely to be missed.

In August 2004, the hedge fund manager buys a five year credit default swap on Fiat and sells a ten year credit default swap on Fiat, in amounts designed to build a duration neutral position. It is a flattening position on the Fiat yield curve.

> With the purchase of a five year credit default swap, the hedge fund manager profits from the underperformance of the five year bond. The investment thesis is that the five year bond will underperform the ten year bond. In stress situations, the issuer yield curve tends to flatten.
>
> The position opened by the fund manager is neutral to the widening or tightening of credit spreads.
>
> If Fiat should default on its bonds, the fund manager would profit from the purchase of the five year credit default swap and would lose from the sale of the ten year credit default swap.
>
> The position of the fund manager has a positive convexity, that is, if the yield curve flattens, the fund manager will profit. Moreover, the position will benefit from any sudden and ample widening or tightening of credit spreads. This position has a negative carry, so the hedge fund tends to lose money in sideway markets.

7.7   LONG/SHORT CREDIT OR CREDIT PAIR TRADING

Credit was at the heart of finance from the inception of the banking industry. Today, it is one of the areas of finance enjoying the strongest growth and hedge funds are active on this frontier to supply the market with liquidity and to make profits, seizing the opportunities emerging from the rising market of credit default swaps.

The US high-yield bond market was worth some $881 billion at the end of 2003 and it accounts for about 20 % of corporate bonds in the United States, while the European market on the same date was worth about €97.8 billion. In 2003, new high-yield bond issues reached $133 billion in the United States and €17 billion in Europe.

In 2003, hedge funds held about 7 % of high-yield bonds. The high-yield bond market is dominated by pension funds, insurance companies and CDO that altogether account for about 61 % of the market.[3] However, in terms of trading volumes hedge funds represent a bigger portion of the high-yield market.

Credit derivatives experienced an explosive growth and currently the nominal outstanding value of derivatives is $5 000 billion.[4] This market is becoming vast, deep, complex and more and more liquid. According to a survey conducted by the International Swaps and Derivatives Association (www.isda.org) on a sample of 120 companies, to mid-2004 the notional amount of outstanding credit derivatives was $5440 billion, up 44 % compared to the beginning of 2004. In the first half of 2003, the growth rate had been 33 %. Surprisingly, the notional amount of credit default swaps has exceeded the value of the entire high-yield fixed-income market, as shown in Figure 7.7.

Today, investing in bonds is not just limited to the purchase and the collection of the coupon waiting for credit spreads to shrink. In 2004 credit spreads were at an historical low level, as shown in Figure 7.8, and in addition the default rate was at its lowest and the number of upgrades exceeded the number of downgrades. Credit spreads practically reflect a low risk premium.

---

[3] 2004 Leveraged Finance Annual Review, CSFB.

[4] British Bankers Association.

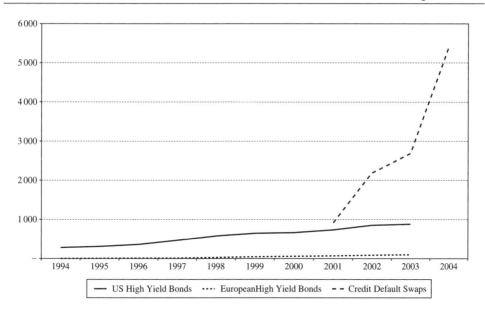

Figure 7.7 High-yield bond market and credit default swap notional mount outstanding from 1994 to 2004 (data in billion dollars). Source: CSFB (US$ and non-$US); www.isda.org

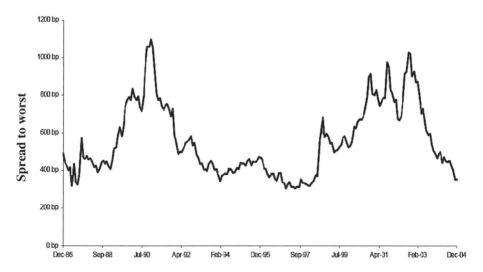

Figure 7.8 JP Morgan high-yield spread to worst (data in basis points). Source: JP Morgan

Such narrow credit spreads have been sustained by a low default rate, strong credit fundamentals and a buoyant demand for high-yield bonds. Credit spreads shrank even more blatantly for speculative grade bonds compared to investment grade bonds.

Credit default swaps make it possible to implement the long/short credit strategy, which is a new approach gaining ground among hedge funds. They allow hedge fund managers to go long or short the credit of a given company without having to trade the underlying bonds.

A buyer of a credit default swap on a company takes a short position on the credit of that company, i.e., he makes money if the credit quality of that company deteriorates, in other words he makes a profit if the credit spread widens. However, a seller of a credit default swap on a company takes a long position on the credit of that company, i.e., he makes money if the credit quality of that company improves, in other words he makes a profit if the credit spread shrinks.

There are hedge funds specializing in the so called crossover names, that is, companies whose bonds have been upgraded or downgraded by rating agencies with regard to their credit quality. Hedge fund managers analyze the credit standing of the companies to anticipate the rating agencies' upgrades or downgrades (Figure 7.9). Over reliance on credit reports generated by rating agencies leads investors to reach similar and undifferentiated investment decisions. By performing independent due diligence, extensive ongoing monitoring and proprietary quantitative analysis, a specialized hedge fund is able to find interesting opportunities to exploit.

Hedge fund managers also carry out a macro analysis to assess the impact of macroeconomic factors on spread direction, on the spreads of single industries and possibly on the spread of single companies. Analysts devote a special attention to currency and commodity markets and to variables such as stock prices, volatility, Z-score, etc. Based on data supplied by external sources, like Moody's and Standard & Poor's for example, a complete analysis covering a single company can be obtained, which includes liquidity, growth outlook, profitability, cash flow, etc.

The hedge fund manager constructs a portfolio with long and short positions on corporate bonds and tries to extrapolate value from his ability to analyze creditworthiness; his net exposure to corporate bonds can change as a function of his macroeconomic view.

The fund manager evaluates the financial position of the issuer to assess the credit standing of the issuer and to identify rating changes that can give rise to investment opportunities. With this strategy it is possible to profit from discrepancies in the relative credit rating between two issuers generally within the same industry.

A fund manager adopting a long/short credit strategy can establish the following positions:

- company A bond versus company B bond having the same maturity date;
- company A long term bond versus company B short term bond;
- credit of sector C versus credit of sector D, etc.

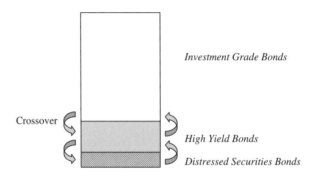

Figure 7.9 Crossover credits

Clariant AG and Rhodia SA are two companies belonging to the chemical industry (see Figure 7.10).

In 2003, the Swiss multinational Clariant AG generated sales of Sfr8.5 billion, employing about 26 500 people. In the same year, the French multinational Rhodia SA reported sales of €5.453 billion, employing about 23 000 people across the world.

A hedge fund manager notices that between Clariant and Rhodia's bonds there is a spread differential that is not justified by fundamentals. These companies have similar financial indices, but according to the fund manager, Clariant's capital structure is more robust. The catalytic event for the deal closure was the narrowing of the credit spread between the two companies.

In 49 days, the fund manager generated a 4.55 % profit without using leverage.

Table 7.1

Deal	Purchase	Short Sale
Security	Clariant 4.25 % 2008	Rhodia 9.25 % 2011
Maturity date	15th March 2008	1st June 2011
Subordination	Senior	Subordinated
Spread	600 bps	560 bps
Entry price on 5th June 2003	0.8800	1.0125
Closing price on 24th July 2003	0.8700	0.9550

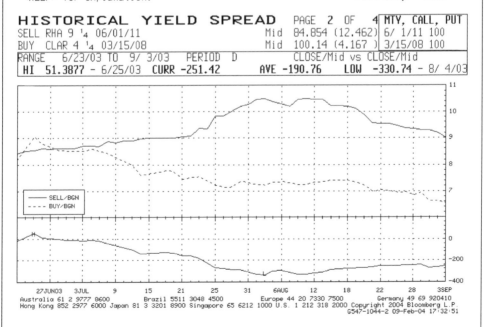

Figure 7.10 Credit pair trading. Used with permission from Bloomberg L.P.

7.8 CARRY TRADE

Carry trade brings you to the grave!
Old Stock Exchange adage

A carry trade consists in buying bonds with yields higher than the cost of money borrowed to purchase them. Clearly, a higher yield entails necessarily a higher risk, because as every investor knows all too well, "there is no free lunch" on the stock market.

A carry trade can be one of two types:

- *intra-curve*: for example, borrowing at the 3-month rate to purchase 10-year bonds;
- *inter-curve*: for example, borrowing in dollars in the United States and purchasing Turkish Treasuries in Turkish Liras. In this case, it is critical to assess the exchange rate risk to which the deal is exposed.

Carry trade is favored by a low cost of capital, when it is easy to obtain funds at a good interest rate. When short-term rates in the United States had reached 1 %, carry trade was widely used by hedge funds. Now that short-term interest rates are rising in the United States, profit opportunities offered by carry trade are shrinking.

7.9 BREAK-EVEN INFLATION TRADES

A break-even inflation trade is executed to take a view on the market's expectations in terms of inflation and it employs a relatively recent type of treasuries, whose yield depends on inflation.

Treasury Inflation Protection Securities (TIPS) are treasuries with a floating rate that depends on the inflation rate and are issued to protect investors from an inflation surge. The coupon's initial rate is fixed below the rate of treasuries having a similar maturity; later on, if inflation goes up, the yield of these securities will follow suit.

If the hedge fund manager believes that inflation will rise, the deal is established by buying TIPS and selling traditional treasuries short, so as to construct a position that is not correlated to interest rates. Vice versa, if the fund manager believes that inflation will go down, he will short sell TIPS and buy traditional treasuries.

If the treasuries used by the fund manager have a 10-year maturity, the fund manager is taking a directional view on the market's expectations in terms of the ten-year average inflation. Whereas, if the treasuries have a 5-year maturity, the deal's success or failure will depend on the average inflation rate over a five year period.

There are however some secondary risks, for example the empirical evidence that often TIPS underperform when approaching auctions of new securities, irrespective of how inflation is performing.

Notice that the break-even inflation trade is a way to take a directional position on a macroeconomic variable such as inflation.

A hedge fund manager buys French Treasuries (OAT) and short sells inflation-linked OAT. It is a directional position on inflation trends, whereby the fund manager will profit if inflation in France goes down. Should inflation rise in France, the fund manager will suffer a loss.

7.10   CROSS-CURRENCY RELATIVE VALUE TRADE

The basic idea underlying this type of deal is that there is one single probability that a given company defaults in a given period of time, irrespective of whether the probability is high or low.

Let's consider for example dollar denominated GM bonds 6.875 % 09/2011 and euro denominated GM bonds 5.375 % 06/2011. There is one single probability that General Motors may default by 2011, irrespective of whether we deem this probability to be high or low.

Therefore, each bond issued by General Motors should pay a credit premium reflecting the default risk and two bonds due in 2011 should be consistently priced, as they are both exposed to the same default risk. If the two bonds embed two different probabilities of default, there is an arbitrage opportunity.

To clarify this deal, we can use the yield spread between the bond and a "risk-free" treasury with the same denomination: a US Treasury Bond for the US dollar denominated GM bond and a German Bund for the euro denominated GM bond. This is the so called credit spread and can be considered as an approximation of the risk or probability of default.

Figure 7.11 shows the credit spread of the two GM bonds, the dollar and the euro denominated.

In theory the spreads should be similar, but there are various reasons explaining the disparity (note that data quality for the dollar denominated GM bond 6.875 % 09/2011 is poor, therefore do not worry about bearish dips):

- the bonds have slightly different maturities (about three months);
- the bonds are traded in different time zones;
- the bonds are held and traded by a different investor base;
- the bonds have different funding costs.

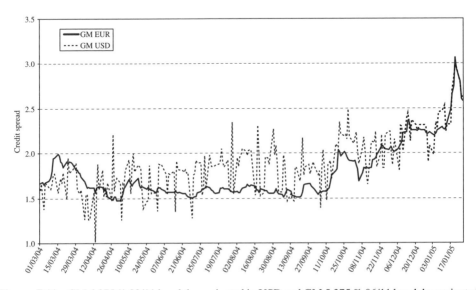

Figure 7.11   GM 6.875 % 09/11 bond denominated in USD and GM 5.375 % 06/11 bond denominated in euro (percentages)

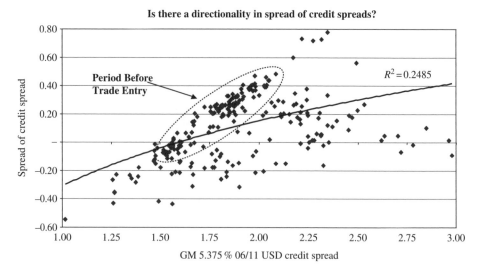

Figure 7.12   GM 6.875 % 09/11 USD spread minus GM 5.375 % 06/11 EUR spread, with two week moving average, versus GM 5.375 % 06/11 USD spread (percentages)

The behavior of a different investor base can also explain the different performance, therefore it is important to test the direction of the "spread of credit spreads".

Figure 7.12 shows the "spread of credit spreads" with respect to the spread level on the GM debt, using the dollar denominated GM bond 6.875 % 09/2011 as an approximation for the general performance of GM debt spreads.

When analyzing Figure 7.12, you may note that the "spread of credit spreads" seems to deteriorate when the spread on the dollar denominated GM bond 6.875 % 09/2011 widens. The best data adjustment is obtained with a logarithmic trendline, but the R^2 indicator is low, therefore the adjustment of square lows to a logarithmic equation is not suited to representing this amount across the whole period (from 27th February 2004 to 26th January 2005). However, note that in the period preceding the deal opening the directional movement appears stronger.

In this case the hedge fund manager has to make a decision because the spreads tend to widen: either he accepts the risk, or he has to give up an attractive position.

Despite the slope of the trendline being slightly supportive of this idea, the hedge fund manager believes that the directional movement cannot persist, i.e., he believes that if the spread on the dollar denominated GM bond 6.875 % 09/2011 widens for some fundamental reason, the spread on the euro denominated GM bond 5.375 % 06/2011 should also widen.

The hedge fund manager is aware that euro denominated bonds do not have as solid an investor base as dollar denominated bonds, which suggests that euro denominated bonds could show a sharper reaction to bad news.

This shows how large and persistent divergences can offer arbitrage opportunities, since it is possible to construct a position with the following characteristics:

- no currency exposure;
- no interest rate exposure;
- no risk associated with the bond issuer default (irrespective of the likelihood assigned to this event).

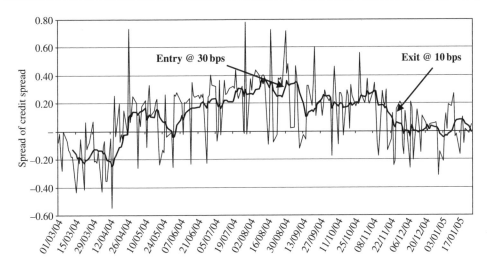

Figure 7.13 GM 6.875 % 09/11 USD spread minus GM 5.375 % 06/11 EUR spread with the two weeks moving average (percentages)

Figure 7.13 shows the "spread of credit spreads" and the entry and exit levels of the position established by the hedge fund manager: long on the dollar denominated GM bond 6.875 % 09/2011 (hedged with a short position on US Treasury Bonds) and short on the euro denominated GM bond 5.375 % 06/2011 (hedged with a long position on German Bunds).

In this case the position was successful and gained 20 bps, but there is always the risk that the spread goes on widening.

In theory, the deal could be held to expiration in 2011 and in this case profit would be guaranteed; but the funding cost might be unsustainable, it could erode profit, it could make it unbearable to carry out a daily mark to market, and it may tie up excessively the hedge fund capital.

Therefore, this example is not a true arbitrage, but rather a good opportunity on the relative value of two correlated securities; an opportunity, however, that has to be analyzed and executed with great care.

7.11   TREASURIES OVER EURODOLLARS (TED) SPREAD OR INTERNATIONAL CREDIT SPREAD

In the deal called "TED spread", the hedge fund manager takes a long position on US Treasury Bonds and a short position on eurodollar contracts having the same maturity.

Also, a TED spread in a broad sense is an investment in government bonds hedged with swaps denominated in the same currency. TED spreads seek to profit from the yield difference between government bonds and the LIBOR rate with equal maturity.

7.12   LEVERAGED LOANS

A bank loan is a private contract priority claim on all or some of the borrowers' assets between a bank syndicate (lenders) and a private or public corporation (borrower). Bank loans are the most senior obligations in the borrower's capital structure. A bank loan is a variable-rate instrument and therefore has a low sensitivity to interest rates.

A leveraged loan is a bank loan made to a highly leveraged company. Leveraged loans are syndicated bank loans granted to non-investment grade borrowers. Leverage loans are typically issued in order to finance LBO, acquisitions, recapitalizations or internal growth. Because they are loans, in the case of default they have a greater recovery value than bonds. The covenants are stricter than those of bonds and loans holders have more visibility and control of the company.

Compared to the high-yield bonds of a same issuer, the leverage loans have a higher rating, a higher recovery rate, are senior secured, are less volatile and are less liquid.

The leveraged loan market was closed to funds until a few years ago because it was a commercial bank business only. There are high barriers to entry because leverage loans primary deals are on an invitation only basis and so the hedge fund must have relationships with major underwriters and private equity firms. The hedge fund has to carry out a detailed due diligence for each trade.

Surprisingly, the leveraged loans market is larger than the high-yield bond market, as shown in Figure 7.14. The benchmark commonly used to evaluate the performances of leveraged loans is the CSFB Leveraged Loan Index. Historical returns have been very positive over the last ten years with a low price volatility. From 1992 to 2004 the CSFB Leveraged Loans Index had an annual return of +6.75 % with a 2.42 % annual volatility.

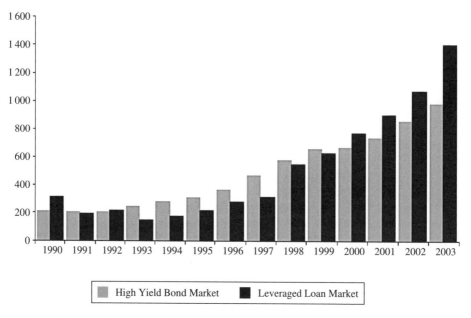

Figure 7.14 Size of the high-yield and leveraged loan markets (data in billion dollars from 1990 to 2003). Source: CSFB, Global Leveraged Finance Research

Amadeus was formed in 1987 by Air France, Iberia, Lufthansa and SAS. The Company operates a global distribution system ("GDS") for travel service providers. The Amadeus system is a computerized reservation system that enables providers to disseminate information about schedules, availability, pricing and also ticketing for these services. The Company also offers IT services, inventory management, reservation management and departure control to the airline industry. In addition, it offers web-enhanced solutions to airlines and online travel agents as well as travel services to consumers through its online travel agencies. A GDS serves as a liaison between two major sets of customers: travel service providers and subscribers (i.e. Travel Agents). The GDS charges the travel service provider a small fee for every booking made using the GDS. Subscribers pay a subscription fee in order to use the GDS, which is offset by incentive fees that they receive from the GDS in return for utilizing their content. The business is therefore driven by volume of travel more than price of travel.

In April 2005, a hedge fund was invited to participate in the €3.4 billion financing for the acquisition of Amadeus by a private equity firm. The hedge fund manager believed that the deal was very attractive from both an equity and debt perspective but not likely to be well received by the market due to the complexity of business and market timing.

The hedge fund went long Amadeus B and C loans but decided to wait before investing in the secondary market. The loan traded down 99.5 then briefly to 99 in the first day of trading. The hedge fund manager went long at an average price of 99.25. During the first few days the loan traded to above par. Following contract wins, the loan has traded up to 100.75.

The downside risk is primarily related to credit risk. Amadeus had long-term contracts and was integrated with its customers. In less than six months, Amadeus had already won a significant proportion of the market share gains expected over a four year business plan. Major airlines continued to be shareholders and senior secured loans have high recovery rates. Significant subordinated debt and equity cushion of approximately 40 %. Liquidity is typically lower than bonds. However, the hedge fund position remained relatively small.

The hedge fund entered at an average price of 99.25 in July 2005 and sold the position at 100.75 in September 2005. The return has been +1.5 % in three months.

7.13 STRATEGY'S HISTORICAL PERFORMANCE ANALYSIS

Let's analyze the historical behavior of this strategy based on the monthly returns of the CS/Tremont Fixed Income Arbitrage Index. Again, the past performance of a given investment is not necessarily indicative of a future return for the same investment. Still, we believe it is useful to examine historical data to understand which scenarios are favorable to this strategy and which are not.

The statistical analysis of the CS/Tremont Fixed Income Arbitrage Index between 1994 and 2004 produces the results shown in Table 7.2.

The Value at Risk (1 month, 99 %) means that "we have a 99 % probability of not losing more than −3.3 % of the investment in the next month". Instead we have observed a monthly performance of −7.0 %. There is nothing wrong because, as usual, we must read statistics

Table 7.2

	CS/Tremont Fixed Income Arbitrage	Morgan Stanley Capital International World in US$	JP Morgan Global Government Bond Global International
Value at Risk (1 month, 95 %)	−1.3 %	−6.4 %	−1.9 %
Value at Risk (1 month, 99 %)	−3.3 %	−10.4 %	−3.6 %
Best month Performance	+2.0 %	+8.9 %	+7.0 %
Average Performance in positive months	+1.0 %	+3.2 %	+1.6 %
Worst month Performance	−7.0 %	−13.5 %	−5.1 %
Average Performance in negative months	−1.1 %	−3.5 %	−1.0 %
% Positive months	81 %	61 %	57 %
Compound Annual Growth Rate (CAGR)	+6.9 %	+6.3 %	+5.4 %
Annualized monthly volatility	3.8 %	14.2 %	6.2 %
Skewness	−3.25	−0.60	0.65
Kurtosis	17.03	0.59	2.21
Largest drawdown*	−12.5 %	−48.4 %	−8.6 %
Duration of the largest drawdown in months	6	30	4
Time to recovery** in months	13	n.a.	9
Drawdown start	31st May 1998	30th Apr. 2000	28th Feb. 1994
Drawdown end	31st Oct. 1998	30th Sep. 2002	31st May 1994

* The largest drawdown is defined as the maximum value of any "peak to trough decline" over the specified period. The subsequent minimum is not determined until it has reached a new high.
** Time to recovery is the time necessary to recover from the largest drawdown.

very carefully. The distribution of monthly returns is asymmetric (Skewness equal to −3.25) with fat tails (Kurtosis greater than 3) and this implies that we cannot use the VaR to estimate an extreme value of the distribution, because we need many more observations.

The percentage of positive months is very high (81 %) and the average performance in positive months is +1 %.

The performance has been positive, with an annualized return of 6.9 % between 1994 and 2004, with a low volatility (3.8 %).

The largest drawdown has been significant (−12.5 %) and lasted for six months. Then the index needed more than one year (13 months) to recover the losses.

Figure 7.15 shows the monthly returns of the CS/Tremont Fixed Income Arbitrage Index from 1994 to 2004.

Figure 7.16 illustrates the historical performance as a function of risk of the CS/Tremont Fixed Income Arbitrage Index between 1994 and 2004. The concentration ellipsoid shows that historically there was a consistent generation of positive returns with a low volatility.

Figure 7.17 shows that between 1994 and 2004 there were three "underwater" dips for hedge funds. The chart must be analyzed taking drawdown data into consideration: throughout the drawdown and the time to recovery period, the hedge funds adopting this strategy were under the high water mark. (See the Chapter 1, Section 1.8, for more details on the setup and meaning of Figures 7.16 and 7.17.) The first dip was the unexpected interest rate rise

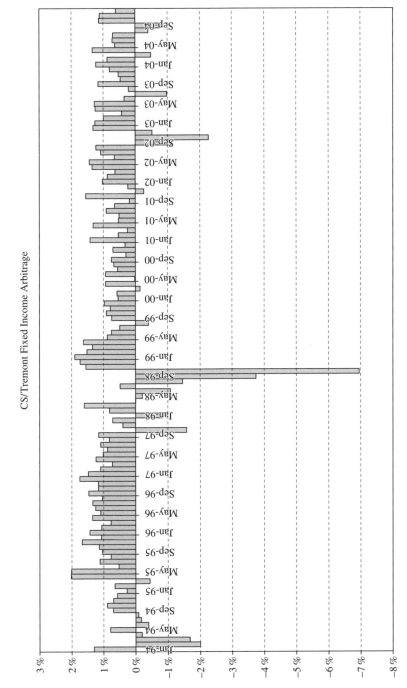

CS/Tremont Fixed Income Arbitrage

Figure 7.15 Monthly returns of CS/Tremont Fixed Income Arbitrage from 1994 to 2004. Source: CS/Tremont Index LLC, www.hedgeindex.com. Copyright © 2006, Credit Suisse/Tremont Index LLC. All rights reserved*

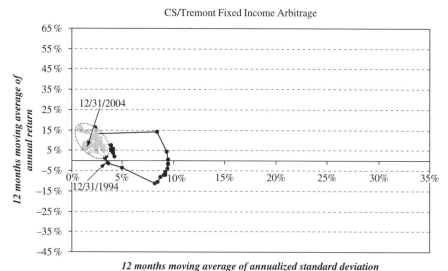

Figure 7.16 Historical performance trend of return as a function of risk for CS/Tremont Fixed Income Arbitrage from 1994 to 2004. Source: CS/Tremont Index LLC, www.hedgeindex.com. Copyright © 2006, Credit Suisse/Tremont Index LLC. All rights reserved*

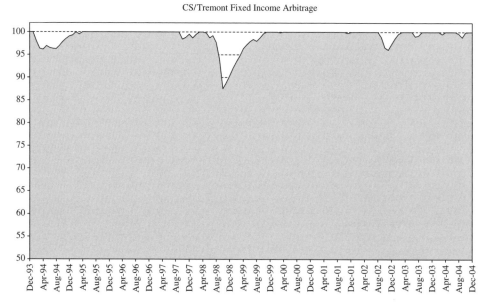

Figure 7.17 Underwater periods for CS/Tremont Fixed Income Arbitrage from 1994 to 2004. Source: CS/Tremont Index LLC, www.hedgeindex.com. Copyright © 2006, Credit Suisse/Tremont Index LLC. All rights reserved*

started in February 1994 by the US Federal Reserve. Then, in August 1998 there was a strong *flight-to-quality* move caused by Russia's default. The final dip came in Summer 2002 when, following the disclosure of the accounting frauds in Adelphia and Worldcom, credit spreads on corporate bonds widened, causing big losses across all credit-oriented strategies.

7.14 CONCLUSIONS

In an actual arbitrage, the fund manager tries to neutralize the interest rate exposure and profit from the identified price inconsistencies, whereas in directional trading the fund manager tries to anticipate correctly interest rate changes, getting close to typical macro-management trades.

In pure arbitrage low hanging fruits have already been picked, whereas in directional trades there are plenty of opportunities.

The most promising areas in fixed income arbitrage are yield curve arbitrage, long/short credit and, as we will discuss in more detail in the following chapters, structured finance and mortgage-backed securities arbitrage.

The EMBI+ Index and the JP Morgan High-Yield Spread to Worst shows that credit spreads are at historically low levels both on corporate bonds and on sovereign emerging market bonds.

The huge amount of liquidity in search of yield, which has been created all over the world by the accommodative policy of central banks, seems to have sustained the high prices for low quality bonds. Often, the risk premia for corporate bonds or emerging market bonds seems really unattractive. A hedge fund manager once said: "It is funny how some fund managers have no problem investing other people's money in countries that they do not have the courage to visit".

The likely widening of credit spreads is a difficult scenario for hedge funds specialized in fixed income arbitrage. As already explained, credit derivatives offer investors the chance to express negative views on credits and to benefit from the widening of spreads. Instead, it's a more favorable environment for those managers with low credit exposure in special situations using both floating rate and bank debt to protect their portfolios from a widening of spreads and interest rate risk.

It is difficult to predict when there will be a credit spread widening. It's easier to say that going forward there will be more volatility in the markets of corporate bonds and emerging market bonds.

8

Strategies on CDOs

A Collateralized Debt Obligation (CDO) is a diversified set of similar financial instruments where credit risk is allocated differently among the various tranches making up the CDO. It gives investors exposure to a customized slice (tranche) of the credit risk of a selected portfolio of reference credits.

Many different financial assets can be used to collateralize a CDO: asset-backed securities (ABS), corporate bonds, bank loans, emerging markets bonds, credit default swaps, etc.

The CDO market has reached a size of $583 billion (Figure 8.1), representing 15 % of the ABS market. According to some observers, the CDO market is still at its infancy and gives rise to many investment opportunities for the more experienced fund managers.

In more detail, a Collateralized Debt Obligation is a basket of bonds or Credit Default Swaps that is cut in different tranches and then sold to investors. Every tranche has a different credit rating and pays a different interest rate. The senior tranche, which has claims to cash flow generated by the underlying securities, has a credit rating of AAA. This is followed by the mezzanine tranche and the equity tranche (completely different from an equity!), which absorbs the eventual losses caused by a default of the underlying securities and receives payments only after all the other tranches have been paid.

In Figure 8.2, the cash flows generated by the pool of securities backing the CDO are portrayed using "Le Jet d'eau de Genève", symbol of the town of Geneva in Switzerland.

The senior bond tranche receives the cash flows first and therefore has a higher rating and pays a lower interest rate compared to the other tranches. The equity tranche gets only the residual cash-flows: The lower the rating of the tranche, the greater the return. Each CDO tranche has a default rate, the lowest for senior tranches and the highest for equity tranches. The definition of a default can be problematic and the rating agencies do not provide it.

The market uses ratings migration to proxy the risk of the various CDO tranches. We can consider downgrades to ratings below B3 as a proxy for "default": i.e., Caa1, Caa2, Caa3, Ca, and C. The Ca and C ratings are traditionally reserved by Moody's for defaulted credits.

Table 8.1 shows the cumulative percent of "defaulted" CDO tranches by rating.

Across all types of CDOs, 0.2 % of Aaa tranches have been downgraded below B3. In other rating categories, the figures are 1.8 % of Aa tranches, 3.7 % of A tranches, 17.1 % of Baa tranches, 21.8 % of Ba tranches and 59.4 % of B tranches. This is the "lifetime" default rate of CDOs that have been outstanding between one and ten years, for a weighted average of four years.

CDOs are a clever credit alchemy whereby low rated bonds are pooled in a super-structure that is subdivided in order to create tranches with a higher credit rating than the constituent bonds. Starting from a pool of bonds that are non-investment grade and assigning different cash-flow allocation priorities to the different tranches making up the CDO, it is even possible to create a tranche with the highest AAA rating. How is this possible? Thanks to the very same principles on which insurance companies rely. The default

100% = 1 839 billion dollars

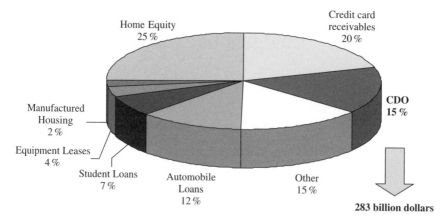

Figure 8.1 ABS Outstanding by Major Types of Credit (as of 31st March 2005). Source: Federal Reserve System, The Bond Market Association

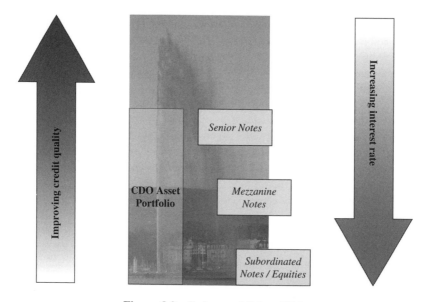

Figure 8.2 Cash waterfall in a CDO

risk of the bonds contained in the CDO is not eliminated; it is only redistributed across the various tranches depending on the risk associated with the single tranches.

With CDOs, investors can participate in the profitability of the underlying financial assets at varying degrees of risk. For example, let's consider a pool of corporate loans collateralizing a CDO. Despite the time of economic recession, within the corporate loan pool a given percentage of companies will avoid financial problems and will pay down debts. Therefore, a given percentage of the corporate loan pool can be considered at very low risk, and can be assigned an AAA rating. In more favorable economic times for credit, a larger percentage

Table 8.1

CDO tranche rating	% of CDO tranche defaults in US
Aaa	0.2
Aa	1.8
A	3.7
Baa	17.1
Ba	21.8
B	59.4

Source: UBS calculations from Moody's rating data.

of corporate loans collateralizing the CDO will be paid down. Hence, a given percentage of the corporate loan pool can be considered as having an A rating and so on, down to the riskier tranches that have no rating.

The CDO Special Purpose Vehicle buys and holds the pool of assets underlying the CDO, also called CDO Asset Portfolio. The CDO Special Purpose Vehicle then issues the senior notes, the mezzanine notes and the subordinated/shares, with a decreasing claim priority along the cash-flow waterfall generated by the pool of assets backing the CDO. In addition to the CDO Trustee, acting as custodian bank for the portfolio of assets underlying the CDO, there is also the CDO Manager, i.e., a company managing the CDO's underlying asset portfolio in compliance with the agreements entered with the CDO SPV. The management can be active or passive and trading can be discretionary or predefined.

The returns of the equity tranche depend on possible trading profits or losses, on the performance of the assets making up the pool collateralizing the CDO, and therefore on possible defaults of securities in the portfolio and changes in the ratings of the CDO tranches.

CDOs are extremely complex investment vehicles, and they are not fully standardized, therefore investing in a CDO calls for a great expertise.

To value the different tranches making up a CDO, a hedge fund manager must set up a credit risk mathematical model, simulate cash-flows, monitor the CDO Manager's activity over time and have a good understanding of the intricacies of CDOs.

We analyze the offering memorandum of a CDO as an example of the complexity of these structured finance vehicles. The offering memorandum is 158 pages long and very complex. The CDO is structured as shown in Figure 8.3.

The issue of the following Notes of the CDO was authorized by resolution of the Board of Managing Directors of the CDO dated 24th June 2002:

- US$171 700 000 Class I Senior Secured Floating Rate Notes due 2009;
- US$103 000 000 Class II Senior Secured Floating Rate Notes due 2009;
- US$38 883 000 Class III Deferrable Interest Secured Floating Rate Notes due 2009;
- US$41 200 000 Class IV Deferrable Interest Secured Floating Rate Notes due 2009;
- US$103 000 000 Subordinated Notes due 2009.

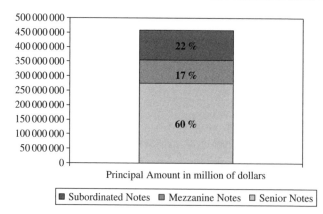

Principal Amount in million of dollars

☐ Subordinated Notes   ☐ Mezzanine Notes   ☐ Senior Notes

Tranche	Principal Amount in millions of dollars	Standard & Poor's Rating	Floating rate	Type of tranche
Class I Senior Secured Floating Rate Notes due 2009	171.700.000	AAA	3m USD LIBOR + 0.55 % yearly	Senior Notes
Class II Senior Secured Floating Rate Notes due 2009	103.000.000	AA	3m USD LIBOR + 0.85 % yearly	Senior Notes
Class III Deferrable Interest Secured Floating Rate Notes due 2009	38.883.000	A	3m USD LIBOR + 1.75 % yearly	Mezzanine Notes
Class IV Deferrable Interest Secured Floating Rate Notes due 2009	41.200.000	BBB	3m USD LIBOR + 3.50 % yearly	Mezzanine Notes
Subordinated Notes due 2009	103.000.000	not rated	3m USD LIBOR + 17 % yearly	Subordinated Notes

Figure 8.3   Example of a CDO structure

So the structure of the CDO is as follows:

- 22 % subordinated notes
- 17 % mezzanine notes
- 60 % senior notes.

The Senior Notes and the Mezzanine Notes are rated Notes.

The portfolio is comprised primarily of US dollar denominated Credit Default Swap Agreements and it is managed by the CDO Manager.

8.1   A BRIEF HISTORY OF CDOS

The first CDO created in 1987 had an underlying high-yield bond portfolio. In 1989, corporate loans and real estate loans were used in CDOs for the first time and the term "collateralized loan obligation" (CLO) was coined. Generally, CLOs are comprised of performing high-yield loans, but a few CLOs, even as far back as 1988, targeted distressed and non-performing loans. The first CDO with underlying emerging market bonds was first created in 1994.

In 1995, CDOs with underlying portfolios of residential mortgage-backed securities were first issued. CDOs with underlying portfolios of commercial mortgage-backed securities and asset-backed securities, or combinations of RMBS, CMBS, and ABS followed.

These CDOs have never found a universally recognized name: nevertheless, Moody's coined the term "resecuritizations".

It is important to note that the collateral diversity mentioned above, between 1987 through 1995, occurred while annual CDO issuance averaged $2 billion and never exceeded $4 billion. CDO issuance only took off in 1996, jumping to $38 billion in 1996, $82 billion in 1997, and $139 billion in 1998. The drop in CDO issuance in 2001 and 2002 was caused by a difficult corporate credit environment. As a result, corporate bond and loan-backed CDO issuance fell 50 % from $100 billion in 2000 to $50 billion in 2002. Since 2002, the steady annual increases in CDO issuance has been fueled by high-yield loan-backed CLOs and resecuritizations.

8.2 HEDGE FUND INVESTMENT STRATEGIES

Hedge funds invest in CDOs with three different strategies:

1. Carry trade;
2. Long/short structured credit;
3. Correlation trade.

These strategies enable hedge fund managers to express certain views on credit markets efficiently.

8.2.1 Carry Trade

This is the easiest and riskiest CDO strategy and consists of buying the equity tranche of CDOs. The return generated by the equity tranche depends on the leverage, the maturity and the composition of the basket of credit forming the CDO. Purchasing CDO equity tranches is equal to selling credit protection.

In June 2003, a hedge fund bought Fixed Income Senior Notes for a par value of $5.5 million (hereafter called simply "Notes") totaling $148 million. These Notes were part of the CDO tranche with the higher claim collateralized by a *private placement* of high-yield bonds carried out in 1998. The issuance also included another tranche of Senior Notes, characterized by a floating rate for a par value of $34 million.

The Notes subscribed by the hedge fund were due on August 2010 and paid a fixed 6.71 % yearly coupon. Technically the issue had defaulted, and the rating of the tranche subscribed by the hedge fund had deteriorated, going from AA3 in 1998 to Baa3 in 2002, turning into a "container" receiving all the capital and interest payments, which were used to pay Senior Notes first, both at a fixed and floating rate, and Subordinated Notes next.

At the time of purchase in June 2003, the par value of the Notes was $4.26 million and the hedge fund bought them for $3.63 million. The Notes were then bought for a price of 85.27 cents, at a substantial discount on the liquidation value of 94.73 cents.

At the time of purchase, the hedge fund had made a conservative assumption according to which 30 % of the high-yield bonds would default and the recovery rate would be of 28 %. As a result, the internal rate of return had been fixed at 13.64 %. The investment was expected to be paid back in 3.5–4 years.

At the time of purchase, the underlying portfolio comprised 117 high-yield bonds characterized by an average price of 74.97 cents, including defaulted securities. The initial analysis conducted by the hedge fund also included the expectation that over the short term the default rate of the collateral high-yield bonds would rise, only to decrease again during the residual life of the securities.

Two months after the Notes had been purchased by the hedge fund, $949 786 had been paid out in terms of capital redemptions for the underlying high-yield notes (accounting for more than 25 % of the initial original cost incurred by the hedge fund), against an initial estimate of $500 000. Over the same period, $142 808 worth of interest were also paid out. Moreover, the price of the Notes grew significantly with respect to the initial cost incurred by the hedge fund.

The improved performance of the collateral and the higher than expected capital redemptions generated a return on investment of 15.88 %, well above the estimated 13.64 %.

8.2.2 Long/short Structured Credit

This strategy's objective is to generate absolute returns, regardless of economic and market conditions such as credit spread moves and the general direction of interest rates. The strategy is naturally long credit and benefits from spread tightening. The effect of market spread widening on long positions can be offset by the manager's ability to short credits that widen more than the general market in a deteriorating environment. The fund employs fundamental credit analysis to determine long and short relative-value positions in different corporate credits. The fund expresses long views through the purchase of CDO equity tranches, and short views through the purchase of single-name Credit Default Swaps.

The long position in CDO equity tranches locks in positive carry. Furthermore, the ability of the hedge fund manager in performing the credit analysis on the companies underlying the CDO generates the trading ideas: a CDO is a basket of credits and the manager can choose inside this basket the credits he wants to be long or short. So the manager can take advantage of opportunities ranging from sector allocation, allocation to single companies and relative-value trading. Finally, the manager can limit the downside from spread widening through the long positions in credit default swaps.

The ideal portfolio built with long positions in CDO equity tranches and with long positions in CDS can have a convexity return profile: an instantaneous equal proportional shift in all spreads, assuming correlation remains constant, should have positive returns irrespective of spread moves.

The most difficult challenge for a hedge fund manager implementing this strategy is the ability to manage the correlation risk among the CDO tranches.

8.2.3 Correlation Trade

CDOs are a recent innovation that enable investors to buy (or sell) limited protection on credit portfolios. The protection attaches (and detaches) once the portfolio realizes certain default losses. The proper compensation for bearing this specialized risk depends not only on the individual portfolio credits, but also on their prospective dynamics, including their prospective interplay. People use the term "correlation" to discuss this interplay, and the term "correlation trading" to capture involvement in these tranched portfolio protection products.

In a correlation trade, credit protection is sold via the purchasing of CDO equity tranches delta-hedged with credit default swaps (CDS).

The correlation trade consists of assuming a long position in the equity tranche of a certain CDO and a simultaneous short position in the mezzanine tranche (or a more senior tranche) of the same CDO, in the attempt to take advantage of the spreads among the different tranches of the CDO. This way the hedge fund is long the implied correlation among the CDO tranches.

Note that the implied correlation is primarily a market-based factor, driven by the demand and supply of protection for each individual CDO tranche.

This trade has a positive carry, and returns can be generated if the credit spreads in the underlying portfolio move in a parallel way, that is, widen or shrink simultaneously.

The correlation trade is exposed to the risk of an unexpected default in the underlying CDO portfolio but, given that in 2005 the prevailing default rate is at historically low levels, many hedge fund managers are comfortable with assuming that risk.

Some investors are reluctant to embrace correlation trading as a model-driven arbitrage strategy.

On 4th May 2005, Tracinda Corp., a company that already owned about 4 % of General Motors, offered $870 million to acquire 4.95 % of General Motors, and GM shares at the end of the day jumped by 18.1 %.

On 5th May 2005, Standard & Poor's had downgraded the GM bonds (from BBB– to BB) to the status of "junk bond", maintaining a negative outlook.

This was a surprising capital structure movement, where the riskiest part of the capital, equities, jumped at a time when the less risky part of the capital, bonds, dropped (Figure 8.4).

Many hedge funds were positioned in a correlation trade: they had short positions (buy protection) in CDO senior tranches and long positions (sell protection) in CDO equity

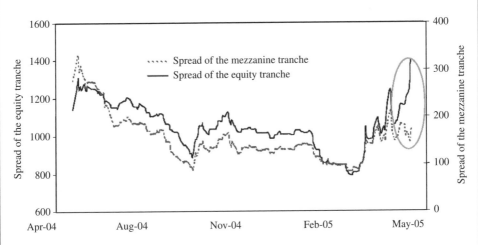

Figure 8.4 Widening of spread between mezzanine tranches and equity tranches in May 2005 (data in basis points)

tranches, delta-hedging with single-name CDS or iBoxx index. This correlation trade expected implied correlation to increase and had positive carry.

Because of the downgrade of GM, the equity tranche of many CDOs declined sharply while the mezzanine tranche soared because of a "fly to quality" movement. This means that the spreads moved in a non-parallel way. Merrill Lynch estimated that the CDO correlation trades in April lost 12 %, and for some hedge funds this loss was worsened by the use of leverage.

8.3   CONCLUSIONS

The important point to note is that these new strategies are relatively untried and untested in periods of market stress, and hence investors could underestimate certain risks, i.e. correlation.

9
Mortgage-Backed Securities Arbitrage

Home sweet loan.
Assonant to the saying:
Home sweet home.

In this chapter, we examine a special type of fixed income arbitrage based on a particular class of securities that are very popular on the US market: mortgage-backed securities (MBS).

A mortgage-backed security is the *securitization* of a set of mortgages collateralized by real estate. Through said securitization, the set of mortgages held by a financial institution is pooled and sold to investors. When a financial institution holds mortgages, pools them and sells units or certificates representing the pooled mortgages, the institution is said to have securitized the mortgages and issued a *pass-through* security, where the cash flows of the pooled mortgages pass from the originating entity to the owner of the *pass-through* security, after deducting the commissions charged by the originator.

To be eligible as underlying of MBS, mortgages must meet a number of minimum requirements, for example the loan maximum size, the required loan documentation, a given ceiling of the loan-to-value ratio, the demand for an insurance, if any, etc.

9.1 A BRIEF HISTORY OF MORTGAGE-BACKED SECURITIES

The practice of packaging mortgages into new securities backed by those pooled mortgages is relatively recent. In 1978 Bob Dall, trader of Salomon Brothers, and Stephen Joseph originated the first private issue of mortgages on behalf of Bank of America. In the autumn of 1981, the Congress approved a tax break that incentivized the securitization of mortgages. At the time, the only well staffed mortgage trading desk was at Salomon Brothers, and this company played a key role in the startup and development of the mortgage securitization market in the United States.

9.2 ORIGINATORS OF MORTGAGE-BACKED SECURITIES

In the United States, *pass-through* securities are issued by Ginnie Mae (Government National Mortgage Association), Fannie Mae (Federal National Mortgage Association) and Freddie Mac (Federal Home Loan Mortgage Corporation). *Pass-through* securities issued by Ginnie Mae and Fannie Mae are called MBS, whereas those issued by Freddie Mac are called *Participation Certificates.*

Ginnie Mae is a government-owned corporation, which is an agency of the US Department of Housing and Urban Development and as such backed by the guarantee of the US government, but Fannie Mae and Freddie Mac are government-sponsored corporations. Although they do not enjoy an explicit guarantee from the US government, they have been set up by the Congress, which is their major shareholder, to contribute to the realization of an American dream: every American being the owner of his or her home.

These agencies issue bonds using the proceeds to purchase mortgages that banks had previously extended to property owners. Thus, commercial banks can securitize mortgages and sell them to these agencies; once the loans have been sold out, banks have cleaned out their accounts to make room to new mortgages extended to people willing to buy a home directly (Figure 9.1).

The agencies pool in a trust the mortgages backed by newly purchased property and issue securities that represent a direct ownership in the trust. Interest payment takes place through (*pass-through*) the commercial banks that had extended the mortgages to get directly to the trust holders.

The agencies profit from the different return between the mortgages they buy and the bonds they issue and sell to investors. One may wonder about the purpose of all this sophistication and complication of mortgage securitizations. The answer is to transfer risk from one market operator that doesn't want to carry the risk to the other that is available to accept the risk.

Fannie Mae and Freddie Mac were granted the top rating for "Senior Long-Term Debt" both by Moody's Investors Service and by Standard & Poor's, even though the US government does not guarantee their bonds directly. Each corporation, however, has a $2250 million credit line open with the US Treasury Department, and is subject to the supervision of the Office of Federal Housing Enterprise Oversight.

At present, market operators are debating whether the US government guarantee towards Fannie Mae and Freddie Mac should be given consideration or not. Fannie Mae is a private company whose stocks are listed on the New York Stock Exchange and belong to the Standard & Poor's 500 index.

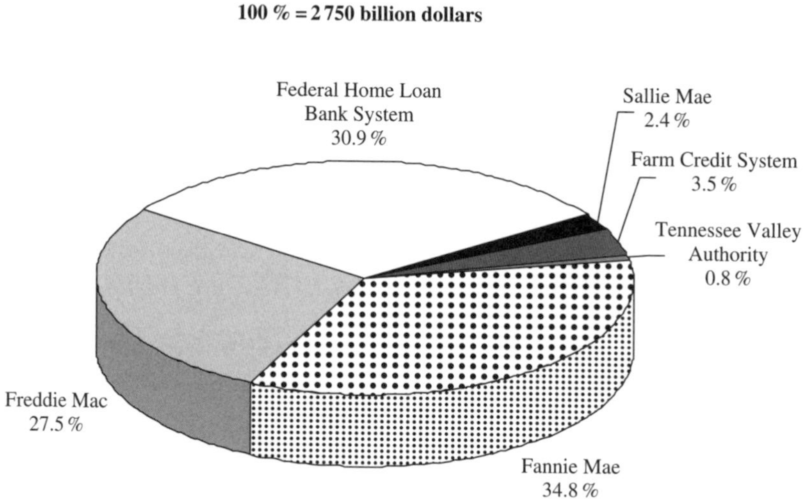

100 % = 2 750 billion dollars

Figure 9.1 Total Federal Agency Debt outstanding as at 30th September 2004 (percentages). Source: Federal Agencies

9.3   THE INDUSTRY OF MORTGAGE-BACKED SECURITIES

The size of the MBS market may cause surprise. The market capitalization of these securities, unknown to most investors, is even greater than that of the US Treasuries. However, the trade volume is smaller than US Treasuries, meaning that MBS are less liquid than US Treasury securities.

The MBS market in the USA was running at $5400 billion at the end of June 2004. This amount well exceeds the amount of all US Treasury Bonds outstanding, which at the same date was $3800 billion[1] (Figure 9.2).

Commercial banks operate on the *primary market*, where mortgages are originated and funds are extended to home-buyers, but they also sell mortgage securitizations on the so-called *secondary market*, to investors such as Fannie Mae, Freddie Mac, pension funds, insurance companies and other institutional investors, like hedge funds. Figure 9.3 shows investors in MBS.

There are different types of MBS, which are described in the following sections:

- *pass-through* securities;
- collateralized mortgage obligations;
- stripped MBS or "Interest Only" (IO) securities and "Principal Only" (PO) securities.

9.3.1   Pass-through Securities

Pass-through securities are a type of MBS allowing investors to receive the cash flows generated by pools of mortgages expressly "repackaged" by the originating company. They have been called "pass-through" because they pass income from debtors through the intermediary

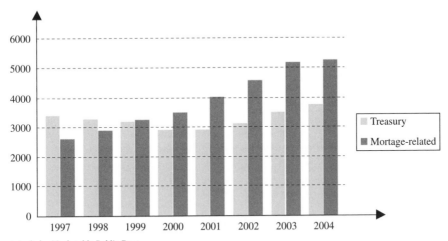

* Includes Marketable Public Dept
* Includes Agency MBS, Agency CMO and Private-Label MBS
  2004 data are updated at the third quarter

Figure 9.2   US Treasury Securities Outstanding* versus Mortgage-Related Securities Outstanding** (data in billion dollars). Source: US Treasury, Federal Agencies, The Bond Market Association

---

[1] *The Economist*, 13th November 2004, "Insecurities"; www.bondmarkets.com.

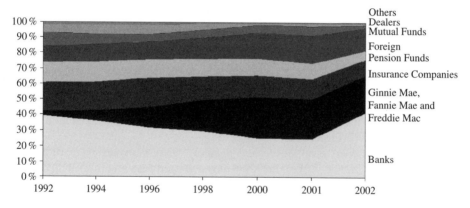

Figure 9.3 Investors in MBS from 1992 to 2002 (percentages). Source: UBS, Morgan Stanley

to investors. Typically, the cash flows produced by an MBS are monthly and are generated by the pool of mortgages underlying the MBS.

In the United States, most *pass-through* securities have the following characteristics:

- 30 year maturity;
- fixed rate;
- monthly payments;
- possibility to repay the principal in advance at any time and with no penalty;
- constant installments comprising an interest component and a return of principal;
- total amortization.

The cash flows generated by a *pass-through* security depend on the cash flows of the underlying pool of mortgages and can vary substantially depending on the prepayment rate, that is, the rate at which mortgages can be prepaid.

9.3.2   Collateralized Mortgage Obligations

Collateralized mortgage obligations (CMO) are groups of MBS issued for the first time in 1983 by Freddie Mac. Whereas with a *pass-through* security the investor is exposed to the risk of prepayment, CMOs envisage different bond tranches with a series of rules whereby the prepayment risk is allocated differently among the various tranches.

These securities have become very popular among investors: consider that in 1997 about 70 % of *pass-through* securities were collaterals for CMOs.

9.3.3   "Interest Only" Securities and "Principal Only" Securities

Payments in mortgages are made up of an interest component and a return of principal. In stripped MBS, interest and returns of principal associated with the pool of underlying mortgages are allocated differently to the "Interest Only" tranche and to the "Principal Only" tranche. The "Interest Only" tranche is paid only the interest originated by the underlying pooled mortgages, whereas the "Principal Only" tranche is paid only returns of principal.

The relative value of the two tranches changes as a function of the rate at which home-owners repay the mortgage in advance or later with respect to the predetermined payment plan.

If mortgage rates go down, an increasing number of home-owners will refinance their mortgages at lower rates, driving down the value of IO securities. Since the changes in the price of IO and PO securities are correlated to interest rates, the purchase of IO or PO is equivalent to taking a directional position on interest rates. To eliminate this directional bias, hedge fund managers can hedge their position with treasuries that usually have the characteristic of moving in the opposite direction with respect to MBS.

Consider that if treasury rates go down, their value increases. Vice versa, if mortgage and treasury rates go up, mortgages are not refinanced and the value of IO goes up, but the value of treasuries goes down. With a correct hedge relation between IO and treasuries, it is possible to wipe out the position's dependence on interest rates and take advantage of possible inconsistencies in the valuation of IO securities.

9.4 THE SENSITIVITY OF MORTGAGE-BACKED SECURITIES TO INTEREST RATES

Unlike traditional bonds, the amount of cash flow generated by an MBS is uncertain because every home-buyer entering any one of the mortgages that have been repackaged into the MBS has the option of refinancing the mortgage or prepaying it. Of course, mortgagors will be induced to refinance their mortgage only if interest rates are lower than they were when the mortgage was originated.

As already mentioned, MBS are highly sensitive to the general performance of interest rates. Unlike *plain vanilla* bonds, interest rates have an additional effect on MBS, due to the prepayment rate. If interest rates go below the mortgage rate, mortgagors will be induced to prepay the mortgage and to refinance it at lower rates, so the prepayment rate will exceed the initial assumptions on which the MBS valuation was based. In the case of lowering interest rates, the increase in the price of *pass-through* securities is lower compared to that of a *plain vanilla* bond. If interest rates go down, there is a *contraction risk,* in that the duration of the MBS gets shorter.

On the contrary, in the case of rising interest rates, the price of *pass-through* securities drops more than that of *plain vanilla* bonds because higher rates tend to slow down the prepayment rate, thus increasing the amount invested at the nominal rate, which is lower than the market rate. At the same time, mortgagors would get no benefit from prepaying the mortgage, thus the prepayment rate will decrease more than the initial assumptions upon which the MBS valuation was based, and the MBS duration gets longer. In this case there is an *extension risk*.

Figure 9.4 shows the refinancing index in the United States, as calculated by the Mortgage Bankers Association, which is an indicator of the refinancing activities on mortgages.

The *prepayment rate* – the rate at which mortgagors carry out prepayments compared to initial assumptions – varies as a function of interest rates, but it depends on many other factors as well, including:

- the interest rate applied on mortgages, which determines the attractiveness of refinancing. If the mortgage rates prevailing on the market drop below the rate paid by home-owners, mortgagors with a fixed rate mortgage will find it more convenient to pay it off before due and open a new mortgage at a lower rate. Of course, this makes sense only if the saving obtained on interest payments is greater than the legal expenses to refinance the mortgage (Figure 9.5);

- the interest rate trend since the mortgage origination;
- relocations, deaths, disasters;
- the characteristics of the mortgage pool underlying the MBS, for example MBS that are backed by residential mortgages will have a lower prepayment rate compared to MBS that are backed by commercial mortgages;
- some seasonal factors;
- mortgage age, because a pool of mortgages that has been newly issued is expected to have a lower prepayment rate compared to an older pool of mortgages, the interest rate being equal, since somebody who has just moved over is less likely to do it again shortly;
- the general economic performance, which affects the credit risk of households with a mortgage. A sustained economic growth also drives a growth in the turnover of residential development due to the increased opportunities for job relocations. The most indicative indices to determine the health ticket of the US real estate market are the number of existing home sales, the number of new home sales and the development of new homes;
- low interest rates that make the purchase of new homes more accessible;
- the trend of real estate prices.

The multiplicity of factors makes it difficult to create a robust and reliable model to estimate the prepayment rate and thus valuate MBS.

We are now going to introduce a very important concept: bond convexity. *Convexity* is the rate of change of the mean duration as interest rates change. Convexity is positive if,

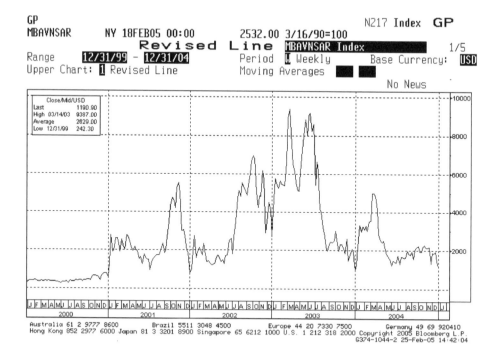

On 03/16/1990 the index started from a conventional value of 100.

Figure 9.4 Refinancing index in the United States, as calculated by the Mortgage Bankers Association, from 2000 to 2004. Source: Mortgage Bankers Association. Used with permission from Bloomberg L.P.

Figure 9.5 Mortgage rates with 30 year maturity and fixed rate in the US (percentages from 1990 to 2004). Source: Mortgage Bankers Association; www.mortgagebankers.org

when interest rates go up, the duration gets shorter, and vice versa, when interest rates drop, it gets longer. Convexity is negative if the duration gets longer when interest rates go up, and gets shorter when interest rates go down.

Typically, MBS show a *negative convexity*, because they are like callable bonds and if interest rates rise, prepayment is less profitable, thus leading to a lengthening of the duration of MBS.

9.5 ARBITRAGE ON MORTGAGE-BACKED SECURITIES

Like convertible bonds, MBS are also hybrid securities that make an ideal arbitrage target for specialized hedge fund managers. From an investor's perspective, an MBS is a fixed-income security embedding a prepayment option. Home-owners can choose to prepay all or part of their loan at any time throughout the entire mortgage. This option makes the mortgage's future cash flow, and therefore also the MBS value, uncertain.

Traditional models are not suited to valuating the prepayment option embedded in MBS. Specialized MBS arbitrageurs use proprietary models to estimate the present value of future MBS cash flows, i.e., to estimate the option-adjusted spread.

The *option-adjusted spread* (OAS) of an MBS is the average spread above the yield curve of Treasury Bonds, and makes the market price of MBS equal to the estimate of the present value of future MBS cash flows. In other words, it is the security's incremental value with respect to Treasury Bonds having a matching maturity, adjusted for the interest rate volatility and the impact of possible MBS prepayments. The higher the option-adjusted spread, the cheaper the MBS.

MBS are therefore classified by option-adjusted spreads, and the MBS that offer the highest OAS values are purchased and hedged with short sales of Treasury Bonds of equal duration or with the sale of Treasury Bond futures, so as to establish a position with zero duration, namely, a position hedged against the interest rate risk. As the spreads between the long and short positions are generally relatively small, hedge fund managers specializing in this strategy can use leverage, which exposes the fund manager to the risk that brokers might make a margin call, forcing the fund manager to liquidate some positions at unfavorable prices at the worst possible time. MBS securities are in fact highly sensitive to treasury yield curve shifts.

MBS arbitrage strategies adopted by hedge funds can be classified based on the different types of MBS on which fund managers decide to operate, as they display different characteristics in terms of risk, yield and liquidity.

For example, a fund manager establishes a complex arbitrage by constructing the following three positions:

- purchase of 30-year FNMA 5.5 % MBS;
- sale of interest rate swaps along all the interest rate curve (2, 5, 10 and 30 years);
- purchase of options as a hedge against the prepayment risk.

9.6   RISK FACTORS

Hedging MBS by short selling treasuries leaves the fund manager exposed to many risks, foremost the liquidity risk, because the liquidity of treasuries is better than the liquidity of MBS as we saw in Figure 7.2: in a *flight-to-quality* move, like the one in August 1998, losses can be heavy.

As already explained above, other risks associated with MBS are the extension and contraction risks. The main macro-economic risks are sudden and unexpected changes in the following factors:

1. interest rate levels;
2. yield curve shape;
3. implied volatility of interest rates;
4. liquidity and swap spreads;
5. prepayment rate;
6. bankruptcy rates.

Hedge fund investors specializing in MBS arbitrages must put special care in the valuation criteria used to price MBS. In fact, MBS are traded over-the-counter. Clearly, it is important that the valuation method adopted by a hedge fund administrator remain unchanged over time.

9.7   STRATEGY'S HISTORICAL PERFORMANCE ANALYSIS

There is no specific CS/Tremont Index associated with the mortgage-backed securities arbitrage. We will resort to an index calculated by Hedge Fund Research, Inc., namely, the HFRI Fixed Income Mortgage-Backed Index, an index that is equal weighted, meaning that the index performance is obtained from the arithmetical mean of the hedge fund performances making up the index.

Let's analyze the historical behavior of this strategy based on the monthly returns of the HFRI Fixed Income Mortgage-Backed Index. Again, the past performance of a given investment is not necessarily indicative of a future return for the same investment. Still, we believe it is useful to examine historical data to understand which scenarios are favorable to this strategy and which are not.

The statistical analysis of the HFRI Fixed Income Mortgage-Backed Index between 1994 and 2004 produces the results shown in Table 9.1.

The Value at Risk (1 month, 99%) means that "we have a 99% probability of not losing more than −4.6% of the investment in the next month". Instead we have observed a monthly performance of −9.2%. There is nothing wrong because, as usual, we must read statistics very carefully. The distribution of monthly returns is asymmetric (Skewness equal to −4.14) and with fat tails (Kurtosis greater than 3) and this implies that we cannot use the VaR to estimate an extreme value of the distribution, because we need many more observations.

The mortgage-backed securities arbitrage strategy historically displays a very high percentage of positive months (89%) and the average performance of positive months is +1.2%. The performance has been very strong, with an annualized return of 10.1% between 1994 and 2004, and a low volatility (4.7%).

The largest drawdown was important (−13.5%), lasted for seven months and was recovered over a very long period (28 months).

Figure 9.6 shows the monthly returns of the HFRI Fixed Income Mortgage-Backed Index from 1994 to 2004. Figure 9.7 illustrates the historical performance as a function

Table 9.1

	HFRI Fixed Income Mortgage-Backed Index	Morgan Stanley Capital International World in US$	JP Morgan Global Government Bond Global International
Value at Risk (1 month, 95%)	−1.1%	−6.4%	−1.9%
Value at Risk (1 month, 99%)	−4.6%	−10.4%	−3.6%
Best month Performance	+3.3%	+8.9%	+7.0%
Average Performance in positive months	+1.2%	+3.2%	+1.6%
Worst month Performance	−9.2%	−13.5%	−5.1%
Average Performance in negative months	−1.9%	−3.5%	−1.0%
% Positive months	89%	61%	57%
Compound Annual Growth Rate (CAGR)	+10.1%	+6.3%	+5.4%
Annualized monthly volatility	4.7%	14.2%	6.2%
Skewness	−4.14	−0.60	0.65
Kurtosis	25.40	0.59	2.21
Largest drawdown*	−13.5%	−48.4%	−8.6%
Duration of the largest drawdown in months	7	30	4
Time to recovery** in months	28	n.a.	9
Drawdown start	30th Apr. 1998	30th Apr. 2000	28th Feb. 1994
Drawdown end	31st Oct. 1998	30th Sep. 2002	31st May 1994

* The largest drawdown is defined as the maximum value of any "peak to trough decline" over the specified period. The subsequent minimum is not determined until it has reached a new high.
** Time to recovery is the time necessary to recover from the largest drawdown.

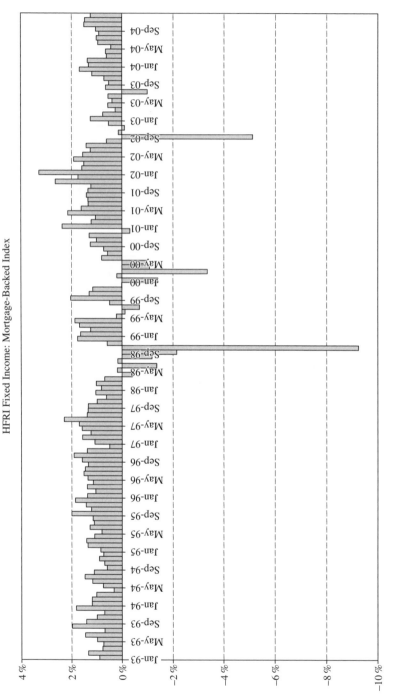

Figure 9.6 Monthly returns of HFRI Fixed Income: Mortgage-Backed Index from 1993 to 2004. Source: Hedge Fund Research Inc., © 2005 HFR Inc., www.hedgefundresearch.com. Reproduced by permission of Hedge Fund Research, Inc.

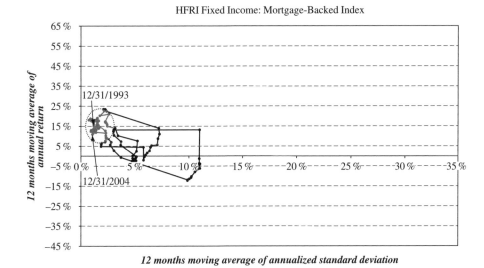

Figure 9.7 Historical performance trend of return as a function of risk for HFRI Fixed Income Mortgage-Backed Index from 1993 to 2004. Source: Hedge Fund Research Inc., © 2005 HFR Inc., www.hedgefundresearch.com. Reproduced by permission of Hedge Fund Research, Inc.

of risk of the HFRI Fixed Income Mortgage-Backed Index between 1994 and 2004. The concentration ellipsoid shows that historically the mortgage-backed securities arbitrage strategy moved very little in the risk/return area, generating consistent performances over time.

As shown in Figure 9.8, between 1994 and 2004 there were two "underwater" dips by hedge funds pursuing this strategy. The chart must be analyzed taking drawdown data into consideration: throughout the drawdown and the time to recovery period, the hedge funds adopting this strategy were under the high water mark. (See Chapter 1, Section 1.8, for more details on the setup and meaning of Figures 9.7 and 9.8.)

The MBS securities market was hit by a spate of prepayments in the spring of 1998, made worse by the strong *flight-to-quality* move in August 1998, triggered by Russia's default.

In September 2002, the prices of government securities rose driven by tumbling returns. Moreover, due to the low level of interest rates, many borrowers prepaid their mortgages to open new ones at lower rates, thus causing losses to investors with long positions on MBS.

In the summer of 2003, Freddie Mac dismissed its chairman and the operating manager, while its chief executive officer and financial officer resigned. On 9th June 2003, the Freddie Mac share shed more than 16 % of its value. Following audits by an independent auditing company, Freddie Mac revised its net income for the years 2000, 2001 and 2002 to factor in gains and losses from derivatives. Income had been undervalued in 2000 by $1.12 billion, overvalued in 2001 by $0.989 billion and undervalued in 2002 by $4.33 billion. This is why in the summer of 2003 there was a sell-off of MBS.

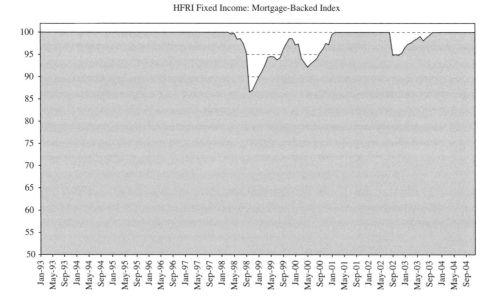

HFRI Fixed Income: Mortgage-Backed Index

Figure 9.8 Underwater periods for HFRI Fixed Income Mortgage-Backed Index from 1993 to 2004. Source: Hedge Fund Research Inc., © 2005 HFR Inc., www.hedgefundresearch.com. Reproduced by permission of Hedge Fund Research, Inc.

9.8 CONCLUSIONS

Looking back at Figure 1.9, let's identify the key factors making up the performance of fund managers following the MBS arbitrage strategy:

- traditional beta: none;
- alternative beta: liquidity risk, prepayment risk, complexity-associate risks, negative convexity;
- structural alpha: none;
- skill alpha: ability to valuate, select and trade MBS, risk management models.

The residential real estate market in the USA is overexposed to interest rate hikes. Interest rate rises in 2004 and 2005 will cause real estate market prices to slow down.

Some hedge fund managers indicate that there is a potential speculative bubble on the US real estate market. US consumers tend to use their home as an ATM to create additional cash to spend. There are some signals pointing at the unsustainability of the price levels reached by the US real estate market.

Debt service remained constant despite the strong drop in interest rates in the past years. How will private consumption fair in an environment of growing interest rates? Will private consumption be in a position to go on sustaining GDP growth in the United States?

The long mortgage refinancing cycle, which lasted while interest rates kept decreasing in the USA, has come to an end. It was the interest rate cuts and the mortgage refinancing that left US households with the additional cash that sustained private consumption.

10
Distressed Securities

Cerbero, fiera crudele e diversa,
con tre gole caninamente latra
sovra la gente che quivi è sommersa.
Li occhi ha vermigli, la barba unta e atra,
e 'l ventre largo, e unghiate le mani;
graffia li spirti ed iscoia ed isquatra.
Dante Alighieri, Inferno, Canto VI, verse 13–18
Translation by H.W. Longfellow

Cerberus, monster cruel and uncouth,
With his three gullets like a dog is barking
Over the people that are there submerged.
Red eyes he has, and unctuous beard and black,
And belly large, and armed with claws his hands;
He rends the spirits, flays, and quarters them.

Cerberus is the name of a hedge fund well known for its restructuring feats in companies going bust. The fund's name, taken from Greek mythology, evokes memories of the *Divine Comedy* in which the Florentine poet Dante meets the three-headed, red-eyed dog Cerberus who guards the gates of hell and barks and rends the spirits of the damned. In the same way, the hedge fund Cerberus feeds insatiably on companies that have been caught by a downdraft and driven to the hell of bankruptcy, and through a creative destruction process seeks to restructure them and sell them out again to make a profit.

The distressed securities market has been a rather obscure area in the last twenty years, and only recently it has been under the spotlight of the press due to the Enron, Adelphia, WorldCom and Parmalat scandals. Certainly, the fact that distressed securities trade mainly over-the-counter contributed to building this image.

In Europe, bankruptcy regulations are complex and differ from country to country, so that settlement procedures call for local expertise and presence. Also, in Europe, bankruptcies tend to turn into negotiated reorganizations. Many reorganization processes in Continental Europe are still relatively new and untested compared to the United States.

In 2002, the number of companies worldwide filing for bankruptcy or whose debt securities were traded under distress conditions was at an all time high, due to the spate of defaults involving the telecommunication, high-tech and energy industries. In 2003, in the United States the default rate[1] of high-yield bonds stood at 4.7%, well below the 12.8% rate reported in 2002, or 9.8% in 2001. And in December 2003, the most flagrant case of default ever experienced on European bond markets occurred: the default of Parmalat and its subsidiaries, which led to a total volume of insolvent bonds issued by the Parmalat group of about €6 billion.

In the United States in 2002 there were 122 bankruptcy filings by publicly held companies[2] with $337.5 billion worth of liabilities before the bankruptcy procedure, whereas in 2003 there were 95 filings associated with liabilities for $337.5 billion.

---

[1] Altman, E.I. and Fanjul, G. (2004) "Special Report On Defaults and Returns on High Yield Bonds: First Quarter 2004," Leonard N. Stern School of Business, New York University Salomon Center; National Bureau of Economic Research Data.
[2] With liabilities of at least $100 million.

In Europe recovery percentages are still rather low (20 % in 2003), about half the amount as in the United States.

For most investors a default is generally a harbinger of bad news. Yet for some hedge funds, which invest only in highly depressed debt securities of distressed companies in the expectation of a price rebound, this represents a great investment opportunity. These funds earned the nickname of "vulture funds", because they pick the bones of underperforming companies clean.

Obviously their role in corporate reorganizations is still controversial. Many observers are philosophically against the idea that some investors may step in during a distressed situation to make a profit, while the company's original shareholders and lenders must suffer material financial losses. This hostility, however, fails to consider the critical role distressed investors may play in the creation of value during a corporate reorganization. After all, even though they might have a repulsive appearance, vultures are appreciated for their useful role as scavengers.

10.1 A BRIEF HISTORY OF DISTRESSED SECURITIES

Investing in distressed securities is not a recent interest. It dates back to the end of the 19th century, and has its origin in the frenzy for railway constructions that developed in the United Kingdom. New plants, new towns, the demographic increase and the need to transport more goods called for a faster transportation system than horses. From 1830 onwards, investments were poured into railway construction companies. The first craze over railways spanned from 1836 to 1840. In the unruly market raid in which many companies had been involved, shares were sent shooting up to the heavens, then many companies went bankrupt: some because they were considered actually distressed, and others by fraud. Despite all this, in England in 1840 the majority of trades were on railway company stock.

The second craze lasted from 1844 to 1847 and inspired many of the themes in Charles Dickens's *Dombey and Son* (1848), which describes the English railway company North Western Railway Company in terms that nowadays are used to refer to a certain software company based in Redmond, Washington. The company, Dickens wrote, "is more prosperous than any other company in the world", transporting in one year many more people than those inhabiting the whole of Scotland and goods exceeding the annual trade of Belgium and Portugal together.

But the craze for railways ended in October 1847 with the so-called "Week of Terror", during which the entire railway industry crashed and the value of railway stock shriveled to one tenth of what it had been during the previous bubble. When the railway stock collapsed, some banks were closed down, and even the Bank of England was left with but a few million pounds in its reserves. Ignoring these alarming signals, a few investors bought the railway shares that were being sold off at ridiculously discounted prices, took an active role in the reorganization process and ended up with hefty profits.

Despite their success, railway distressed securities, and distressed securities at large, had no appeal to most investors. Only a few specialized investment boutiques would dare include them in their portfolios.

It is only recently that the all time high levels of bankruptcy procedures, debt restructurings and junk bond issues, in the United States and in Europe, opened the doors to an active secondary market for distressed securities. The catalyst of this heightened interest has been the rise of the junk bond market in the 1980s, thanks to Drexel Burnham Lambert Inc. and in particular its star, the trader Michael Milken. This growth profoundly changed the junk

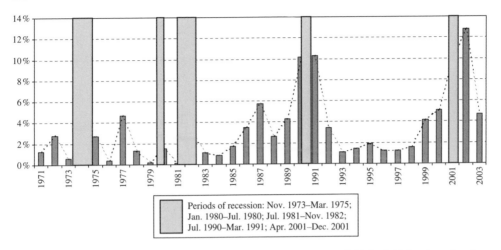

Figure 10.1 Historical default rates and recession periods in the US high-yield bond market from 1971 to 2003 (percentages). Sources: Edward I. Altman, Gonzalo Fanjul, April 2004, Special Report On Defaults and Returns on High Yield Bonds: First Quarter 2004, Leonard N. Stern School of Business, New York University Salomon Center; National Bureau of Economic Research Data

bond market, from a highly illiquid bazaar for few specialized purchasers, to a robust secondary market for highly discounted debt securities.

A collateral effect of the credit expansion was that many distressed companies gained access to new funding sources. Thus, at the beginning of the 1990s, the fall of Drexel Burnham Lambert led to a record number of issuers of junk bonds going under distress, including large companies like LTV, Eastern Airlines, Texaco, Continental Airlines, Allied Stores, Federated Department Stores, Greyhound and Pan Am. To make things worse, some other companies (for example Maxwell Communication, Olympia & York, etc.) were caught up in complicated actions involving several jurisdictions. Their divested assets, however, started once again to appeal to vulture investors. In the movie *Pretty Woman* of 1990, the actor Richard Gere plays a brilliant businessman who buys companies in financial straits, then takes them apart and sells them piece by piece to gain more than he paid for the entire company.

Recently, the economic slowdown that started in March 2000 also caused a significant increase in bankruptcy rates (Figure 10.1), as well as a jump in credit spreads. According to Moody's, the average spread between high-yield bonds and 10-year Treasury Bonds skyrocketed from 746 bps in June 2000 to an astounding 1029 bps in September 2000, a level comparable to the high spreads reported in the years 1990 and 1991. As a result, a big pile of "paper" from bankrupt companies flooded the markets, thus giving rise once again to great opportunities for investments in distressed securities.

10.2   THE DISTRESSED DEBT MARKET

It is difficult to measure the entire market of distressed securities, mainly due to the lack of transparency. Whereas information on the amount of public debt or defaulted shares is readily available, similar data are not available on privately placed debt securities or bank loans.

As shown in Table 10.1, on 30th June 2004, the estimated market value of distressed and defaulted securities in the United States came in at about $321 billion, well below the record

Table 10.1 Estimated market value of distressed and defaulted debt in the United States (data in billion USD) Source: Estimated by Professor Edward Altman, NYU Stern School of Business from Salomon Smith Barney's High Yield Bond DataBase, NYU Salomon Center Defaulted Bond DataBase, New Generation Research.

	Face Value			Market Value			Market Value/Face Value		
	31/12/02	31/12/03	30/06/04	31/12/02	31/12/03	30/06/04	31/12/02	31/12/03	30/06/04
Defaulted Public Debt	187.7	193.6	156.6	37.5	87.1	78.3	20 %	45 %	50 %
Distressed Public Debt	204.7	50.5	48.7	102.4	32.8	31.7	50 %	65 %	65 %
Total Public Debt	392.5	244.1	205.3	139.9	119.9	109.9	36 %	49 %	54 %
Defaulted Private Debt	262.8	271.0	219.2	157.7	189.7	153.4	60 %	70 %	70 %
Distressed Private Debt	286.6	70.7	68.7	215.0	60.1	58.0	75 %	85 %	85 %
Total Private Debt	549.5	341.7	287.4	372.7	249.8	211.4	68 %	73 %	74 %
Total Public and Private Debt	**941.9**	**585.8**	**492.7**	**512.6**	**369.8**	**321.3**	**54 %**	**63 %**	**65 %**

Private debt is considered mainly as bank debt

$513 billion in 2002 or the $370 billion in 2003. The cause underpinning this sharp drop lies in the lower percentage of distressed securities out of the total high-yield bond market, as illustrated in Figure 10.2.

The market supply is much greater than the demand for distressed securities by investors, which professor Edward Altman of New York University estimated to be running at $70–80 billion. This imbalance between demand and supply appears to be structural. There is evidence corroborating the conclusion that the supply of distressed securities is and will remain high in the near future:

- default cases reached historically high levels in 2001 and 2002;
- the rise of the high-yield market implies a substantial source of defaults;
- the leveraged loan market grew at a record pace in the 1990s, leveraged loan yields reached their all time low and the quality of issues is deteriorating, and while all this is happening, loan extension standards in banks are softening, as illustrated in Chart 15.2.

The New York University Salomon Center estimates that the face value of default and distressed loans at the end of 2003 was $585.8 billion, which breaks down into $244.1 billion of public debt and $341.7 billion of privately placed debt securities. This is well below the amount of debt reported at the end of 2002, soaring at $941.9 billion. The situation that developed in 2001 and 2002, including several cases of fraud and default among large US issuers, appears to be over (Table 10.2).

Figure 10.3 shows the historical performance of the default rate and the recovery rate for default corporate bonds.

In the 1990s, banks would require very high standards to grant loans, which led to record issues of high-yield debt securities. According to Moody's Investors Service, in 2004 only 34 issuers worldwide defaulted, representing a bond value of $16 billion. In 2003, 79 issuers defaulted involving bonds for $34.2 billion, which is in turn a big reduction over 2002, when 145 issuers had defaulted with $163.6 billion worth of bonds.

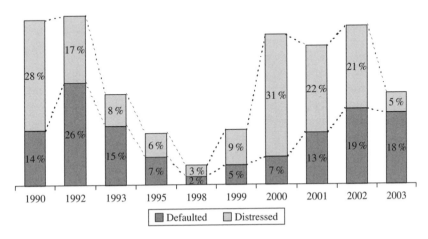

Figure 10.2 Evolution of the size of the distressed and defaulted bond markets as a percentage of the total high-yield bond market from 1990 to 2003. Source: Edward I. Altman, Gonzalo Fanjul, April 2004, Special Report On Defaults and Returns on High Yield Bonds: First Quarter 2004, Leonard N. Stern School of Business, New York University Salomon Center

Table 10.2   The largest bankruptcies in the US from 1980 to 28th October 2005 Source: www.BankruptcyData.com; New Generation Research, Inc. Boston, MA

Company	Bankruptcy Date	Total Assets pre-bankruptcy in billion USD
Worldcom, Inc.	Jul. 21, 2002	103.9
Enron Corp.*	Dec. 02, 2001	63.4
Conseco, Inc.	Dec. 18, 2002	61.4
Texaco, Inc.	Apr. 12, 1987	35.9
Financial Corp. of America	Sep. 09, 1988	33.9
Refco Inc.	Oct. 17, 2005	33.3
Global Crossing Ltd.	Jan. 28, 2002	30.2
Pacific Gas and Electric Co.	Apr. 06, 2001	29.8
UAL Corp.	Dec. 09, 2002	25.2
Delta Air Lines, Inc.	Sep. 14, 2005	21.8
Adelphia Communications	Jun. 25, 2002	21.5
MCorp	Mar. 31, 1989	20.2
Mirant Corporation	Jul. 14, 2003	19.4
Delphi Corporation	Oct. 08, 2005	16.6
First Executive Corp.	May. 13, 1991	15.2

* The Enron assets were taken from the 10-Q filed on 19th November 2001. The company has announced that the annual financials were under review at the time of filing for Chapter 11.

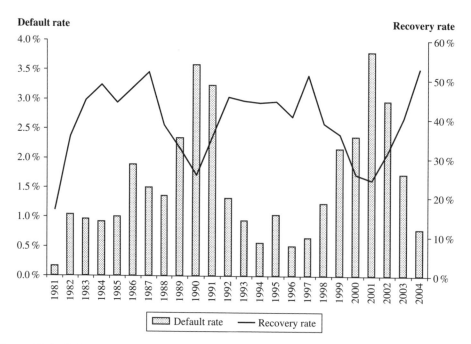

Figure 10.3   Default rate and recovery rate from 1981 to 2004. Source: Moody's Investors Service. © Moody's Investors Service, Inc. and/or its affiliates. Reprinted with permission. All rights reserved

The high-yield bond market seems to confirm this trend, as the percentage of distressed companies in the high-yield universe dropped drastically in 2003, as shown in Figure 10.2.

The sum of the percentage of default companies and the percentage of distressed companies over the total high-yield market dropped considerably from about 40 % in 2002 to about 23 % in 2003. Note that between 2002 and 2003 the percentage of distressed companies out of the total high-yield market declined from 21 % to 5 %.

Also, yields are falling: issues with a CCC rating slipped from a high yield of 25.7 % in September 2003 down to 12.2 % at the end of 2003. Similarly, issues with a B rating went from a yield of 13.5 % down to 7.6 %. The prevailing rationale appears to be that with a growing economy and a shakeout of tottering companies, surviving issuers can stay in good shape for some time.

It is important to clarify outright that the distressed securities market in Europe is totally different from the situation in the United States.

The European market of high-yield bonds was virtually non-existent before 1997 and the distressed securities market was essentially made up of bank loans, appealing to a select number of specialists only. It was only with the advent of the European Union that the distressed securities market started to take off and earn a reputation. The European single currency changed the attitude of companies towards financing their operations, and the high-yield bond market stood out as a viable alternative to borrowing from banks. The single currency erased currency and interest rate trades among EU member states, and forced investors to develop new strategies based to a greater extent on credit spreads. This favored the rise of a full-blown high-yield bond market, followed by a parallel secondary market of distressed high-yield debt securities.

To date, the European market of distressed securities is still lagging behind that of the United States both in terms of maturity and market size. According to Moody's, between 1970 and 2001, 77 % of all defaults and 85 % of volumes were based in the United States.

The European market of distressed securities is still expanding, supported by a strong demand by both European and American investors. Up to now, growth was mainly driven by the telecommunications industry, for two reasons. First, the advent of the European Union coincided with a booming demand for funds by telecommunication companies (with GSBM and UMTS mobile phones, the next generation of broadband mobile telephony). Second, the entire telecommunications sector slipped towards the lower spectrum of credit ratings. In one year, the seven major European phone companies issued more than $170 billion debt securities. In an industry in which the cost of capital represents the key to competitiveness, the burden of huge interest payments could significantly bear down on issuers and create a new set of truly distressed securities. No doubt, there are also reasons that could slow down the rise of the European market of distressed securities. First of all, European distressed securities are typically issued by a holding company, compared to what happens in the United States where the issuers are the operating companies. This makes it more difficult to force a default, which, coupled with the claims of secured bank lenders, limits the possibilities for the distressed security holder of taking part in the company's restructuring. In addition, the US legislation is typically more transparent and simpler compared to the host of bankruptcy laws and procedures riddling the European jurisdictions. A unanimous consensus by the European Union member states on bankruptcy procedures, accounting standards and reporting requirements combined with a single regulatory authority might be the tip-off that the European market of non-investment grade securities is taking off. It should also be noted that Eastern Europe is becoming an interesting source of distressed securities. For example, the Czech Republic was a trendsetter in post-communist Central Europe, introducing the first auctions of large packets of non-performing loans. This gave rise to the most developed market of distressed securities in Central Europe. The example set by the Czech Republic was followed by Slovakia and Poland, and now the latter is trying to learn from the lessons taught by the auction program. Yet, it is still rather difficult for investors to make a profit, due to the cumbersome regulatory framework that makes loan and default application a rather lengthy process.

Finally, in Asia the opportunity to buy distressed companies and reorganize them has grown significantly. However, in Japan, despite the huge amount of non-performing loans, institutions are still extremely averse to disclosing information on these activities so as to avoid embarrassing publicity to companies that borrowed funds and are now under distress. Despite all this, the purchase and sale of these securities has become a very profitable business.

10.3 BANKRUPTCY LAWS

To understand how the investment in distressed securities works, first of all it is necessary to review the basic criteria of bankruptcy laws. We deliberately decided to focus our analysis on US bankruptcy laws, even though they are significantly different from the rest of the world. Elsewhere filing for bankruptcy generally means that the corporate management is ousted, a new trustee is appointed and assets are liquidated, while the US Bankruptcy Code offers essentially two options: a distressed company can choose whether to go for a reorganization in order to recover from crippling debt, or more simply, go out of business and opt for liquidation. The section of the US Bankruptcy Code, which deals with both options, regulates two different types of bankruptcy. Generally, winding up companies file for bankruptcy under "Chapter 7" of the Code, which provides for the liquidation of the debtor's property and the distribution of liquidating dividends to creditors. Distressed businesses instead typically file for bankruptcy under "Chapter 11", known also as "reorganization in bankruptcy".[3] Bankrupt companies under Chapter 11 retain possession of their assets, but operate under the supervision of a court that oversees the bankruptcy process to safeguard creditors. Indeed, the debtor in possession of the business and in control of its operation acts as a fiduciary for creditors. If its management is ineffective or dishonest, an independent manager, or trustee in bankruptcy, is appointed by the court and a creditor's committee can be created, chosen from among the 20 largest unsecured creditors who are not insiders. The committee represents all creditors in the supervision of the debtor's operations, and it is an entity with which the debtor can negotiate an acceptable reorganization plan.

The US Bankruptcy Code offers this dual option to bankrupt companies to facilitate the liquidation of "bad" companies, while allowing healthy companies to reorganize their debt and go on doing business. By "bad" companies we mean companies whose assets can be put to a better alternative use compared to the current one. These companies should sell their assets, return the proceeds of this sale to their investors and set them free to invest in

---

[3] In France the equivalent of Chapter 11 is called "déclaration de cessation des paiements", in Ireland "examinership", in the United Kingdom "receivership" and in Belgium "concordat". In Italy, the legal reference is set by the Civil code, bankruptcy laws and in particular by law decree n. 270 of 8th July 1999 on the receivership of defaulted large companies: "Nuova disciplina dell'amministrazione straordinaria delle grandi imprese in stato di insolvenza, a norma dell'articolo 1 della legge 30 luglio 1998, n. 274", published by the *Official Gazette* n. 185 of 9th August 1999.

more productive businesses. In contrast, by "healthy companies" we mean companies that can still create more value by doing business than if they were liquidated. These companies might have burdened themselves with too much debt or have short-term cash-flow problems that call for a debt restructuring, but this temporary financial distress does not imply that the company must be wound up.

Most US distressed publicly held companies file for bankruptcy under Chapter 11 rather than Chapter 7, because by doing so they can still go on doing business and retain control over the bankruptcy process. Under Chapter 11, at least in the short term, all court procedures, tax collection activities, foreclosures and reintegration of ownership against the bankrupt company are suspended. A reorganization plan must spell out clearly the rights of all investors and what they can expect to receive from the company. Generally, bond-holders will stop receiving interest payments and returns of principal and in exchange for their old bonds will receive new shares, new bonds or a combination of both. Generally shareholders will stop receiving dividends and might be forced to exchange their old shares with new shares from the reorganized company. New shares may be less in number and be worth less than the old shares. In any case, it is important to understand that the long-term result of a company filing for bankruptcy under Chapter 11 is still uncertain. At times, companies successfully squeeze out of bankruptcy and go back to being profitable, whereas in other cases they will end up being liquidated anyway.

In the case of liquidation, bankruptcy laws define the priority of payments. As a general rule, investors who took the least risk have the higher claim and are paid first. For example, secured creditors take on a lower risk because the credit they granted is generally collater-alized, for example by a mortgage or other corporate assets. They know they will be paid first if the company files for bankruptcy. Similarly, bond-holders have a higher claim than shareholders, because bonds stand for the company's debt and the company accepted that it would give bond-holders interest payments and return the principal. Shareholders own the company and take on the greatest risk. They can make more money if the company performs well, but at the same time they can lose their money if the company goes bust. Owners are the last to be paid if the company goes bankrupt. Now, as a general legal rule, an investor buying a distressed security enjoys the same "rights and incapacities" as the original holder. With a few exceptions, the investor can claim the full nominal value of the security in a bankruptcy or in a reorganization, irrespective of how much the investor paid to buy it.

If in the case of corporate distress the different parties come to an agreement, it is possible to have an *out-of-court* reorganization, which is much more rapid.

10.4 STRATEGY DESCRIPTION

10.4.1 Securities Involved

There are many different opinions as to what to include under distressed securities and one should always be wary of what a fund manager actually implies when he uses this definition. In general, distressed securities are shares, bonds, trade receivables or financial loans of companies on the verge of, in the middle of, or emerging from bankruptcy or financial distress.

A strict definition would include only debt and equity securities – publicly held and traded – of companies that defaulted their debt obligations and/or filed for bankruptcy protection, such as under Chapter 7 or 11 of the US Bankruptcy Code. A broader definition may also include debt securities that are publicly held and traded at a big discount to their issuing price, and that, if the issuer does not default, offer a significant yield (yield-to-maturity), typically 10 % over comparable maturity US Treasury Bonds. But distressed securities can also include those bank loans and other privately placed debt of the same or similar entities with rather acute operating and/or financial problems.

The quality of any bond is based on the issuer's financial ability to oblige payments of interest and return the full principal when due. Rating services help with assessing the creditworthiness of bonds and are also a good indicator of the quality of an issuer compared to other bonds. Two of the major independent rating agencies that rate bonds are Moody's and Standard & Poor's. Both show at the end of their ratings an indicator illustrating where the bond ranks within the same class of notes. Moody's uses a numeric indicator. For example, A1 is better than A2, but not as good as Aa. Standard & Poor's uses the plus and minus signs as indicators. For example A+ is better than A and A is better than A−.

Typically, investors also group bond ratings into three main categories: "investment grade" refers to bonds with a Baa/BBB rating or greater; high-yield (also called "speculative grade") refers to bonds with a rating below Baa/BBB; and the low end of high-yield ratings is made up of the distressed securities market (Figure 10.4).

Although investment grade bonds can be downgraded at any time, or may even default, it is less likely for a high-rated bond to incur a downgrading or a default.

Figure 10.5 shows for each rating the historical probability of default or changes in credit quality for corporate bonds rated by Moody's. The figure shows the average annual percentages of rating transitions between 1985 and 2003 for both Europe and North America to aid comparability. The rating migration matrix shows that on average in one year in Europe only 7.6 % of all bonds with an Aaa rating have been downgraded to an Aa rating. In the United States this percentage drops to 5.9 %. Moreover, in Europe only 0.1 % and in the United States only 0.2 % of Baa bonds defaulted during the year. However, we should always remember that these are averages of downgrade or default rates, and that during economic downturns these rates can get much higher.

Each percentage in Figure 10.5 indicates the weighted average percentage of issuers that at the beginning of the year had been assigned a given rating (shown in the column on the left)

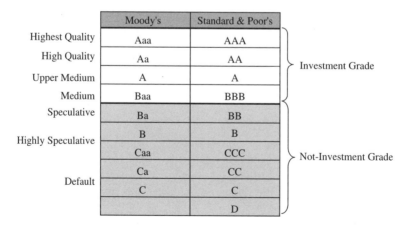

Figure 10.4   The bond rating system. Source: Bloomberg L.P.

The average annual percentages of rating transitions between 1985 and 2003 for Europe and North America.

To Ratings →
From Ratings ↓

Europe

	Aaa	Aa	A	Baa	Ba	B	Caa-C	Default	Withdrawn
Aaa	89.1 %	7.6 %	0.3 %	0.0 %	0.1 %	0.0 %	0.0 %	0.0 %	2.9 %
Aa	1.4 %	87.2 %	8.8 %	0.1 %	0.0 %	0.0 %	0.0 %	0.0 %	2.6 %
A	0.0 %	4.4 %	85.0 %	4.2 %	0.2 %	0.1 %	0.0 %	0.0 %	6.1 %
Baa	0.0 %	0.2 %	4.9 %	81.1 %	3.8 %	1.2 %	0.1 %	0.1 %	8.5 %
Ba	0.0 %	0.0 %	0.8 %	9.8 %	72.2 %	8.7 %	0.4 %	1.0 %	7.1 %
B	0.0 %	0.0 %	0.3 %	0.8 %	10.7 %	66.9 %	8.3 %	3.2 %	9.8 %
Caa-C	0.0 %	0.0 %	0.0 %	0.0 %	0.0 %	19.1 %	46.3 %	21.2 %	13.4 %

North America

	Aaa	Aa	A	Baa	Ba	B	Caa-C	Default	Withdrawn
Aaa	89.0 %	5.9 %	0.2 %	0.0 %	0.0 %	0.0 %	0.0 %	0.0 %	4.9 %
Aa	0.8 %	85.7 %	8.3 %	0.4 %	0.1 %	0.0 %	0.0 %	0.0 %	4.7 %
A	0.1 %	2.2 %	86.9 %	5.7 %	0.6 %	0.2 %	0.0 %	0.0 %	4.3 %
Baa	0.1 %	0.3 %	5.0 %	83.1 %	4.8 %	1.1 %	0.2 %	0.2 %	5.3 %
Ba	0.0 %	0.0 %	0.6 %	4.9 %	73.7 %	9.1 %	0.6 %	1.4 %	9.6 %
B	0.0 %	0.1 %	0.2 %	0.6 %	4.9 %	74.1 %	4.4 %	6.7 %	8.9 %
Caa-C	0.0 %	0.0 %	0.0 %	1.1 %	1.5 %	5.1 %	59.9 %	21.5 %	10.9 %

Figure 10.5 Inferring the likelihood of default from ratings. Source: Moody's Investors Service Global Credit Research April 2004. © Moody's Investors Service, Inc. and/or its affiliates. Reprinted with permission. All rights reserved

and that at the end of the year had the credit rating shown on top of each column. The sum of all the percentages of the same line (including the columns "Default" and "Withdrawn") adds up to 100 %. Percentages are weighted based on the number of issuers. The higher values in the transition matrix fall along the main diagonal in that it is likely every issuer will end the year with the same rating it had at the beginning of the year.

For example, a European issuer that at the beginning of the year had a Baa rating has an 81.1 % historical probability of retaining the same rating to the end of the year, a 4.9 % probability of closing the year with an A rating, a 3.8 % chance of being downgraded to a Ba rating and 0.1 % of defaulting.

Rating transition percentages for European issuers are quite similar to those of North American issuers. Figure 10.5 shows that only rarely does a rating transition jump beyond the next rating category.

A useful indicator to measure creditworthiness is the ratio between rating upgrades and downgrades: if this ratio shows an increase over a given period, this means that credit quality has improved; on the other hand, if the ratio has decreased, it points to a worsening of credit quality.

When the ratio between issuer upgrades and downgrades is greater than one, it means that the number of rating upgrades exceeds the number of downgrades (Figure 10.6).

In 2001 and 2002, downgrades exceeded upgrades, which is consistent with the increase in default percentages reported over those years. Credit quality as a function of rating changes showed a marked improvement in 2004. The ratio between issuer upgrades and downgrades rose to 1.55 in 2004 from 0.44 in 2003; 14 % of issuers were promoted, while 9 % were demoted. It is important to note that in 2004 the number of rating upgrades was greater than downgrades for the first time since 1997. It is almost unnecessary to point out that credit quality improves in economic expansionary periods, and deteriorates during recessions.

Of course, bond ratings are not the only way investors can value bonds. News about an issuer can be known to the market before a rating agency has the time to update its rating or put the issuer on the watch list. As a result, a bond rating cannot reflect current information.

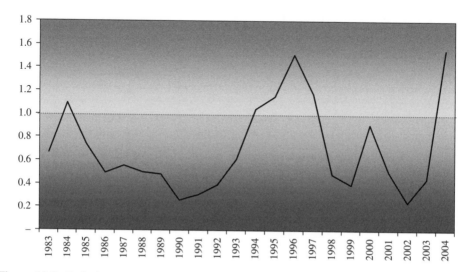

Figure 10.6 Ratio between issuer upgrades and downgrades. Source: Moody's Investors Service, Default and Recovery Rates of Corporate Bond Issuers, 1920–2004. © Moody's Investors Service, Inc. and/or its affiliates. Reprinted with permission. All rights reserved

Hedge fund managers actively research the industry, the municipality and the issuer, to determine whether there has been any recent piece of news that might negatively affect the bond or its issuer. They are on the look out for companies with good survival probabilities but whose debt securities have been excessively punished by the market. In the pursuit of this strategy, fund managers can then invest in distressed securities, debt securities perceived as distressed (stressed debt) or in *orphan shares*.[4]

Orphan shares are issued to satisfy creditor rights when a company is going through a reorganization in bankruptcy. These shares tend to be undervalued for recovering companies that are coming through bankruptcy with a deleveraged balance sheet and that are neglected by most institutional investors. The creditors of a bankrupt company often want to quit when the company's reorganization plan has been confirmed and the debt converted in new shares, which generates a technical pressure on shares, pushing them down by 20–40 % without the company's fundamentals being at fault. Some fund managers estimate that between 2003 and 2006 there will be more than 500 companies in the United States that will have weathered bankruptcy and issued "orphan shares", so some interesting opportunities may well lie ahead.

We can identify four types of distressed securities depending on the situation of the issuer:

- *Pre-reorganization securities*: securities of companies that are entering restructuring and where it is easy to sell the company's securities short. The risk profile is high, but the risk premium is sizeable.
- *Interim-reorganization securities*: securities of companies that are complying with the restructuring plan. A wide range of investors hold the new debt securities and the securities liquidity is good. The reorganization process can lead to the issue of orphan shares.
- *Mature distressed*: the reorganization plan is operational and the securities of the restructured company start to reflect the company's improved health conditions.
- *Deeply distressed*: the defaulting company is wound up and distressed securities trade at a discount to the company's recovery rate, also under the worst scenario. It is possible to identify inexpensive options on potentially positive events, such as higher recovery values or lower number of legal actions and liabilities than expected.

Besides the debtor's insolvency, the characteristic shared by all these securities is their illiquidity, which can be caused by different reasons:

- *Delisting*: in most cases, companies filing for bankruptcy under Chapter 11 of the US Bankruptcy Code are generally unable to meet the listing requirements to continue to be traded on the NASDAQ or on the New York Stock Exchange. Hence, they are delisted from these major stock exchanges. Since there is no federal law prohibiting the trading of shares of a bankrupt company, their shares can continue to be traded either on the over-the-counter market (OTC) or on Pink Sheets.[5]
- *Legal constraints*: many institutional investors cannot buy distressed securities because their articles of association, their fiduciary responsibilities or their regulatory authorities forbid them to hold speculative grade securities, even though the issuer can generate profits.
- *Lack of coverage by analysts*: coverage by analysts tends to decline significantly when a company is under distress, until it almost disappears in the case of bankruptcy. Clearly, the low interest by investors and the specific nature of the bankruptcy procedure erode

---

[4] Also called restructured equity, orphan stock or orphan equity.

[5] Pink Sheets® LLC is a provider of financial information and prices for over-the-counter markets (www.pinksheets.com).

the incentive for equity analysts to devote time to collecting and analyzing information. Lack of information in turn generates low interest by investors.

• *Lack of knowledge*: the valuation of distressed securities requires a lot of work and several skills, together with a constant access to the latest information on issuers. Creditors often prefer to sell their securities at a strongly discounted price, because they do not have the knowledge, the interest, the skills or the time to conduct the necessary analyses.

This situation results in a disorganized and illiquid distressed securities market that does not have a solid offer price structure. Most orders are on the sale-side, with traditional investors unwilling to buy. This allows hedge funds to inject liquidity onto the market and profit from its inability to appreciate the intrinsic value of these securities.

NES Rentals Holdings, Inc. ("NES" or the "Company"), one of the largest companies in the equipment rental industry, rents over 750 different types of machinery to industrial and construction end-users. The Company also distributes new equipment for nationally recognized original equipment manufacturers, sells used machinery as well as complementary parts and supplies, and provides repair and maintenance services. NES operates in two different segments: general rental and traffic safety. General rental equipment includes aerial work platforms, forklifts, cranes, water equipment, industrial equipment, air compressors and other construction-related equipment. Traffic safety equipment includes arrow boards, message boards, barricades, cones, warning lights and pavement marking systems. The Company serves approximately 87 000 customers, ranging from large, multi-national corporations to small companies and general contractors in a wide variety of industries. In 2002 and 2003, equipment rental rates decreased considerably as an overall economic downturn and a decrease in non-residential construction spending softened the equipment rental market. In addition, the resale market for used rental equipment weakened, resulting in a decrease in the value of NES' rental fleet, which secured its credit facility. In June 2003, as a result of this difficult market environment, combined with the Company's highly leveraged capital structure, a decline in collateral value and upcoming debt maturities, NES filed for bankruptcy protection. Subsequently, in July 2003, the hedge fund began purchasing the senior secured bank debt of NES in the high 80s confident of an industry-wide turnaround, management's ability to realize cost savings and ultimately the Company's ability to refinance bank debt upon its emergence from Chapter 11. In February 2004, the Company emerged from bankruptcy with a considerably lower debt burden and refinanced the facility in August 2004. The hedge fund realized a return in excess of 20 % on the investment.

10.4.2 Investment Thesis

While academic literature mostly suggests that shares on the distressed securities market are priced efficiently, the popular press has often speculated that share prices could be inefficient during the bankruptcy period. For example, Continental Airlines shares continued to be traded on the AMEX at about $1.50 per share even after the company had negotiated a plan with its creditors, based on which there would be no distribution to those who held the shares before the petition. Indeed, vulture investors have attracted a sizable amount of risk-capital, offering the possibility of high returns and taking advantage of apparent market anomalies.

Distressed businesses can give rise to many opportunities for prospective buyers. Often the market value of distressed securities does not reflect their intrinsic value due to the "automatic" behavior of some type of investors, who are subject to constraints that guide their investment behavior, for example bank *capital ratios*, and what to do in case of rating downgrades or of bond defaults.

Many institutional investors, in keeping with their articles of association, cannot invest in speculative grade bonds. These investors tend to dispose of their positions in advance of a default event or a downgrading to speculative grade, often exerting a strong downwards pressure and opening up opportunities for distressed investors who enjoy greater latitude.

A restructuring or a business discontinuation may lead to the disposal of business operations (or entire companies) at exceptional values. As we will see later on, hedge funds specializing in these types of transactions are very close to private equity investors.

Stocks drop in advance of financial straits when owners decide to sell rather than to keep investing in a company that is in financial trouble. For example, sellers can have an emotive reaction to bankruptcy, neglecting or ignoring the company's true value due to the stigma associated with a reorganization or bankruptcy procedure. Institutional investors may be forced to sell, and many banks and other creditors, who are managing their assets from a global portfolio perspective rather than from an accounting standpoint, are also selling *non-performing loans* or *sub-performing loans* at appealing discounts to get rid of them.

In many countries there are legal instruments that allow buyers to choose the desired assets, while leaving behind over-leveraged financial accounts and undesired contracts. In all these cases, professional investors specializing in securities research analyses, who appreciate the risks and values involved, can buy these securities or options at a discount, and see the light at the end of the tunnel.

In addition, often the low valuations accompanying investments in distressed debts bring with them a significant advantage in joining the capital structure as senior creditor rather than as shareholder. A private equity investor in a typical bid to take over a business has to face the normal risks and premiums inherent in an equity investment (for example, theoretical unlimited upside coupled with the corresponding downside risk of potentially losing the invested capital), whereas investments in distressed debt instruments can often offer a more limited expected downside, while capturing most if not all of the potential upside. Due to their privileged status within the capital structure, distressed debt instruments are less affected by value erosions. At the same time, although a recovery on debt securities is often equal to a limited upside with respect to the par value or par value plus accrued interest, some distressed debt instruments can be converted into shares as a result of the reorganization, thus creating an additional upside.

The identification of good opportunities has to rely on a complex legal and financial analysis. The validity of an opportunity and the offered price will depend on the adopted valuation approach, which may include cash flows, market multiples, industry benchmarking and liquidation values.

Contract rights will determine how to corroborate the analysis by using the value of guarantee, off-balance-sheet debt, claim priorities, and the possibility of enacting rights and guarantees. Finally, the length of the analysis process will depend on how events evolve: the length of the legal procedure, persons entitled and regulatory issues. Above all, there is no one standard model for distressed investments; each and every distressed situation calls for a unique approach and solution. It should be borne in mind that, in case of default, bond-holders receive but a fraction of the value of their original credit. There are many determinants underlying recovery rates, including the company's structure characteristics, the position of the debt instrument within the company's capital structure, as well as the macroeconomic conditions. The time trend of default bond recovery rates and their correlation with default rates are other additional factors affecting the recovery of bonds in the case of default. All these elements must be assessed and validated before making any investment decision.

Professor Altman of New York University identified three investment styles characterizing distressed securities investors. His classification is general and not limited to hedge funds, but it still perfectly suits our purpose.

Investors of the first kind seek to gain control of the company by acquiring the company's shares or debt.[6] Once they have control over the company and its assets, these types of hedge funds participate directly in the bankrupt company's management and try to make a profit either by redirecting the flow of corporate resources towards higher-value uses or by cutting costs. This process takes much time and work, and its implementation is expensive, in that it calls for long-term investments and a significant involvement of the hedge fund during the reorganization. The time necessary to exit the investment is two or three years, and target returns range from 20–25 %.

The second kind of investor invests in preferred securities, and takes an active role in the corporate reorganization without controlling the company. The exit strategy is based on selling the distressed securities on equity or bond markets at the end of the corporate reorganization. The time-to-exit is one or two years, with 15–20 % target returns.

The third kind of investment is rather passive: it acquires the debt on expectation that its future value will be higher than the purchase price, or that a skilled owner may increase its value. When a company undergoes a reorganization, its securities (or the existing reintegrated securities, or the new securities received in exchange) tend to appreciate when the crisis is over and the securities start being traded again on traditional fixed income and equity markets. The time-to-exit is six months to a year, with 12–20 % target returns.

10.4.3   The Valuation Process

The DCF analysis (discounted cash flows) and relative valuation approaches (like for example the price/earning ratio, the price/book value ratio, the price/sales ratio, etc.) are primarily designed to value healthy companies, but they fail miserably when used to value companies facing a substantial probability of default in the near future due to their inability to meet debt obligations or operating expenses. The degree to which traditional methods do not make a correct valuation of companies varies, depending on the accuracy with which expected cash flows are estimated, the ease-of-access to capital markets enjoyed by the companies, as well as on the effects of the crisis.

The DCF analysis is carried out by projecting expected cash flows over a given period, estimating the terminal value at the end of the period, so as to project the company's value

---

[6] When shares have no value or no voting rights, often the outstanding debt is purchased in expectation that it will be converted into shares with voting rights. When a sufficient amount is purchased, this can give the holders control over the company's activities after the reorganization. However, the purchase of outstanding shares prior to the reorganization is rarely an appealing option due to the dilution caused by the reorganization.

at that point in time, and then discounting cash flows at a discount rate that factors in the company's cash-flow risk. This is a highly flexible approach, which can be used to value a wide range of companies: from those with foreseeable profit and low growth, to those with a high growth and negative cash flows. Still this approach rests on the assumptions that the company is and will remain a going concern for a potentially unlimited period, and that it is possible to reinvest the cash flows at the company's same internal rate of return. The terminal value is generally estimated by assuming that profit keeps on growing at a stable rate (a perpetual growth rate). Also, when the terminal value is estimated based on revenue or profit multiples, this multiple can be derived by looking at publicly traded, but generally only healthy, companies. In practice, if there is a high distress probability, if capital access is restricted (by internal or external factors) and/or if distress sale proceeds are significantly lower than those of a healthy company, the outcome of a discounted cash-flow valuation will overestimate the company and its share value, even if the cash flows and the discount rates have been correctly estimated.

Hence, it is necessary to adopt the discounted cash-flow valuation technique to reflect some or most of the effects on the corporate value caused by the crisis. To do so, it is necessary to include the crisis effects both in the expected cash flows and in the discount rates. In its most comprehensive form, this will require that all possible scenarios be taken into consideration, from best to worst case, that all scenarios be assigned probabilities and cash flows under every scenario, and that expected cash flows be estimated for every year. A shortcut, although one allowing for some approximation, requires the estimation of only two scenarios: the functioning company and the bankrupt company. For the functioning company scenario, expected growth rates and estimated cash flows can be used under the assumption that the company will be taken good care of until it fully recovers. In the bankrupt scenario, it is assumed that the company will be wound up in exchange for the proceeds from the auction sale. A correct assessment of the probabilities to be assigned to each scenario is key to the final valuation.

10.4.4 Hedging Techniques

Unlike all other assets, typically distressed securities are not lent out for short sales. Once a company is identified as being under distress, all investors wish to sell and the time to short sell is generally over. Hence, generally speaking, borrowing distressed securities is not viable, or requires the payment of high returns to the creditor. In addition, minor events or news may easily trigger strong rallies, which make selling short rather dangerous. Also other hedging mechanisms, like credit default swaps or equity options, tend to be very expensive to establish and/or to carry. And short positions on high-yield equity and indices have a limited use, in that in any case the hedge works only against the change in the default premium, but not against the specific default risk of an issuer. As a result, the only effective way to reduce the risk of a distressed securities portfolio is to diversify. By investing in many issuers, sectors and countries, it is possible to avoid, or at least limit, the contagion effect of a big default.

10.5 RISKS

Hedge funds that are managed along a distressed securities strategy have a net long position on distressed securities, or in other terms, they have a long bias. This characteristic exposes distressed securities hedge funds to the risk of credit spread widening, which by driving prices down would cause them to report a negative performance.

As already mentioned, an additional relevant risk associated with distressed securities investments is the liquidity risk. Typically, distressed securities hedge funds have a quarterly, six-month or annual liquidity due to the illiquidity of the securities and the long time horizons to finalize the manager's strategy.

There are additional risks associated with the complexity of bankruptcy laws and the intricacies of default situations: claim priority, the setting up of the creditor's committee, the bankruptcy negotiation process, etc.

Generally, leverage is not used, as distressed securities already have a high implied leverage, since they are traded at a substantial discount to par value.

Finally, there is the problem of the valuation of distressed securities: in the absence of trades, prices do not change and are often based on a purely accounting reckoning. Hence, investors must make sure that the distressed securities portfolio is valued by an independent administrator, who prices the securities based on criteria that must not change over time.

10.6 A BRIEF CONSIDERATION OF THE DIRECTIONAL NATURE OF DISTRESSED SECURITIES HEDGE FUNDS

It is important to understand that hedge funds investing in distressed securities are directional funds.

Downside protection can be obtained by purchasing credit default swaps, or put options on the issuer's stock, or by selling short the main credit indices, as for example the CDX 100 High Yield Index or iTRAXX, or again through the short sale of bonds. The idea associated with the long/short factor in credit-oriented funds is unfounded and often people tend to draw a similarity with long/short equity funds. A good long/short equity fund can make a profit during bullish as well as bearish markets, by changing its net exposure to the market. But how many credit-oriented funds can perform well when the relevant credit indices are negative? Almost none, because in order to profit from a credit spread widening, the hedge funds should have a negative net exposure to the market, hence a negative carry.

These funds seek to capture a return through the appreciation of bonds, but also by pocketing the yield, and these fund managers will short sell a bond only if they are convinced that the bond will shed value, the only reason why they would be willing to give up the accrued interest and pay it out to the counterparty who is lending the bond.

There are two catalytic events leading to the short selling of a bond, namely, the identification of failing business models at the issuer's and bonds with very high prices that are traded close to par or above par. Critical keys to success are the analysis of a company's credit fundamentals and the right expertise in interpreting the issuers' financial accounts and business models.

In the fourth quarter of 2003, a hedge fund manager decided to buy defaulted convertible bonds issued by the company DDi Corp., a manufacturer of electronic components (*Electronic Contract Manufacturing*, ECM), based in North America and the UK. DDi became insolvent in March 2003. In August 2003 the company started a corporate reorganization plan under the protection of Chapter 11. The hedge fund manager decided that it was a good investment opportunity.

The hedge fund initially purchased the convertible bonds at 50 cents. This price was quite far from past historical lows reached by the securities, which had plummeted to as low as 10 cents in March 2003. Despite this, the hedge fund manager still considered the investment opportunity as being appealing. In fact, the manager saw that the ECM industry was sending recovery signals with respect to past troublesome circumstances. In addition, the price of many industry stocks had markedly soared in the months preceding the purchase, in some cases by more than 100 %.

Moreover, the hedge fund manager believed that DDi Corp.'s reorganization plan submitted to creditors in the summer of 2003 was based on highly conservative assumptions and on valuation multiples based on peers from the ECM sector, whose share prices had substantially increased in recent times.

The analyses conducted by the hedge fund analysts suggested a price forecast well exceeding 100 cents, once the securities had been converted into shares, and more precisely between 200 and 400 cents. While establishing this deal, however, the hedge fund was not going to be exposed to the ECM industry risk, and therefore it short sold a basket of similar companies belonging to the same industry.

At this point the hedge fund waited for the approval of the reorganization plan and for it to be up and running. Surprisingly, the major worry for the hedge fund managers was the possibility that the company's fundamental value would become too obvious too soon, and that subordinated creditors (in this case practically only shares) would file an appeal to oppose the excessive redemptions paid to senior creditors with a higher claim, which included, of course, the hedge fund. Indeed, had the bankruptcy court approved the validity of said appeal, it could require that the reorganization plan be changed. In this case, the convertible bonds bought by the hedge fund would probably have gone very close to 100 cents.

This possibility entailed an additional drawback: following the significant rise in the price of ECM shares, the hedge fund would no longer be hedged against the ECM industry risk. Actually, it could be argued that the hedge fund in this case is in the same position as a call option writer on the ECM sector, with the exercise price equal to the threshold value that would have triggered the change in the reorganization plan by the bankruptcy court.

In the end, the plan was approved with no changes by the Bankruptcy Court and was rapidly put in place. The bonds were converted into the shares of the restructured company, which started to be traded over-the-counter. In the following months, the shares were given an average coverage by the analysts of some small investment banks and definitely overperformed the basket of shares from the ECM sector that the hedge fund had sold short. The hedge fund then sold the convertible bonds for 200 cents.

10.7   TRADE CLAIMS[7]

Under section 101(5) of the Bankruptcy Code, a *claim* is the title to demand for payment or the right for a fair remedial action against a performance default, if said default may give origin to a right for payment. A claim can be a defined as a sum of money, such as a loan. These rights to payment are sold and bought based on the expectations of the buyer and the seller as to the final recovery value.

In the event of bankruptcy under Chapter 11, claims subdivide into secured and unsecured. In any distribution plan, secured claims are generally recognized as having a higher priority of payment over unsecured claims. A claim seller can be a creditor (typically a supplier of goods and services) who has extended an unsecured credit line to a debtor company that went bankrupt, or a secured creditor (typically a financial institution) who obtained a collateral to secure a credit advanced to the debtor.

Creditors who cannot wait the time necessary to reorganize the indebted company may decide to sell their claims at a discount to obtain an immediate liquidity without having to wait maybe years to be refunded by the bankrupt company. Other creditors who find themselves in a situation in which a debtor company filed for bankruptcy under Chapter 11 are not in a position to define the correct value of the claim they have, and therefore may be willing to sell it off at a cut-rate price.

The reason for buying a trade claim is that the buyer believes the trade claim will be fully refunded after having purchased it at a discount, or that as part of a probable restructuring it will be converted in debt or equity having a greater value than the price paid to buy it. The reason for selling a trade claim is to transfer the risk and take in at least part of its nominal value.

Typically, in the event of bankruptcy under Chapter 7, there are not enough assets to allow for a claim trade. Moreover, companies filing for bankruptcy under Chapter 7 generally are liquidated too rapidly to give creditors time to trade the claim. Therefore claim trades occur mainly in bankruptcies under Chapter 11.

Creditors who own a claim have a voting right with regard to the reorganization plan in keeping with the procedure envisaged by Chapter 11. Hedge fund managers can therefore buy from creditors their claims against bankrupt companies so as to profit from the restructuring under way. Even though the claim trade is often carried out directly between the parties involved, more often the transaction is executed with the help of a broker.

Claim investors can take an active or a passive role. Those who take a passive role make an estimate of the expected recovery value and the time needed to complete the bankruptcy procedure. If the claim's present value is lower than the seller's bid, it is enough to wait for the bankruptcy procedure to come to an end to make a bargain. However, so many variables come into play that an unexpected delay in the bankruptcy procedure may eat up most of the return on investment.

Let's assume for example that we bought a claim for $100 000 and that upon completion of the bankruptcy procedure $150 000 are refunded. If the bankruptcy procured lasts one year, the return on investment will be +50 %, but it will drop to +22 % if the bankruptcy procedure lasts two years, tumbling to +8 % if it lasts five years.

---

[7] Barbarosh, C.A. and Freeman, W.B. (1998) *Buying and Selling Claim in Bankruptcy: Maximizing Returns* (www. pillsburywinthrop. com).

A claim investor can however decide to take an active role in the bankruptcy procedure, trying to participate actively in the reorganization process, and vote for a reorganization plan that would maximize the value of the claim he owns.

In a claim trade it is important to make sure that the seller's rights are fully passed on to the buyer. Often it is such a complex matter that both the sellers and the buyers of claims resort to expensive law firms for legal advice.

In this regard, the role the Bankruptcy Code attaches to the bankruptcy court is of paramount importance. Under the law, the court is given a certain latitude in assisting a company that is reorganizing to gain back its financial stability. Therefore, following the bankruptcy proceeding, the US courts have a major influence on the bankruptcy outcome.

Trade claims are generally traded over-the-counter, but there are brokers who are specialized in trade claims and who act as intermediaries between the buyer and the original creditor.

Leap Wireless International, Inc. is a mobile communication company, based in San Diego, California, established in 1998 from a spin-off from Qualcomm Inc. to meet the requirements of consumers who were unhappy with traditional mobile phone services. As with all the providers of mobile communication services, in the process of building the network and its customer base the company was practically draining its liquidity. In 2002 the company suffered from a cash shortage and had no access to capital markets, so it started discussing the restructuring with its creditors. With a debt of more than $2 billion, it negotiated a reorganization plan in advance and on 13th April 2003 filed for bankruptcy under Chapter 11 with the US Bankruptcy Court of the Southern district of California in San Diego. On 22nd October 2003, the Bankruptcy Court approved the reorganization plan.

The reorganization plan called for old bond-holders to receive beneficial interests in a liquidating trust which in turn was to receive 3.5 % of the new common stock, approximately $68 million in cash (after a reserve for administrative claims), a few small wireless licenses and some miscellaneous other assets and litigation claims.

The reorganization plan gave suppliers, or holders of the suppliers' credits before the restructuring, 96.5 % of new common shares and $350 million in new secured and senior 13 % Payment-In-Kind notes.[8]

Leap Wireless International, Inc. markedly improved and restructured its operating processes. Starting from the fourth quarter 2002 the company cut operating costs by more than $100 million per year and was able to achieve these savings while retaining its customer base. The company reduced its sales and G&A costs, eliminated and renegotiated several contracts and made many other operational changes. For example, it reduced its gross expenses associated with the acquisition of new customers because it stopped granting a free first month service with the purchase of a phone handset in the fourth quarter 2002. The company also reduced its cost per user from $21.43 in the fourth quarter 2002 to $18.47 in the second quarter 2004 and decreased the gross expenses for the acquisition

---

[8] In contrast to normal bonds, where the issuer must pay a periodic interest in addition to the redemption of the nominal value upon expiration, Payment-In-Kind bonds (PIK) give the issuer the option of avoiding the cash payment of accrued interest, with the issue of new bonds having a nominal value equal to the accrued interest and having the same expiration date as the original bond. The newly issued bonds are also interest-bearing. Briefly, the issuer may choose to make no payments during intermediate periods, but on expiration must pay the nominal value plus all the interest accrued during the intermediate periods. This type of note is used by companies in need of ready cash that want to defer interest payment for an undefined period of time.

of a new customer from $277 to $141 over the same period. The following tables show the projections present in the reorganization plan of 30th July 2003.

Historical data in million dollars:

Year	EBITDA	Debt	Liquidity	Net Debt	Net debt/ EBITDA	Liquidity	EBITDA/ Liquidity
2000	−142.7	1 702.9	338.9	1 364	Negative	112.4	Negative
2001	−309	2 210	243	1 967	Negative	178.1	Negative
2002	−123.3	2 210	100.9	2 109.1	Negative	229.7	Negative
2003	130.5	2 650.2	84	2 566.2	19.664	0	N/A
2004E	238.2	573.4	86.8	486.6	2.043	27.9	8.538
2005E	291.9	573.4	256.3	317.1	1.086	48.3	6.043

Share distribution (every $1000 nominal value of trade payables):

	Nominal value	New secured senior notes at 13 %	New shares	Nominal amount
Lucent	$1000	230.12	38.07	$1 062 148 333
Nortel	$1000	227.98	37.71	$300 217 498
Ericsson	$1000	227.65	37.66	$122 771 686
				$1 485 137 517

Lucent Technologies, one of its suppliers, extended Leap Wireless International, Inc. a credit line to purchase some equipment. This credit line had not been repaid at the time of bankruptcy under Chapter 11 and had turned into a claim. The claim was senior and secured, so at the time of bankruptcy there was a relatively small risk that the amount would not be paid back.

However, Lucent Technologies, who owned the claim, could sell the claim as if it were a bond, in that it represented a debt security of the company Leap Wireless International, Inc. The hedge fund manager, in turn, could buy the claim and the rights to any payment regarding the amount due in virtue of the credit line, taking on the risk that the claim may not be repaid.

On 3rd June 2004, the hedge fund manager bought $90 000 trade claims of Leap Wireless International, Inc. for 110.375 % the nominal value at a purchase price totaling $99 337. The fund manager did not purchase the trade claims directly from the suppliers of Leap Wireless International, Inc. but instead went through a broker.

Purchase of the trade claim:

Date	Quantity	Price	Market value
3rd June 2004	90 000	110.375 %	$ 99 337

During the restructuring of Leap Wireless International, Inc. under Chapter 11, the trade claim was converted into part of the company's new debt and new shares. In exchange for the $90 000 trade claims, the hedge fund received 3.81 % of this amount in shares (equal to 3429 shares) and 23 % of this amount in bonds (equal to 20 700 bonds). At the time of reorganization, the share price was $25, and the bond price was 107 % the nominal value. So at the time of reorganization the share cost was $85 725, the bond cost was $22 149 and the total cost was $107 874. The shares accounted for 79.47 % of the cost and the bonds the residual 20.53 %. If we apply these percentages to the purchase price of trade claims ($99 337), we obtain the actual cost of the newly issued shares and bonds. The costs are $78 941 for the new shares and $20 396 for the new bonds.

Conversion following the reorganization plan:

Received	Quantity	% of quantity	Price at the time of reorganization	Cost at the time of reorganization	% of cost	Actual cost
Shares	3429	3.81 %	$25	$85 725	79.47 %	$78 941
Bonds	20 700	23 %	107 %	$22 149	20.53 %	$20 396

The total cost at the time of reorganization was $107 874 while the actual cost was $99 337. Now we can analyze the profit and loss on shares and bonds separately.

On 25th October 2004, the hedge fund sold the bonds and at the time of writing this book still holds the shares. The average selling price of bonds was $107.75 % of the nominal value equal to a total amount of $22 304. The share price as of 25th October 2004 was $21.36 and the market value of the stock position 73 243.

Thus the hedge fund made a profit on the bond sale (equal to $1908) and on 25th October 2004 had an unrealized loss on the stock position (equal to $5698): the net total loss is $3790.

The gains were:

Security	Sold?	Quantity	Price	Market value	Cost	Profit or Loss
Shares	No	3429	$21.36	$73 243	$78 941	$−5698
Bonds	Yes	20 700	$107.75	$22 304	$20 396	$1908

The Net Loss = $−3790.

When the trade claim was purchased by the hedge fund, the fund manager expected the share price to go well beyond the level reached on 25th October 2004.

What we have been discussing in this example is but one of the numerous purchases of Leap Wireless International Inc. trade claims made by the hedge fund, and purchasing prices ranged from 110 % to 75 % of the trade claim nominal value. Since a significant amount of trade claims was bought close to the 75 % price, most likely the overall transaction will close with a net profit for the hedge fund once all the positions are closed. To understand this outcome better, Table 10.3 illustrates the sensitivity analysis with all the profits made by the hedge fund as a function of the Leap share price and as a function of trade claim prices.

Table 10.3 Sensitivity analysis (profit on trade of 90 000 units)

				Price of Trade Claim (Percent of Par)				
LEAP – Stock Price (USD)	75	80	85	90	95	100	105	110
17.36	$14.332	$9.832	$5.332	$832	$(3.668)	$(8.168)	$(12.668)	$(17.168)
18.36	$17.761	$13.261	$8.761	$4.261	$(239)	$(4.739)	$(9.239)	$(13.739)
19.36	$21.190	$16.690	$12.190	$7.690	$3.190	$(1.310)	$(5.810)	$(10.310)
20.36	$24.619	$20.119	$15.619	$11.119	$6.619	$2.119	$(2.381)	$(6.881)
21.36	$28.048	$23.548	$19.048	$14.548	$10.048	$5.548	$1.048	$(3.452)
22.36	$31.477	$26.977	$22.477	$17.977	$13.477	$8.977	$4.477	$(23)
23.36	$34.906	$30.406	$25.906	$21.406	$16.906	$12.406	$7.906	$3.406
24.36	$38.335	$33.835	$29.335	$24.835	$20.335	$15.835	$11.335	$6.835
25.36	$41.764	$37.264	$32.764	$28.264	$23.764	$19.264	$14.764	$10.264

10.8 STRATEGY'S HISTORICAL PERFORMANCE ANALYSIS

Let's analyze the historical behavior of this strategy based on the monthly returns of the CS/Tremont Event Driven – Distressed Index. As always, the past performance of a given investment is not necessarily indicative of a future return for the same investment. Still, we believe it is useful to examine historical data to understand which scenarios are favorable to this strategy and which are not.

The statistical analysis of the CS/Tremont Event Driven – Distressed Index between 1994 and 2004 produces the results shown in Table 10.4.

The Value at Risk (1 month, 99 %) means that "we have a 99 % probability of not losing more than –4.1 % of the investment in the next month". Instead we have observed a monthly performance of –12.5 %. There is nothing wrong because, as usual, we must read statistics very carefully. The distribution of monthly returns is asymmetric (Skewness equal to –2.83) and with fat tails (Kurtosis greater than 3) and this implies that we cannot use the VaR to estimate an extreme value of the distribution, because we need many more observations.

Figure 10.7 shows the monthly returns of the CS/Tremont Event Driven – Distressed Index between 1994 and 2004. The average annualized return on this index is +13.7 % with an average annualized volatility of 6.7 %: this excellent risk/return ratio placed the distressed securities strategy among one of the historically most efficient hedge fund strategies. Even the percentage of positive months is very high (80 %) with an average monthly performance of +1.7 %.

The largest drawdown was very important (–14.3 %), lasted five months and was recovered in eight months.

Figure 10.8 illustrates the historical performance as a function of risk of the CS/Tremont Event Driven – Distressed Index between 1994 and 2004. The concentration ellipsoid shows

Table 10.4

	CS/Tremont Event Driven – Distressed	Morgan Stanley Capital International World in US$	JP Morgan Global Government Bond Global International
Value at Risk (1 month, 95%)	−1.40%	−6.40%	−1.90%
Value at Risk (1 month, 99%)	−4.10%	−10.40%	−3.60%
Best month Performance	4.10%	8.90%	7.00%
Average Performance in positive months	1.70%	3.20%	1.60%
Worst month Performance	−12.50%	−13.50%	−5.10%
Average Performance in negative months	−1.50%	−3.50%	−1.00%
% Positive months	80%	61%	57%
Compound Annual Growth Rate (CAGR)	13.70%	6.30%	5.40%
Annualized monthly volatility	6.70%	14.20%	6.20%
Skewness	−2.83	−0.6	0.65
Kurtosis	17.46	0.59	2.21
Largest Drawdown*	−14.30%	−48.40%	−8.60%
Duration of the largest drawdown in months	5	30	4
Time to recovery** in months	8	n.d.	9
Drawdown start	31st May 1998	30th Apr. 2000	28th Feb. 1994
Drawdown end	30th Sep. 1998	30th Sep. 2002	31st May 1994

* The largest drawdown is defined as the maximum value of any "peak to trough decline" over the specified period. The subsequent minimum is not determined until it has reached a new high.
** Time to recovery is the time necessary to recover from the largest drawdown.

that the distressed securities strategy has historically moved prevailingly within an excellent area of the risk/return plane. Recently, the strategy's volatility has shown a strong decrease with respect to its historical average.

Figure 10.9 shows that between 1994 and 2004 there were some "underwater" dips for hedge funds. The chart must be analyzed taking drawdown data into consideration: throughout the drawdown and the time to recovery period, the hedge funds adopting this strategy were under the high water mark. (See Chapter 1, Section 1.8, for more details on the setup and meaning of Figures 10.8 and 10.9.)

As shown by the "underwater" chart, there have been three important drawdowns between 1994 and 2004 that can be easily associated with events that had relevant consequences on the markets. First, the unexpected interest rate rise started in February 1994 by the US Federal Reserve. Second, in August 1998, there was a strong *flight-to-quality* move caused by Russia's default and at the same time a worsening in this strategy's drawdown (in the month of August 1998 the strategy shed 12.45%): the drawdown lasted five months and it took eight months to recover the loss. Third, in summer 2002, following the disclosure of the accounting frauds in Adelphia and Worldcom, credit spreads on corporate bonds widened, causing big losses across all credit-oriented strategies.

The main factor underpinning the performance of this strategy is the availability of distressed paper, which primarily depends on the economic cycle and on the evolution of credit spreads.

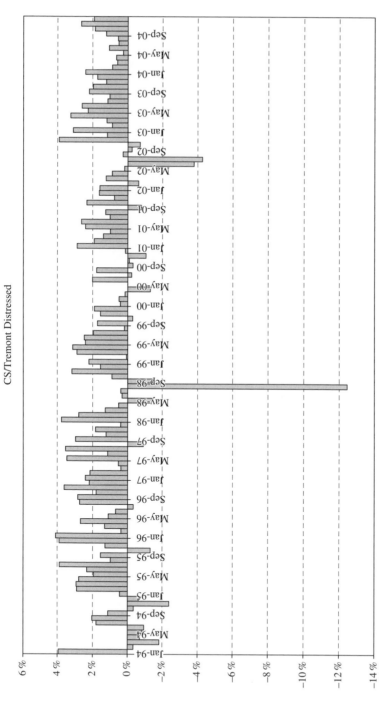

Figure 10.7 Monthly returns of CS/Tremont Event Driven – Distressed from 1994 to 2004. Source: CS/Tremont Index LLC, www.hedgeindex.com. Copyright © 2006, Credit Suisse/Tremont Index LLC. All rights reserved*

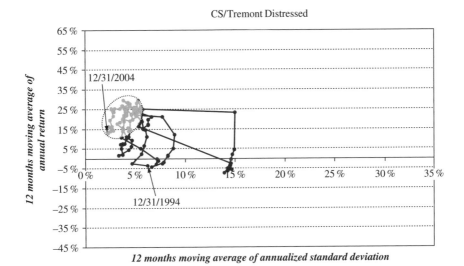

Figure 10.8 Historical performance trend of return as a function of risk for CS/Tremont Event Driven – Distressed from 1994 to 2004. Source: CS/Tremont Index LLC, www.hedgeindex.com. Copyright © 2006, Credit Suisse/Tremont Index LLC. All rights reserved*

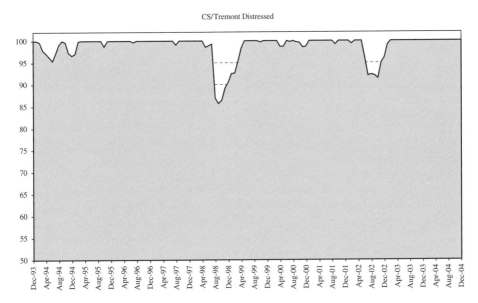

Figure 10.9 Underwater periods for CS/Tremont Event Driven – Distressed from 1994 to 2004. Source: CS/Tremont Index LLC, www.hedgeindex.com. Copyright © 2006, Credit Suisse/Tremont Index LLC. All rights reserved*

10.9   CONCLUSIONS

Default rates are highly correlated to credit spreads. In 2004, credit spreads were at their lowest in the last twenty years. At the end of 2004, the JP Morgan High Yield Spread to Worst Index was worth 350 basis points, whereas the index's long-term average from 1986 to 2004 is 559 bps. From the peak of 1100 bps reached in 2002, credit spreads dropped to 68 %. The market was driven by the improvement of corporate accounts and the decrease in default rates, which reached historically low levels. Many hedge fund managers perceive a substantial risk level in the dynamics of speculative grade bond returns. As a matter of fact, there is the risk of a credit spread widening during an economic slowdown, which would make the present debt level unsustainable for business companies. Probably it is not a generalized risk: there is volatility and a differentiation in the credit performance of the different industries.

Finally, looking back at Figure 1.9, let's identify the key factors making up the performance of fund managers who follow a distressed securities strategy:

- traditional beta: equity market beta and credit spread beta;
- alternative beta: liquidity risk, bankruptcy or default risk, complexity-linked risks and legal risks;
- structural alpha: regulatory constraints prevent many institutional investors from investing in distressed securities;
- skill alpha: ability to valuate, select and trade distressed securities.

11
Event Driven or Special Situations

The event driven investment strategy, also called special situations, refers to opportunities that arise throughout a company's life and that are created by extraordinary, or special, corporate events, such as spin-offs, mergers, acquisitions, business consolidations, liquidations, reorganizations, bankruptcies, recapitalizations, share buy-backs, hostile takeover-bids, changes in benchmark or index composition, sale or purchase of assets, discrepancies in the value of share classes, agreements, legal disputes and even investments in real assets.

So-called special situations are characterized by catalytic events, i.e., events that can drive the price towards a new value. Depending on the opportunities available on the market, fund managers dynamically allocate their capital across the different sub-strategies.

To this end, analysts carry out thorough research on the operating and financial profiles of companies. It is a subjective and creative task that relies on the analyst's talent and calls for great experience. All investment decisions rest on a bottom-up analysis, which puts the burden of emphasis on fundamental analysis and a good knowledge of industrial sectors.

It is not necessary to anticipate events: more often fund managers try to manage events. The complexity of events makes it difficult to predict when the positions opened by hedge fund managers will show a return. When the expected catalytic events do not take place, the positions can remain dormant or shed value, eroding the fund's global return.

The event driven strategy consists in trying to predict the outcome of a given deal, as well as the best time to allocate capital in the investment. The uncertainty surrounding the final outcome of these events creates investment opportunities for those fund managers who are correct in assessing the outcome and timing of these complex situations in advance. The event driven strategy includes also other strategies, such as merger arbitrage and distressed securities.

The performance of hedge funds pursuing an event driven strategy does not depend on market direction. However, weak equity markets may cause some deals to fail or others to be redefined, thus negatively affecting the performance of this strategy. However, buoyant equity markets tend to act as catalysts, opening up investment opportunities for the event driven strategy.

According to the LIPPER TASS database, as of 31st December 2004, event driven funds accounted for 16% of the hedge fund industry.

In November 2002, ENI SpA, the Italian energy group, announced a €2.5 billion takeover offer for the 56% stake it didn't already own in Italgas SpA, the leading gas distributor in Italy and one of the largest in Europe. ENI offered €13 a share in cash and the offer marked an aggressive effort to create a seamless gas operation stretching from exploration and extraction to distribution into homes and businesses. By taking full ownership of Italgas and its five and a half million customers ENI could leverage its own power generation and gas supply businesses to cross-sell products and protect margins. The offer was solely conditional upon anti-trust approval. The hedge fund manager was comfortable about anti-trust approval because ENI already controlled Italgas. Furthermore, under the European Directive on the liberalization of the gas market, no gas company will be able to supply more than 50 % of a national final consumption market by 2003. ENI had 27 % of the Italian retail gas market. Together with Italgas, that market share totaled 39 %, well below the quota of 50 % authorized by the Italian energy regulator. The hedge fund realized an annualized return of about 8 % when the transaction closed in January 2003.

Anchor Glass Container Corporation is one of the largest manufacturers of glass containers in the US. Most of the company's containers are for the beverage and food industries, mainly beer bottles, supplied through a large long-term contract. Since the industry rationalization of the mid-1990s, Anchor and its competitors have enjoyed pricing power as glass container demand has exceeded capacity. This spurred strong financial performance. Starting in late 2000, a string of events occurred causing a negative impact on the company's liquidity. First, the price of natural gas – a key requirement in the glass manufacturing process – increased dramatically. Second, the company's pension plan became increasingly under funded, leading to projected funding requirements. Lastly, in May 2001, Anchor's parent company, Consumer Packaging Inc. filed for bankruptcy protection in Canada. The bankruptcy triggered a put in Anchor's mortgage bonds, which could not be satisfied. A private equity investor accumulated a controlling position in the unsecured debt of the company in order to convert the bonds to equity and control the entity post reorganization. In May 2002, the hedge fund purchased first mortgage bonds. The bonds paid an 11.25 % coupon, and, in addition to being over secured by the company's assets, had the downside of the put back to the company at 101 %. The private equity investor – the company's future owner – needed to bypass this put in order to restructure the company successfully. The hedge fund joined the ad-hoc committee of first mortgage bonds to negotiate the treatment of the bonds. After agreeing to receive a 3.75 % fee to forgo the put, the company filed a prearranged bankruptcy plan in June 2002 and emerged soon thereafter. In February 2003, on the strength of the business, a newly equitized balance sheet and a cash injection by the private equity investor, the company completed a refinancing plan that retired the bonds at par. The hedge fund realized an annualized return of approximately 16 % on the senior secured position.

11.1   ACTIVIST INVESTORS

For event driven hedge funds, the ability to assess the probability and forecast the timing of potential catalysts is a key success factor. A delay in a catalyst may dilute the return of a fund. Some hedge fund managers prefer to be able to control the timing of catalysts fully by causing them directly.

Activism is a particular style of event driven investing, where hedge funds managers have an active role in generating catalyst events that unlock shareholders value. Whereas the event driven strategy is focused on finding companies with a near-term catalyst event, activist investors act directly to generate events themselves.

Active investing features a new breed of hedge funds that intensively focus on shareholder value and have an active role in the corporate governance. In an effort to maximize shareholder value, the activists typically take an active role as a shareholder or bondholder. Activists invest in cash rich companies or undervalued companies, where they believe they can influence change to enhance shareholder value and generate returns on investments. According to these activists, there are many undervalued assets where management could be doing a number of things to enhance shareholder value but for one reason or another is reluctant to do so.

Activists can act directly alone, or be followers of other activists, or join forces with other activists or even with mutual funds. (Traditional investors, like mutual funds and pension funds, have strict concentration and diversification constraints that for example forbid the investment of more than 10 % of net asset value in a single issuer or more than 20 % in a single sector.)

The investment space represented by participations of more than 5 % of the company's capitalization is out of reach for most traditional investors, and was not accessible to hedge funds when this industry started to grow. Nowadays, with huge assets under management, these investments have become affordable, and a new frontier has opened up for exploration.

The activist's approach to top management at the beginning is usually friendly, but can soon become hostile if top management rejects the hedge fund's proposals.

As a key part of the investment strategy, the manager takes active participation in the management of most, if not all, of the companies held in the fund's portfolio, interacting proactively with top management.

The approach generally leads to getting involved with companies by sitting on the board of directors or credit committees of companies, offering advice to management, participating in key negotiations, or initiating the sale of a company (e.g. leveraged buyout) or proxy fights in order to influence the company's activities.

The actions taken to create value are:

- reorganization of companies and battle for strategic change;
- disposal of non-core assets;
- spin-off of business units;
- distribution of cash flow to shareholders through a share buy-back program or the payment of a special dividend.

To achieve these changes, activists often oust top management. They use public letters sent to top management, the financial community and newspapers, to force companies to change their strategies.

In the United States, any fund manager who has become actively involved in the management of a company has to file the 13-D filing[1] with the SEC. 13-D filing is a public document that the SEC requires investors to file when they buy or sell shares if they own more than 5% of a company's outstanding stocks and intend to influence how the company does business. It requires a considerable amount of time to file proxy and 13-D.

Activists take large stakes in companies whose shares have underperformed. The fund typically holds very concentrated positions in a small number of stocks and the fund frequently may hold more than 5% of the issued capital of a company. Usually, in their reports, activists measure their positions as an owned percentage of the capital of the target company and not as a percentage of the fund's assets under management. Often, rumors that shares are being purchased by corporate raiders drive the share price up, because the market anticipates that activists will raise big stakes in target companies.

Activist investors seldom act alone: instead they join forces. In the hedge fund industry, there is a growing cooperation among hedge funds, ranging from takeovers to leveraged buyouts, syndicated loans and activism. This is a keiretsu-like[2] phenomenon, where many hedge funds have positions similar to the Japanese practice where companies have interlocking business relationships and shareholdings.

Activism is a seasonal activity that has its peak during the spring. This is because the fiscal years for most listed companies end on 31st December and annual general meetings are held in April, May and June.

The three main risks of this investment strategy are:

- portfolio concentration risk;
- liquidity risk because activists are insiders and they might be restricted in buying or selling;
- reputational risk.

By taking an active role, activists are likely to be involved in investment litigations against the top management of target companies, which increases their risk profile. Although the fund manager pays for all investment related legal expenses, the existence of litigation increases the firm's reputational risk. Also, activists may take board positions in target companies. This means they may be aware of material confidential information that could prevent them from transacting in the securities of target companies.

Between December 2004 and March 2005, activist investors came to dominate the Deutsche Börse's shareholder base. Two hedge funds led a revolt against Deutsche Börse's bid for the London Stock Exchange. They forced a withdrawal of the London Stock Exchange offer, demanded a return of excess capital, and ousted the top management. Deutsche Börse returned €1.5 billion to shareholders through share buyback. Figure 11.1 shows the appreciation of the stock in the first three quarters of 2005.

---

[1] Schedule filed to report acquisition of beneficial ownership of 5% or more of a class of equity securities.
[2] Source: *Absolute Return*, September 2005

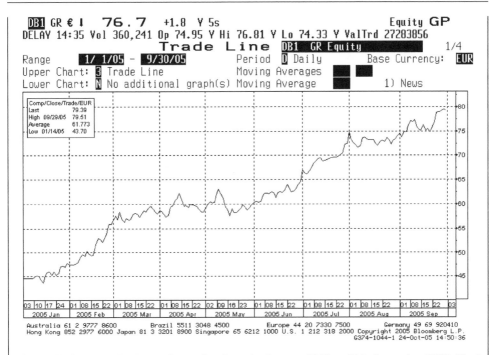

Figure 11.1 Deutsche Börse share price from 1st January 2005 to 30th September 2005. Used with permission from Bloomberg L.P.

Note: The Bloomberg command PHDC allows one to search for institutional and insider holders, whose trading activity may influence the price of a selected security. PHDC can be used to discover which investors are building or unwinding positions.

11.2   STRATEGY'S HISTORICAL PERFORMANCE ANALYSIS

Let's analyze the historical behavior of this strategy based on the monthly returns of the CS/Tremont Event Driven Index. Again, the past performance of a given investment is not necessarily indicative of a future return for the same investment. Still, we believe it is useful to examine historical data to understand which scenarios are favorable to this strategy and which are not.

The statistical analysis of the CS/Tremont Event Driven Index between 1994 and 2004 produces the results shown in Table 11.1.

The percentage of positive months is very high (81 %) and the average performance of positive months is +1.5 %. The performance has been very strong, with an annualized return of 11.8 % between 1994 and 2004, with a modest volatility (5.8 %).

The Kurtosis has an extreme value caused by the outlier in August 1998, when the monthly return has been −11.8 %. A negative value of the Skewness means that the statistical distribution of monthly returns is not symmetric. So we can conclude that this distribution is not Gaussian.

Table 11.1

	CS/Tremont Event Driven Index	Morgan Stanley Capital International World in US$	JP Morgan Global Government Bond Global International
Value at Risk (1 month, 95 %)	−1.1 %	−6.4 %	−1.9 %
Value at Risk (1 month, 99 %)	−3.1 %	−10.4 %	−3.6 %
Best month Performance	+3.7 %	+8.9 %	+7.0 %
Average Performance in positive months	+1.5 %	+3.2 %	+1.6 %
Worst month Performance	−11.8 %	−13.5 %	−5.1 %
Average Performance in negative months	−1.3 %	−3.5 %	−1.0 %
% Positive months	81 %	61 %	57 %
Compound Annual Growth Rate (CAGR)	+11.8 %	+6.3 %	+5.4 %
Annualized monthly volatility	5.8 %	14.2 %	6.2 %
Skewness	−3.47	−0.60	0.65
Kurtosis	1.025	0.59	2.21
Largest drawdown*	−16.0 %	−48.4 %	−8.6 %
Duration of the largest drawdown in months	5	30	4
Time to recovery** in months	10	n.d.	9
Drawdown start	31st May 1998	30th Apr. 2000	28th Feb. 1994
Drawdown end	30th Sep. 1998	30th Sep. 2002	31st May 1994

* The largest drawdown is defined as the maximum value of any "peak to trough decline" over the specified period. The subsequent minimum is not determined until it has reached a new high.
** Time to recovery is the time necessary to recover from the largest drawdown.

The Value at Risk (1 month, 99 %) means that "We have a 99 % probability of not losing more than −3.1 % of the investment in the next month". Instead we have observed a monthly performance of −11.8 %. There is nothing wrong because, as usual, we must read statistics very carefully. The distribution of monthly returns is asymmetric (Skewness equal to −3.47) and with fat tails (Kurtosis greater than 3) and this implies that we cannot use the VaR to estimate an extreme value of the distribution, because we need many more observations.

The largest drawdown has been very important (−16 %), lasted for five months and it was recovered in ten months.

Figure 11.2 shows the monthly returns of the CS/Tremont Event Driven Index between 1994 and 2004. The chart shows that with the exception of two big drawdowns, returns have been consistent over time: the percentage of positive monthly returns is high (81 %).

Figure 11.3 illustrates the historical performance as a function of risk of the CS/Tremont Event Driven Index between 1994 and 2004. The concentration ellipsoid shows that the risk/return profile of the event driven strategy throughout most of the 1994–2004 period remained within a restricted area of the risk/return range, which is a highly desirable characteristic.

Figure 11.4 shows that between 1994 and 2004 there were three important "underwater" dips by hedge funds pursuing the event driven strategy. The chart must be analyzed taking drawdown data into consideration: throughout the drawdown and the time to recovery period, the hedge funds adopting this strategy were under the high water mark. The first drawdown occurred following the unexpected interest rate hike in February 1994 introduced by the

CS/Tremont Event Driven

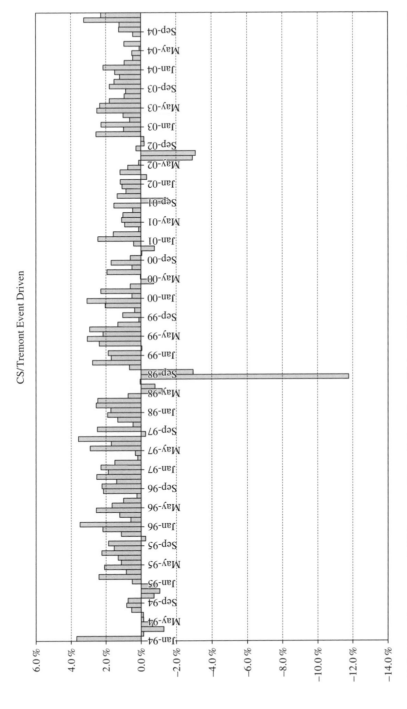

Figure 11.2 Monthly returns of CS/Tremont Event Driven from 1994 to 2004. Source: CS/Tremont Index LLC, www.hedgeindex.com. Copyright © 2006, Credit Suisse/Tremont Index LLC. All rights reserved*

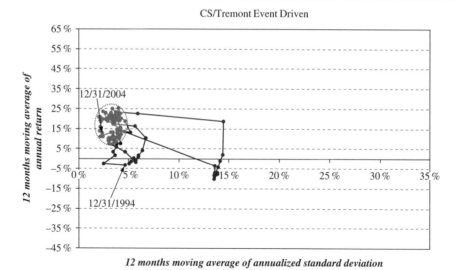

Figure 11.3 Historical performance trend of return as a function of risk for CS/Tremont Event Driven from 1994 to 2004. Source: CS/Tremont Index LLC, www.hedgeindex.com. Copyright © 2006, Credit Suisse/Tremont Index LLC. All rights reserved*

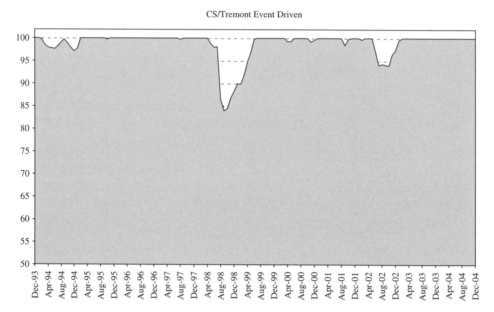

Figure 11.4 Underwater periods for CS/Tremont Event Driven from 1994 to 2004. Source: CS/Tremont Index LLC, www.hedgeindex.com. Copyright © 2006, Credit Suisse/Tremont Index LLC. All rights reserved*

US Federal Reserve. The second and more severe drawdown took place in August 1998 for the strong *flight-to-quality* move caused by Russia's default. Finally, the third drawdown occurred in the summer of 2002, when in the aftermath of the discovery of the Adelphia and Worldcom accounting frauds, credit spreads on corporate bonds widened, causing sizeable losses across all credit-oriented strategies. (See Chapter 1, Section 1.8, for more details on the setup and meaning of Figures 11.3 and 11.4.)

12

Multi-Strategy

12.1 MULTI-STRATEGY FUNDS

Multi-strategy funds generally specialize in convertible bond arbitrage, fixed income arbitrage, distressed securities, event driven and merger arbitrage. Depending on the opportunities offered by the markets, the fund manager decides which percentage of his capital he intends allocating to the single strategies: this way the fund manager can seek to capture multiple opportunities, without having to invest along a specific strategy that under given market circumstances could prove unprofitable. Another advantage brought by multi-strategy is the diversification of return sources across multiple strategies. Due to these characteristics, it is impossible to associate these funds with any of the strategies analyzed up to now.

Generally, the front offices of the management companies of multi-strategy hedge funds are organized into trading groups, each specializing in a specific investment strategy. The hedge fund's chief investment officer is the person deciding the hedge fund's capital allocation across the various trading groups, and he changes this allocation dynamically depending on the opportunities he predicts the single strategies are going to present.

In addition to the above strategies, some multi-strategy funds allocate part of their capital to long/short equity, statistical arbitrage and other minor strategies, like PIPEs or energy trading, which we will cover more extensively in Chapter 13.

Multi-strategy funds are similar to global macro funds from the point of view of the fund manager's discretionary powers in allocating capital across the various strategies, but they differ in terms of lack of investment directionality. Sometimes they also share with global macro funds the large size of the assets under management and the organizational structure of the management company.

12.2 STRATEGY'S HISTORICAL PERFORMANCE ANALYSIS

Let's analyze the historical behavior of this strategy based on the monthly returns of the CS/Tremont Multi-Strategy Index. Again, the past performance of a given investment is not necessarily indicative of a future return for the same investment. Still, we believe it is useful to examine historical data to understand which scenarios are favorable to this strategy and which are not.

The statistical analysis of the CS/Tremont Multi-Strategy Index between 1994 and 2004 produces the results shown in Table 12.1.

The percentage of positive months is very high (84 %) and the average performance of positive months is +1.2 %. The performance has been strong, with an annualized return of 9.4 % between 1994 and 2004, with a surprisingly low volatility (4.4 %).

The distribution of monthly return is asymmetrical (Skewness lesser than zero) and the tails are fatter than those of the Gaussian distribution (Kurtosis greater than 3).

The largest drawdown has been important (−7.1 %), lasted for five months and was recovered in five months.

Figure 12.1 shows the monthly returns of the CS/Tremont Multi-Strategy Index between 1994 and 2004. There are very few months with a negative performance: 84 % of months had a positive performance. The worst month performance (−4.8 %) took place in August 1998 as a result of the strong *flight-to-quality* move caused by Russia's default.

Figure 12.2 illustrates the historical performance as a function of risk of the CS/Tremont Multi-Strategy Index between 1994 and 2004. Note that the concentration ellipsoid includes almost all the amounts in the figure, suggesting an important regularity of the strategy, which is its attractive characteristic.

Table 12.1

	CS/Tremont Multi-Strategy Index	Morgan Stanley Capital International World in US$	JP Morgan Global Government Bond Global International
Value at Risk (1 month, 95 %)	−1.6 %	−6.4 %	−1.9 %
Value at Risk (1 month, 99 %)	−3.4 %	−10.4 %	−3.6 %
Best month Performance	+3.6 %	+8.9 %	+7.0 %
Average Performance in positive months	+1.2 %	+3.2 %	+1.6 %
Worst month Performance	−4.8 %	−13.5 %	−5.1 %
Average Performance in negative months	−1.3 %	−3.5 %	−1.0 %
% Positive months	84 %	61 %	57 %
Compound Annual Growth Rate (CAGR)	+9.4 %	+6.3 %	+5.4 %
Annualized monthly volatility	4.4 %	14.2 %	6.2 %
Skewness	−1.31	−0.60	0.65
Kurtosis	3.71	0.59	2.21
Largest drawdown*	−7.1 %	−48.4 %	−8.6 %
Duration of the largest drawdown in months	5	30	4
Time to recovery** in months	5	n.d.	9
Drawdown start	31st Jul. 1994	30th Apr. 2000	28th Feb. 1994
Drawdown end	30th Nov. 1994	30th Sep. 2002	31st May 1994

* The largest drawdown is defined as the maximum value of any "peak to trough decline" over the specified period. The subsequent minimum is not determined until it has reached a new high.
** Time to recovery is the time necessary to recover from the largest drawdown.

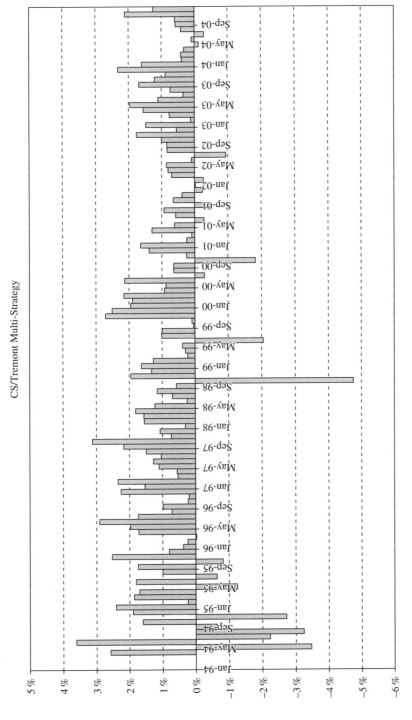

CS/Tremont Multi-Strategy

Figure 12.1 Monthly returns of CS/Tremont Multi-Strategy from 1994 to 2004. Source: CS/Tremont Index LLC, www.hedgeindex.com. Copyright © 2006, Credit Suisse/Tremont Index LLC. All rights reserved*

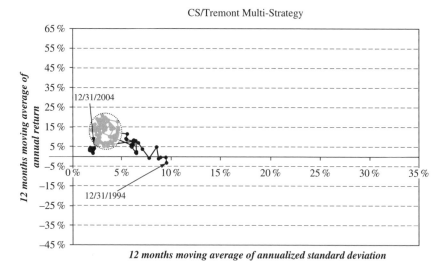

Figure 12.2 Historical performance trend of return as a function of risk for CS/Tremont Multi-Strategy from 1994 to 2004. Source: CS/Tremont Index LLC, www.hedgeindex.com. Copyright © 2006, Credit Suisse/Tremont Index LLC. All rights reserved*

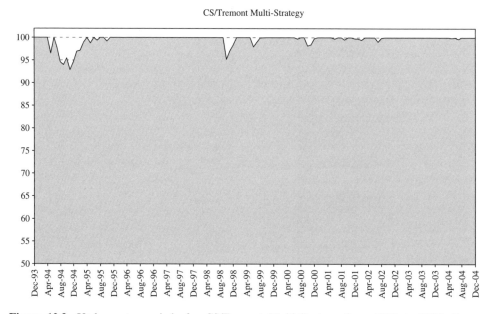

Figure 12.3 Under water periods for CS/Tremont Multi-Strategy from 1994 to 2004. Source: CS/Tremont Index LLC, www.hedgeindex.com. Copyright © 2006, Credit Suisse/Tremont Index LLC. All rights reserved*

---

* See page 298 for full copyright notice.

Figure 12.3 shows that between 1994 and 2004 there were very few "underwater" dips. (See Chapter 1, Section 1.8, for more details on the setup and meaning of Figures 12.2 and 12.3.)

Finally, it is interesting to note that the dynamic strategy allocation in 2004 led these funds to reduce their exposure to the convertible bond arbitrage and to the merger arbitrage strategies.

13
Managed Futures

Trading systems don't care what the answers are: we will let
the market tell us the answers by what it does.
A hedge fund manager

Inappropriately, this strategy is also called CTA, from the name of the type of management company adopting it. A Commodity Trading Advisor (CTA) is any individual or firm that for compensation or profit, directly or indirectly, advises others on the opportunity to buy or sell commodity futures or options contracts. Under the Commodity Exchange Act of the United States, all individuals and firms that intend to operate in the field of futures contracts, albeit with some exceptions, are required to be registered with the Commodity Futures Trading Commission (CFTC, www.cftc.gov) and be members of the National Futures Association (NFA, www.nfa.futures.org).

Some CTAs exercise a discretionary management over hedge funds that invest in options and futures. Initially, they restricted their activities to commodity futures or options trading, which is clearly why they were called Commodity Trading Advisors.

A Commodity Pool Operator (CPO) is an organization soliciting funds from a variety of investors for the purpose of investing in commodity futures or options. With the exception of a few special exemptions, a CPO must be registered with the CFTC. In the United States, CPOs are organized as Limited Partnerships or Limited Liabilities Companies: both types of organizations protect investors from a loss exceeding the original investment.

Let's clarify this point, which is often a source of misunderstandings. Let's say that a hedge fund managed along a managed futures strategy suffers from a loss exceeding the capital, who would pay?

If the hedge fund is organized as a Limited Partnership or a Limited Liabilities Company, for investors the loss cannot exceed the initial capital. So, who pays for the losses exceeding the fund's capital? The answer is that the banks that extended lines of credit to the hedge fund to let it use leverage are going to incur the loss. This is however a very rare situation, because investment banks monitor a hedge fund's credit risk very carefully before starting to do business with it, and at the same time they act as a custodian bank for the hedge funds. As a custodian bank, they keep custody of the hedge fund's securities and can at any time call the securities and settle the positions to protect their credit lines.

Starting in the 1970s and 1980s, hedge fund managers following a managed futures strategy expanded their scope of action and started to trade listed derivatives on commodities, raw materials, precious metals, equity indices, interest rates and treasuries from all over the world.

Note: Managed futures are not literally hedge funds, in that they do not hedge, but are in fact highly directional funds.

Some people do not count CTAs as being among hedge fund strategies. However, we do consider managed futures funds as hedge funds, since most of them have the same legal structure as a hedge fund, the same type of offering memorandum, the same way of calculating performance fees with the high watermark and, because many funds of hedge fund managers invest in managed futures funds to benefit from the low correlation, these funds are displayed with the other hedge fund strategies.

According to the LIPPER TASS database, as of 31st December 2004, managed futures funds accounted for 5 % of the hedge fund industry.

13.1   WHAT IS A FUTURES CONTRACT?

A *futures* contract is a standardized agreement between two parties to buy or sell a specific amount of a commodity (raw materials, agricultural produces) or a financial instrument (shares, interest rates, indices or currencies) at a particular price on a stipulated future date. However, the amount actually exchanged between the parties is not the amount of the assets underlying the futures contract, but instead the margin. The *margin* of a futures contract is the amount of money a hedge fund deposits with a broker to start a trade on a futures contract and keep open positions on futures contracts.

The initial margin varies over time depending on the performance of the futures contract underlying assets and may decrease or increase, and therefore may even require the hedge fund to put up more money to meet margin requirements.

Margin requirements are relatively low and typically range from 5–10 %, and futures trades allow for a very high leverage. As a result, relatively small futures price movements may lead to sizeable losses or gains.

According to the Futures Industry Association (www.futuresindustry.org), in 2003 futures and options trades worldwide reached 8.11 billion contracts, growing by about 30 % with respect to the previous year. In 2003, 49 % of traded contracts were on indices, 23 % on interest rates and 19 % on individual stocks. In the last decade there has been an exponential growth in the number of traded futures contracts.

13.2   A BRIEF HISTORY OF MANAGED FUTURES

This section details some of the milestones in the history of managed futures.

The first futures contracts on agricultural produces started to be traded on the Chicago Board of Trade. The Chicago Board of Trade (www.cbot.com) was founded in 1848 by a group of Chicago merchants, who in the following years started to use *to arrive* contracts for the future delivery of agricultural produces such as flour and hay. The earliest *forward* contract, for 3000 bushels of corn, was recorded in 1851.

In 1859, the Chicago Board of Trade received a charter from the State of Illinois and was mandated to set standards of quality, product uniformity and routine inspections of grain. In 1865, it formalized grain trading by developing standardized agreements called *futures contracts*. The Chicago Board of Trade also began requiring performance bonds on its grain markets, called "margins".

In 1922, the federal government formed the Grain Futures Administration to regulate grain trading, and in 1936 soybean futures trading began.

A crucial figure in the history of futures is Richard Donchian (1905–1993), known as the father of the modern trend of following systems for his pioneering works in the field of commodity futures management. Donchian's original methods involved the use of a moving average as entry/exit indicator. After World War II, he shifted his focus from securities to commodity trading. In 1948, he created the commodity fund Futures, Inc., based on the principle of diversification. He developed a technical trading system, called *trend following,* which presupposed that commodity prices would move in long sweeps like bull and bear markets. He did not concentrate on market fundamentals, and would rather use a mathematical system based on moving averages of commodity prices. He authored many articles on futures trading. From 1960 to 1993, he was an associate with Hayden Stone Inc., as Director of Commodity Research and Senior Vice President. In 1960 he started writing a successful weekly newsletter entitled *Commodity Trend Timing,* which he continued to author for another 19 years.

Another notable milestone in the history of managed futures is the installation in 1967 of new electronic price display boards on the walls above the trading floors, which meant that prices were reported in real time.

In 1973, the Chicago Board Options Exchange was formed. Since then futures trades rapidly expanded into many new markets in addition to traditional agricultural and physical commodities.

In 1975, CBOT launched the first futures contract on a financial instrument: a futures on Government National Mortgage Association mortgage-backed certificates. It introduced the US Treasury bond futures contracts in 1977 and options on US Treasury Bond futures in 1982. In 1984, trading in options on agricultural futures began with soybean futures, followed by the launch of interest rate futures and options on futures in 1987. In 1997, CBOT introduced the Dow Jones Industrial Average Index futures and options on futures contracts, and in 2001, 10-year interest rate swap futures were launched.

In recent years, there has been a proliferation of futures and options on a wide variety of underlying commodities, such as crude oil, heating oil, gasoline, natural gas and a wide variety of financial instruments, such as currencies, treasuries and equity indices. In addition, innovative futures contracts have been launched on electric power and weather derivatives.

Together with the Chicago Board of Trade, the London Metal Exchange (www.lme.com) is one of the main exchanges where commodities are traded. The London Metal Exchange is to date the world's premier non-ferrous metal market with a turnover of about $2000 billion per annum, and its history is instructive. In the 19th century, Britain's industrial revolution led to a massive increase in metal consumption in the United Kingdom, which required the import of enormous quantities from abroad. Merchants were investing large sums of money in this activity and were exposed to great risks, not only because voyages were hazardous, but also because the cargoes could lose value if there was a fall in price during the time it took for the metal to reach the UK. Merchants began meeting in coffee houses where they traded metal cargoes as forward contracts so as to protect themselves against the risk of a fall in the prices of the sea-borne goods during the long voyages from the colonies. The London Metal Exchange was founded in 1877, to bring order to this activity with a single marketplace, recognized times of trading and standardized contract specifications.

13.3 MANAGED FUTURES STRATEGY

The managed futures strategy is similar to the macro strategy: both are directional strategies investing prevailingly in futures listed worldwide. The primary difference is that in the managed futures strategy the fund manager's emotions are eclipsed by the use of computerized models that automatically make trading decisions. The fund manager can only periodically re-adjust the trading model parameters.

CTAs develop many models that are processed by a computer in real time in order to pick a trend in each of more than 100 different futures markets and on different time horizons.

They follow the trend until it dies out, first with a *back testing* on historical data, then with the management of a test portfolio, and finally with the management of true data in real time. A good trading system must minimize the brokerage fees paid by the fund to brokers, minimize volatility and minimize slippage, which curbs the strategy's profitability. In fact, an overly intensive trading may accumulate high brokerage fees that negatively affect performance. Risk management is very important, and to this end sophisticated risk management systems are put in place. For example, losing positions are gradually reduced through *stop loss* techniques, or net market exposure is limited, or the fund manager tries to increase positions that are inversely correlated with those that are reporting a loss. Some fund managers link the position's size with its volatility.

Pattern recognition systems seek to identify market trends on different time horizons, i.e., to spot whether a weekly trend is forming on soybean futures, a fortnight trend on oil futures, or a 3-hour trend on NASDAQ futures.

Often *back testing* is misleading, in that it is relatively easy to find a model that suits the historical data. However, the application of a similar model to a computer-assisted trading system rests on a very potent assumption: that the future will behave exactly as the past. A very questionable assumption indeed! Just think of events such as the outbreak of the Gulf war, the terrorist attacks of 11th September 2001, etc.

Managed futures can be concentrated in a limited number of positions or offer a diversification on a wide variety of futures markets: currencies, interest rates, equity indices, bond indices, energy, base and precious metals, agriculture commodities, etc.

In periods of *trading range* or sideways markets, managed futures that follow medium to long-term periods are at a disadvantage, as there is no trend to profit from. Classical trend following models are also at a disadvantage when a medium to long-term trend suddenly shifts direction, because they can recognize the reversal of a main trend only with a certain delay.

In order to assess the solvency of a managed futures fund it is important to verify its *margin-to-equity*, that is the existing ratio between the margins put up as a guarantee to the futures contracts and the hedge fund's net equity. Generally, a high leverage is used.

CTAs have a different approach compared to the hedge fund managers analyzed up to now: they do not consider fundamental analysis, and instead conduct only technical analysis. Most futures fund managers operate with highly technical trading systems that they apply through sophisticated risk management systems. The people dealing with the research and implementation of these futures trading strategies are mathematicians, physicists, engineers, chess champions, software engineers, cryptography scientists, etc. Managed futures also differ from hedge funds managed by other strategies due to an asset management activity that focuses only on derivatives, the high leverage being used, and the great transparency delivered to their investors, so as to incur no capacity problems, and retain good liquidity, low correlation and low volatility.

Figure 13.1 spells out the fundamental parameters to classifying managed futures. We can distinguish two types of CTA based on the trading approach:

- *discretionary*, which use a qualitative approach. Entry/exit decisions are based on the manager's subjective opinion;
- *systematic*, which make trade decisions based on mathematical models. Trades are based on the systematic application of quantitative trading rules. Purchase and sale signals are generated by the computer and risk control is also automated. Systematic strategies are based on quantitative and computational investment techniques developed by the fund managers based upon experience and empirical research.

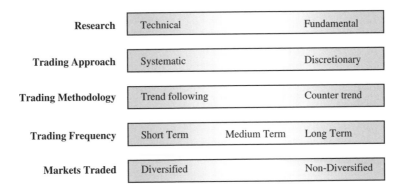

Research	Technical		Fundamental
Trading Approach	Systematic		Discretionary
Trading Methodology	Trend following		Counter trend
Trading Frequency	Short Term	Medium Term	Long Term
Markets Traded	Diversified		Non-Diversified

Figure 13.1 Classification of managed futures investment strategy. Source: free adaptation from Fimat

Based on the trading methodology, we can distinguish the following strategies:

- *trend following*, where transactions are opened in the same direction as the trend and closed when the trend reverses;
- *counter trend*, where positions are counter to the trend to try and anticipate reversals.

(Discretionary CTAs will be covered in Chapter 14 when we discuss global macro funds.) Systematic CTAs can operate on over 100 different markets worldwide, 24 hours a day in real time. Trading is automated by mathematical models that sample input signals, filter them to eliminate background noise, detect the market signal, and analyze and interpret said signals to generate buy, hold or sell decisions automatically. Input signals are the time series of prices, volumes and open interest, that is, the total number of contracts in an options market that are still open at a given time.

The managers of this type of hedge funds are "software engineers", who design the trading logic and then implement programs that run automatically on markets. CTAs trade with proprietary software programs that have been developed in-house with programming languages like Java, and that electronically send buy or sell orders to brokers or directly on the market.

If we see price as an electric signal, we realize there is a very interesting analogy: looking for short, medium and long-term trends is like looking for the frequency of a signal after filtering the "good" signal from background noise. It is very difficult to assess the mathematical models that filter and process input signals, and for this reason they are called black box models.

Figure 13.2 illustrates a diagram that resembles an electronic device, receiving an electric signal as an input and sending out a signal processing as output. To analyze signals we can therefore apply the theories of filtering, prediction and model identification, which have been long-developed in electronics. In fact, we can leave it up to the data to tell us which model is best-suited. Interestingly, the theory of model identification draws a very important conclusion: a time series can be best interpreted by models that change over time.[1]

Currently, the futures industry is in great turmoil and many specialists are looking for *money machines*, capable of inputting market prices and making money through automated

---

[1] Bittanti, S. (1992) *Identificazione dei Modelli e Controllo Adattativo*, Bologna: Pitagora Editrice; Bittanti, S. (1992) *Teoria della Predizione e del Filtraggio*, Bologna: Pitagora Editrice; Bittanti, S. and Schiavoni, N. (1994) *Modellistica e Controllo*, CittàStudi.

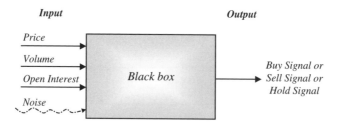

Figure 13.2   The transformation function

trading. As previously started, chess champions, physics researchers, nuclear engineers, PhDs, mathematicians and many others are all at work developing models.

Once the trading mathematical models have been designed, a test is carried out by "running" the model with past time series. If the model works, then real money is invested on a compelling, yet dangerous assumption: if the model worked with past data, it will be able to work in the future as well. Once again, it has to be reiterated that in the author's opinion assuming the future will be similar to the past is totally unfounded; and if the assumption does sometimes work, it is just by pure chance.

Trading systems used by CTAs can be specialized in researching market price trends (trend follower) or in the research of market price trend reversals (counter trend). Trend followers seek to ride a trend as soon as it appears, and try and do so until the trend fades out.

CTAs also differ from other strategies in terms of length of time horizon, that is the frequency of moves they try to follow: long-term trends are those lasting from one to six months, medium-term trends are those lasting eight to 30 days and short-term trends last from one to seven days.

Short-term trend followers are specialized in the analysis of the market micro-structure and the price formation mechanism. They try to identify the faster trends. They will enter a position immediately after the first strong movement that takes place after a trend reversal. This will lead to a high frequency of deals with limited gains or losses and with a high trading cost incidence.

Long-term trend followers try to identify long-term trends, i.e., the slower trends. They will ride a trend while it is developing and will need generally more time to identify a trend reversal. As a result, they will carry out less trade with respect to short trend followers, and will make greater gains or losses.

The trading frequency is equal to the reverse of the time period analyzed by the strategy to produce a trading signal:

$$f = \frac{1}{T}$$

Figure 13.3 illustrates an example showing the graphical meaning of moving averages. We have overlapped the chart with the daily closing prices of West Texas Intermediate oil with the moving averages at 15, 50 and 180 days, i.e., a short, a medium and a long-term moving average.

The frequency of the moving average line increases as the number of days, based on which it is calculated, decreases: the frequency of the 15 day moving average for example is greater than the frequency of the 50 day moving average.

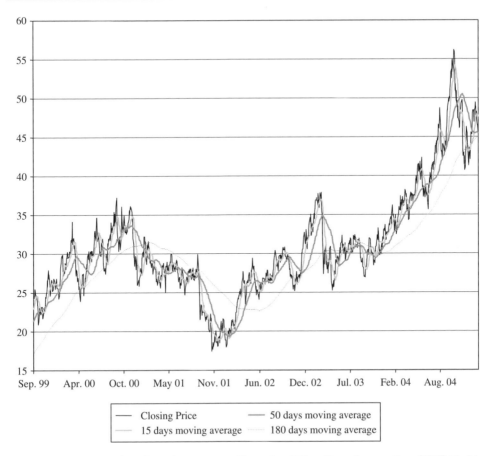

Figure 13.3 Frequencies of moving averages: Example of West Texas Intermediate (WTI) Cushing Crude Oil Spot Price in dollar/barrel. Source: Bloomberg L.P.

Figure 13.4 shows the daily closing euro–dollar exchange rate and the moving averages at 15, 50 and 180 days. The moving averages are lagging behind price trends. In bullish markets, this lag causes the moving average to be below the price, whereas in bearish markets the moving average is above. When the price changes direction, the trendline and the priceline intersect because the line price is slow in reflecting the new direction. These intersections provide a very simple example of trading signals:

- buy when rising prices intersect trendlines;
- sell when falling prices intersect trendlines.

Figure 13.5 shows an example of moving average curves to highlight their intersections and the buy and sell signals that are suggested by these intersections.

This example shows only the theoretical rationale underlying a trading system based on sell and buy signals. For a practical application it would be necessary to better clarify what we mean by priceline (opening price, closing price, highest price, lowest price or averages of different kind) and which are the moving averages we used (for example, is it better

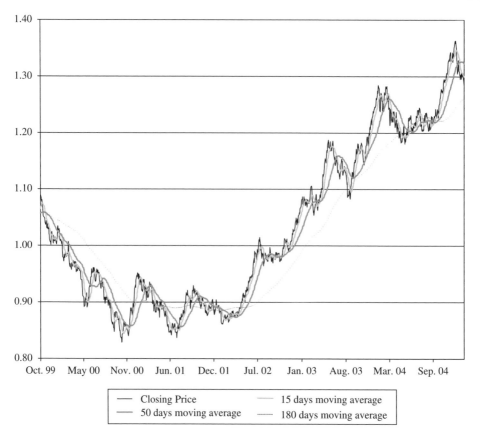

Figure 13.4 Frequencies of moving averages. Example of Euro–Dollar exchange rate. Source: Bloomberg L.P.

to use the 7-day, the 10-day or the 50-day moving average?). Once again, this is another demonstration of how simple the strategy may be, but how complex it is to implement.

Most CTAs tend to trade on many futures markets in order to seize the largest number of investment opportunities. The exposure to single markets may vary over time, even automatically, depending on the opportunities arising on the different markets.

Risk management is part and parcel of every trading strategy used in the mathematical models of CTA. A variety of models and systems can be employed. The author met one CTA who tried to take advantage of the volatility expansions and contractions of a price time series. All these techniques are long volatility: the greater the market volatility, the greater are the opportunities for the hedge fund manager.

There are also a variety of indicators being used: regression analysis (for example, the ARIMA model), moving averages (some even with exponential smoothing), momentum indicators (momentum and oscillators), overbought and oversold analysis, Bollinger bands, etc. Many of the present development areas in the research of mathematical models used by CTA coincide with research theories on the frontier of mathematics and statistics: theory of chaos, fractal geometry, neural networks, genetic algorithms, theory of games, fuzzy logic, artificial intelligence, etc.

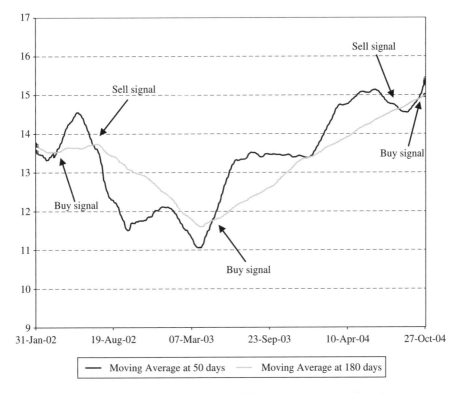

Figure 13.5 Buy and sell signals that are suggested by the intersections of moving average curves with different frequencies. An example

The study of economic time series is a pioneering research area in the scientific field. We might recall that in 2003 Robert F. Engle III won the Nobel Prize for Economic Sciences for his contribution to methods for analyzing economic time series with time-varying volatility. Clive W.J. Granger shared the Nobel Prize with him for his contribution to methods for analyzing economic time series with common trends. Engle and Granger's studies are of great interest to managed futures hedge fund managers.

A key element determining the profitability of a trading strategy based on quantitative models is the amount of transaction costs, as already illustrated in Chapter 2. CTA hedge funds generating greater trading volumes have a greater bargaining power with brokers in the definition of lower brokerage fees, which gives them a competitive advantage because they can take advantage of a greater number of opportunities.

In general, analyzing managed futures fund data on the LIPPER TASS database we noticed that these funds have commission and performance fees populating the top end of the hedge fund market. Performance fees are generally 25 % and management fees are generally 2.5 %.

The weight invested on the different markets can change depending on opportunities. Managed futures trade very liquid instruments and long and short positions can be established very easily through the purchase or sale of futures. Valuating the portfolio is simple because practically it is no more than assigning market price to the futures present in the portfolio. The high liquidity of futures contracts allows managed futures funds to offer a good liquidability to its investors and often they offer a daily, weekly or fortnight liquidity to its subscribers.

Some quantitative models are based on the principle of *mean reversion*. Mean reversion is the tendency of a stochastic process to stay close or return over time close to its long-term mean. Intuitively, a share that has performed well recently, will tend to underperform, whereas a share that recently performed less well will tend to recover: a share's price time series will tend to return to its mean. Of course, some phenomena can be explained efficiently by a mean reversion model and others cannot.

Other quantitative models are based on the concept of *momentum*. Momentum is the share's tendency to persist along a medium-term trend. Intuitively, shares that recently have performed well will go on performing well in the medium-term, while shares that recently have performed less well will go on underperforming in the medium-term.

Figure 13.6 illustrates a pound sterling futures trade in the time period from 1st January 2004 to 3rd December 2004. The left axis shows the number of futures contracts on the pound sterling bought or sold by the fund manager, while the right axis shows the dollar-denominated closing price of the pound sterling futures contracts with a 1-month maturity. Historical data were processed to factor in the periodic recalculation of positions following the expiration of futures contracts.

Figure 13.6 British pound futures trade example

> The hedge fund manager uses a combination of moving averages, short-term volatility and trade volume data to determine the buy, hold or sell signals. Moving averages are a good approximation for trends, but the fund manager does not rely on them alone to make an investment decision.

13.4   "DO STORKS DELIVER BABIES?" AND THE PREDICTABILITY OF FINANCIAL TIME SERIES

One of Neyman's[2] fictitious friends, in an empirical attempt to prove the theory that storks deliver babies, calculated the correlation between the number of storks every 10 000 women and the number of babies every 10 000 women in a sample of countries. He found a statistically highly significant correlation, and prudentially concluded that "despite [the fact] there is no evidence that storks really deliver babies, there is overwhelming evidence that, for some mysterious process, they affect the birth rate!".

This amusing example teaches us to distinguish between interpretational models (causality) and predictive models.

The modalities by which market prices are formed are being researched both by academics and by market operators and their aim is to highlight non-causal, that is, predictable behaviors. In the finance literature, we can find some very interesting interpretations.

Keynes' historic example of the beauty contest where judges do not vote for the most beautiful girl, but instead the girl they think is considered the most beautiful by most of the jury is indicative: the same behavior causes prices on financial markets to uncouple from the intrinsic value of the goods traded on the markets, relating them to psychological mass dynamics.

Regarding the validity of mathematical-statistical models, it is worth focusing special attention on the assumptions upon which they rest. For example, the highly useful modelings that can be made based on the Black–Scholes formula are obviously associated with the validity of the assumption on which it lies, that is, that financial time series are represented by a random walk of prices.

Finally, there is George Soros's interpretation, who argues that price dynamics do not only reflect available information, but play an active role in forming the interpretation of the same information.

13.5   STRATEGY'S HISTORICAL PERFORMANCE ANALYSIS

Let's analyze the historical behavior of this strategy based on the monthly returns of the CS/Tremont Managed Futures Index. Again, the past performance of a given investment is not necessarily indicative of a future return for the same investment. Still, we believe it is useful to examine historical data to understand which scenarios are favorable to this strategy and which are not.

The statistical analysis of the CS/Tremont Managed Futures Index between 1994 and 2004 produces the results shown in Table 13.1.

---

[2] Neyman, J. (1952) *Lectures and Conferences on Mathematical Statistics and Probability*, 2nd edition, Department of Agriculture, Washington DC, USA, pp. 143–154.

Table 13.1

	CS/Tremont Managed Futures Index	Morgan Stanley Capital International World in US$	JP Morgan Global Government Bond Global International
Value at Risk (1 month, 95 %)	−5.2 %	−6.4 %	−1.9 %
Value at Risk (1 month, 99 %)	−8.2 %	−10.4 %	−3.6 %
Best month Performance	+10.0 %	+8.9 %	+7.0 %
Average Performance in positive months	+3.0 %	+3.2 %	+1.6 %
Worst month Performance	−9.4 %	−13.5 %	−5.1 %
Average Performance in negative months	−2.3 %	−3.5 %	−1.0 %
% Positive months	55 %	61 %	57 %
Compound Annual Growth Rate (CAGR)	+7.0 %	+6.3 %	+5.4 %
Annualized monthly volatility	12.2 %	14.2 %	6.2 %
Skewness	0.03	−0.60	0.65
Kurtosis	0.44	0.59	2.21
Largest drawdown*	−17.7 %	−48.4 %	−8.6 %
Duration of the largest drawdown in months	8	30	4
Time to recovery** in months	15	n.a.	9
Drawdown start	30th Apr. 1995	30th Apr. 2000	28th Feb. 1994
Drawdown end	30th Nov. 1995	30th Sep. 2002	31st May 1994

* The largest drawdown is defined as the maximum value of any "peak to trough decline" over the specified period. The subsequent minimum is not determined until it has reached a new high.
** Time to recovery is the time necessary to recover from the largest drawdown.

The difference between the best and the worst months is very wide, indicative of the fact that there is a great breadth of changes. The percentage of positive months is relatively low, therefore months with negative performance are frequent, and it is essential for the fund manager to implement an effective risk management to limit losses. The percentage of positive months is modest (55 %) and the average performance of positive months is +3 %.

The performance has been strong, with an annualized return of 7 % between 1994 and 2004, but with a very high volatility (12.2 %): so the risk/return has been quite disappointing in general. Nevertheless, the great strength point of this investment strategy is the low correlation with the other hedge fund investment strategies. The distribution of monthly return is symmetrical (Skewness close to zero) and the tails are shorter than those of the Gaussian distribution (Kurtosis lesser than 3). The largest drawdown has been very high (−17.7 %), lasted for eight months and was recovered in more than one year (15 months).

Figure 13.7 shows the monthly returns of the CS/Tremont Managed Futures Index between 1994 and 2004.

Figure 13.8 illustrates the historical performance as a function of risk of the CS/Tremont Managed Futures Index between 1994 and 2004. The figure does not show the concentration ellipsoid due to the historical erratic behavior of the risk/return profile of these hedge funds.

Figure 13.9 shows that between 1994 and 2004 there were many "underwater" dips by hedge funds pursuing this strategy. The chart must be analyzed taking drawdown data into consideration: throughout the drawdown and the time to recovery period, the hedge funds

CS/Tremont Managed Futures

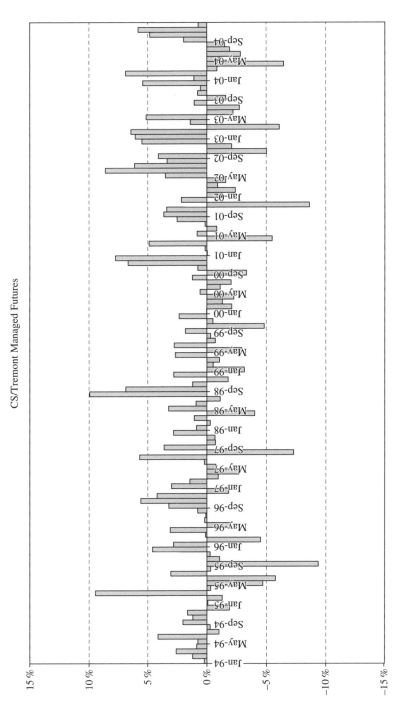

Figure 13.7 Monthly returns of CS/Tremont Managed Futures from 1994 to 2004. Source: CS/Tremont Index LLC, www.hedgeindex.com. Copyright © 2006, Credit Suisse/Tremont Index LLC. All rights reserved*

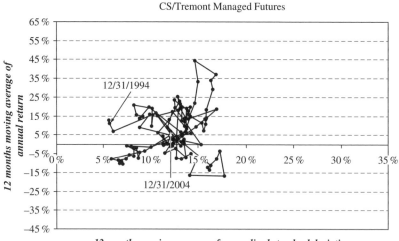

Figure 13.8 Historical performance trend of return as a function of risk for CS/Tremont Managed Futures from 1994 to 2004. Source: CS/Tremont Index LLC, www.hedgeindex.com. Copyright © 2006, Credit Suisse/Tremont Index LLC. All rights reserved*

adopting this strategy were under the high water mark. (See Chapter 1, Section 1.8, for more details on the setup and meaning of Figures 13.8 and 13.9.)

In 2004 there was the largest drawdown in the last ten years caused by trend reversals in all sectors, followed by sideway markets with no trends. It lasted from March to August.

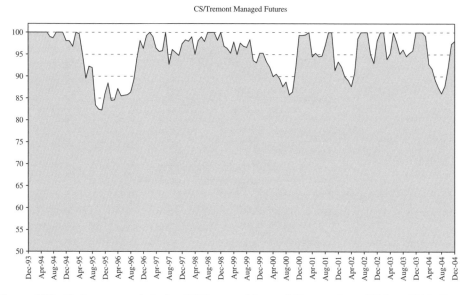

Figure 13.9 Underwater periods for CS/Tremont Managed Futures from 1994 to 2004. Source: CS/Tremont Index LLC, www.hedgeindex.com. Copyright © 2006, Credit Suisse/Tremont Index LLC. All rights reserved*

* See page 298 for full copyright notice.

Managed futures in April 2004 suffered losses due to the strong trend reversal on interest rates and on metals, and then due to false trend signals in particular on currency markets. However, the strong trend shown by oil throughout 2004 was highly profitable for fund managers adopting this strategy.

The low volatility on equity markets (Figure 6.10), as indicated by the VXO index that is at its lowest in the last six years, determined a trendless environment, with a dearth of opportunities for managed futures.

What do these apparently disparate events have in common? In all these cases, there were volatility peaks on the markets. It is interesting to note that managed futures performed well in periods of great market shocks: the black Monday in 1987, Russia's default in 1998 and the Gulf crisis in 1990.

In the past, managed futures have demonstrated a low correlation with other investment strategies. When there are trends to be followed on the futures market, this strategy performs well. Whereas, if the market moves sideways, there are many false signals and the mathematical models will switch between buy and sell decisions while prices find no direction. Therefore, we can state that low volatility is an adverse scenario for managed futures managers.

Although in the past managed futures were highly correlated with one another, today they may show no correlation or at times even a negative correlation. As we have seen in Figure 13.1, there are various types of managed futures that have designed widely differing mathematical models.

Figure 13.10 shows the 20 worst monthly downturns of the Morgan Stanley Capital International World Index in dollars between 1994 and 2004. In 70 % of cases, managed

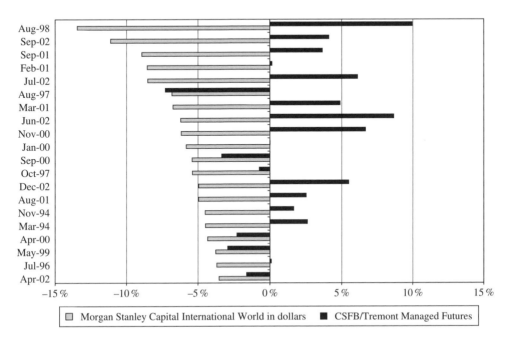

Figure 13.10 Return of CS/Tremont Managed Futures Index during the 20 worst monthly losses of the Morgan Stanley Capital International World Index in dollars from 1994 to 2004. Sources: Bloomberg, CS/Tremont

futures funds were able to get a positive return, thus offering to their investors a protection in times of strong downturns on financial markets.

13.6 CONCLUSIONS

Looking back to Figure 1.9, let's identify the key factors making up the performance of fund managers pursuing the managed futures strategy:

- traditional beta: equity, fixed income and currency market beta;
- alternative beta: commodities, risks associated with following trends;
- structural alpha: trend behavior on all financial markets;
- skill alpha: trend following system quality, risk management, for example stop loss or position sizing.

2004 was a bad year for this hedge fund strategy due to the trend reversals that took place in all sectors, followed by sideways markets. It is difficult for markets to remain trendless for long. There are a host of factors that can inject volatility and start trends on the treasury, currency, equity and commodity markets: oil prices, the US trade deficit, growth in China, growth in the US, geo-political factors, etc.

Directional strategies do not suffer from overcrowding, with lots of market operators who try to seize the same opportunities. Markets are driven by macro-economic forces that are much more powerful than those started off by hedge fund managers. If some trends start showing again on markets, these fund managers are well positioned to capture them.

14

Global Macro

We open this chapter by recalling Plato's allegory of the cave, in order to tackle the topic of how to discern reality, or truth. In this context, market prices can be seen as the shadows of a reality that is all too difficult to comprehend. George Soros, with the theory of reflexivity, teaches us that market participants try to understand market performance and obtain the desired results by modifying reality without ever fully comprehending it. Therefore, prices are a manifestation of reality, but in turn they can influence and modify reality.

Global macro fund managers have the broadest investment mandate among the various types of existing hedge funds. Managers can invest on almost any market, using any financial instrument.

Their investment approach is typically top-down, as their choices are prevailingly based on the analysis of macro-economic variables associated with the different countries in which they have decided to allocate their capital. Market forecasts are generated by econometric models, trying to leverage the inconsistencies perceived by the statistical analysis of macro-economic variables, such as gross domestic product, balance of trade, public deficit, population and demographics, treasuries yield, equity market returns, prices of raw materials, exchange rates, etc.

Fund managers form their own view as to the prevailing trends on financial markets, and then try to capture returns by trading the main world macro-economic indices. They trade all asset classes (treasuries, currencies, corporate bonds, precious metals, commodities), use all financial instruments (securities, indices, options, spot, forward and futures contracts, swaps, etc.) and use short selling and leverage. Some invest in commodities only by way of derivatives, whereas others even invest in physical commodities. Generally, there are no predetermined geographical restrictions to their investments, therefore they can trade all over the world, from G7 countries to emerging markets.

Macro fund managers try to anticipate price changes on capital markets and often establish directional positions, i.e. unhedged. To identify events that will produce price changes, they focus on the analysis of how political events, global macro-economic factors, economic and financial fundamentals and other external factors influence the valuation of financial instruments. At the same time, they also analyze capital markets directly, and the risk/return potential of a given investment.

If through the top-down analysis of fundamentals the fund manager decides to anticipate a market trend, he is going to use the financial market analysis to determine the market timing and the financial instruments that best suits his opinion.

Every trading decision must necessarily be consistent with the manager's macroeconomic view, but it also has to be consistent with the risk profile of the entire portfolio. In addition, for global macro hedge funds, the main objective is capital preservation.

Due to the directional bias of their investments, global macro fund managers generally offer little transparency to their investors. They deny interviews to journalists and if they do discuss their performance with the investors at all it will be several months later and in very general terms.

In the case of macro funds, however, the key player is the manager, who with his insight and skill generates investment ideas and seeks to seize the less obvious investment opportunities. Profits will be reaped if the fund manager correctly anticipates the price movements on global financial markets. Their investment philosophy is opportunistic, as they trade in any capital market sector presenting profit opportunities and with any financial instrument, in that they opportunistically replicate the most specialized strategies belonging to the other fund classes. Macro funds are similar to multi-strategy funds, except that they carry out directional investments and many discretionary hedge funds are very similar to managed futures funds.

In comparison to the hedge funds managed along the strategies analyzed up to now, global macro hedge funds are generally characterized by a larger size in terms of assets under management. They trade on highly liquid markets, for example the currency, commodity and treasury markets, and since they do not go for niche strategies, they can handle their positions without affecting market prices to their disadvantage.[1]

One of the most important indicators used by hedge fund managers is the average number of days necessary to settle a position.[2]

Directional strategies represent a substantial departure from the original hedge fund philosophy according to the Alfred Winslow Jones model. In broad terms, macro funds are also defined as being hedge funds, not because they provide a hedge, but rather because they are not subject to the constraints and limitations of mutual investment funds. Instead of hedging market risks, they seek to profit from the direction of movements on financial markets, establishing directional positions that reflect their predictions in terms of market direction. As a result, their performance fully depends on the quality and timing of their predictions. Macro funds tend to invest on capital markets of highly developed countries as well as of emerging countries. They rapidly jump from one investment opportunity to the other and from one asset class to the other. Sometimes they make a wide use of leverage and of derivatives, and their returns are often highly volatile with respect to the other types of hedge funds.

Using a metaphor, we can say that macro funds are comparable to the queen on the chessboard, the most powerful chess piece who can move in any direction.

14.1   A BRIEF HISTORY OF MACRO FUNDS

Although the first hedge fund was created in 1949 by Alfred Winslow Jones, these "alternative" investment instruments did not start to attract the attention of the media and the financial community until 1992, when George Soros's Quantum Fund brought the Central Banks of England and Italy to their knees. By selling short an enormous amount of Italian lira and British pounds and making an extensive use of leverage, Soros caused a significant devaluation of the two currencies and made huge profits. The exit of the British pound and

---

[1] *Slippage* is that phenomenon whereby the trades executed by a manager are so huge as to cause a market movement that erodes the potential profit. Beyond a given AuM size, the portfolio is no longer nimble and the manager cannot enter and exit at his own whim from his positions without affecting the market to his detriment. When a long position is established, the market price goes up, and when the market position is liquidated, the market price goes down, i.e., the originated movement goes against the fund manager.
[2] This indicator is generally calculated as the value of the position subdivided by the daily average trading volume of that security.

the Italian lira from the European Monetary System in September 1992 allowed Soros to rake in the breathtaking profit of $2 billion.

The first years of the 1990swere the golden age of macro funds. Robertson, Soros and Steinhardt made a *style drift* from the long/short equity to the global macro strategy, when the success of their hedge funds caused their assets under management to grow enormously and they could not move without affecting market prices to their detriment. The global macro strategy gave them access to the currency, commodity and treasury markets, which are highly liquid, and therefore confronted them with no *capacity* problem. Consider for example that the currency market has a daily estimated volume of $1200 billion.[3]

On 4th February 1994, the Fed unexpectedly raised the interest rates by one quarter of a percentage point, causing treasuries to topple and market liquidity to temporarily drain out. The twin impact of market panic and leverage proved disastrous for Steinhardt Partners, which in 1994 suffered a 31 % loss. Steinhardt decided to retire at the end of 1995, despite partly recovering the losses suffered the previous year, and ending the year up 26 %.

In October 1998, when the Japanese yen appreciated against the dollar, Robertson suffered a loss of about $2 billion. In 1999, his long/short equity strategy, based on the fundamental analysis of listed companies, did not work at all on a market driven by the tail wind of the New Economy. After withdrawals from investors, assets under management had plunged from $25 billion in August 1998 to less than $8 billion at the end of March 2000. By the end of March 2000, when the "dot.com" speculative bubble was at its peak, Robertson announced the liquidation of the Tiger fund. Fate played him a nasty trick, because the bubble burst right then.

In April 2000, George Soros changed his chief investment strategist and soon after the CEO of Soros Fund Management LLC as well. Soros announced to his investors that he would stop making large leveraged macro investments. To reduce the risk he would downsize his return objectives.

In 1990, global macro funds accounted for 71 % of the hedge fund industry, according to Hedge Fund Research, whereas at the end of 2004 they were down to only 10 %, according to the LIPPER TASS database. Currently, the number of global macro funds is small, but they tend to have a greater size than hedge funds pursuing other strategies. Consider that at the end of 2004, one of the largest hedge funds was Caxton, with about $10 billion managed along a global macro strategy.

Some macro funds became famous for their performance, their size and, because they are very reserved and closed to new investors, the aura of mystery surrounding them. The key player in macro funds is the manager, and investment strategies rely on his insight and skill: this is why the history of the major macro hedge funds is intrinsically linked to the life experience of their managers.

Soros, Robertson and Steinhardt are now retired from the active management of their hedge funds. These legendary figures can be rightly considered the founding fathers of the modern hedge fund industry. They were central to the developmental history of hedge funds in the 1980s and 1990s and reared a legion of disciples who went on to set up their own successful hedge funds.

Who will be the next Soros, Robertson and Steinhardt? Maybe Bruce Kovner, Paul Tudor Jones or Louis Moore Bacon? Only time will tell.

---

[3] Natsuko Waki, *Banks intensify FX prime broker competition*, Reuters, 15th April 2004.

14.2   INVESTMENT STRATEGIES ADOPTED

Through the use of short selling and leverage and by resorting to the most disparate financial instruments, it is possible to make a profit from the following kind of circumstances: Swiss franc as a safe haven; gold as a safe haven; Russia's economy depends on oil; East European economies are converging towards the European Union; oil prices rise when there are geopolitical risks, etc. Traditional investors are not able to benefit from these financial themes with the same effectiveness as hedge funds.

14.3   THE CHARACTERISTICS SHARED BY GREAT TRADERS

Managing a hedge fund calls for devotion: George Soros tried to remain detach emotionally in order to identify himself with the fund he managed. Michael Steinhardt called himself a humble servant of his investors.

Successful traders are not greedy and are not afraid; they have an in-depth knowledge of themselves and their minds. From a psychological point of view, we could say that they sublimate the survival instinct into their business, they fully identify with the fund they manage and are totally involved in its management, body and soul.

Greed and fear cause the manager to become undisciplined and lead him to disaster. Successful traders see things that others do not see: they make connections that are not apparent to others. They are not victims of money and success: they have a detached attitude towards money and money is only their scorecard. Emotions end up playing a negative role in trading decisions, leading many traders to let losses run bigger than they should and to cash in profits too soon. Successful traders do not change their lives when they gain and do not despair when they lose. Above all, they are hard workers.

Pride can cause traders to make serious mistakes: they must be able to acknowledge their mistakes very rapidly. No trader can fall too much in love with his ideas, especially if they are based on extremely complex analyses. Great traders are able to admit when they are wrong and are able to reduce their risks accordingly.

A trader must be able to be patient: if he sees no investment opportunities, he must not trade. He must take on a risk only when he clearly spots an opportunity.

According to Van K. Tharp, a psychologist who dedicated his career to researching the psychology of winners in the financial markets, the traits of a successful trader are listed as follows:[4]

- money is not important;
- trading is a game;
- it is acceptable to lose with some trades;
- it is important to put one's ideas to test.

In contrast, losers think that money is important and have a difficult time accepting losses.

The personality traits of losers are stress, impatience, personality conflicts, a negative attitude towards life, and a tendency to both follow the herd and blame others when things go wrong.

---

[4] From an interview with Jack D. Schwager in the book *Market Wizards.*

14.4   THE LEGS OF A TRADE

Divide et impera.   *Divide and rule.*

Latin phrase

Generally, macro fund managers construct their long and short positions on financial markets gradually and with several counterparties, so that brokers are not aware of the size and direction of their trades.

In general, securities positions held with a counterparty are partially hedged by the securities positions held with other counterparties. The reason why trades are broken down across various markets stems from the attempt to defend themselves from the possibility that other counterparties understand the fund manager's true intentions and might corner him by causing a squeeze.

For example, to sell British pounds spot does not necessarily mean that one has a negative sentiment on the pound: a global macro manager might have a very positive sentiment on the British pound, but he might be simply cashing in profits by selling pounds against an opposing and dominant portfolio position.

The analysis of a hedge fund portfolio is not very obvious at first sight: the book of long positions and that of short positions are but two legs of a trade, or in more complex cases, the branches in which a trade is split. To understand the true intentions of a fund manager, it is necessary to couple the positions that give rise to a relative value trade, and this is possible only with the fund manager's help.

The devaluation of the British pound

In 1990 the United Kingdom joined the European Monetary System, a system seeking to fix the value of European currencies as preparation for the introduction of the single European currency. The EMS required the member states to maintain their currencies within a 2.25 % fluctuation band above or below the fixed parity rate, and the maximum fluctuation of the individual currencies against the dollar was fixed at 4.5 %.

However, in 1992 the divergences in the economic conditions of European countries strained the interest rate necessary to maintain the exchange rate within the required fluctuation bands and the one required by the state of domestic economies. In particular, the German reunification caused a strong growth and heavy inflationary pressures in the country, and thus German interest rates were high. In the United Kingdom things were quite the opposite: the country was just getting out of a recession, had a slow growth and a decreasing inflation. To keep the British pound within the European Monetary System, the British Central Bank could not cut interest rates as an incentive to the UK economy.

In September 1992, Soros brought off a successful trade that turned him into a famous public figure and had him dubbed by *The Times* of London as "The Man Who Broke the Bank of England". In Soros's opinion, the British pound could not maintain its value against the other currencies belonging to the European Monetary System, and as for the reasons we explained above, would have to be depreciated at some point. Soros believed that central banks could not defend the British pound from market forces and so used leverage to short sell $10 billion worth of British pounds.

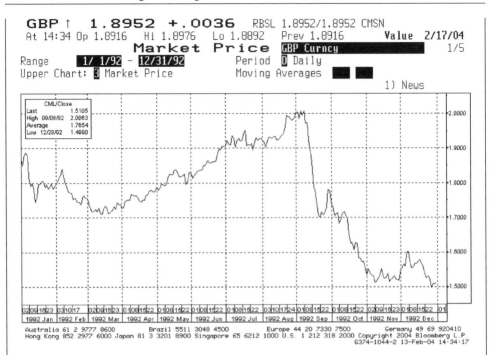

Figure 14.1 The devaluation of the British pound in September 1992 (exchange rate British pound/USD). Used with permission from Bloomberg L.P.

Together with other investors, Soros exerted such a pressure against the British pound that he forced it to exit the European Monetary System: the British pound exchange rate against the dollar plummeted in just a few days by 15 % and then went on tumbling down in the following months (Figure 14.1). The macro-economic situation caused a downward pressure on the British pound exchange rate, which reached its peak on 16th September 1992 with the exit of the United Kingdom from the European Monetary System and a sudden devaluation of the British pound.

Soros's Quantum Fund and his investors made a profit of about $1 billion with this one deal.

The devaluation of the Italian lira

The situation of Italian public accounts in 1992 was disastrous: the public deficit was skyrocketing; the balance of trade deficit was unsustainable; interest rates were high; inflation was high; and the unemployment rate was high. Public expenditure was out of control and was mainly focused on current expenditure. The high interest rates burdened the public deficit, generating a vicious circle between growing debt service, balance deficit and growing debt. A fixed exchange rate was penalizing Italy; it could not devalue its currency despite the high inflation and the high interest rates.

Having analyzed Italy's unsustainable macro-economic situation in 1992, Soros short sold the Italian lira. From 10th to 16th September 1992, the Italian lira depreciated by 14.2 % against the dollar and quit the European Monetary System (Figure 14.2).

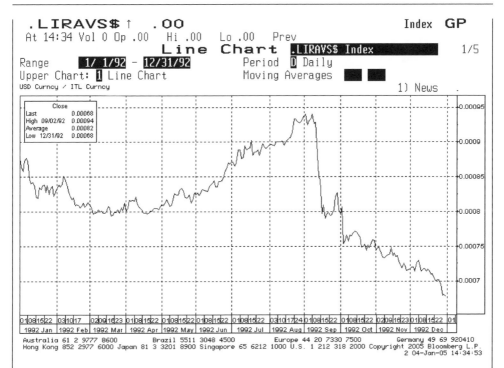

Figure 14.2 The devaluation of the Italian lira in September 1992 (exchange rate Italian lira/USD). Used with permission from Bloomberg L.P.

In the months of September and October 1992, with his bearish trades on the British pound and Italian lira, Soros raked in the awesome profit of $2 billion.

Swiss Franc as safe haven

In 2003 the Swiss franc had appreciated as a result of being considered a safe haven. The Swiss economy was weak both in absolute as well as relative terms in comparison to its trade partners. The Swiss national bank was striving to maintain expansionary monetary conditions. Overnight interest rates were below 1 %. The Swiss National Bank had reiterated its concern over the strength of the Swiss franc, corroborating these statements with actions on the monetary markets and by cutting overnight interest rates. The exchange rate volatility between the euro and the Swiss franc showed an imbalance. The volatility of out-of-the-money put options on the euro (or call options on the Swiss franc) were higher than the volatility of the corresponding out-of-the-money put options on the Swiss franc (or call options on the Euro). This imbalance was caused by the Swiss franc's characteristic of being considered a safe haven (Figure 14.3).

The strategy followed by a fund manager was to sell out-of-the-money put options on the euro while buying an equal amount of put options of the Swiss franc, which were, however, less out-the-money than the former. The sale of euro put options financed the purchase of the Swiss franc put options, therefore the fund manager paid no price to open this position.

Figure 14.3 Exchange rate Swiss franc/euro. Used with permission from Bloomberg L.P.

There were two possible scenarios:

- if the euro goes down, the euro put option holder exercises his option, obliging the fund manager to buy euro. In this case the fund manager will be long on euro at a low level due to the asymmetry;
- vice versa, if the euro goes up, the fund manager exercises his call options on the euro.

Convergence towards the European Union

The currencies of East European countries have displayed a long-term growth trend triggered by a number of causes: the expected convergence towards the European Union; direct foreign investment flows in view of lower costs; and treasury investments in view of higher yields. The convergence trade is very crowded and is subject to periodic sudden write-offs, because participants all try to settle their positions at the same time, clashing against a low liquidity market.

The currency, yield and macro-economic convergence took place at different rates in the different East European countries. The rate convergence in the Czech republic has been practically completed and now its rates are lower with respect to the European Union. In contrast, the Slovakian crown is much less expensive based on the purchasing power parity (the exchange rate at which the price levels in the two nations are equal) and the macro-economic data (per capita GDP, wages, etc.) are much lower compared to the Czech republic.

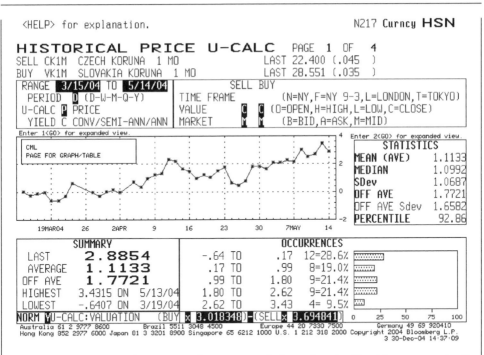

Figure 14.4 The hedge fund manager buys one month forward on the Slovakian crown and sells one month forward on the Czech crown (from 15th March 2004 to 14th May 2004). Used with permission from Bloomberg L.P.

A hedge fund manager buys one month forward on the Slovakian crown and sells one month forward on the Czech crown. By doing this, he collects a significant carry (Figure 14.4).

The fund manager expects the ongoing convergence to cause an appreciation of the Slovakian crown over the Czech crown because direct foreign investments and treasury investments find more appealing opportunities in Slovakia. He is protected from the risk of sudden write-offs because his position is not correlated to euro movements.

Other examples

Global macro managers generally trade on currency markets by acting on relative value position of currencies such as the ones shown below:

- long Polish zloty versus short euro;
- long Swedish crown versus short euro;
- long Australian dollar versus short New Zealand dollar. Fund managers believe that New Zealand's Central Bank has raised interest rates too much, opening the way to an economic slowdown in New Zealand in 2005;
- long Korean Won versus short Japanese yen;
- long Korean Won versus short euro.

14.5   THE THEORY OF REFLEXIVITY BY GEORGE SOROS

In any situation in which there are participants who think, there is a two-way interaction between the thought of the participants and the situation in which they are participating. On one side, the participants try to comprehend reality, and on the other side they try to reach the desired goal.

When a participant tries to comprehend reality, the reality is a fact. However, when a participant acts, the constant is the understanding of reality. Understanding and action can interfere with one another, turning what is assumed to be a fact into a contingency. The interference between understanding and action is what George Soros calls *reflexivity* (Figure 14.5).

Reflexivity impairs the participants' understanding of reality, and causes their actions to lead to undesired consequences. As a result, there is a divergence between expectations and results. Since thought and reality are interconnected, an analytical approach to capital markets proves inadequate, whereas an integrated approach is more suited. One's vision of the world is part of the real world itself, and therefore people's thoughts shape reality.

One of the fundamentals of the paradigm prevailing on financial markets is that future results are fully reflected in market expectations. Hence, market prices are considered as being passive reflections of corporate fundamentals. The assumptions generated on efficient markets are that market prices reflect all existing information. However, Grossman-Stiglitz's paradox states that: "If markets are perfectly informed, then there is nothing to be gained from gathering more information; but if nobody gathers information, then markets will not be perfectly informed".

People behave very differently from what is described by the theory of rational expectations. Emotions often prevail over reason due to the time factor: decisions must be made rapidly, and the less time available to take all the relevant considerations, the greater is the role played by instinct and emotions.

George Soros maintains that market participants base their actions not on reality, but rather on what they believe is reality, and the two things are not the same. Therefore, since the decisions of market participants are not based on their knowledge of reality, but on their vision of reality, results can differ from expectations.

Although the theory of rational expectations states that markets are always rational, George Soros argues that financial markets are almost always wrong, but often try to validate themselves by influencing not only market prices, but also the fundamentals that market prices are supposed to reflect.

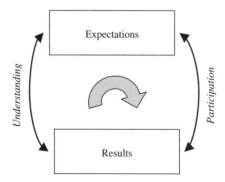

Figure 14.5   Reflexivity

Epistemological studies led George Soros to become fascinated by Heisenberg's Principle of Indetermination (1927), whose consequences deeply modified some convictions as to the meaning of the laws of physics used to interpret the phenomena of quantum mechanics, as well as the role of observers in the theory of measure. Heisenberg's Principle of Indetermination asserts that the more we know about the position of a particle, for example an electron, the less we know about its momentum at that point in time and vice versa. This principle implies that measuring a phenomenon necessarily entails interfering with it, and this is an insurmountable barrier in the human knowledge of nature. Soros recognizes a similar behavior in financial markets: it is not possible to obtain a perfect knowledge of the market because the cognitive act affects the market itself, which in turn reacts to the perception of participants. There is a divergence between the participants' expectations with regard to the events that characterize financial markets and the actual outcome of said events. Sometimes the difference is negligible, in other cases it becomes a relevant element in the course of events.

Drawing from this principle of quantum mechanics, George Soros established what he called the *human uncertainty principle*. The principle holds that people's understanding of the world in which they live cannot correspond to the facts and be complete and consistent at the same time. Results are affected but not determined exclusively by expectations.

George Soros interprets capital markets as a historical process: although a scientific model can be submitted to repeatable experiments, it is not possible to conduct experiments on the theory of reflexivity because situations are not repeatable.

In the new emerging paradigm, the rational behavior hypothesis is replaced by the concept of adaptive behavior. Whereas the hypothesis of rational behavior leads to a deductive logic, adaptive behavior is an empirical concept.

The theory of reflexivity can explain the sequences of the onset of speculative bubbles and the subsequent burst, and the persistency of conditions away from equilibrium. For example, adaptive behavior is more suited at explaining the boom of Internet companies than rational behavior. Reflexivity goes beyond the concept of adaptive behavior, asserting that market participants have an adaptive behavior and this creates an adaptive environment that is interconnected in a reflexive way.

An equity market boom is a self-feeding process in which inflated stock prices improve expectations, which in turn inflate stock prices. These expectations are reinforced by positive changes in the fundamentals: for example, increasing revenues and profits. Expectations are inflated to the point of becoming unsustainable. The trend reversal point arrives when results disappoint, do not support expectations anymore, and markets go bust. When stocks start going down, the trend starts self-feeding in the opposite direction.

The *boom/bust* model does not qualify as a scientific theory because it cannot be falsified. However even the theory of rational expectations cannot be falsified, in that any deviation from expected results can be attributed to exogenous shocks. Karl Popper maintains that the ability of a theory to be falsified is what qualifies it as scientific. Therefore, the theory of reflexivity is a philosophical theory and not a scientific one because it cannot be falsified.

14.6 DEBT EMERGING MARKETS

This strategy is linked with funds that trade mainly treasuries issued by emerging countries or recently industrialized countries, such as Latin America. Eastern Europe, Asia or Africa.

Investments flowing in and out of emerging markets are the consequence of global market dynamics, and therefore are residual. Fund managers who trade on emerging markets must try to anticipate correctly the macro-economic changes intervening on those markets, and this is why we consider *debt emerging markets* funds as macro funds specialized in emerging countries. Macro fund managers take directional positions on a wide range of financial instruments in order to anticipate trends.

On 30th September 2004, emerging markets funds accounted for 3.79 % of the hedge fund industry.[5]

The JP Morgan Emerging Markets Bond Index Plus (EMBI+) tracks total returns for traded external debt instruments in the emerging markets. These debt instruments include external-currency-denominated Brady bonds, loans, Eurobonds and US dollar local market instruments.

EMBI+ is concentrated on instruments from Latin American countries (Argentina, Brazil and Mexico), and reflects the size and liquidity of these external debt markets. The other main nations represented in the index are Bulgaria, Morocco, Nigeria, the Philippines, Poland, Russia and South Africa. The financial instruments included in the EMBI+ must have a minimum of $500 million outstanding (Figure 14.6).

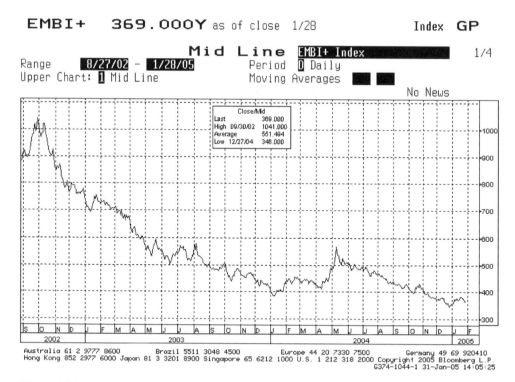

Figure 14.6 EMBI+ from 27th August 2002 to 28th January 2005. Used with permission from Bloomberg L.P.

---

[5] TASS Asset Flows Report, Third Quarter 2004.

Other fund managers purchase treasuries issued by emerging markets and denominated in local currency (Turkish lira, Polish zloty, Brazilian pesos, Russian rubles, etc.), with short durations, in the belief that the high carry trade can ensure a good profitability despite currency fluctuations. However, the short-term interest rate hike in the United States is reducing the profitability of carry trade and with it the risk appetite associated with emerging markets.

Bullish position on Brazil

Let's first consider a traditional trade (*outright trade*): the purchase of treasuries of the Federal Republic of Brazil with a fixed rate of 8.875 % and maturity date on 15th April 2024 for a nominal position of $10 million (Figure 14.7).

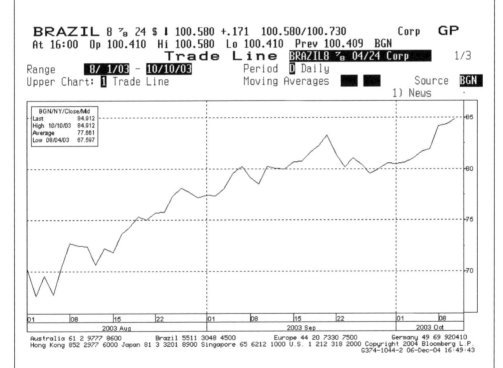

Figure 14.7 Outright trade on Brazil from 1st August 2003 to 10th October 2003. Used with permission from Bloomberg L.P.

The potential profit is $1 385 000 as shown below:

			Price	Cash
1st Aug. 2003	Purchase	Brazil 8.875 % 2024	$71.00	$7 100 000
10th Oct. 2003	Sale	Brazil 8.875 % 2024	$84.52	$8 485 000
			Profit	$ −1 385 000

However, should Brazil default, the loss is $4 600 000:

			Price	*Cash*
1st Aug. 2003	Purchase	Brazil 8.875 % 2024	$71.00	$7 100 000
10th Oct. 2003	Sale	Brazil 8.875 % 2024	$25.00	$2 500 000
			Loss	**$ −4 600 000**

So, in the case where Brazil defaults, the long position on treasuries causes a much greater loss than the profit that can be made in the case where Brazil is solvent. This is not a hedged position, and therefore it does not satisfy the good hedge fund manager.

Let's now consider another trade constructed on the relative value of two Brazilian treasuries.

Relative Value Trade

Let's couple the purchase position on treasuries of the Federal Republic of Brazil with a fixed rate at 8.875 % and maturity date on 15th April 2024, with a short sale position on Brazil C-Bond, maturity date 15th April 2014 and fixed rate at 8 % (Figure 14.8).

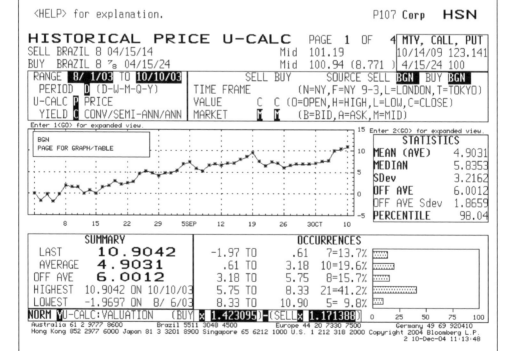

Figure 14.8 Relative value trade on Brazil from 1st August 2003 to 10th October 2003. Used with permission from Bloomberg L.P.

On 1st August 2003 the following positions are established:

Name	Amount	Offer price	Yield to maturity[6]	Spread against Treasury Bond	Value in $ for every 1 bps change
Brazil C-Bond	$–10 million	85.12	11.93	780	4.11
Brazil Global Bond	$10 million	71.00	12.94	813	5.36
		14.12	**−101**	**−33**	**0.77**

Cash	Cash with accrued interest
$10 481 639[7]	$13 264 384
$ −7 100 000	$ −7 531 424
$3 381 639	**$5 732 961**

If Brazil is solvent, on 10th October 2003 the two above transactions are closed as follows:

Name	Amount	Offer price	Yield to maturity	Spread against Treasury Bond	Value in $ for every 1 bps change
Brazil C-Bond	$10 000 000	93.52	9.64	552	4.61
Brazil Global Bond	$–10 000 000	84.85	10.71	591	7.22
		8.67	**−107**	**−39**	**0.64**

Cash	Cash with accrued interest
$ −11 515 654	$ −14 770 191
$8 485 000	$8 916 424
$ −3 030 654	**$ −5 853 767**

Name	Profit or loss
Brazil C-Bond	$–1 034 015
Brazil Global Bond	$1 385 000
Total	**$350 985**

---

[6] yield to maturity in the discount rate, which equates the present value of future cash flows to the bond price (the same for all the tables of this example)

[7] Value factoring in a capitalization factor.

What if Brazil was insolvent? On 1st August 2003:

Name	Amount	Offer price	Yield to maturity	Spread against Treasury Bond	Value in $ for every 1 bps change
Brazil C-Bond	$−10 000 000	85.12	11.93	780	4.11
Brazil Global Bond	$10 000 000	71.00	12.94	813	5.36
		14.12	**−101**	**−33**	**0.77**

Cash	Cash with accrued interest
$10 481 639	$13 264 384
$ −7 100 000	$ −7 531 424
$ 3 381 639	**$ 5 732 961**

On 10th October 2003:

Name	Amount	Offer price	Yield to maturity	Spread against Treasury Bond	Value in $ for every 1 bps change
Brazil C-Bond	$10 000 000	25.00	65.02	6,089	0.44
Brazil Global Bond	$−10 000 000	25.00	35.61	3,081	0.72
		0.00	**2940**	**3008**	**0.61**

Cash	Cash with accrued interest
$ −3 078 525	$ −4 380 626
$2 500 000	$2 931 424
$ −578 525	**$ −1 449 203**

Nome	Profit or loss
Brazil C-Bond	$7 403 114
Brazil Global Bond	$ −4 600 000
Total	**$2 803 114**

The following table summarizes the profits and losses incurred by the hedge fund manager depending on whether Brazil defaults or not.

Profit or loss	Positive scenario	Brazil insolvency scenario
Outright Trade	$1 385 000	$ −4 600 000
Relative Value Trade	$350 985	$ 2 803 114

The relative value trade between the two Brazilian treasuries is profitable irrespective of the scenario in terms of Brazil's creditworthiness. Is the market giving out a "free lunch"? No, once again on the market "There is no free lunch". Even the position constructed on the relative value of the two Brazilian treasuries is subject to a risk. The risk for this trade is a sideway market: the carry is negative, hence it generates interest payable for the fund manager. Another risk is if interest rates rise because the position does not have a zero duration. Also a change in the shape of the yield curve can negatively affect the performance.

14.7 STRATEGY'S HISTORICAL PERFORMANCE

Let's analyze the historical behavior of this strategy based on the monthly returns of the CS/Tremont Global Macro Index. Again, the past performance of a given investment is not necessarily indicative of a future return for the same investment. Still, we believe it is useful to examine historical data to understand which scenarios are favorable to this strategy and which are not.

The statistical analysis of the CS/Tremont Global Macro Index between 1994 and 2004 produces the results shown in Table 14.1.

The performance of global macro funds is historically the highest among all the other hedge fund strategies, with an annualized return of 14 % between 1994 and 2004, although

Table 14.1

	CS/Tremont Global Macro	Morgan Stanley Capital International World in US$	JP Morgan Global Government Bond Global International
Value at Risk (1 month, 95%)	−4.5%	−6.4%	−1.9%
Value at Risk (1 month, 99%)	−7.0%	−10.4%	−3.6%
Best month Performance	+10.6%	+8.9%	+7.0%
Average Performance in positive months	+2.6%	+3.2%	+1.6%
Worst month Performance	−11.6%	−13.5%	−5.1%
Average Performance in negative months	−2.5%	−3.5%	−1.0%
% Positive months	72%	61%	57%
Compound Annual Growth Rate (CAGR)	+14.0%	+6.3%	+5.4%
Annualized monthly volatility	11.6%	14.2%	6.2%
Skewness	0.00	−0.60	0.65
Kurtosis	2.39	0.59	2.21
Largest drawdown*	−26.8%	−48.4%	−8.6%
Duration of the largest drawdown in months	14	30	4
Time to recovery** in months	18	n.d.	9
Drawdown start	31st Aug. 1998	30th Apr. 2000	28th Feb. 1994
Drawdown end	30th Sep. 1999	30th Sep. 2002	31st May 1994

* The largest drawdown is defined as the maximum value of any "peak to trough decline" over the specified period. The subsequent minimum is not determined until it has reached a new high.
** Time to recovery is the time necessary to recover from the largest drawdown.

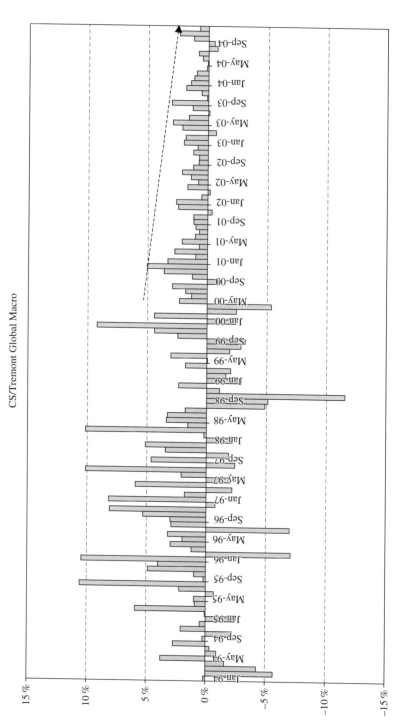

CS/Tremont Global Macro

Figure 14.9 Monthly returns of CS/Tremont Global Macro from 1994 to 2004. Source: CS/Tremont Index LLC, www.hedgeindex.com. Copyright © 2006, Credit Suisse/Tremont Index LLC. All rights reserved*

CS/Tremont Global Macro

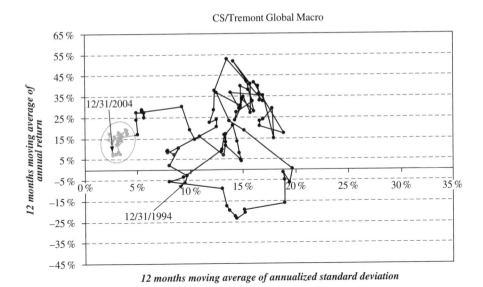

Figure 14.10 Historical performance trend of return as a function of risk for CS/Tremont Global Macro from 1994 to 2004. Source: CS/Tremont Index LLC, www.hedgeindex.com. Copyright © 2006, Credit Suisse/Tremont Index LLC. All rights reserved*

CS/Tremont Global Macro

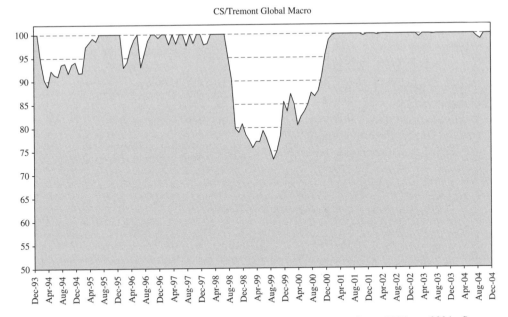

Figure 14.11 Underwater periods for CS/Tremont Global Macro from 1994 to 2004. Source: CS/Tremont Index LLC, www.hedgeindex.com. Copyright © 2006, Credit Suisse/Tremont Index LLC. All rights reserved*

---

with a high volatility (11.6 %). The distribution of monthly return is symmetrical (Skewness equal to zero) and the tails are shorter than those of the Gaussian distribution (Kurtosis lesser than 3). The largest drawdown was significant (−26.8 %). It lasted for more than one year (14 months) and took 18 months to recover the losses.

Figure 14.9 shows the monthly returns of the CS/Tremont Global Macro Index between 1994 and 2004. The dotted line shows what appears to be a trend of the last three years: a volatility fall and downturns. The figure highlights the strong and sudden drawdown started in August 1998. In that month there was a strong *flight-to-quality* move caused by Russia's default.

Figure 14.10 illustrates the historical performance as a function of risk of the CS/Tremont Global Macro Index between 1994 and 2004. The concentration ellipsoid shows that the risk/return profile of the global macro hedge funds in the last three years shifted as a whole towards a low volatility. We can associate this fact with the growing implementation of risk management techniques aiming at containing volatility. Figure 14.10 must be analyzed taking drawdown data into consideration: throughout the drawdown and the time to recovery period, the hedge funds adopting this strategy were under the high water mark.

Figure 14.11 shows that between 1994 and 2004 there were two important "underwater" dips by hedge funds: In February 1994 the onset of the unexpected interest rate rise by the US Federal Reserve; and in August 1998, as already mentioned, the crisis triggered by the Russian default. This drawdown lasted 14 months and it took 18 months for global macro hedge funds to get back to the value before the Russian crisis. (See Chapter 1, Section 1.8, for more details on the setup and meaning of Figures 14.10 and 14.11.)

14.8 CONCLUSIONS

Looking back to Figure 1.9, let's identify the key factors that make up the performance of fund managers following the global macro strategy:

- traditional beta: beta of equity markets, bond market beta, beta of currency markets, beta of credit spreads;
- alternative beta: market makers and suppliers of liquidity to the market;
- structural alpha: flexibility, speed and size;
- skill alpha: macro-economic research and risk management skills.

15
Other Strategies

To make money in the next decade, you must be willing to invest in
new ideas. The easy money in hedge funds may already have been made.
A hedge fund manager

As we extensively covered in Chapter 1, the hedge fund industry has been changing the makeup of its investment strategies since the beginning of the 1990s, reflecting the rising and falling performance of the various strategies. The search for new areas of investment is to be considered an evolutionary process, linked to the struggle for survival fought by hedge funds. At present, the hedge fund industry is rapidly shifting towards new frontiers and the emerging strategies are PIPEs, long/short credit, energy trading and structured finance. At the same time, long-standing strategies are being revised, in particular investments in commodities and real estate.

Not surprisingly, market operators who use the same research and the same investment approach, try to seize the same opportunities, invest on the same markets, and end up with similar results. To obtain different results, it is often necessary to operate along different modalities from those prevailing among most competitors.

The following strategies can be single strategies used by hedge funds, but more often they are one of a series of strategies adopted by multi-strategy funds:

- holding company arbitrage;
- closed-end fund arbitrage;
- statistical arbitrage;
- index arbitrage;
- volatility trading;
- split-strike conversion;
- lending;
- PIPEs or Regulation D;
- real estate;
- natural resources;
- energy trading;
- natural events.

15.1 HOLDING COMPANY ARBITRAGE

There are abnormalities in the intricate capital structures of holding companies. The market capitalization of a holding company trades at a premium or, more frequently, at a discount to the *Net Asset Value* (NAV) of shareholdings.

Generally, a fund manager will take a long position on the holding company and short sell the listed companies held by the holding company. The fund manager will make a profit

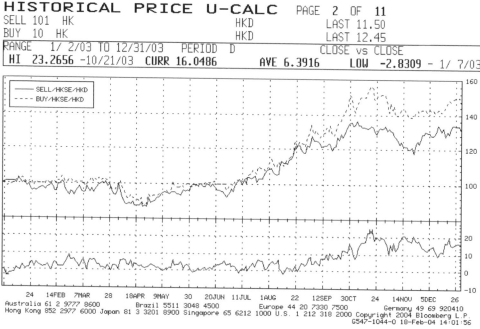

Figure 15.1 Holding company arbitrage. Used with permission from Bloomberg L.P.

if the discount narrows down, and in practice it is as if he had sold short the discount to the NAV. The fund manager can also construct an opposite position if he believes that the discount to NAV is too small. The discount reflects the risk that the majority of shareholders may impair the interest of minority shareholders (Figure 15.1).

15.2   CLOSED-END FUND ARBITRAGE

Arbitrages on listed closed-end funds seek to capture the premium or discount changes between the net asset value of the listed closed-end funds and the market capitalization of their shares. The following example will better clarify how this strategy works.

In 2002, a hedge fund invested in some closed-end funds listed on the Greek market. In 16 months, the hedge fund gathered from the market the shares of a dozen scarcely traded Greek closed-end funds, buying them at a high discount to the fund's net assets. Later, the hedge fund launched a tender offer for the remaining shares of one of these funds, attracting the market's attention on the sector and causing a revaluation of funds, which allowed the hedge fund to make a big profit. The assessment of the investment opportunity had been carried out in February 2002.

It was considered that Greece had gone through a phase of strong demand for shares and bonds by investors, in expectation of Greece's entry into the European Union. To meet the demand, banks and insurance companies created some closed-end funds.

At the peak of equity markets in 1999, the enthusiasm of investors drove the share price of these closed-end funds beyond the net asset value of the fund with a premium of occasionally 20–30%. However, in February 2002, the equity index Athens Stock Exchange[1] had shed about 60% from its 1999 peak and the share prices of closed-end funds were at a discount to the fund's net asset value ranging between 25% and 35%.

Many of these closed-end funds owned shares of highly capitalized Greek companies and held substantial amounts in cash. The hedge fund calculated that the closed-end funds' asset risk could be hedged with a position combining Athens Stock Exchange futures and index swaps with short positions on single stocks.

The hedge fund analyzed the prospectuses of the closed-end funds and decided that there was the potential to take an active role in the management of the closed-end funds to reduce the share price discount on the fund's net asset value. In May 2003, the hedge fund launched a tender offer on all the residual shares outstanding of the closed-end fund New Millennium at a price discounted by about 16% to the fund's net asset value. This called the investors' attention to the undervalued market of Greek closed-end funds and drove prices up by about 5–10% for all closed-end funds and by 12% for the New Millennium fund, which allowed the hedge fund to make a sizeable profit.

15.3 STATISTICAL ARBITRAGE

This strategy seeks to capture imbalances in expected values of financial instruments, while trying to be market-neutral. Typically, said imbalances stem from the segmentation of the financial instrument market and the specialization of market operators in a single segment.

The identification process of a trading opportunity starts by estimating the theoretical value of thousands of financial instruments, using the current price flow downloaded from *information providers* and the hedge fund's database containing historical data.

The quantitative analysis process continues with the analysis of the difference between the theoretical value and the market current value. Considering a specific stock, the possible pricing abnormality[2] can be confronted with historical data or with similar financial instruments. The divergence between the theoretical value and the market value of a given financial instrument does not imply by itself a prediction of future price movements, therefore it does not imply a profit opportunity. There could be for example an explanation in some market dynamics, such as fiscal reasons, economic reasons, the desire by some investors to replicate an index, etc. This is why it is important for the fund manager to carry out a qualitative analysis when assessing potential investment opportunities. Arbitrage opportunities are the outcome of a quantitative filtering process and a qualitative evaluation process.

Fund managers use proprietary mathematical processes to analyze thousands and thousands of financial instruments in a wide range of asset classes and countries in search of potential abnormalities in market valuations.

---

[1] L'ATX is the index of stocks listed on the Athens stock exchange. The index was developed based on a 100 value on 31st December 1980.
[2] We use the term abnormality and not inefficiency because it is the author's strong conviction that day to day behavior of financial markets shows that markets are not efficient at all and that emotions felt by operators play an important role in the abnormalities of the markets.

In-house research analysts construct databases that they keep updated with historical financial data of various kinds, and which all company employees can access. Pricing abnormalities are typically identified through an assumption formulation, testing and a rigorous validation process. Valuation abnormalities that prove statistically significant are then used in trading strategies, which typically operate in real time based on an almost continuous flow of financial data fed by Bloomberg, Reuters and other information providers.

The identification of multiple market pricing abnormalities is very difficult: it takes time and is expensive.

Experimental results are then used to refine the adopted models. Optimization software products help to construct and dynamically change the portfolio makeup, with the aim of maximizing the portfolio's expected return, minimizing risk, controlling the portfolio's liquidability and minimizing transaction costs.

15.4   INDEX ARBITRAGE

This strategy seeks to profit from the spread convergence between a futures contract and the basket of securities it is made up of. If the fund manager believes that the spread is going to narrow down, he will simultaneously buy a basket of securities having the exact weight they have in the futures contract and sell the futures contract short. He will do the opposite if he believes that the spread is going to widen.

Fund managers specializing in this type of arbitrage actively trade on the days that index changes have been announced, when there are securities entering and exiting indices.

A classical strategy is the purchase of a security that has to be added to the index and the concurrent sale of an equal amount of futures on the index so as to hedge the position against market risk. This deal is based on the observation that passive funds rebalance their positions on the day in which the index is actually changed.

15.5   VOLATILITY TRADING[3]

We examined volatility trading in Chapter 6, Section 6.7.2. It is a strategy whereby the hedge fund manager seeks to profit from volatility changes, without being affected by the direction of the price movement. In volatility trading, fund managers trade on derivatives, like options, warrants and futures, on securities of a single issuer as well as on market indices. The fund manager can go long or short the volatility depending on the expected changes in the volatility of the underlying security, as well as on changes in implied volatility.

Volatility can be considered as the most intuitive and basic – but undoubtedly not the only – form of measuring risk when investing in a financial asset.

Volatility is the square root of the average of the sum of squared deviations of returns recorded by said financial asset with respect to its average return in a given time period. The greater the deviations of the financial asset from its average value, the greater its volatility within the defined time horizon.

For this reason, many investors have always considered volatility as a characteristic of other financial asset classes, and not as a financial asset class in its own right that can be traded, that is, "bought" or "sold". Even investors who trade instruments that are closely

[3] Mason, C. and Weingram, S. (2004) *Volatility Trading Hedge Fund: A Primer*, SwissHedge.

related to volatility, like options and convertible bonds, generally have never looked at volatility as the starting point for a dedicated investment strategy.

In spite of this widespread conception, lately *volatility trading* has become more and more popular as a result of a combination of factors, including the wide movements the equity markets went through during the 1990s. This explains the desire of some investors to protect themselves against volatility, but at the same time profit from it.

Nowadays, *volatility trades* are easier to execute than in the past, thanks to new risk management technologies, easier access to financial information and the introduction of listed and unlisted dedicated products, which allow investors to express their view on volatility more rapidly and easily.

As hedge funds are undoubtedly among the most frequent volatility traders, we will try to understand the strategies and instruments they use.

Volatility traders are typically looking for options that "misprice" volatility. In fact, volatility is one of the main factors affecting option prices. Given an option's market price, it is possible to derive the *implied volatility* inherent in the option price, for example by using the Black–Scholes formula.

In order to understand volatility trading better, it can be useful to take an overview of the option market, whose main actors are brokers and investors. Typically, investors buy or sell options through brokers, to hedge their portfolios or to take a directional risk. Generally, brokers do not take speculative positions on the underlying stocks and get immediately hedged by buying or selling the option's underlying stocks.

In order to be neutral with respect to the price performance of the option's underlying, when the price of the underlying changes, the broker must immediately buy or sell other stocks through a continuous hedging process that is called *delta hedging*. This is because the option value as a function of the price of the underlying stock is curve-shaped, and therefore its sensitivity to the stock price changes as the stock price goes up or down.

By delta hedging, the broker eliminates the exposure to the directional price movements of the underlying, but he introduces an exposure to the daily volatility of the underlying. When a broker buys an option, he goes long volatility, gaining from delta hedging when volatility goes up.

In addition to the above methods of trading options and delta hedging, many hedge funds also use other instruments, including *variance swaps*. In the following sections, we will examine in turn the four main ways in which traders express their views on volatility:

- option trading;
- delta hedging;
- variance swaps;
- other instruments.

15.5.1 Option Trading

The simplest way to carry out volatility trades is to establish a directional position on financial options. The funds adopting these types of strategies often make use of a very thorough research analysis. Said funds pursue strategies that search for options that are consistent with the value of the underlying and offer a price premium based on volatility.

For example, if we believe that the price of a certain share belonging to our portfolio will not move rapidly in any direction, we can decide to sell an out-of-the-money call option on that share. If the price of a given share does not move closer to the exercise price, we will benefit from the premium generated by selling the call; however, if the share price on expiration is above the exercise price, we will be obliged to sell the share at the exercise price, and will suffer a loss exceeding the collected premium.

Finally, if we believe that a share price will not change much and we assume that implied volatility is high, we may decide to speculate by selling an option with this share as an underlying.

15.5.2 Delta Hedging

If option trading makes it possible to trade volatility, it does not however allow the investor to have an exposure to the daily volatility of the underlying. Actually, profits in option trading depend on where the underlying price is at maturity, and not on the course followed to get there.

One way to gain exposure to the daily volatility of a given share may be delta hedging an option. For example, if we believe that the future volatility of a stock will be lower than the current implied volatility, we will sell the option and delta hedge it (or, vice versa, we will buy an option and delta hedge it).

Delta hedging is however quite complicated to put into practice. It calls for sophisticated trading systems and software products, to measure one's exposure daily.

15.5.3 Variance Swaps

At the end of the 1990s, some new products were designed to help investors express their views on volatility. The most common form is variance swaps.

In a variance swap, on the day the deal is opened, a "strike" volatility level is defined, linked to the market's current implied volatility levels. On the same day, no money is exchanged between the counterparties. On the day the variance swap expires, a money payment is exchanged between the party having a long position and the party with a short position. If the realized volatility is greater than the implied volatility, the counterparty with a short position will settle the difference in cash to the counterparty having a long position (and vice versa if the opposite occurs). In practice, a variance swap is based on a basket of options and on the corresponding delta hedging. It carries two major advantages, which led to its popularity: simplicity and the fact that its profit/loss profile depends on the difference between the actual volatility and its strike level, irrespective of any other factor.

15.5.4 Other Instruments

By delta hedging and trading options, it is possible to take a directional position on the fact that the realized volatility will be higher or lower than implied volatility. It is also possible to open a position based on the fact that the implied volatility may rise or fall. This can be done by trading a combination of listed options.

In recent years, brokers have introduced *over-the-counter* products, including forward-starting options and forward-starting variance swaps, which allow investors to express their views on volatility in a more simple and rapid way. The growing interest devoted to these products contributed to the development of pure volatility products. The most popular is the

VXO Futures Contract traded at the CBOE, which allows investors to express their view on the volatility of the S&P 500 index.

Related to this, Figure 6.10 in Chapter 6 clearly shows the steep drop of volatility on equity markets starting from the beginning of 2003.

15.6 SPLIT-STRIKE CONVERSION

This strategy is based on the construction of the following positions:

- A long position on a basket of 30–35 of the largest cap shares in the S&P 100, proportional to their weight in the index. Globally, the basket displays a high index correlation.
- The sale of S&P 100 *out-of-the-money* call options with an underlying value equal to the value of the shares belonging to the above basket.
- The purchase of an equal amount of S&P 100 *out-of-the-money* put options.

The sale of S&P 100 call options against a basket of shares aims at increasing the rate of return, while allowing the equity portfolio to move upside towards the call options' exercise value. The put options, partly financed with the proceeds from the sale of the call options and from any dividends, protect the equity position from a downside risk.

The long put and short call position is a so-called short synthetic market position, hedging against the long position on the share basket.

With the help of IT systems, the fund manager constantly optimizes the share basket, and the put and call options are actively managed, so that in response to market movements their exercise prices and their maturity dates are constantly changed.

15.7 LENDING

Se vogliamo che tutto rimanga come è, bisogna che tutto cambi.
    Giuseppe Tomasi di
    Lampedusa, Il Gattopardo, 1958

If we want everything to stay the same, everything has to change.

Everything must change for everything to remain the same. This saying appears to be substantiated by the fact that corporate lending now represents one of the evolutionary frontiers of hedge funds. Hedge funds are back doing the same business as the first bankers in history. Actually, this should not come as too much as a surprise, because through the extension of loans hedge funds provide companies with venture capital. Moreover, hedge funds can be considered as spin-offs of investment bank units and as such they also originate corporate loans, also called *direct lending* or *private lending*.

In their lending activity some hedge funds offer competitive rates compared with banks, and especially a more rapid lending process compared with commercial banks. Typically, these hedge funds diversify their loans, in that they grant loans of limited sizes, ranging from $1 to 5 million, trying to guarantee a wide sector distribution among borrowing companies.

Generally, a hedge fund grants convertible loans collateralized by assets of the borrowing company, and there is a downside protection, because the hedge fund is a senior creditor on said collateral. The loan is subject to many other legal provisions aimed at limiting the hedge fund's loss in the case of default of the borrowing company. As it is a convertible loan, the hedge fund will profit most if the market price of the borrowing company's stock exceeds the conversion price.

By granting this special type of convertible loan, the hedge fund has created a very interesting return profile: a positive carry due to the loan interest receivable, a limited downside in the case of borrower default and the share in the upside of the borrowing company's stock. The success of this strategy rests on the fund manager's expertise and on his ability to select the right borrowing companies. The main risk is an increase in the corporate bankruptcy rate as happens in specific times of economic recession. Another important aspect is the competition in the lending arena by banks and other financial companies.

In 2004, US banks softened the lending standards, having reached the highest stringency level of the last decade in September 2001. This softening was a reaction to the soaring competition among banks in the United States and to the wide range of alternative credit sources (Figure 15.2).

Direct lending can be of very many types: bridge loans, loans before a high-yield issue, loans before an initial public offering, bail-out loans, placing of an issue among a selected number of financial intermediaries and equity recapitalizations.

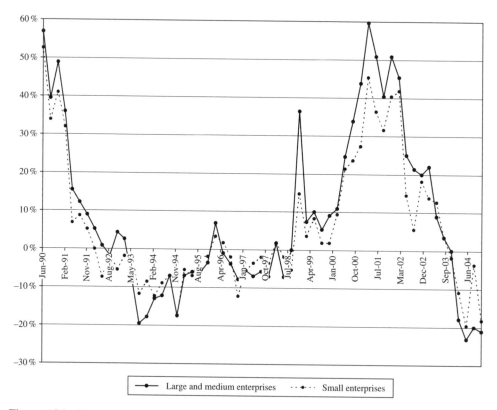

Figure 15.2 Net percentage of banks that are tightening their lending standards (percentages). Source: Board of Governors of the Federal Reserve System, The October 2004 Senior Loan Officer Opinion Survey on Bank Lending Practices; www.federalreserve.gov

The *direct lending* market seems to be characterized by a lower competitiveness with respect to high-yield bonds or private equity.[4] Recently, commercial banks and lending companies have staged an aggressive comeback to the market of corporate lending, cutting way back on spreads, mainly in large cap companies that comply with defined requirements.

The consolidation of the banking industry in the United States is giving rise to many investment opportunities, especially in the market of SME lending.

In 2003, a hedge fund granted a loan to a company engaged in the energy sector (hereinafter called "Company"). The fund had been exchanging views with the Company's CEO for quite some time, and a series of possible transactions had been vetted. The Company purchases, surveys and produces natural gas and oil, and historically had also been engaging in the purchase of reserves, that is, priority rights on future gas and oil shipments.

The hedge fund arranged the organization and extension of a $90 million loan through the issue of senior and secured debt securities (Senior Secured Credit Facility), subdivided into a tranche A of $30 million and a tranche B of $60 million. In particular, the hedge fund managed and placed the entire tranche A, while it underwrote tranche B directly. All the Company's assets were used as a collateral for tranche B; however, in the case of liquidation, tranche B was subordinated to tranche A.

The collateral assets were represented by 60% of already developed reserves under production, 40% of already developed reserves not yet under production and 20% of not yet developed reserves, under the restriction that not yet developed reserves could not exceed 10% of the loan collateral.

The hedge fund had calculated that tranche B would generate yearly returns of 16%, 17% and 18%, had the investment lasted for one, two or three years, respectively.

Note: the hedge fund also acted as agent for three other investors participating in the lending transaction.

The Company's debt structure was subdivided into three parts: the two tranches of the above issue and a small banking credit line.

When the bonds came close to maturity, the hedge fund structured the banking credit line in such a way as to allow the Company to refinance its debt when due, increasing the sum available under the existing banking credit line. The increased cash availability allowed the Company to turn some idle property into production activities.

The Company's activity base included mainly gas reserves that had already been developed by 71%. Based on conventional reserve valuation models, the hedge fund was covered with collaterals representing 3.4 times tranche B. The transaction was also resting on a conservative EBITDA forecast for 2003, which allowed the hedge fund to expect higher future cash flows than estimated.

Next, the Company benefited from the oil and gas price rise, generating higher than expected revenue flows and, at the time of writing this book, was able to pay back 50% of the entire $90 million loan.

---

[4] Private equity indicates investments in venture capital, with specific reference to investments carried out in periods of the corporate life cycle subsequent to inception.

> In addition, the hedge fund is confident that the following quarters will see a further increase in revenues since, according to its analysts, the positive impact of the soaring oil and gas prices has not yet been fully factored in by the Company's financial accounts. The hedge fund's expected return on investment is about 17%.

15.8 PIPES OR REGULATION D

The burst of the New Economy speculative bubble came with a sudden credit market crunch. The stringent requirements necessary to be granted a loan by investment banks, and every tightening in lending by commercial banks to companies carrying a speculative credit rating, offer hedge funds the opportunity to provide non-traditional financing solutions, such as *private investments in public entities,* or PIPEs. Historically, demand has been dominated by high-tech, healthcare and biotech companies, but at present the recourse to PIPEs is also spreading to other industries.

To place securities directly with a select number of investors, most hedge funds operating in the United States adopt *Regulation D.*

Regulation D governs the limited offer and sale of securities without registration under the Securities Act of 1933, exempting *private placement* transactions from the stringent registration requirements with the Securities and Exchange Commission (SEC). However, Regulation D is also widely used by small public companies that are finding it difficult to raise additional capital and as a result turn to private placements. In particular, PIPEs allow publicly-held companies to issue new shares not registered with the SEC and sell them in a private transaction.

Generally, securities issued under Regulation D take two forms:

- share issue: investors purchase the company shares at a discount to the market price;
- convertible issue: upon maturity the convertible bond can be converted into a precise dollar consideration of the underlying share, at an unknown unit value. Therefore, even the number of shares to be received upon conversion is unknown: what is known is the dollar consideration. Also these convertible notes are sold at a discount on market price.

For investors in securities issued under Regulation D, profit comes from the initial discount between the purchase price and the market value at the time of issue. However, investors take upon themselves some risks:

- the risk of issuer default;
- the lack of liquidity of PIPEs.

Under the current regulations, it is necessary to hold securities issued under Regulation D for at least two years before reselling them publicly. To avoid this restriction, generally the issuer files the registration of these securities with the SEC within 180 days of issue, thus allowing the issued securities to be publicly traded. In this case, for the first 180 days after their issue, these securities can be traded among "accredited" investors, as defined by the US rule.

In a typical PIPE, the fund manager buys common shares or convertible bonds directly from an issuer that is trying to raise capital through a private placement under Regulation D. Due to the illiquidity of these securities, the purchase price paid by the hedge fund manager (or the conversion price in the case of convertible bonds) is typically set at a discount on the market price of the issuer shares at the time of the transaction.

Generally, the issuer is also contractually obliged to try and register the securities with the SEC within a defined period of time to permit the issued securities to be publicly traded. If the issuer cannot register these securities with the SEC within the defined deadline, the transaction may envisage that the hedge fund manager is given the right to purchase an additional number of securities at a discount; however, the fund manager will not be able to sell these until the registration process is completed. Therefore, PIPEs entail a liquidity risk.

If the issuer is not be able to register with the SEC the securities held by the hedge fund, the securities can be sold only in a private transaction and generally at a lower price than the hedge fund originally paid, on the off chance that a buyer can be found. Also, where the securities have been registered so as to be sold publicly, their market might be thin or illiquid, making it difficult or at times impossible to sell the securities at the desired price and in the desired quantity.

Although the price paid by the fund manager is generally at a discount to the market price at the time of purchase, by the time the fund manager can dispose of the securities by selling them on the public market, their market price might have dropped with respect to the price paid by the fund manager; or the concurrent sale by the fund manager and by other investors having similar registration rights might drive the market price of the issuer securities deeply down.

In the past, many of the issuers that executed PIPEs were in stringent need of liquidity or were not in a position or could not raise money through capital increases. When a fund manager invests in companies that may be experiencing financial straits, he gets exposed to the risk that the issuer may default.

Figure 15.3 shows the number of PIPEs and their value in the United States, excluding Structured Equity Lines, 144-A Convertibles, Reg S Placements and Canadian companies.

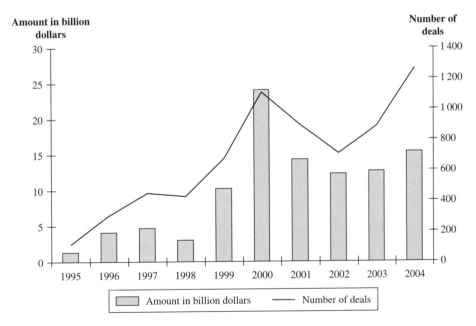

Figure 15.3 Size of the PIPEs market from 1995 to 2004. Source: www.placementtracker.com

The PIPE market is a niche market and often investing in these securities is but a small part of the strategies adopted by multi-strategy funds.

In Europe, Basel 2 regulations spell out a series of operational standards that are reshaping the relations between banks and business organizations, in particular with regard to lending modalities. In brief, Basel 2 aims to match banks' regulatory capital with the true economic risk of different assets and investments. The main change comes from the introduction of sophisticated methods to assess credit risk. Each company will be assigned a rating, based on which it will be possible to obtain a closer correlation between the borrowing company risk level and the bank's capital requirements to cover risks. The higher the risk associated with a given client, the credit line being equal, the greater the capital absorption, and therefore the higher the interest rate imposed to the client. This will cause a credit crunch with respect to small and medium-sized enterprises in Europe. Therefore, when the new Basel 2 regulations come into effect, there will be room in the lending arena for operators other than banks, for example hedge funds specializing in private lending.

15.9   REAL ESTATE

Real estate is a strategy in which a fund manager invests in rental property with long-term rents, mortgages or property that is undervalued, badly managed or financed.

When defining the purchase price, the fund manager generates a projection, generally based upon the assumption of a property restructuring or improvement and its sale to a traditional buyer, or the liquidation of the property after splitting it in smaller units.

15.10   NATURAL RESOURCES

The growth in China and India should drive the demand for energy significantly up, as we have already illustrated when talking about the "long/short equity strategy on emerging markets" in Chapter 4.

Recently, China's massive growth propelled the price of many raw materials up, oil in particular. Whether the Chinese growth is sustainable is still uncertain, and this should suggest a conservative attitude with regard to the persistency of this trend. The worst scenario for this strategy is the onset of a global recession, which would undermine the prices of raw materials. During a time of recession, the demand for natural resources is expected to remain rather low and sluggish, and the performance of commodities is expected to turn negative.

A strategy investing in natural resources generates positive returns in a scenario of global recovery, and negative returns in a scenario of global recession. Only a macro-economic analysis can help the fund manager assign a probability to these scenarios and act accordingly.

Commodity markets are extremely wide and diversified, and comprise base metals, precious metals, energy and agriculture produce. Historically, commodity markets have generated better returns in times of growing inflation. Raw materials can be classified as follows:

- energy: oil, natural gas, coal;
- power: electric power;
- base metals: steel, aluminum, copper, nickel, lead, tin;
- precious metals: gold, silver, platinum, palladium;

- forest products: wood, paper, cellulose pulp, rubber;
- soft commodities: wheat, corn, soybean, coffee, sugar, cocoa, orange juice, cotton, wool, meat and cattle.

The Goldman Sachs Natural Resources Index is a market capitalization weighted index, and it includes companies engaging in the energy, extracting and manufacturing sectors, owners and operators of timber tracts, forestry services, producers of pulp and paper and owners of plantations. Figure 15.4 clearly shows that at the beginning of 2003 there has been a strong rise in the price of raw materials.

Raw materials each have their own particular attributes. Precious metals behave like a currency whose attractiveness depends on the strength of the dollar, and they are perceived as havens in times of financial crisis. Historically, precious metals are a hedge in times of a weak dollar. Base metals depend on the production of mines and on the level of international production activity. Some raw materials display a basic imbalance between demand and supply, giving rise to investment opportunities. For example, China is building many new nuclear power stations for the production of electric power, which will push the price of uranium up, considering its limited supply.

Natural resources have a low correlation with traditional asset classes due to the different performance *drivers*, which is why many sophisticated investors are rekindling an old interest for natural resources. Figure 15.5 shows the factors that have historically affected the valuation of the different raw materials.

The index was created on 30th April 1998 based on a fictitious value of 100.

Figure 15.4 Goldman Sachs Natural Resources Index from 2000 to 2004. Used with permission from Bloomberg L.P.

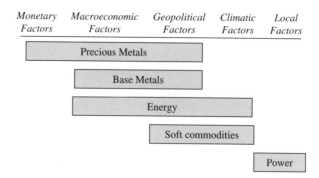

Figure 15.5 Factors that have historically influenced the evaluation of different raw materials. Source: Free adaptation from Barep Asset Management

As summarized in the figure, the main factor affecting agriculture produce is the weather, which is difficult to forecast. The valuation of energy resources depends on geo-political, macro-economic and also climatic factors, for example a bitterly cold winter drives up the demand for heating fuel. In particular, the oil price is subject to sudden and deep changes in the aftermath of international political events, like for example wars or terrorist attacks.

Hedge funds can invest in natural resources by several trading techniques, which can be grouped under two main families: directional and *relative value* deals. Relative value deals are more complex and seek to profit from the following abnormalities that can occur on the marketplaces:

- *calendar spread*: abnormality in the term structure of a raw material price, that is, a price abnormality between different delivery months of a single raw material;
- *geographical spread*: price abnormality between two similar products with different delivery locations;
- *inter-commodity spread* or *cross-commodity spread*: price abnormality between two raw materials within the same class of natural resources, displaying an apparent fundamental relation and traded at prices that do not reflect their relative value;
- *commodity-related equity spread*: price abnormality between two shares whose price depends on the performance of raw materials, like for example a long/short equity strategy on stocks of the extracting sector or a long position on stocks whose valuation is linked to the price of raw materials and the sale of futures on these same raw materials.

Fund managers can construct several investment strategies. For example, the valuation of oil stocks discount a given oil price. The oil futures price can be widely different. This may open up an arbitrage opportunity between the oil price implied in the valuation of oil stocks and the oil futures. Note that this position has no correlation with oil price movements.

Years of weak investment by the major oil companies in upstream assets has created a situation were the oil-industry contractors have consistently under-invested themselves: the worldwide fleet of jack-up oil rigs is on average 22 years old, with the peak of investment dating back to 1982. As exploration and production budgets have increased, there has been substantial tightening of supply in the drilling business with continuous increases in utilization rates and rental fees.

The drilling sector has performed strongly as a result. The sector has recently pulled back, however, on concerns over new capacity. Several new jack-up orders have been announced. According to the hedge fund analysis, those rigs will not be delivered in time to match the increase in drilling demand and the prevailing rental rates do not allow acceptable returns on new-build prices. Hence most of the new orders have been placed in anticipation of rising fees.

A hedge fund manager opened a long position in Ensco International Inc, an international offshore contract drilling company, which also provides marine transportation services in the Gulf of Mexico.

Ensco has a fleet of 44 jack-up units, half of which are in the high-end segment. The hedge fund manager estimates it would cost approximately $38 per share to replicate the fleet by buying similar units in the secondary market.

The fund manager has hedged this long position against two risks: oil prices and sector shocks. Strong increases in exploration and production budgets are estimated to be supported only by a $35–40 oil price environment. The fund manager used 12 month futures to hedge 50% of the Ensco long exposure. The remainder of the long exposure was delta-hedged using put options on a basket of oil services stocks.

Ensco shares performed very well in second half of 2005 as shown in Figure 15.6.

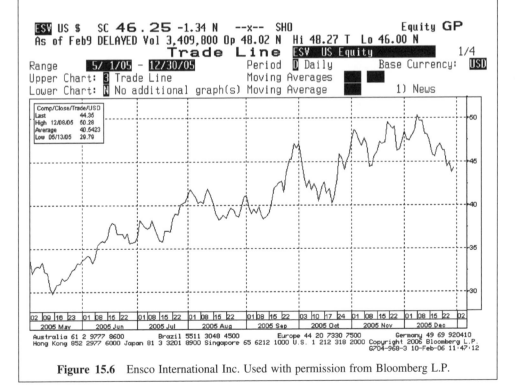

Figure 15.6 Ensco International Inc. Used with permission from Bloomberg L.P.

15.11   ENERGY TRADING

In this strategy the fund manager can establish positions on securities, raw materials, assets and derivatives whose value depends on the global production, stockage, distribution and consumption of energy. For example, positions can refer to the prices of the future delivery of crude oil, natural gas and electric power in different geographical locations.

The fund manager can invest in derivatives on the following energy forms:

* oil[5];
* coal;
* natural gas;
* refined oil products;
* electricity.

Oil futures are the most traded among natural resources. The high volatility characterizing energy markets opens up plenty of trading opportunities.

Some fund managers who trade energy limit themselves to trading derivatives on energy raw materials, whereas others reach further and trade on the emerging markets of electricity. Electric power cannot be stocked, except in very small quantities, and therefore production must adjust to the demand. Also the transferability of electric power is limited, in that leaks from electrodes make it ineffective to transport electricity beyond a given distance, and therefore demand and supply must meet on a local marketplace. The electricity market is characterized by high fragmentation into local marketplaces, and being still in its infancy, it offers many trading opportunities. Moreover, in the United States many new investment opportunities have been generated by the liberalization of the electricity market and by Enron's collapse.

Many factors can affect the markets of electric power:

* the operational conditions of distribution networks;
* tariff regulations;
* weather-correlated events;
* government interventions;
* unexpected market conditions, for example the discontinuation of power supply due to atmospheric events.

In order to execute given energy strategies, a hedge fund, or any entity associated with the hedge fund, may be required to register with the US Federal Energy Regulatory Commission as *power marketer*.

In energy trading, hedge funds compete against public utilities, which have the advantage of producing all or part of the energy they trade, thus reducing their exposure to market price fluctuations. Since hedge funds do not produce electric power, in order to meet contract obligations some hedge funds may be forced to buy energy at the market price, suffering a heavy loss. In order to be level with utilities, some hedge funds have set up *ad hoc* entities in the United States for the production of electric power, to which the hedge funds extend loans. The operating profit or loss reported by these entities is transferred to the hedge fund under the form of interest service, obtaining a highly efficient fiscal management.

---

[5] Brent is a light sweet crude oil from the North Sea. Despite the limited quantities, it has become a benchmark for the European market, through the exchanges at the International Petroleum Exchange in London. WTI, acronym of West Texas Intermediate, is a crude oil that stands as a benchmark for the North American market. Its prices generally differ from Brent prices.

Other hedge funds decided not to restrict their trades to financial instruments, and included investments in physical assets, for example power transmission lines, natural gas pipelines, refineries, oil production and stockage equipment, oil or natural gas field research and surveying companies, oil and natural gas extraction companies, etc. These investments entail unusual risks: for example they are particularly illiquid, it is difficult to value them, and they run significant potential risks of causing environmental damage, for example water or soil contamination.

15.12 NATURAL EVENTS

Cat-bonds, short for catastrophe bond, are bonds associated with natural catastrophes like earthquakes, hurricanes, volcano eruptions, landslides, storms, tornados, typhoons and cyclones. At the end of 2003, the market of these innovative financial instruments reached $4.34 billion (Figure 15.7).

The issuers of this type of bonds are re-insurers. The issuer insures against catastrophic events like earthquakes and hurricanes, and the risk is transferred over to institutional investors who are willing to take on the environmental risk in exchange for the bond's cash flows.

Recently, the frequency of catastrophic events led to an increase in the demand of insurance policies, driving written premiums up: this incremented the claim risk and the re-insurance cost for insurance companies. It is the re-insurance cost increase itself that prompted insurance companies to look for hedging solutions on the market through the issue of cat-bonds.

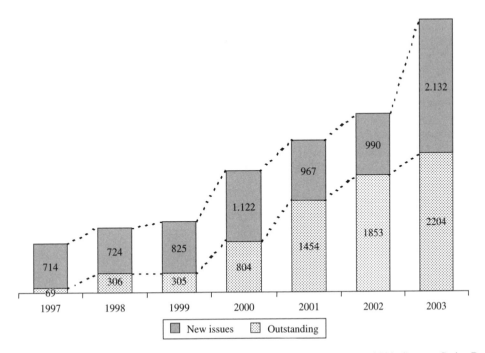

Figure 15.7 Catastrophe bonds market size in billion dollars from 1997 to 2003. Source: Swiss Re Capital Markets Corporation, Sigma: Natural catastrophes and man-made disasters in 2003

A *Special Purpose Vehicle* (SPV) issues the cat-bonds. The proceeds raised from the bond subscribers are then re-invested in money market securities or segregated as a provision for bond redemption, in case the catastrophe does not occur, or on the contrary as a provision for claim settlement.

Cat-bonds pay a rather high interest rate that depends on the likelihood a given natural disaster may occur. If the catastrophic event does occur, the investor who bought the bond will receive no interest consideration and may also lose the principal, which goes to the bond issuer. Thus, the issuer gets protected against a series of natural catastrophes like earthquakes and hurricanes. The issuer re-insures with the bond market instead of other insurance companies. This transaction allows the issuer to find a less expensive protection with respect to the traditional re-insurance.

There are two types of cat-bonds: indemnity bond and parametric bond:

- *Indemnity bonds* are bonds whereby the redemption of the face value depends on the losses suffered by the issuer as a result of a catastrophic event. They are quite similar to re-insurance contracts. It may take months to define exactly the claims an insurance company may have to settle after a catastrophe, therefore investors do not know exactly the extent of the issuer's exposure at the time a catastrophe occurs.
- *Parametric bonds* are bonds whereby the percentage redemption of the face value depends on a calculation based on physical parameters measured during the catastrophe. For example, specialized companies like EQECAT (www.eqecat.com) calculate a catastrophe's severity index, which is compared to the attachment point; that is, the threshold defined in the bond's offering memorandum affecting the bond's redemption percentage. If the ultimate loss is greater than the attachment point, the bond redemption is not affected, otherwise only part of the bond's face value will be refunded, depending on the severity of the damages inflicted by the catastrophe.

Recently, companies like Risk Management Solutions, Inc. (www.rms.com) have been springing up. These specialize in the provision of services for the measurement and management of catastrophe risks caused by natural events such as earthquakes, hurricanes, storms and tornados, as well as in modeling disasters caused by man, for example terrorist attacks.

In the summer of 2004, four powerful hurricanes, Charley, Frances, Ivan and Jeanne, hit first the Caribbean and then Florida, leaving death and destruction in their wake. We have to go back to 1886 to find the last time four hurricanes hit the same state of the United States. Estimated losses for insurers reached $24 billion, while the economic loss was about double that amount.

Also in the summer of 2004, Japan was hit by the worst typhoon season in its history: nine different storms hit different areas in Japan. Estimated losses for insurers reached $5 billion.

In addition to the death and suffering they caused, these natural events also affected the 2004 profitability of the insurance and re-insurance industry.

And, of course, it did not end there. In August 2005, the Gulf of Mexico was hit by hurricane Katrina, one of the most destructive natural disasters ever to hit the United States. Estimated losses for insurers should range between $40 and $60 billion. In October 2005, hurricane Wilma hit the southwest Florida coast, causing estimated insured losses from $8 to $12 billion.

Are these catastrophic events in 2004 and in 2005 to be considered as exceptional events? The Geophysical Fluid Dynamics Laboratory in Princeton designed a mathematical model that has projected a strong increase in the number of hurricanes due to global warming caused by the increase in carbon dioxide in the atmosphere. According to *The New York Times*,[6] the intensity and frequency of extreme climatic events is bound to increase progressively over the coming decades.

In December 1999, a quarter of the electric lines of Electricité de France (EDF) were damaged by winds blowing at over 200 km/h, bending poles and uprooting trees that tore down electric lines. In that same month, Electricité de France launched two cat-bonds to insure against damages to transmission lines caused by windstorms.

The cat-bonds issued by the special purpose vehicle Pylon Ltd. were issued on a private placement in two tranches, €120 million and €70 million respectively, both with a maturity date on 29th December 2008. The two tranches pay floating rate coupons: the first tranche pays EURIBOR +3.9% and the second EURIBOR +1.5%. Subscribers do not receive the coupon payment or even the principal if an index calculated on the wind speed in France exceeds a given threshold.

---

[6] Revikin, A.C. (2004) "Global Warming Is Expected To Raise Hurricane Intensity," *The New York Times*, 30th September.

16
Hedge Fund Performance Analysis

Performance analysis must always be associated with risk analysis, because every performance is connected to the assumption of some risks.

16.1 RISKS INHERENT IN HEDGE FUND INVESTMENTS

Risk management is an extremely important activity for the success of a hedge fund. In order to survive in highly volatile markets, stock picking skills are no longer a sustainable competitive advantage for the fund manager. This skill must be accompanied by a well-designed and rigorously managed risk management system.

The risks associated with the strategies adopted by hedge funds are more complex than those entailed in traditional investments. In order to appreciate the actual risk a subscriber of these funds may run, it is necessary to carry out an in-depth analysis of the peculiarities of the investment strategy and of the risk management techniques adopted by the fund. There are basically three types of risks:

- market risk;
- credit risk;
- liquidity risk.

Figure 16.1 highlights the overlapping areas of these three risk classes in a hedge fund investment.

Market risks are associated with the performance of the variables affecting capital markets (prices of financial instruments, interest rates, exchange rates, etc.). The possible use of leverage magnifies the market risks to which a hedge fund is exposed. Depending on the investing style, the fund manager has the possibility of acting so as to reduce this risk.

Credit risk is associated with the reliability of the operational structure and the organizational processes of the hedge fund and its service suppliers. A credit risk may stem from an insolvent financial counterparty, or from the impairment of a security due to the downgrading of the issuer's credit rating.

A critical liquidity risk is the fact that one of the typical characteristics of hedge funds is that redemption by subscribers is possible only at pre-determined and fixed deadlines (for example monthly, quarterly or annually). The liquidity risk is also represented by the liquidity of the financial instruments in which the hedge fund manager has invested. A liquidity risk rises when a given hedge fund must exit a position, but due to a liquidity squeeze on the market can do so only at unfavorable prices.

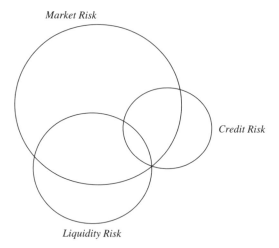

Market Risk

Credit Risk

Liquidity Risk

Figure 16.1   Three risk classes in a hedge fund investment. Source: Free adaptation from "Sound Practices for hedge fund manager", February 2000

These three risk classes entail different impacts depending on the specific investment strategy followed by the hedge fund. For example:

- distressed securities funds hold illiquid assets in companies under restructuring that expose them to liquidity and default risks;
- merger arbitrage funds are exposed to the risk that the merger may fail;
- funds specializing in emerging countries are exposed to the country risk;
- long/short equity funds are exposed to the short-squeeze risk by their brokers (where the fund manager has short sold securities, the broker who lent the securities may make a supplementary margin call in the case of adverse market movements leading to an excessive value erosion of the position);
- fixed income arbitrage funds are exposed to the risk of credit spread widening.

The use of leverage exposes hedge funds to the risk of a sudden withdrawal of funds by brokers, which may force the hedge fund to close out its positions rapidly, even at unfavorable prices.

The operational risk is associated with the inefficiency of organizational and information systems that may cause the fund manager to make wrong decisions.

The global risk to which a hedge fund subscriber is exposed can be effectively reduced with diversification, turning to fund of hedge funds instruments, whose portfolio construction rationale entails the creation of a product that can minimize the risks that would otherwise be borne directly by the investor. A fund of hedge funds diversifies its investment on multiple strategies and multiple managers, reducing the overall volatility of the portfolio as a result of the correlations among the strategies, offers a better liquidability than single hedge funds and performs a constant portfolio monitoring and rebalancing.

The different types of risks we have just analyzed demonstrate clearly that volatility does not capture all the risk factors inherent in a hedge fund. Classical risk measurement methods must be modified, because the hedge fund returns do not follow a Gaussian distribution but an asymmetrical one, which for example can be characterized by events that may be less frequent, but have a higher impact.

The quantitative analysis is affected by a data paucity caused by both the frequency of the fund *Net Asset Value* (NAV) calculation, and by the fact that often open-end hedge funds have a short track record. For example, since fund units are measured monthly, the short-term volatility is hidden by the lack of liquidity: if a fund drops in the middle of the month and then recovers, the hedge fund hides the problem with a valuation of the monthly NAV.

As a result, it is preferable not to calculate the Value at Risk along a classical approach (variance/covariance), but rather use all those simulation methodologies that are not based on the assumption of a normal distribution of returns (historical simulation method or Monte Carlo simulation).

In order to fully measure investment risks, it is necessary to remember that:

- correlations depend upon market conditions;
- leverage induces an acceleration of both profits and losses;
- in times of crisis, correlations rise;
- in times of crisis, the liquidity of financial instruments drops drastically.

16.2 HEDGE FUND STRATEGIES INDICES

In order to cover the general performance of hedge fund investment strategies and highlight the determinant factors, we use the performance of the CS/Tremont indices and the LIPPER TASS database, which is one of the most comprehensive on the market.

All hedge fund databases, however, display biases at performance data level. The main distortions carried by databases are:

- self selection bias;
- survivorship bias.

The self selection bias stems from the fact that the contribution of data to databases is voluntary, therefore only best funds tend to report data. Generally, hedge fund start-ups tend not to report their performance to databases: they may be more willing to do so after 6 or 12 months if the attained performance is positive. Of course, hedge fund start-ups showing a negative performance will have no propensity to disclosure.

The survivorship bias is caused by the exclusion from databases of funds that over the years have disappeared, maybe due to their negative performance. This bias tends to affect data samples positively, and therefore to overstate the real-world returns. By excluding hedge funds that have been started less than one year before, practically all those hedge funds are excluded that having turned out a negative performance from the start, decide to close down their business even before one year has passed. By excluding hedge funds that stop sending reports to CS/Tremont, funds that go out of business are also automatically excluded.

In the book *Absolute Returns: The Risk and Opportunities of Hedge Fund Investing*, Alexander M. Ineichen estimates that CS/Tremont indices overestimate the hedge funds' real-world performance by about 2.5–3.5 % a year.

CS/Tremont indices start by defining the universe of hedge funds. The chosen funds carry the following characteristics:

- they are included in the LIPPER TASS database;
- they have a minimum $10 million NAV;
- they have been in business for at least one year;
- they have certified accounts covering the previous fiscal year.

Funds are then subdivided into categories based on the manager's investment style:

1. CS/Tremont Hedge Fund Index
2. CS/Tremont Hedge Convertible Arbitrage
3. CS/Tremont Hedge Dedicated Short Bias
4. CS/Tremont Hedge Emerging Markets
5. CS/Tremont Hedge Equity Market Neutral
6. CS/Tremont Hedge Event Driven

   - CS/Tremont Hedge Distressed
   - CS/Tremont Hedge Event Driven Multi-Strategy
   - CS/Tremont Hedge Risk Arbitrage

7. CS/Tremont Hedge Fixed Income Arbitrage
8. CS/Tremont Hedge Global Macro
9. CS/Tremont Hedge Long/Short Equity
10. CS/Tremont Hedge Managed Futures
11. CS/Tremont Hedge Multi-Strategy

CS/Tremont indices are asset-weighted, that is, the performance of each fund is weighted with respect to the fund's assets under management, so as to provide a more accurate description of the hedge fund industry behavior. The index is measured and rebalanced on a monthly basis. Funds may be reselected on a quarterly basis.

To minimize the survivorship bias, funds are not removed from indices until they have been completely liquidated or stop sending reports.

Finally, it is important to note that CS/Tremont indices are not automatically investable, that is, some funds making up the index are closed to new investors. However, as of 1st August 2003, the CS/Tremont Investable Hedge Fund Index started being measured.

16.2.1 Benchmarking

There have been several attempts to construct worthwhile benchmarking tools for the hedge fund industry (Table 16.1), but none has been used as a mainstream tool to the same extent and in the same manner as benchmarks in traditional asset management.

Benchmarking with an index only makes sense if the index is representative, rule-based, fully investable, transparent, diversified, timely reporting and liquid. To address some of

Table 16.1 List of major hedge fund index providers (non-investable)

Provider	Launch date	Provider	Launch date
Hennessee	1987	Altvest	2000
LJH	1992	Zurich	2001
Van Hedge	1994	S&P	2002
HFR	1994	Eurekahedge	2002
CISDM	1994	MSCI	2002
Bernheim	1995	Blue X	2002
EACM	1996	Feri	2002
HF net	1998	MondoHedge	2002
CSFB	1999	Barclay	2003

Table 16.2   List of investable indices

Provider	Launch date
CS/Tremont	2003
HFRX	2003
S&P Hedge Index	2002
MSCI/Lyxor	2003

Table 16.3   Index methodology

	CS/Tremont	HFRX	S&P Hedge Index	MSCI/Lyxor
Weighting	Asset weighted	Asset weighted	Equally weighted by strategy	Asset weighted
Return source	Funds	Managed accounts	Managed accounts	Managed accounts
Rebalancing frequency	Semi-annually	Quarterly	Annually	Quarterly

these issues, several index providers have created some investable hedge fund indices (Table 16.2).

Each investable index is designed to represent the overall composition of the hedge fund universe. The indices differ in their construction methodology, weighting preference, assets under management and number of strategies covered. Now that the marketplace offers investable hedge fund indices, it is easier to identify alpha creators by comparing them to their relevant sub-sector investable indices.

The correlation between the different indices is high and the return profiles are similar. Since inception, however, the cumulative performances vary from one index to the other. This can be attributed to the construction of the indices and to the underlying constituent funds. The calculation methods of these indices can differ considerably, as shown in Table 16.3.

The great advantage of investable indices is that they do not suffer from the usual distortions of non-investable hedge fund indices. It is however important to note that investable indices continue to underperform non-investable indices.

16.3   STATISTICAL ANALYSIS OF INDICES

As part of the index analysis we have performed we should not forget that the behavior of single hedge funds might deviate – at times substantially – from the behavior of the reference index.

Volatility, or even VaR, cannot conceivably represent the risk associated with investing in a hedge fund because historical data are too scarce: first, because funds are valued on a monthly basis and, second, because funds change over time. In addition, there are risks that are difficult to assess, for example, tight liquidability. This is why we say that it is not possible to measure the risk inherent in hedge funds, but it is possible to think that it can be characterized.

As a comparison to hedge fund performance, we selected two indices: the dollar denominated Morgan Stanley Capital International World index to represent international equity markets and the dollar denominated JP Morgan Global Government Bond Global International Index to represent international fixed income markets.

Let's examine some important statistics describing the monthly return distribution.

All strategies, with the exception of short selling and fixed income arbitrage, are more efficient than traditional investments, as they are positioned above the capital market line. The capital market line is formed by a linear combination of equity and bond investments. In Figure 16.2 it is the line between JPM Global Bonds and MSCI World.

The annual return dispersion is high both within investment strategies as well as across the different investment strategies, which underscores the importance of investing in the best hedge funds.

The return scatter in the hedge fund industry is much greater than that measured in traditional investment funds, where returns tend to be clustered close to their reference benchmark.

In order not to disrupt the ordinary properties of time series, data have been analyzed after having trimmed out extreme distribution data, but the outcome has not changed with respect to the one obtained with the complete time series. The analysis of the empirical distribution and the comparison with the Gaussian distribution show a marked left skew in general, with the exception of Dedicated Short Biases. This means that all distributions display negative extreme values, for example for returns generated in August 1998.

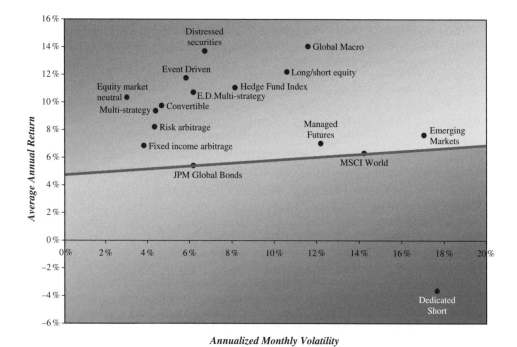

Figure 16.2 Risk/Return profile of the hedge funds strategies from 1994 to 2004. Copyright © 2006, Credit Suisse/Tremont Index LLC. All rights reserved*

---

* See page 298 for full copyright notice.

In contrast, the return distribution of CS/Tremont Hedge Fund Index, Convertible Bond Arbitrage, Dedicated Short Bias, Emerging Markets, Equity Market Neutral, Global Macro and Long/Short Equity show a right skew.

Indices carrying a symmetric distribution are:

- CS/Tremont Hedge Fund Index
- Global Macro
- Managed Futures

Let's now examine the distribution momentum: if kurtosis is greater than 3, tails are high and skewness is above or below zero, distributions are asymmetric.

The analysis of the distribution momentum shows that most have high tails:

- Convertible Arbitrage
- Emerging Markets
- Event Driven
- Distressed
- E.D. Multi-Strategy
- Risk Arbitrage
- Fixed Income Arbitrage
- Long/Short Equity
- Multi-Strategy

The conclusion is that data distribution is not normal, and to identify the distribution it is necessary to carry out parametric density estimates or resort to gamma distribution or the generalized normal distribution.

In all asymmetric distributions, volatility is not a good risk index: remember that the tails of the monthly return distribution are high, which means that the probability is not negligible that these extreme events may occur.

The return distribution of hedge funds is characterized by extreme events like the return profile of an insurer: the payoff profile of many hedge fund strategies is similar to that of the sale of put options, that is selling to the market an insurance against the extreme events.

Index performance data do not display a residual self-correlation, meaning that data are independent and uncorrelated, and therefore the linear regression model appears not to be oversimplified.

The data statistical analysis shows that over 11 years no strategy displays significant trends.

Between 1994 and 2004, the convertible bond arbitrage index shows a 1-month delay correlation equal to 0.6, which means that data display a slight inertia. The descriptive analysis of data allows us to detect a recent volatility compression within the strategies:

- global macro
- convertible bond arbitrage
- emerging markets

In the case of global macro funds, this can be explained by the growing implementation of risk management techniques aimed at containing volatility.

In the past, hedge fund strategies showed a low correlation with both equity and fixed income markets. In Figure 16.3 we have calculated the correlation matrix of markets and

	CS/Tremont Hedge Fund Index	Convertible Arbitrage	Dedicated Short	Emerging Markets	Equity Market Neutral	Event Driven	Distressed Securities	E.D. Multi-Strategy	Risk Arbitrage	Fixed Income Arbitrage	Global Macro	Long/Short Equity	Managed Futures	Multi-Strategy	Salomon Treasury Benchmark 30Y	MSCI World
CS/Tremont Hedge Fund Index	+1.00															
Convertible Arbitrage	+0.40	+1.00														
Dedicated Short	−0.48	−0.23	+1.00													
Emerging Markets	+0.65	+0.31	−0.57	+1.00												
Equity Market Neutral	+0.33	+0.32	−0.33	+0.22	+1.00											
Event Driven	+0.66	+0.58	−0.64	+0.68	+0.36	+1.00										
Distressed Securities	+0.57	+0.50	−0.63	+0.59	+0.33	+0.94	+1.00									
E.D. Multi-Strategy	+0.68	+0.59	−0.55	+0.68	+0.34	+0.93	+0.76	+1.00								
Risk Arbitrage	+0.39	+0.40	−0.50	+0.42	+0.30	+0.68	+0.56	+0.65	+1.00							
Fixed Income Arbitrage	+0.45	+0.53	−0.08	+0.29	+0.07	+0.39	+0.31	+0.43	+0.13	+1.00						
Global Macro	+0.86	+0.29	−0.13	+0.41	+0.21	+0.37	+0.31	+0.42	+0.13	+0.45	+1.00					
Long/Short Equity	+0.78	+0.26	−0.72	+0.59	+0.34	+0.66	+0.58	+0.64	+0.50	+0.20	+0.42	+1.00				
Managed Futures	+0.12	−0.19	+0.19	−0.10	+0.13	−0.19	−0.14	−0.22	−0.19	−0.07	+0.25	−0.03	+1.00			
Multi-Strategy	+0.16	+0.35	−0.07	−0.03	+0.20	+0.17	+0.11	+0.21	+0.07	+0.26	+0.11	+0.15	−0.01	+1.00		
Salomon Treasury Benchmark 30Y	+0.15	+0.06	+0.08	−0.10	+0.10	−0.07	−0.02	−0.09	−0.10	+0.11	+0.24	+0.05	+0.33	+0.05	+1.00	
MSCI World	+0.47	+0.10	−0.76	+0.53	+0.35	+0.59	+0.57	+0.51	+0.46	+0.03	+0.18	+0.61	−0.13	+0.12	−0.08	+1.00

Figure 16.3 Correlation matrix between hedge funds strategies and financial market indexes from 1994 to 2004. Copyright © 2006, Credit Suisse/Tremont Index LLC. All rights reserved*

* See page 298 for full copyright notice.

hedge funds with index data between 1994 and 2004. The matrix is symmetric, and therefore we reported only the data located in the lower triangular part of the main diagonal. The value in each box represents the correlation between the index of the corresponding line and the index of the corresponding column. The darker the tone, the greater the data correlation.

By analyzing this matrix, we see that the following correlations are statistically significant:

- The Dedicated Short Bias strategy has a negative correlation with all the other strategies, except the Managed Futures strategy, where in any case the correlation is low.
- The Managed Futures strategy has a negative correlation with all the other strategies, except the Dedicated Short Bias, Equity Market Neutral and Global Macro strategies, where in any case the correlation is low.
- The Long/Short Equity strategy has a positive correlation with Emerging Markets, Event Driven, Distressed Securities and Risk Arbitrage.
- The Fixed Income Arbitrage strategy has a positive correlation with the Convertible Bond Arbitrage strategy.
- The Risk Arbitrage strategy has a positive correlation with the Event Driven and Distressed Securities strategies.
- The Distressed Securities strategy has a positive correlation with the Convertible Bond Arbitrage, Emerging Markets and Event Driven strategies.
- The Event Driven has a positive correlation with Convertible Bond Arbitrage and Emerging Markets.
- All hedge fund strategies have a low correlation with the Salomon Treasury Benchmark 30 Years index.
- The Emerging Markets, Event Driven, Distressed Securities and Long/Short Equity strategies have a positive correlation with the MSCI World Index.

Finally, it is important to note that in times of market crisis, correlations are disrupted and hedge fund strategies tend to show a downside correlation with one another.

16.4 VALUE AT RISK

VaR measures the worst expected loss over a given time horizon under normal market conditions and with a given confidence interval. The reason for calculating VaR is to allow for the following statement: "We have an $X\%$ probability of not losing more than $Y\%$ of the portfolio in the next N days". $Y\%$ is the portfolio's VaR (Figure 16.4).

VaR is a function of two parameters: time horizon N and confidence interval $X\%$.

The natural time horizon in our analysis is one month because hedge funds calculate and disclose their performance on at least a monthly basis. Typically, the confidence intervals are 95% or 99%.

VaR can be calculated through various practical methods. Each of them is based on an assumption about the statistical distribution of returns: what counts is that the employed method does not assume the distribution to be normal.

Figure 16.5 highlights the débâcle that took place in August 1998 triggered by Russia's default, which caused unexpected huge losses.

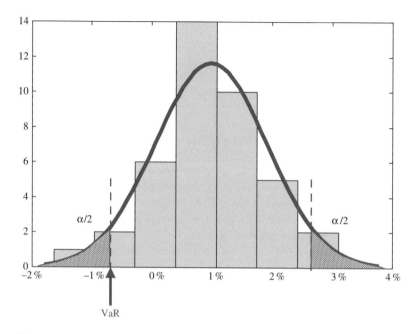

Figure 16.4 Graphical meaning of the VaR in the returns empirical distribution

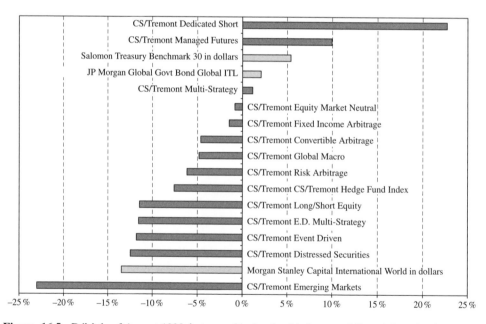

Figure 16.5 Débâcle of August 1998 (returns of hedge fund indexes and financial market indexes in August 1998). Copyright © 2006, Credit Suisse/Tremont Index LLC. All rights reserved*

---

* See page 298 for full copyright notice.

16.5 STATISTICAL ANALYSIS OF DATA FROM THE LIPPER TASS DATABASE

We considered the performance generated in the five-year period from 2000 to 2004 and obtained 911 hedge funds showing returns throughout the period. Then we asked ourselves whether there is an empirical answer to some common sense questions:

- Closed funds overperform funds that are still open to new investments?
- Less liquid funds overperform more liquid funds?
- Small-sized funds overperform larger-sized funds?

We followed a rigorous methodology to avoid biasing the results with our expectations. We created various samples: closed funds; funds that are still open to new investors; funds with monthly liquidity; and funds with at least a quarterly liquidity. Finally, we have identified three sizes: medium-sized funds, with NAV between $100 and 500 million; small-sized funds, with less than a $100 million NAV; large-sized funds, with a NAV in excess of $500 million. At first we carried out the "Two-sample F test" to verify if taken on a two-by-two sampling they had the same variance. Based on the outcome, we analyzed the data again to see whether the sample means were the same, with the "Two-sample T test" taking the same or different variances depending on the results obtained from the "Two-sample F test".

Let's skip further details of the procedure and jump directly to the outcome:

- There is no statistical evidence that closed funds overperform funds that are still open to investors.
- There is no statistical evidence that less liquid funds (with a liquidity in excess of one month) overperform more liquid funds (with a monthly liquidity).

Instead, we identified an interesting correlation between the performance and the size of funds: the average performance of mid-sized hedge funds is greater than that of small-sized hedge funds, whereas large hedge funds and mid-sized hedge funds show a similar average.

We can draw the conclusion that on a sufficiently long time horizon closed funds do not offer a performance premium, and less liquid funds do not offer a return premium. However, the fact that larger hedge funds overperform smaller hedge funds leads us to believe that there are barriers to entry with regard to performance. Larger funds are those with larger organizations, and state-of-the-art technological and research infrastructures. Larger organizations are no doubt in a better position to try and generate a consistent performance over time.

17
Conclusions

No, this is not the end. Not even the
beginning of the end. But it is, perhaps,
the end of the beginning (. . .).
Sir Winston Spencer Churchill,
Speech at The Lord Mayor's Luncheon,
Mansion House, 10th November 1942

There are people who are pessimistic with regard to the future of the hedge fund industry, but even though some concerns may be reasonable, there is little doubt that hedge funds are going to play a key role in the development of the asset management industry. We are not experiencing the demise of hedge funds, nor the beginning of their end: rather, we are witnessing the end of the beginning of their development.

In this book we have described the different investment strategies adopted by hedge funds, examining all the nooks and crannies of the finance world. For all strategies we underlined that profits and losses are not correlated to the general performance of capital markets, a characteristic that makes hedge funds an important diversification tool when managing a portfolio. The very fact that hedge fund returns tend to be uncorrelated to the general performance of capital markets means that the presence of a hedge fund basket within a traditional portfolio made up of stocks and bonds improves portfolio efficiency.

In recent years, the hedge fund industry grew exponentially in terms of assets under management and number of offered funds; it has remodeled its investment strategy composition and is constantly undergoing deep changes.

The hedge fund industry is now going institutional, thanks to the strong capital flow from pension funds, banks and funds of hedge funds. In order to meet the requirements of institutional investors, many hedge funds are investing in their infrastructures, trading systems, internal processes, auditing and risk management. Progress is also being made in terms of market transparency and disclosure. Since February 2006, the largest hedge fund management companies have been required to register with the US Securities and Exchange Commission. Registration forces management companies to report regularly on their organization and makes them subject to periodic inspections by commissioners.

Still, the hedge fund world is driven by supply and not by demand, since asset management talents, as in many other fields, are scanty. The offer of new funds will certainly keep up with demand, but most probably this will take place to the detriment of quality, because new talent is not coming to the market at the same rate at which money is flowing into the hedge fund industry. There will be a growing number of mediocre fund managers, and it will be more and more difficult to find top class fund managers.

We are witnessing the mushrooming of many new funds as a result of several factors: an extremely appealing commission structure and the provision of *capital introduction* services, as well as technological and risk management infrastructures by investment banks. This explosive concoction caused the industry to experience an extraordinary growth: today it is fashionable to be a hedge fund manager, and it is one of the most coveted professions in Wall Street.

We saw how the proprietary trading desks of large investment banks are very similar to hedge funds. It is therefore natural to consider hedge funds as spin-offs of investment banks. The finance tree in Figure 17.1 shows which investment bank departments compete against hedge funds.

Hedge funds provide very important services to the market, such as liquidity, risk transfer and in general financial intermediation services that traditionally were offered exclusively by financial institutions.

As we have said, the hedge fund industry is changing its composition in terms of investment strategies. Arbitrage strategies are exhausting their ability to generate a performance because they are overcrowded, so their appeal is withering away. But whereas merger arbitrage or convertible bond arbitrage strategies are suffering from overcrowding, which is causing market opportunities to be rapidly used up, the hedge fund industry is quickly turning to new strategies: PIPEs, private lending, long/short credit, energy trading, natural events, sector long/short equity and structured finance. At the same time, long-standing strategies are being revamped, like real estate and natural resources. Moreover, there are many investment opportunities in illiquid investments, with a time horizon ranging between two and five years, beyond which we trespass on private equity or real estate. The most successful hedge funds are those that adapt the most.

Will supply be able to keep up with demand without causing a performance deterioration? Directional strategies have no capacity problems because there will always be some trend to follow and because the markets they trade on are very liquid. The long/short equity strategy will benefit from the popularity of indexed passive funds, and the long/short credit strategy will benefit from the growing liquidity on the credit derivative market. *Relative value* strategies have big capacity limits: the huge flow of capitals directed towards these strategies has caused an overcrowding effect and this is why we believe that the weight of this type of hedge funds is bound to decrease in the near future.

Capacity management is key to the success of a hedge fund: it must grow up to the asset capacity that proves to be optimal from a management viewpoint. The role of fund managers as intermediaries capable of trading capacity with funds will become more and more important.

Should we then talk about a hedge fund bubble? Each expansion may be closely tied to the potential danger of excesses, and maybe we are witnessing excessive demand by customers. The risk is that people might resort to improvisation, and this is why we believe that the best way to access the hedge fund world is through the funds of hedge funds doorway. This financial instrument allows investors to delegate the selection of funds to a specialized company and with it the solution of all the issues associated with an industry that is experiencing such extraordinary growth.

The hedge fund industry is rapidly changing, and the same is true for the profession of fund pickers. The rapid growth of demand is pushing investments towards younger funds, and the fund picker profession is becoming more and more similar to that of a talent scout.

Investing in closed funds is similar to investing in private equity: the available investment is determined, and then private equity calls for capital when investment opportunities arise. There is no empirical evidence showing that closed funds perform better than open ones: clearly, often behind successful hedge funds there are organizations staffed by hundreds of people who know how to obtain a consistent performance over time.

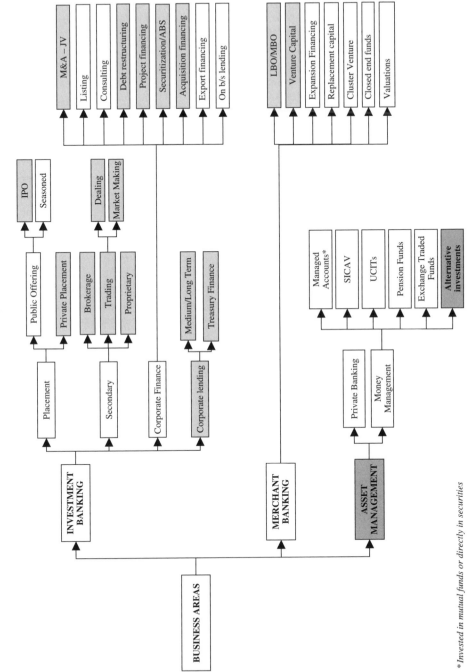

Figure 17.1 The finance tree. Source: Accenture

*Invested in mutual funds or directly in securities

As a direct consequence of the success enjoyed by some hedge funds, and the fact that the demand for good hedge funds is growing stronger, a recent trend is to require longer lock-up periods, worse liquidability terms and higher commissions. Although these fund managers do not want their managed assets to grow beyond the level they consider optimal, they are prepared to take advantage of their privileged position by imposing increased sacrifices on investors. Of course, the stability of the fund's capital base is a great advantage for a hedge fund manager, because he will not be forced into an ill-timed sell by investors who try to exit during market crises.

Another interesting trend was started by a very peculiar solution that the largest groups have found to the capacity problem nagging at hedge funds: in 2004 some of the most successful hedge fund management companies started to manage traditional mutual funds, which are less exposed to the problem of capacity.

The hedge fund industry is under consolidation.[1] This is shown by the fact that in 2004 numerous hedge funds and funds of hedge funds have been acquired by large investment companies looking for high margins and a stable commission income. The volatility of trading income leads to a stock market valuation with lower corporate multiples. The ability to create market-uncorrelated returns combined with a high distribution capacity represents a highly appealing opportunity for investment banks.

Whereas the best hedge funds can afford to close their funds earlier and diversify their customer base as they wish, funds of hedge funds are often forced by their size to "overdiversify", a phenomenon that may level down returns. Due to the capacity limits and the need of large funds of hedge funds to overdiversify, we believe that at least in the near future this industry will not experience the same consolidation process that took place in the mutual fund industry.

In this gold rush, with caravans of pioneers stalking the still unknown trails of financial markets, somebody will discover a goldfield and become rich. But most will never find gold and instead will remain poor or go bust. One thing is sure: in this gold rush, the ones who make money will be those who sell to the pioneers the shovels and picks they need to dig, namely, investment banks.

---

[1] "Boom or bust? Hedge funds are booming. That doesn't mean banks should buy them", *The Economist*, 9th October 2004.

Bibliography

Altman, E.I. (1993) *Corporate Financial Distress and Bankruptcy: A Complete Guide to Predicting & Avoiding Distress and Profiting from Bankruptcy*, New York: John Wiley & Sons, Inc.

Altman, E.I. (1999) *Distressed Securities: Analyzing and Evaluating Market Potential and Investment Risk*, Washington DC: Beard Books.

Altman, E.I. and Fanjul, G. (2004) "Special Report On Defaults and Returns on High Yield Bonds: First Quarter 2004," Leonard N. Stern School of Business, New York University Salomon Center; National Bureau of Economic Research Data.

Andrade, G., Mitchell, M. and Stafford, E., (2001) "New Evidence and Perspectives on Mergers," *Journal of Economic Perspectives*, **15**(2), 103–120.

Asensio, M.P. and Barth, J. (2001) *Sold Short: Uncovering Deception in the Markets*, New York: John Wiley & Sons, Inc.

Barbarosh, C.A. and Freeman, W.B. (1998) "Buying and Selling Claims in Bankruptcy: Maximising Returns" (www.pillsburywinthrop.com).

Beliossi, G. (2001) Prendere la via lunga e quella corta, *Risk Italia*, December 2001.

Bernstein, P.L. (1996) *Against the Gods: The Remarkable Story of Risk*, New York: John Wiley & Sons, Inc.

Bittanti, S. (1992) *Identificazione dei Modelli e Controllo Adattativo*, Bologna: Pitagora Editrice.

Bittanti, S. (1992) *Teoria della Predizione e del Filtraggio*, Bologna: Pitagora Editrice.

Bittanti, S. and Schiavoni, N. (1994) *Modellistica e Controllo*, Milan: CittàStudi.

Brealey, R. and Myers, S. (2000) *Principles of Corporate Finance*, 6th edition, New York: McGraw-Hill.

Burton, K. and Tudor Jones, P. (2004) "Adapt or Die," Bloomberg Markets.

Calamos, J.P. (1998) *Convertible Securities: The Latest Instruments, Portfolio Strategies, and Valuation Analysis*, New York: McGraw-Hill.

Calamos, N.P. (2003) *Convertible Arbitrage: Insights and Techniques for Successful Hedging*, New York: John Wiley & Sons, Inc.

Chancellor, E. (1999) *Devil Take the Hindmost: A History of Financial Speculation*, New York: Plume, a division of Penguin Putnam Inc.

Chanos, J. (2002) "Developments Relating to Enron Corp.," (Prepared Witness Testimony to The House Committee on Energy and Commerce), 2nd February 2002; http://energycommerce.house.gov.

Chanos, J. (2003) "Hedge Fund Strategies and Market Participation," US Securities and Exchange Commission, Roundtable On Hedge Funds, Panel Discussion: 15th May 2003; www.sec.gov.

Connolly, K.B. (1998) *Pricing Convertible Bonds*, Chichester: John Wiley & Sons, Ltd.

Cottier, P. (2000) *Hedge Funds and Managed Futures: Performance, Risks, Strategies, and use in Investment Portfolio*, Berne: Haupt.

Cox, J.C., Ross, S.A. and Rubinstein, M (1979) "Option Pricing: A Simplified Approach," *Journal of Financial Economics*, October, **7**, 229–263.

Dunbar, N. (2000) *Inventing Money*, Chichester: John Wiley & Sons, Ltd.

Endlich, L. (1999) *Goldman Sachs: The Culture of Success*, London: Little, Brown and Company.

Faber, M. (2002) *Tomorrow's Gold: Asia's Age of Discovery*, Hong Kong: CLSA Books.

Foster, R. and Kaplan, S. (2001) *Creative Destruction: Why Companies That Are Built to Last Underperform the Market – And How to Successfully Transform Them*, New York: Doubleday, a division of Random House Inc.

Gabbi, G. (1999) *La previsione nei mercati finanziari: trading system, modelli econometrici e reti neurali*, Rome: Bancaria Editrice.

Ghiringhelli, P. (2004) *Hedge funds e gestione di portafogli mobiliari*, Milan: Egea.

Graham, B. (1973) *The Intelligent Investor: The Classic Bestseller on Value Investing*, New York: HarperBusiness.

Gurwitz, A.S. (2000) *Managing a Family-Fixed Income Portfolio*, Frank J. Fabozzi Associates.

Hope, A. (2000) *Convertibles; Wandelanleihen – neu entdeckt*, Verlag Finanz und Wirtschaft.

Hull, J.C. (1987) *Opzioni, futures e altri derivati*, Milan: Il Sole 24 ORE SpA.

Hull, J.C. (2000) *Futures, Options and Other Derivatives*, 4th edition, Englewood Cliffs, N.J.: Prentice Hall.

Ineichen A.M. (2003) *Absolute Returns: The Risk and Opportunities of Hedge Fund Investing*, New York: John Wiley & Sons, Inc.

Ingersoll, J. (1977) "A Contingent-claims Valuation of Convertible Securities," *Journal of Financial Economics*, **4**, 289–321.

Izzo, C. (1992) *Titoli a reddito fisso*, Milan: Il Sole 24 ORE SpA.

Kaufman, P.J. (1998) *Trading Systems and Methods*, New York: John Wiley & Sons, Inc.

Kerschner, E. and Geraghty, M. (2004) *Riding the Wave: An Elongated M&A Cycle*, Citigroup.

Krieger, A. (1992) *The Money Bazaar: Inside the Trillion-dollar World of Currency Trading*, Times Books.

Lewis, M. (1989) *Liar's Poker: Rising Through the Wreckage on Wall Street*, New York: Penguin Books.

Lhabitant, F. (2002) *Hedge funds: Myths and Limits*, Chichester: John Wiley & Sons, Ltd.

Lhabitant, F. (2004) *Gestion alternative: comprendre et investir dans les hedge funds*, Paris: Dunod.

Lofthouse, S. (1994) *Equity Investment Management: How to Select Stocks and Markets*, Chichester: John Wiley & Sons, Ltd.

Lowenstein, R. (2000) *When Genius Failed: The Rise and Fall of Long-Term Capital Management*, New York: Random House.

Malkiel, B.G. (1973) *A Random Walk Down Wall Street*, Eighth edition, New York: W.W. Norton & Company.

Manuli, A. and Manuli, E. (1999) *Hedge funds: i vantaggi di una forma di investimento alternativa*, Milan: Gruppo Editoriale Futura SpA.

Mason, C. and Weingram, S. (2004) *Volatility Trading Hedge Fund: A Primer*, SwissHedge.

Merton, R.C. (1974) "On the Pricing of Corporate Debt: The Risk Structure of Interest Rates," *Journal of Finance*, **29**, 449–470.

Moore, K.M. (1999) *Risk Arbitrage: An Investor's Guide*, New York: John Wiley & Sons, Inc.

Neill H.B. (2003) *The Art of Contrary Thinking*, Caldwell, ID: Caxton Press.

Neyman, J., (1952) *Lectures and Conferences on Mathematical Statistics and Probability*, 2nd edition, Washington DC: Department of Agriculture, pp. 143–154.

Nichele, D. and Stefanini, F. (2002) *Hedge Funds: Investire per generare rendimenti assoluti*, Milan: Il Sole 24 ORE SpA.

Nicholas, J.G. (2000) *Market-Neutral Investing: Long/Short Hedge Fund Strategies*, Bloomberg Press.

Phillips, K.S. and Surz, R.J. (2003) *Hedge Funds: Definitive Strategies and Techniques*, New York: John Wiley & Sons, Inc.

Revikin, A.C. (2004) "Global Warming Is Expected To Raise Hurricane Intensity," *The New York Times*, 30th September.

Robinson E. (2003) *The Outsiders*, Bloomberg Markets.

Schwager, J.D. (1989) *The New Market Wizards: Conversations with America's Top Traders*, New York: HarperBusiness, a division of HarperCollins Publishers.

Schwager, J.D. (1992) *Market Wizards: Interviews with Top Traders*, New York: HarperBusiness, a division of HarperCollins Publishers.

Soros. G. (1994) "Hedge Funds and Dynamic Hedging" (Testimony to US House of Representatives Committee on Banking, Finance, and Urban Affairs), 13 April 1994.

Soros, G. (1995) *Soros on Soros: Staying Ahead of the Curve*, New York: John Wiley & Sons, Inc.

Soros, G. (2003) *The Alchemy of Finance*, New York: John Wiley & Sons, Inc.

Staley, K.F. (1997) *The Art of Short Selling*, New York: John Wiley & Sons, Inc.

Steinhardt, M. (2001) *No Bull: My Life In and Out of Markets*, New York: John Wiley & Sons, Inc.

Strachman, D.A. (2000) *Getting Started in Hedge Funds*, New York: John Wiley & Sons, Inc.

Strachman, D.A. (2004) *Julian Robertson: A Tiger in the Land of Bulls and Bears*, New York: John Wiley & Sons, Inc.

Swensen, D.F. (2000) *Pioneering Portfolio Management: An Unconventional Approach to Institutional Investment*, New York: The Free Press.

Taleb, N.N. (2001) *Fooled by Randomness: The Hidden Role of Chance in the Markets and in Life*, New York: Texere.

Teitelbaum, R. (2003), *Wall Street Refugees*, Bloomberg Markets.

Temple, P. (2001) *Hedge funds: The Courtesans of Capitalism*, Chichester: John Wiley & Sons, Ltd.

Thorp, E.O. and Kassouf, S.T. (1967) *Beat the Market*, New York: Random House.

Weinstein, M.H. (1931) *Arbitrage in Securities*, Harper Brothers.

WEBSITES

www.aima.org

www.altvest.com

www.awjones.com

www.bankruptcydata.com

www.bondmarkets.com

www.dbconvertibles.com

www.edhec-risk.com

www.eurohedge.co.uk

www.frmhedge.com

www.hedgefund.net

www.hedgefundresearch.com

www.hedgeindex.com

www.hedgeworld.com

www.macroanalytics.com/html/convertible_arbitrage.html

www.mondohedge.com

www.stern.nyu.edu/~ealtman

www.soros.org

www.vanhedge.com

Copyright notice for Credit Suisse/Tremont Index LLC figures appearing in this book

Index

Index compiled by Terry Halliday